The
Laurel's Kitchen

BREAD BOOK

by Laurel Robertson
with Carol Flinders &
Bronwen Godfrey

The Laurel's Kitchen

BREAD

BOOK

A Guide to Whole-Grain Breadmaking

Random House, New York

New York • Toronto • London • Sydney • Auckland

Published in the United States by Random House, Inc., New York,
and simultaneously in Canada by Random House of Canada Limited,
Toronto.

Grateful acknowlegment is made to the following for permission to
reprint published material:
Stan Dworkin: Recipe on page 308 from The Good Goodies by Floss
and Stan Dworkin. Rodale Press, Emmaus, Pennsylvania, 1974.
Used with permission.
Woodbridge Press Publishing Co.: Recipe on page 305 from the Oats,
Peas, Beans & Barley Cookbook, Revised edition. Woodbridge Press,
Santa Barbara, California, 1980. Used with permission.

Library of Congress Cataloging in Publication Data:

Robertson, Laurel.
    The Laurel's kitchen bread book.

    1. Bread.   I. Flinders, Carol.   II. Godfrey, Bronwen.
III. Title.   IV. Title: Whole-grain breadmaking.
TX769.R65   1984   641.8'15   83-43208
ISBN 0-394-53700-9
        Ingram   4/10 23.00   42408
Manufactured in the United States of America

BVG 01

Table of Contents

A Breadmaking Handbook

Acknowledgments

Like *Laurel's Kitchen,* this book is the work of many hands. In addition to those who contributed so many hours and loaves, much appreciation is due

❧ to our good friends Maura Bean and Kazuko Nishita of the Cereals Group at the USDA Western Regional Laboratory in Berkeley, California, whose vast experience in the scientific aspects of breadmaking gave this book one of its most important, unique, and useful dimensions

❧ to Hy Lerner, who pioneered and bakes the wonderful bread of Baldwin Hill Bakery near Boston, for helping us develop the home-kitchen version in this book

❧ to Manuel Friedman, for sharing his experience as a professional whole-foods baker and giving us a great boost toward better breadmaking

❧ to Al Giusto, whose generous advice on everything from wheat farming to milling and baking solved many puzzles for us along the way

❧ to Charlotte Mayerson, with gratitude and affection

❧ and to all the people who have taken *Laurel's Kitchen* into *their* kitchens and let us know how much it has changed their lives.

From Laurel

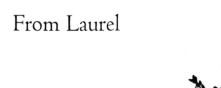

Ever since we wrote *Laurel's Kitchen* people have been asking us what we actually eat. Thinking it over, we realized that along with fresh vegetables and fruits, some beans and dairy products, the real mainstay of our diet is whole grains — in particular, bread. Because we are Westerners, bread is the natural staff of life for us; having fresh delicious homemade bread makes it easy to enjoy a simple way of eating.

Even so, for a long time, though we made a lot of good bread, we had our disasters, too. It wasn't until we really got serious about the subject that we could bake bread we liked every time. What we learned over the course of these years is what we want to share with you.

There are a lot of bread books, even many that purport to be whole-grain books, but as far as we could discover, all of them approach the subject as if whole wheat flour is the same as white flour — only worse. The mixing method these books advise is a white-flour method, and when it is applied to whole wheat flour, a lot of the time it doesn't work. The natural response to this kind of failure is, "Oh, well, what do you expect from whole wheat? Next time, let's make it lighter — put in some white flour or gluten flour."

People just assume that to make good bread you have to include refined flour. We once asked the owner of a big bakery supply company if he could point us to a really good old-fashioned *whole-grain* rye bread. He sent us to a tiny bakery in an old San Francisco neighborhood. It was late in the afternoon by the time we got there and only one loaf was left — black, encrusted with caraway, fragrant, lovely. I couldn't resist, and hefted the solid-looking loaf in my hands. (You know the feeling. You pick up a milk carton you think is full, and it's empty—featherlight?)

"Gee, what kind of flour did you use in this?" I asked.

"Rye flour," he beamed back proudly.

"Surely there must be some wheat flour too?"

"Oh no, no wheat flour. Only rye flour—and regular flour, of course," he said, pointing to a huge bin of the pure white stuff.

Without wanting to sound like fanatics, we just don't think you need white flour for good bread. After all, people baked well before white flour came along. What we've learned, and what we want to pass on to you, is a traditional method that does not depend on the uniformity of white flour, but rather expects, accommodates, and even celebrates the variability of good whole wheat flour.

We would be the first to admit that getting some of the ingredients we call for—especially good flour—can require ingenuity and persistence. Not only bakers but natural food clerks, supermarket managers, and others who should be well informed often don't know the various kinds and qualities of flour, don't appreciate the differences between them, and sometimes don't even know how to store flour properly. As a matter of course, you'll soon be a lot more knowledgeable than many of the experts if you are serious about baking with whole wheat, and use the information we've gathered here.

ð

Start with A Loaf for Learning and bake with it more than once. It has eased lots of beginners into breadmaking, and we know it works. In fact, even when you are following recipes later on in the book, turn back to Loaf when you're feeling uneasy, uncertain, or unhinged.

The basic Whole Wheat Bread is another good one to try early on, before you branch out to the rest of the recipes. It is good everyday eating and welcomes a lot of variation. Later sections in the book cover the use of a variety of ingredients—dairy products, fruits, nuts, beans, other grains than wheat, and more. Each is introduced by some hints about its special problems and its special joys. People on restricted diets will want to have a look at the Saltless Breads or the section on Rice Breads.

The Breadmaking Handbook at the end provides a reference to techniques, ingredients, and equipment. Refer to it, like A Loaf for Learning, when you need to know more.

And there is always more to know. We've baked, by modest calculation, more than 20,000 loaves and still, every baking is an adventure, every baking seems to reveal some new secret. Maybe that's one reason breadmaking is so satisfying: there's no end to the learning.

We would like to present this book to you like a loaf fresh from the oven. It is warm with our affection and with our hope that it will inspire, inform, and cheer you on to create wonderful, satisfying bread.

Always a Choice

Always a Choice

EIGHT YEARS have passed since *Laurel's Kitchen* first appeared, and in that time our approach to whole-foods cookery has evolved considerably. For one thing, we've learned to bake bread.

It's true that back in 1976 we talked a good bread story. And we probably did know as much about baking with whole-grain flours as any of the other people who were writing books about it.

But over time, we became increasingly impatient with the occasional disasters Laurel mentions, and not quite so ready to blame them on factors out of our control. So began the long and painstaking enquiry that resulted at last in *The Laurel's Kitchen Bread Book* which, as it turns out, may be more of an apprenticeship than a book. Though the instructions are not hard to understand or particularly technical, the art of bread-baking is set forth here in depth and with a regard for detail you might expect to find in a professional baker's manual. There are good reasons for this, which you are most likely to appreciate if you have already tried to bake with whole-grain flour and seen what a challenge it presents.

Given the inherent difficulties, one might reasonably wonder why such partiality to 100 per cent whole-grain bread. Need we be fanatical about all this, and join the ranks of what English food writer Elizabeth David calls, with unconcealed distaste, "wholemeal cranks"? After all, a compromise loaf still has a good grainy flavor and many of the benefits of whole grain, only it's more likely to be light enough for almost anyone to enjoy.

Readers of *Laurel's Kitchen* will recall that we've favored whole grains all along. Their special importance for vegetarians had become clear when we first began to look into the nutritional requirements of a meatless diet. The reason meat is so "nutrient dense" a food, we learned, is that the *animals* concerned eat whole grains, leafy greens, root vegetables, and legumes. As vegetarians, we saw that we would need to eat these foods ourselves, directly.

I might add that deciding to switch over to whole grains when we stopped eating meat didn't have to do solely with nutritional considerations. It was a very natural changeover that had as much to do with how things tasted. White bread, refined pasta, and rice have very little flavor or texture of their own—they're companionable enough, but relatively innocuous. In a meat-centered diet, that's fine, but once meat is out of the picture, one really welcomes the stronger flavors and chewiness of brown rice, kasha, and whole wheat bread. A great many people are making this discovery today who are not all-out vegetarians, but who are simply trying to cut back on meat consumption.

Today, we are still vegetarians, but what really defines our diet now isn't so much that we don't eat meat as that whole cereal grains predominate, eclipsing most of the dairy products, eggs, and even redoubtable foods like tofu to which we had given top priority in the past.

This development took place gradually over the years after *Laurel's Kitchen* came out. It was a matter of finally assimilating information that was right there in the nutrient charts at the back of the book, and applying it to our own engrained (or ungrained) habits.

Long after we should have known better, for instance, many of us continued to look upon bread rather warily as being what the British call "stodge"—something to fill up on, really, with no terrific value of its own—the first thing that should go, therefore, if you're trying to keep your weight down. Today, we know that because foods high in dietary fiber are also filling, they can be exceedingly helpful in a reducing diet. And their nutritional value appears to be nothing short of terrific after all.

With passing time we have become far more appreciative of the precision with which unrefined cereal grains—whole wheat, brown rice, kasha, and oats—reflect *actual* human nutritional needs. Take protein, for instance. As long as we thought more was better, we really could not see whole grains as anything but accessories to milk, cheese, eggs, tofu, etc. But now that excessive protein has been linked with a wide range of disorders that includes osteoporosis, hypertension, kidney problems, and cancer, the relatively modest protein content of whole grains appears to work to our advantage. (Let me point out, though, that half a loaf of plain whole wheat bread does offer 24 grams of protein—no mean contribution to anyone's daily needs, even considering that wheat's amino acid pattern is not quite complete by itself.

"Starch" was almost a dirty word ten years ago. But today, under the more respectable designation of "complex carbohydrate," it is universally recognized as the fuel the body is tuned to use most efficiently. When starchy foods like bread, cereal, and pasta are eaten unrefined, moreover, they include the full battery of B vitamins necessary for the assimilation of that fuel. They also include the most complex form of carbohydrate, called "dietary fiber." Passing unaltered through the digestive tract, it does tremendous good along the way—good that medical research makes more apparent by the year.

On nutritional and gastronomic grounds, then, we are more convinced than ever that whole cereal grains are the foundation of the ideal diet. But there's more to life than a smoothly functioning digestive system or a baby-smooth complexion—more, for that matter, than longevity itself. There is the vast rest of the world, too.

When we first published *Laurel's Kitchen*, the information brought out in Frances Moore Lappé's *Diet for a Small Planet* was still new to most of us. The connections she had drawn between hunger abroad and the meat-based diet of the wealthier West gave us enhanced motivation for pursuing a diet "low on the food chain." Today, as we rely even more heavily (and happily) on whole cereal grains, and feel even less need than before of relatively expensive concentrated protein foods like cheese and eggs, it seems more ironic than ever that there should *seem* not to be enough food in the world to feed everyone.

It is abundantly clear now that the diet which is most healthful for the individual is also the supremely democratic one; the one that offers the best chance of feeding us all. It *has* in fact fed most of us down through the ages. Cereal grains supplemented with legumes are the basis of a host of ethnic specialties ranging from falafel and fejoida, to pasta fazool and peanut butter sandwiches.

Today we know—Ms. Lappé has been among the first to alert us—that it will take a whole lot more to alleviate world hunger than just cutting out hamburgers. But it is equally clear that adopting a cereal-based diet is a most suitable place to start. In Ms. Lappé's own words, ". . . Where do we get the courage to begin? I believe part of the answer lies in making ourselves more powerful people—more convincing to ourselves and therefore to others. For me, part of that process is making our individual life choices more and more consistent with the world we are working towards." (F.M.Lappé, Food First News, Summer, 1982).

Ms. Lappé's remarks have exceedingly wide application: changing one's diet is really only a small part of what is implied. But my own grasp of what she is saying, and my whole-hearted agreement, does have to do with food: There was a particular moment, in fact, when it all came home to me with special force.

My son was three, and I was watching him eat one of his favorite breakfasts: cornmeal ground fresh the day before, cooked into a buttery yellow mush, cooled down with home-brew soy milk, and sweetened with a trickle of maple syrup. He tucked it away with voluptuous appreciation. Watching, I recalled suddenly the picture I had been looking at just the day before of refugee children somewhere in the Third World. From huge kettles, relief workers were ladling into battered tin basins a porridge of corn and soy, mixed, as was my boy's, in a proportion intended to maximize nutritional benefits. It would take a lot of that porridge, though, eaten over many weeks, to flesh out the matchstick arms on those children, bring light to their shadowed eyes, and return to normalcy bellies distended from chronic hunger.

Knowing that my son's diet is simple, grain-based, and inexpensive did not begin to mitigate the sorrow I had felt on looking at his counterparts in that refugee camp. Nor should it have. But it did help keep that sorrow from turning into despair: which seems very important if we're to work toward solutions. To a small, yet meaningful degree, deciding to simplify one's diet and limit oneself to foods that *could* conceivably be enjoyed by everyone on earth, begins to diminish the terrible and disempowering gulf between "them" and "us"—between "those children" and our own.

I WOULD ADD, finally, that our profound attachment to whole grains has also to do with a feeling that has deepened steadily over many years' experience as bakers and eaters of these splendid foods, and which can only be called, at the risk of sounding somewhat balmy, reverence.

There it sits—a single kernel of wheat, maybe three sixteenths of an inch long, creased along one side and rounded on the other. At the bottom nestles a tiny oval compartment, the minute beginning of the plant's rebirth, called the germ. Above the germ is the endosperm, a protein- and calorie-rich food reservoir that will fuel the plant as it germinates. Enveloping both is a hard seed coat, impermeable for decades to anything but the warmth and moisture that will bring the seed to life.

What's so marvelous about this simple structure is that everything that helps the grain preserve and reproduce itself also suits the needs of human beings and animals superbly well. It comes close to being a complete food, needing to be supplemented only by small amounts of animal products and/ or legumes, and the leafy green and yellow vegetables that almost any environment between the polar caps will provide in some form. The same hard seed coat that protects the seed's capacity to reproduce itself has also made possible for human-kind the almost indefinitely long storage of a wholesome food supply.

There are those who can look on this kind of arrangement and keep their wits about them. There are others who can't conceive of it as anything but a sure, small sign of some larger benevolence, hidden deep behind the appearance of things — and who feel, too, that nothing could be more fitting in response than to summon up all that is skilled and artful in themselves to bake a fine, high-rising loaf of uncompromisingly whole-grain bread.

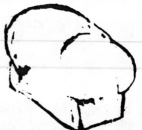

YES, BREAD. For no matter how much we enjoy whole grains in other guises — creamy oatmeal, kasha cooked with mushrooms and potatoes, and platters of yellow polenta topped with tomato sauce and cheese — no matter how much we value the sheer variety for nutritional reasons as well as pleasure, we always come back to bread — the convenience food *par excellence,* ready at hand, good with anything or almost nothing, synonymous, in the West, with "food" itself.

So all right, whole grains — one hundred per cent whole, and no fudging. *Bread,* moreover, and not just a pot of steamed wheat berries. Are you ready, though, for the "home-baked and regularly" clause? For between the safely impersonal admission that, Yes, whole grain is a lovely food, optimal in every way, and, Yes, I'd adore to bake it twice a week from this moment on, there yawns a chasm wide and deep.

Right now, your week almost certainly does *not* include great chunks of hanging-around-the-house time. This doesn't have to stop you. Look long and hard at Laurel's suggestions for fitting bread into your life (page 73), and you may find that your current schedule need not be disrupted as much as you imagine.

It might possibly be, too, that someone else in your household would like to help. Many hands don't just make light work, they can also make high-quality work. Today, when there are so many more pressures on all of us to be out and away from home, the "divide and conquer" principle has become standard kitchen practice. Just because no one's home to cook all afternoon doesn't mean nobody's interested in good meals anymore. It *may* mean more innovative solutions are required to produce them: At one end of the spectrum, Friday night potluck with friends, at the other, communal householding.

One of my favorite cases in point is the annual Christmas-Hanukkah supper a friend stages each year, towards which everyone involved contributes one absolutely spectacular item. It's understood that Jeff will bring the pies, because he always does, and that they will be exquisite, because they always are, and that they will be described in lingering detail on the also exquisite hand-lettered menus that are Rhoda's gift to the evening.

The principle is infinitely variable—do you have a friend who'd love to trade homebaked bread for a panful of chili rellenos? A clipped hedge, maybe?

But let's suppose the worst. Suppose none of Laurel's optional timing schemes will work for you, and suppose that in response to all your gambits ("Wanna help? Wanna trade?") no one has flickered an eyelid. Still, you really yearn to see that bread coming out of the oven twice weekly.

For a long time, you may just be It, and being It may well mean giving up some activity you're not at all happy to part with.

If so, let me try to sweeten the cup. For there *are* compensations, not immediately apparent. Bring together four or five committed bread bakers, loosen them up with a strong pot of tea, and listen closely as they talk about the subtle, far-reaching, and distinctly positive changes that can take place when you begin to bake regularly. . .

First, on the personal level, there's the purely therapeutic effect. Watch a four-year-old burst in the door after a long morning with his buddies, still exultant, talking nonstop, but exhausted, too, from the sustained stress of it all. Watch him fall with instinctive good sense on a pile of play-dough, and pull, push, pummel and squeeze until finally all the tension has flowed out through his fingertips and he is at peace. Watch him, and wonder why on earth grownups shouldn't have access to the same very healing, very basic kind of activity. And in fact, they can. For kneading bread dough, forming it into coffee-cake wreaths or cottage loaves or long baguettes affords exactly this kind of satisfaction.

Good breadbaking is much more, though, than just a good outlet. At certain critical junctures, you really have got to block out extraneous goings-on and attend meticulously to small details. Far from being onerous, these more exacting phases of the baking process can also be the most calming— precisely because they do require such powerful concentration. And the very fact that so much of oneself is called upon, in the way of artistry and resourcefulness, makes the whole business that much more gratifying—enhances the quality of life over-all.

That breadbaking—as well as gardening, spinning, bee-keeping, and animal husbandry—is in fact creative and exact-ing is often overlooked. Instead, they are regarded as "subsis-tence skills"—what you have to deal with to scratch out a bare living, reeling, as you do, from the endless labor entailed. You can hardly blame our parents and grandparents for having set firmly behind them so rigorous and chancy a way of life, and for thinking a bit daft those of us who cast a rueful glance backwards. For it was with full, trusting, and grateful consent that people began to buy what they needed, use "convenience foods," and adopt a full complement of helpful household machines. Hardly a voice was raised in protest when our tradi-tionally home-centered, small-scale system of food production gave way, little by little, to what has been called "the corporate cornucopia."

Today, though, there is good reason to question whether our present food system can be sustained—so profoundly de-pendent on petroleum is it, and so flagrantly wasteful of other resources as well. Good reason, too, to seek out more direct ways of meeting our food needs, and to breathe a little easier when you find them. This ease of mind is yet another source of satisfaction that comes of being a competent whole grains baker. Revival of what is, yes, a subsistence skill, means you know yourself able to turn just about any flour or grain that might come your way into something that will nourish and even delight. Knowing this, you feel that much less vulnerable to circumstance. It's a subtle change, but it goes deep.

Reinstate breadbaking as a home-based activity, and you begin to change the home, too. Once you have established a regular baking pattern and the people who live with you *know* that on, say, Tuesday evenings and Saturday mornings there will be fresh bread, and good smells, and you there, too, manifestly enjoying yourself, there begins to be more reason for *them* to be there as well. The place starts to exert its own gentle tug, a strong counterforce to the thousand-and-one pulls that would draw them out and away.

The creature comfort of a warm kitchen and people to chat with accounts only in part for this magnetic force. It's the baking itself: the artistry, the science, the occasional riddle of it. People of all ages, but particularly children, seem to draw immense satisfaction from hanging around a place where work is taken as seriously as we've come to take baking. We observed this when we first began the kitchen research that preceded *Laurel's Kitchen*, and had a chance to reaffirm it just last year, when we constructed the oven where our beloved "desem" bread is baked.

Building the oven, which extended along the top of an enormous fireplace as part of a large new kitchen, was a formidable undertaking. It drew in an architect, bricklayers, carpenters, a blacksmith, and several master bakers. It also drew in every toddler in the vicinity. At every opportunity, there they'd be, watching unblinking as each brick was laid in place and each fitting was forged. My own son was among them, and for months afterward, once the oven was working, he would watch twice weekly with equal fascination as the bread itself came out of the oven—loaf after round, brown loaf, sliding out on a wooden paddle we learned to call a "peel," caught in leather-gauntleted hands and then pitched onto racks to cool. Back in his room later, he would re-enact the entire sequence, molding loaves out of clay, using a spatula and my old driving gloves to unload the "oven" he'd built out of wooden blocks.

Now, at four, Ramesh proudly brings in firewood for the baking—and he's not likely to stop there. He is as crazy about the desem bread as we are, and he's well aware how much care goes into its making. To him, a kitchen is a place where unquestionably important things go on, and where everyone has a contribution to make. I'm profoundly glad he feels that way.

Much of what gives traditional communities their special character and form has to do with the way they go about meeting basic life needs. In the past, to get crops harvested, wheat ground, or a well dug and maintained, people had to come together in respectful cooperation, suspending for the moment any private grievances they might be nursing. Often, they even managed to get some fun out of what they were doing—enough, even, to lay some of those grievances to rest. It was in the course of carrying out all that work—the "bread labor" of which Leo Tolstoy was so enamored—that the essential values of a particular society got hammered out and then transmitted to the young people growing up and working in its midst.

Until quite recently, this has been true for families as well as communities. Just about everything people ate, wore, slept under and sat on was produced at home. Everyone took part in the producing and everyone knew he or she was needed. It was in work carried out together that relationships deepened and values were handed on. Kitchens, gardens, woodshops—workplaces of any sort that aren't dominated by machines too loud to talk over—are ideal places to exchange confidences as well as acquire skills. There's no more effective situation to impart "the way we do things here" than in the throes of a specific job—no better place to show by example the patience to see out a task, or the good humor and ingenuity to set things right when they go awry.

In today's world, the home tends not to be as productive a place as it once was. We take jobs elsewhere, earn money, buy things and bring them home to use. If we want our families to benefit from work undertaken together, we have deliberately to set up situations where that can happen. A great many families are doing just that today, in a variety of ways. Breadbaking maybe, or a vegetable garden, the tasks assigned by age and skill. One family of friends maintains a cottage-scale spinning and weaving industry using wool from their goats. The proceeds from what they sell go into a college savings fund.

Still another friend, a single mother and full-time librarian, missing the fine, fresh milk of her native Scotland and feeling vaguely that something was missing in her admittedly hectic life, decided that what she and her teenaged daughter needed more than anything . . . was a cow. Skeptical friends like me have been chastened to observe that she may have been right. Having the common, and thoroughly endearing focal point of a soft-eyed Jersey cow, knowing that she's got to be milked no matter who's overslept or who has a cold, having to arrange for grain, and hay, and visits from the vet, actually has *not* stressed the relationship of mother and daughter to the breaking point or sent either of them into exhaustion. Rather, it seems to have compelled them to stay in closer touch than they would have otherwise, and they both find the outdoor work, the contact with the animal herself, to be a perfect restorative. Not for everyone, a cow, but it does illustrate the principle and makes a twice-weekly baking seem small potatoes by comparison!

AS LONG AS we've known each other, Laurel, Bron, and I have shared with others at Nilgiri Press a strong interest in the life and teachings of Mahatma Gandhi. (The first book we published, in fact—which Laurel helped design—was *Gandhi the Man*, by Eknath Easwaran.) That interest was rekindled last year by Richard Attenborough's film masterpiece "Gandhi." More and more of late, along with a great many other people, we have been looking to the man and his writings, seeming to find there solutions to the mounting problems of our day—solutions, or at least inspiration to go on looking for them.

The fact that Gandhi is always in the back of our minds now has led us to see in the baking of whole-grain bread even greater possible significance than I've already proposed. This might seem odd, if you think of Gandhi primarily as a political figure. Baking bread, after all, is a domestic and private preoccupation—far removed from political goings-on. But the fact is, overtly political activity took up a relatively small amount of time in Gandhi's life.

For years and years at a time, throughout the nineteen thirties and forties, Gandhi virtually buried himself in village India, preoccupied exclusively with the daily minutiae of "rural uplift." This was because his idea of revolution was "from the bottom upward." He believed that the people of India, the vast majority of whom lived in the villages, would be in no position to take responsibility for governing themselves effectively until they were also able to feed, clothe, and shelter themselves. This is where the spinning wheel or "charkha" came in: all-important symbol of Gandhi's effort to achieve authentic self-rule in India—symbol, but direct means, too.

Prior to British imperial rule, manufacture of cotton into textiles had been a cottage industry. Homespun had been the ideal complement to agriculture, enabling the villagers to clothe as well as feed themselves, and providing work that could be carried on throughout the rainy season. Everyone could take part, moreover—the elderly and disabled, even the very young.

Over the years, though, the British had systematically suppressed the cottage textile industry. By the turn of the century, Indian cotton was exported to Britain, manufactured into calico in the Lancashire mills and returned for sale to Indians —to be bought with money they had an ever-diminishing chance to earn. While spinning wheels collected dust in attics, the villagers themselves grew poorer, more dispirited, and ever more dependent on the British *raj*.

Gandhi offered a deceptively simple solution. Drag out

those wheels, he urged. If you don't know how to use them, get your grandmothers to teach you. Boycott foreign-made cloth, and wear only what we can produce ourselves.

Homespun cotton was just the beginning. Gandhi encouraged use of village-ground whole wheat, too, instead of mill-refined white flour; of locally processed raw sugar, called "gur," instead of white sugar, and greatly increased use of leafy green vegetables. He advocated employment of local materials for housing, and indigenous herbal medicines — every conceivable form, in short, of individual and local self-reliance.

The poor of India did not need alms, Gandhi maintained, they needed work. Finding themselves able, after all, to meet basic life needs through their own skills, they would begin to trust their capacity to govern themselves as well — and they would have the courage to try. A people thus transformed would be free in the most meaningful sense whether they were officially recognized to be or not. It would be only a matter of time before political institutions caught up. Gandhi saw in this transformation of the individual the very essence of nonviolent revolution — its driving power.

It would be very easy to look at India today — at the serious problems she has yet to solve — and conclude that Gandhi's ideas haven't worked there. Easy, unless you realize that in fact, they haven't really been tried. The overall direction of development efforts in India has not been that of the Constructive Program. Even Gandhi's closest followers did not all share his passion for homespun or his faith in what it promised for India. It seemed so terribly slow, after all, and the needs were so acute. Hoping to relieve their people's suffering more quickly, many of these individuals were attracted instead to the industrialized models of the West, and they strove mightily, once they were in political office, to adopt similar patterns for India.

It's quite understandable that Gandhi's successors would have chafed at the long, slow process of change his approach entails. The darker side of life in the West probably didn't look *as* dark to them as it did to him, and they may not have been as convinced as he was that our highly industrialized and primarily urban mode of life was largely to blame.

In the long run, Gandhi's teachings might turn out to have fallen on more fertile ground here in the West, amidst people who have lived out the consequences of a highly industrialized, materially abundant way of life, and who have, like many of us, our own reasons to question it.

THE POSSIBLE relevance of homespun to life in the West is suggested in a scene that occurs well along in the Attenborough film. A bemused Margaret Bourke-White is struggling under Gandhi's direction to master the *charkha*.

"I just don't see it," she says wryly, holding up the hank of cotton her efforts have produced, "as the solution to the twentieth century's problems."

He smiles and demonstrates the process once again. They joke a little, and getting back to her challenge in what seems an oblique way, he says, "But I know happiness does not come with things — even twentieth century things. It can come from work, and pride in what you do. It will not necessarily be 'progress' for India if she simply imports the unhappiness of the West."

What Gandhi was insisting upon with that spinning wheel — he never quit talking about it, and carted it all over Europe as well as India — was the absolutely vital importance of how we accomplish the most mundane things in life: the putting of clothes on our backs and food on our tables. There is always a simpler way to meet these needs, he taught, and a more self-reliant one — always an adjustment to make that will foster better health and draw you into more richly interdependent relationships with others. There is always a choice.

Are Gandhi's ideas applicable in this country today, so vastly different from British-ruled India? A great many people would appear to think so, for they are at work in every area of life, introducing reforms of enormous diversity that would have won Gandhi's wholehearted approval: agricultural marketing projects; research into low-cost solar-heated housing; instructional programs in natural childbirth and breastfeeding; worker ownership of factories and co-operative food-buying clubs; urban gardening schemes and a growing number of home-based businesses.

Whole-grain bread baking has a very special place along this spectrum — particularly because it's so immediate and personal, and so well within nearly everyone's reach. It's an ideal first step towards a way of life that is more self-reliant, and at the same time more consciously interdependent. We're tempted to see it, in fact, as the *khadi* of our own day.

We're tempted to think, too — taking our cue from Gandhi and judging from our own experience — that when you begin to adopt the kind of changes in life style outlined above, you aren't *only* making choices more consistent with the world you're trying to bring about. Rather, you actually are bringing it about. The compass of that new world might at first seem no longer than the distance from your kitchen stove to the front door — but don't be deceived. The fact of what you are doing will most certainly make itself felt by everyone who comes in contact with you (by people, in fact, who happen only to walk past your house on baking day). Your personal example assures them that indeed life *can* be both simpler and more challenging, but much more satisfying in the bargain. It encourages them in the most irresistible way possible to take that first step themselves.

In short, the idea that life's really important and far-reaching changes come "from the bottom upwards" no longer seems to us romantic or overly optimistic at all. Let's begin, then, at the beginning . . .

A Loaf for Learning

A Loaf for Learning

The very best way to learn to make bread is to bake often, alongside someone who is really good at it, with lots of leisure for questions. This section is meant to be as much like that as we can get without being in your kitchen with you. You could say the Loaf for Learning is a short course on breadmaking; repeat for credit any number of times.

It isn't that you can't learn to make bread by yourself, by trial and error (or error and trial, as it usually turns out!), but breadmaking has so many variables that it is tricky to pin down what makes the same recipe turn out light one time and heavy the next, or why it tastes funny this week when it was fine last week. When you have an idea of what is actually going on in the dough during mixing, kneading, rising, and baking, your skill will increase and you will be much more in control.

We have been baking for (good grief) more than fifteen years, but really until we worked on this book, we never approached mastery, the kind that lets you observe wisely, learn from what you see, and convey what you learn clearly. (Some of us thought we had, but it was actually not mastery but an affectionate mixture of unchecked experience, canny hunches, homegrown psychology, and bravado. These never lose their usefulness, just as breadmaking never loses its mystique; but the process is simply a whole lot more fun when you know what you are doing—and that is what the Loaf for Learning is about.)

Beginners: don't be intimidated! Perhaps you'll feel there's an awful lot to read here, a lot to understand, but plunge right in anyway, and get your hands on the dough. It all makes much more sense much more easily when you're *doing,* rather than staring at the pages. Besides, nobody takes it all in the first time through. Beginners and old hands alike find that each time they follow Loaf, some aspect of baking falls into place, or some mystery is resolved.

Some people seem to think that learning more about it will make a dreary science out of what should be a joyful art, and this is quite an understandable viewpoint. But as we worked to make this book we found that every discovery not only made our bread better, but gave us a sense of control, even a thrill of understanding. As for the challenge and excitement, the suspense and mystery, the sense of loving cooperation with the living thing that is dough—this grows with every baking even still, after nearly five years' immersion in the process. Maybe a pertinent analogy would be a musical one: learning to read a score or play a cello doesn't decrease your enthusiasm for Bach, but rather makes you all the more appreciative; and as you learn to play really well, your own enjoyment increases along with the quality of your music.

A Loaf for Learning concentrates on the skills that you need to master if you want to make Light Bread. It isn't that the only good bread in the world is the puffy sort—far from it! But once you know what to do to produce a high-rising loaf, you can turn confidently to any bread recipe and expect good results.

The first part of Loaf for Learning goes through the baking process from beginning to end in detail. In the second part are questions and answers about breadmaking—about the ingredients, the techniques, the dough. . . .To make these pages as helpful as possible, we have drawn upon advice of professional bakers, cereals scientists, and friends who bake a lot at home—and then put it all to work in our own kitchens. The result, we think, is a unique and helpful guide to baking good bread.

Rockbottom Essentials

These few things are essential. There is much, much more about each of these ingredients elsewhere in the book and for more information, refer to the pages noted. But whatever recipe you choose in this book, please follow the simple guidelines given here.

FLOUR

Freshness Whole wheat flour, unlike white flour, is perishable and must be fresh to make good bread. If you buy packaged flour and can't read the "pull date" on it, ask your storekeeper. Don't try to make bread with whole-grain flour that has been on the shelf for more than 2 months. If you are in doubt, taste a pinch. There should be no bitterness. When you get the flour home, refrigerate it, wrapped airtight. The day before you bake, take what you will need out to come to room temperature before you use it.

Type To achieve a light loaf of yeasted bread you need flour that is high in protein. Look for "bread" flour or flour milled from *hard red spring wheat, hard red winter wheat,* or *hard white wheat.* Hard red spring wheat usually makes the lightest loaves. If none of these are on the bag, but there is a nutrition profile, look for a protein content of 14% or more, by weight.

"All purpose" flour and pastry flour make tender quick breads, muffins and pancakes, but they do not have enough gluten protein to make light yeasted breads.

Grind A very fine grind will make the lightest loaves, all other factors being equal, but many people prefer coarser stoneground flour for flavor and texture in some breads. *More about flour and milling on pages 363–376.*

YEAST

We call for active dry yeast because it is available everywhere and is reliable. The usual amount called for is two teaspoons, which is one packet. If you prefer moist yeast, one cake is the equivalent of one packet. Moist or dry, if the yeast is not fresh—within its expiration date, and properly stored—it cannot raise your bread.

More about yeast on pages 377–381.

OIL OR BUTTER

Make sure it is fresh: rancid fat will spoil your bread. We strongly recommend storing both oil and butter in the refrigerator.

More about fat in general on page 389. More about butter on page 173.

WATER SALT & SWEETENERS

Any water that is good to drink—not extremely hard or soft—will do fine. Normal table salt is adequate for baking. For sweetening, we usually call for honey, but if you prefer something different there are many possibilities, and within bounds, they will all work.

More about water, salt, and sweeteners on pages 382–388.

You Will Need

EQUIPMENT

china cup or mug
chef's thermometer
mixing bowl
(3 to 4 quarts)
small mixing bowl
1-cup dry measuring cup
liquid measuring cup
set of measuring spoons
rubber spatula
dough cutter or spatula
kneading board or other
flat surface
rolling pin (optional)
greased metal loaf
pan 8"×4"

Thermometer

Yeast performs best when it is dissolved at the right temperature. Also, to time your rising accurately and come out with the best bread, you need to know the temperature of your dough and of the place it will rise. Both of these are so important to good baking that we really do recommend using a thermometer. The "Chef's" kind, with a metal spike and an instant-reading dial that registers from freezing to boiling, is the most practical we have found.

Measuring cups

You'll need both kinds: dry—usually opaque plastic or metal—where you level the cup at the top to get the proper amount; and wet—usually glass or clear plastic with the amounts marked on the side—where you fill the cup only up to the mark you need.

Mixing bowl

Your mixing bowl can be of almost any sort. We like to use a thick crockery bowl that can be prewarmed and will hold the heat. Plastic is not bad, but once it is scratched the dough will stick to it. If you use a metal bowl, be particularly careful to protect your dough from drafts. Save your wonderful seasoned wooden salad bowl for salads; dough will leach the oil and seasoning right out of the wood.

Kneading board

You will want a place that is comfortable and steady for kneading the dough. For most of us that's a tabletop, but you can use any smooth surface at least 1½ by 2 feet. If you use a breadboard, setting it on a damp towel will help it stay put.

The height of the place you knead is important. You should be able to rest your palms flat on the surface with your elbows slightly bent. Proper height makes your kneading more efficient and less tiring, so take the time to adjust the place you're going to work so that you'll be comfortable.

Loaf pan

Whole-grain breads bake better in the middle-sized, 8"×4" pans than in larger ones, and this recipe (like most of ours) provides the right amount of dough for that size. We suggest metal pans only because glass and pottery pans often require special treatment.

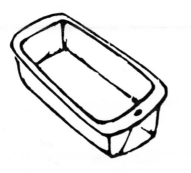

This recipe is enough for only one loaf because that amount of dough is easy for beginners to handle. If you want to make two, just double all the measurements *and the kneading time.* All the other timings remain the same.

INGREDIENTS

*6 tablespoons warm water
   (90 ml)*
*1 teaspoon active dry yeast
   (⅛ oz or 3.5 g)*
*3 cups whole wheat bread
   flour, finely ground
   (450 g)*
1 teaspoon salt (5.5 g)*
*⅓ cup cold yogurt
   (80 ml)**
*⅔ cup hot tap water
   (160 ml)**
2 tablespoons oil (30 ml)
*1½ tablespoons honey
   (25 ml)*
*for greasing the pan:
   the lecithin and oil
   mixture on page 390,
   or vegetable shortening.*

**If you don't want to use
yogurt, use
1¼ teaspoons salt
1 cup lukewarm water*

1. Preparing the Yeast

Warm your china cup or mug by rinsing it with warm tap water, and then measure the warm water into it. Follow the directions on the yeast package, if there are any; otherwise, let the water be slightly warmer than body heat, from 105 to 115°F. Test with your thermometer. Sprinkle yeast into the water while stirring with a spoon, so that each granule is individually wetted. Be sure the yeast is completely dissolved.

2. Mixing the Ingredients

Using your dry measure, stir the flour in its storage container briefly. Scoop up three full cups, leveling the top with a knife or other straight edge. Measure both flour and salt into the bowl and stir them together lightly, fluffing the flour with air.

Put the yogurt in your liquid measuring cup and add very hot tap water to make a full cup total. (If you are omitting the yogurt, measure one cup lukewarm water.) Mix with the oil and honey in the small mixing bowl.

Make a well in the center of the dry ingredients and pour the wet ingredients and the yeast mixture into it. Using a rubber spatula or your hand, begin stirring from the center, gradually spiraling outward. In this way the flour will come into the liquid without lumping up—you can feel how smooth it is. Bring the flour gradually in from the sides of the well until the mixture reaches the consistency of a thick batter, and then fold in the rest of the flour, combining it all to make dough.

Squeeze the dough between your wet fingers until you are certain that it is evenly mixed. It will be very sticky.

3. *Adjusting the Consistency*

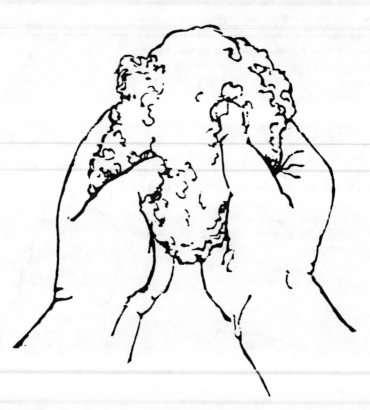

Now, before you continue, take a moment to evaluate the dough and decide if it is too slack or too stiff. You can learn to do this by feeling the dough. Clean your hands and moisten them slightly. Pick up the dough and squeeze it. Feel deep into the dough, not just the surface. It's sure to be sticky and wet, but is it soft, or is it stiff? A soft, pliable dough makes lighter bread.

Does the dough resist your touch? Does it strain the muscles in your fingers when you squeeze it? Then it is too stiff. On the other hand, the dough must have enough flour to hold its shape. Does it feel waterlogged, as if the flour is not contributing much substance to it? Does it have a runny, liquid quality? Then it is too slack. Again, feel deep into the dough.

If the dough is either too stiff or too slack, return it to the bowl and flatten it out. If it is too stiff, sprinkle a couple of tablespoons of water on it; if too slack, 3 or 4 tablespoons flour. Fold the dough over and squeeze again until it is well mixed. Reevaluate the dough and add more water or flour if necessary until it feels right. Remember that even perfect dough will be moist and sticky at this stage, so don't look for a firm, claylike dough—you'll end up with a brick.

Whatever the ingredients in your recipes, if you are attentive when mixing, you will learn to feel small differences in the amount of water the dough holds. Developing this sensitivity is not difficult, and it will make an enormous difference in the quality of your bread—especially how high it rises.

4. Kneading the Dough

Kneading makes the dough resilient and stretchy, so the bread can rise high.

There are many styles of kneading. The important thing is to aim for a pleasant, easy rhythm that is not tiring. The traditional method is to work the dough with both hands, which gives maximum pushing power. You can also squeeze the dough between your fingers, or pound or push into it with your fists, or even throw it down on the table. Since this recipe calls for a very small amount of dough, and it is sticky, we suggest here a method that lets you use only one hand to push on the dough. In the other hand you hold a dough cutter or small spatula and keep that hand clean.

First, turn the dough out of the bowl onto your kneading surface. Clean out the bowl and pour in a cup or so of warm water. Most people knead with flour under the dough to keep it from sticking. Today, though, use a little water instead, just at the beginning, so that you will be able to watch the dough change. If there is water or flour on the kneading surface throughout the process the changes will be masked.

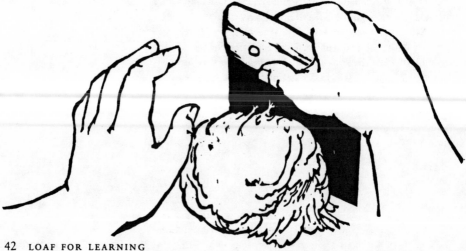

To knead with one hand, scrape the dough from the table with your dough cutter or spatula. Use the spatula to fold the dough in half. Then, with the palm of your other hand, push into the dough from the front, deep into the center—but before your hand becomes embedded in the sticky mess, pull back quickly and lightly. Aim for a touch that is both light and firm. Now give the dough a quarter turn and repeat the fold and the push. Keep turning, folding, and pushing the dough.

Kneading with a food processor: page 410.
Kneading with a dough hook: page 413.

At first you will want to touch the sticky dough lightly, but as it becomes more resilient, your stroke can be bolder. Try to keep the dough in a ball, stretching it from underneath and folding it back into itself above. Keeping the dough in a ball makes your kneading more effective because all of the dough receives the benefit of each push. For a while the dough will stick to the table and to your palm, but just keep on scraping it up with the spatula. Gradually the ball will become more coherent and less sticky, and your kneading more rhythmic and enjoyable.

Kneading (cont.)

As you work, watch and feel what is going on in the dough. Somewhere around halfway through the kneading, as the dough loses its stickiness, it will also get more springy and elastic, though if you try to stretch it out, it will still rip easily. Looking closely at the surface, you can begin to see brown flecks of bran against a *beige* background. Although the surface of the dough is much smoother than before, it is still a little bumpy, pocked with tiny craters. (Unabsorbed flour or water from the board would temporarily make the surface appear smooth, if they were present.)

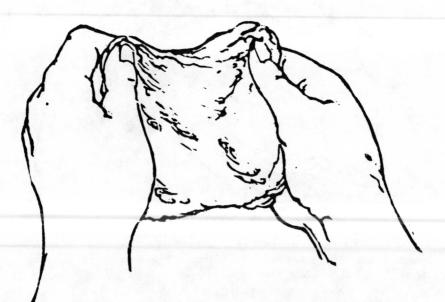

Halfway through kneading you can gently tug and pull the dough out flabby-thin. The surface will still be plenty rough, with little craters all over; the dough will tear easily.

If you stop kneading at this halfway point, your bread *will* rise, but it won't be nearly as good as it can be if you continue. Kneading is the secret of truly splendid bread, so continue until the dough is silky smooth. Now when you pull gently on the dough, it should stretch out without tearing. It will lose its wet quality, although on the surface it is still sticky. If your flour is finely ground, you will see a *whitish* cast to the beige color. If your flour is coarser, brown flecks of bran will be embedded in a bright, white sheet of gluten, looking like freckles on fair skin.

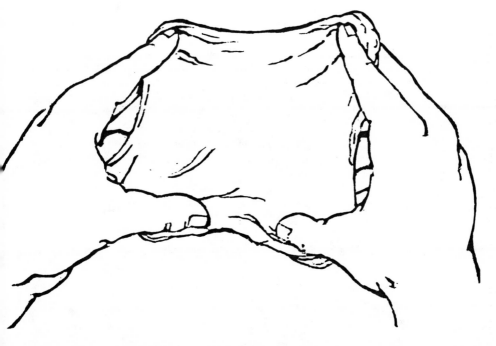

When the dough is fully developed, it will pull into a paper-thin sheet, smooth and bright. When you hold it to the light, you can see the webbing of the gluten strands in the sheet.

Kneading is much easier if you use the weight of your body rather than just the strength of your arms. (Anybody who's ever held a baseball bat or tennis racket or calligraphy pen has heard *that* before!) If your table is the right height, your work can be rhythmic and nearly effortless. The motion will be relaxing and, as one friend put it, even therapeutic: "Tell them that kneading a loaf of bread can cure a migraine headache better than medicine." When you are just learning, though, you will have to work pretty hard, which is why we suggest starting out with only one loaf's worth of dough. Count your strokes, and stop to rest any time you feel like it. (If for some physical reason this is too hard for you, please consider kneading with a machine. See pages 410 to 415.)

For one loaf, 300 substantial strokes or about 10 minutes' worth of kneading should develop the dough. Two loaves, the standard recipe quantity, really does take twice as long. Beginners may find that they take more time to achieve a really smooth, elastic dough. There is no substitute for kneading if you want high, light, even-textured loaves. But if you are alert to what is happening under your hands and can relax into the rhythm of the process, kneading is interesting as well as pleasant work.

5. *Letting it Rise: I*   (About 1½ to 2 hours at 80°F)

Once you have finished kneading, it's time for you to rest while the yeast does its part. Keep the dough at an even 80°F if you can, and it will rise beautifully in just the allotted hour and a half.

Warm the clean bowl by rinsing it with warm water. Shape the dough into a smooth round, and put it in seam side down. Cover the bowl snugly with a platter, a plastic sheet, or whatever to keep the dough from drying out. The bowl should allow plenty of room for the dough to rise without bumping the cover—it may double or even triple in volume. *Don't oil or grease the bowl.* Unabsorbed fat can make holes in the finished loaf.

A good method of providing steady heat is to place the bowl of dough on a towel on a heating pad, using newspapers or towels to protect it from drafts. Here again, the thermometer enables you to tinker with the arrangement to get the temperature just right.

If your oven has either a gas pilot or electric bulb to maintain warmth, maybe the easiest place to keep the rising dough is inside. Ovens have the advantage of being very good at protecting the dough from drafts, but be sure to check the temperature: many ovens with pilots are far too warm inside when the door is shut. Use a rolled-up towel or some other innovation to prop the door open a little, and keep your thermometer inside to check on the temperature, making adjustments with the door opening to maintain 80°F.

6. Deflating

Often, you will see bread recipes that tell you to let your dough rise "until it doubles in volume." But the amount the dough has come up in the bowl doesn't really provide much reliable information about its state, at least not when you are using whole-grain flours. It may have risen as much as it can long before it doubles—or it may have the power to rise much more.

There is a more accurate way to tell whether dough has risen as much as it should, one we learned from a professional baker: the finger-poke test. When the dough has just been kneaded, it will feel firm and a little sticky when you press on it. After a time, though, it becomes light and spongy. When it has risen substantially, you can check to see how it is progressing: moisten your finger with water so it won't stick and gently poke it about ½ inch deep into the center of the dough. Does it feel firm or spongy? If it feels firm and the hole fills in somewhat when you take your finger out, more rising is needed. If the hole does not fill in, and its circumference sighs slightly downward, the dough has probably gone just a little bit longer than it should. Go on to the next step and make sure to catch the dough in time on the second rising. Be sure that the rising temperature is not too hot. At 80°F, the first rise should take just about an hour and a half.

If the dough feels spongy and the hole does not fill in at all, the first rising is over; the dough is ready to be deflated.

The dough is now full of tiny gas bubbles that need to be released. This is best done gently, without tearing the gluten, and for this reason we like to call this step "deflating" rather than the more traditional "punching it down." More care here means higher bread.

Moisten your hand with water and press it gently into the center of the dough first; then flatten the dough all around the sides. Next, using a rubber spatula, carefully dislodge the underside of the dough from the bowl. (You can see the gluten strands where you do this.) Fold the dough under itself all around the edge until you have a small, firm ball again. Cover the bowl and return it to its warm spot to let the dough rise once more.

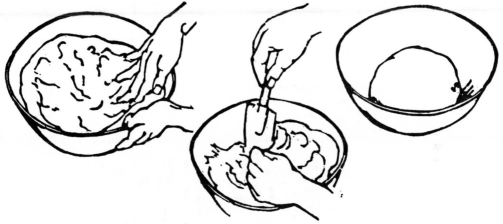

7. Letting it Rise: II (About 45 minutes to 1 hour at 80°F)

Because the yeast has been growing and multiplying, the dough will rise about twice as fast the second time. The dough develops while it is rising until the gluten attains its maximum strength and elasticity. When the dough completes its second rise, you can look for the signs that show it is *ripe* and ready to shape.

To tell if the dough is ready, test it with your moistened finger again, as just described. Now the dough should have lost all its stickiness, even on the surface. It should be dry and pleasant to handle (but not dried up or dried out!).

8. Rounding

Before shaping, deflate the dough and *round* it to invigorate the yeast and prepare the smooth gluten film to form the top of the loaf. This step is frequently omitted, but we have found that it invariably gives a higher-rising loaf.

To round the dough, dust the surface of your kneading board *lightly* with flour so the dough won't stick to it. Using a rubber spatula, carefully dislodge the dough from the bowl and turn it gently out onto the board top side down. (The smooth top surface of the dough will form the crust of your finished loaf, so try not to tear it.)

Moisten or flour your hands and flatten the dough into a circle about an inch thick, pressing gas bubbles out of it. Notice how stretchy and pliable the dough is when it is fully risen — the gluten is completely relaxed.

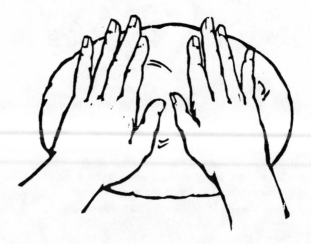

Imagine the dough as a flower whose petals you are going to fold into the center. Fold one edge just past the center, then overlap the next part of the edge and work your way around the circle, pressing them all down as you go until you have formed a ball. If the dough is very soft, you may need to go around the circle more than once to get a ball. Turn the piece over so the smooth side is up.

Next, hold the dough ball on the table with your hands on each side and move the full surface of your hands downward until they almost meet underneath, forming a little foot of dough between them on the bottom. Give the ball a turn and repeat the motion. Continue until the gluten film is smooth and tight, being careful not to tear it. You have now rounded the dough.

Deflating and rounding invigorates the yeast, but it also tenses the gluten. The dough will need to rest a few minutes before you can shape it into a loaf. Cover it with a damp cloth or inverted bowl and allow it to rest. Depending on the dough, it will gas up enough to relax in 10 minutes or so. Use this time to wash out your bowl, to grease your loaf pan, and to prepare a warm place for the final rising.

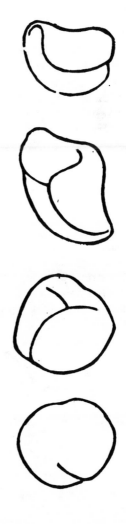

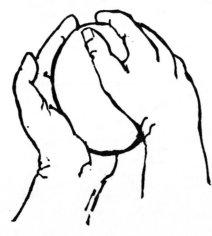

9. Shaping

There are many ways to shape a loaf. The idea is to provide an orderly structure so that it can rise its highest. A well-shaped loaf is even-textured, unlikely to crumble when sliced or to fall apart when the slice is spread.

The rounded dough is ready to shape when it has softened, or *relaxed*. Shape it in easy stages, gently, because while shaping invigorates the dough and improves its texture and structure, you want to avoid rough handling that might tear the gluten. Use either your hands or a rolling pin, whichever works better for you.

1. Dust your board lightly with flour if the dough seems sticky at all, and turn the relaxed round of dough upside down on it. Press into a circle about an inch thick.

2. Fold the dough down not quite in half, so the bottom edge smiles at you. Press the dough from one side to the other, letting the gas pop when it comes out the edge.

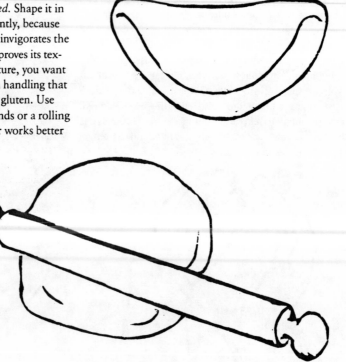

3. Fold this piece in from the sides, overlapping the ends slightly, so that the dough is about two-thirds the length of your loaf pan. Use the side of your hand or a rolling pin to press out the gas bubbles, rolling or pressing until the dough is about the length of the loaf pan.

4. Pull the dough toward you as if you were going to curl it up like a jelly roll. Since the piece is not very long, it may not actually roll up, but just about fold in half: either way is fine, as long as it's rolled snugly so that it doesn't trap air pockets.

5. Press the seam to seal it, and press the ends down to seal them.

6. Place the loaf in the center of the greased pan with the seam on the bottom, in the middle. Press the dough with the palm of your hand or the back of your fingers, so that it covers the bottom of the pan.

Mastering shaping takes a little practice; don't expect perfection the first time through. If you have to, you can go back to the rounding step, but unless your loaf looks totally ludicrous, it is better not to reshape because of the likelihood of tearing the gluten with too much handling. (Anyhow, some of the weirdest-looking breads taste the best because they're so crusty.)

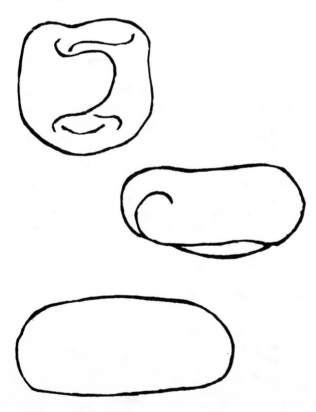

The rising in the pan, known as the proof, takes about half the time of the second rising. Because it is good to give the yeast a boost at this point, the temperature of the proof can be as much as 10° higher than it was for the previous risings, or about 90°F. If you used a heating pad, you can just turn it up a bit. If you used your oven, you can close the door a little more until it is time for preheating.

A humid atmosphere during the proof will keep the top of the loaf from drying out into a hard crust. One simple and effective way to achieve this is to rinse or spray the inside of a plastic bag with water, then put the loaf inside, puff the bag up with air, and seal. Or just place a lightweight damp cloth directly on the surface of the loaf. The ripe dough is dry enough now that the cloth won't stick; be sure it stays damp, though.

About halfway through the proof you will want to start heating the oven. Before you turn on the gas, adjust the height of the racks so that you can put your loaf as nearly in the middle as possible. Preheat the oven in time to have it up to 350°F by the time the bread is ready to go in. If you have kept the bread in the oven to rise, remove it now to a draft-free place while the oven preheats. Protecting the loaf from chills by putting it on a heating pad under a box—or devising some other way of warming it while the oven preheats—helps keep the texture of the loaf even. If the nearly risen loaf gets chilled, the crust may be thick and tough.

During the proof the dough rises fast, so watch it closely; it can get away from you. To check its progress, moisten your finger and press on the dough gently with your fingertip. Early on, it feels firm and the indentation fills in quickly. Halfway, it feels spongy on the surface but firm underneath. The dough is ready for the oven when it feels altogether spongy and the indentation fills in slowly. Don't wait until the dent from your finger remains, because by then the dough is in danger of losing its capacity to continue rising in the oven. If the dough is ripe and strong, it will rise in the pan to the top of the sides and make a satisfying arch over the middle by the time it is ready to bake. But the bread will be plenty good if the rise is a little short of that (for one reason or another), and if after 45 minutes or so you suspect it has done all the rising it is going to do, bake it even if it is less than mammoth. It's better to put bread in the oven a little early than a little late.

If your dough has risen very well, arching over the top of the pan, with plenty of resilience when you press with your finger, you can slash the top to give it extra room to spring in the oven. This bread is very pretty with one straight slash down the middle. (For general tips on slashing, see page 86.)

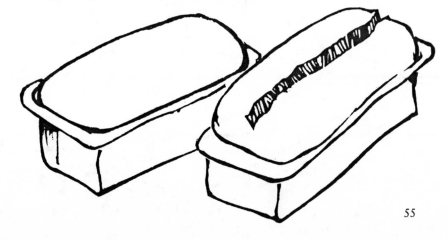

11. Baking

When the bread is ready and the oven hot, place the loaf very gently on the rack as close to the center of the oven as you can. Ideally, you will bake your bread for an hour at 350°F. But ovens vary a lot so after about half an hour (*not* before then, please!) check on the loaf to see how it looks. If it is quite brown at this point, reduce the temperature setting to 325°F and check after 15 minutes or so to see if the bread is done.

If, on the other hand, the bread is pale—pinkish rather than golden—raise the setting by 25°F and give it more time. Either way, for the next baking you will want to make suitable adjustments when you preheat. (Note that convection ovens take less time at a lower setting.)

When you check at the half-hour point, you may find that the bread is baking unevenly, brown on one end and pale on the other. Often ovens have hot spots. If yours does, gently turn the pan so that the loaf bakes evenly. (More about ovens on page 420.)

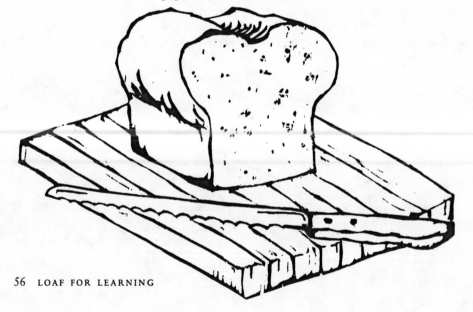

12. Is It Done?

If this is the first time you have baked the Loaf for Learning in your oven, looking at the crust will not give you much help in deciding whether it is done. After a few bakings, when you have adjusted the heat, the color of the crust will tell you a lot. In a very accurate oven with even heat, this loaf, because it has both milk protein and sweetener in it, will be a rich deep golden brown when it is done. Especially look at the upper parts of the sides of the loaf, just below the place where the top crust ends. If they are pinkish rather than brown, that loaf needs more baking.

After checking the color of the crust:

ꝫ Tip the bread out of the pan. Does it slide out easily with just a little tap? That's a good sign, because when it is done, a loaf will shrink slightly away from the baking pan.

ꝫ As you hold it, gently squeeze the sides. Do they seem bouncy? Finished bread is resilient; if it is undercooked, the loaf may retain an impression even from your gentlest squeeze.

ꝫ With your fingertips, tap the bottom sharply. Is the sound thick and muffled? Back into the oven for 15 minutes! If your thump makes a hollow sound, the loaf is done. (Don't throw up your hands at this. You won't guess wrong, however far-fetched it seems.)

ꝫ If you don't think it is a sin to cut into a loaf before it has cooled—and you have a really good, sharp wavy-bladed knife that can cut a fresh loaf without mangling it—there is an infallible test for doneness: slice off one end close to the crust and gently poke the inside. If the bread is done, the poke will spring back; if it is not done, your fingerprint will remain: back into the pan and the oven for another ten minutes or so.

13. *Looking at Your Bread*

Though you shouldn't be too critical of your early efforts, it may be fun — and helpful — to look at your finished bread from the viewpoint of professional bakers who have specific criteria for judging their product. These criteria can pinpoint areas that need more attention, and show up places you have done things right that you might never have suspected.

THE LOAF To start with, look at the loaf as a whole. Is it symmetrical? A big break down the side can be pretty, but if the loaf dips in the middle or has a big hump, the shaping has been careless. A symmetrical loaf, pleasingly slashed or with an even break down the top of each side, is likely to have strong, even slices too.

CRUST Next look at the crust. How is the color, or "bloom"? It should be neither too pale nor too dark, but warm and rich. Is it evenly colored all the way around? How does the crust feel: is it thick or thin? From this recipe you can expect a mouthwatering crust that is parchment thin, with a delicate crispness quite noticeable when you press your finger into it.

CRUMB Once the bread has had a chance to cool, slice it open and look at the inside, or "crumb." Use the same thin, sharp wavy-bladed knife we described above and cut with a light, long sawing motion, with very little downward pressure. It's easy to squash fresh bread, particularly if it is still warm.

* Look at the pattern of air cells in the crumb. Is it even throughout the slice? Are the individual cells tiny, with an elongated shape? Is each cell wall transparent and shiny? If it is the crumb will be bright and light-colored, and each slice will have enough strength to be buttered without tearing.

ِ♪ To a baker, "texture" is how the crumb feels when you stroke it with your finger. It should be velvety soft, and flaky as opposed to crumbly: that is, if you tear a piece of crumb away from the loaf, it should pull off as a flake rather than crumble up. A crumbly loaf can sometimes be soft and springy, like a cake, but often it is rough and dry.

ِ♪ You may find fine, velvety areas together with rough and dense areas in the same slice. That is a good clue that your dough was good, but needed more care during the final handling.

Well. You've had quite a day—and we hope you have a magnificent loaf, too, and a head and hands full of new sympathy for bread dough. If this is your first try at breadmaking and you've had a real success, there's no need to encourage you to keep at it; a good bread provides its own congratulations. If only we could be there to sit down with you and sample your masterpiece!

If it didn't turn out quite so well, think back on the day and see if you can pinpoint the problem areas. (The troubleshooting section on page 358 may help.) The next time *will* go better, and you have learned much more than you may suspect.

A Loaf for Learning:
Questions & Answers

How can I tell if the yeast is okay?

If you have bulk yeast, or packet yeast whose expiration date is at hand and you want to make sure it is alive and well before you start, stir only a few drops of honey (or a tablespoon of flour) into the water with the yeast, and let the mixture stand. In about ten or fifteen minutes it should foam up to the surface. If there is no sign of activity after about twenty minutes, put off the baking until you can get some livelier yeast.

Note that some kinds of yeast will foam up if they are alive, even if you don't add the honey or flour; others won't go to work until they have some fuel. If you are sure your yeast is all right, there is no need to wait till it foams in its dissolving cup: you can use it as soon as it is completely dissolved in the warm water.

Why dissolve the yeast separately?

Active dry yeast has endured some very fancy high-tech processing and needs a certain amount of care when you bring it out of its state of suspended animation.

For one thing, when yeast is dried, its cell walls become porous and fragile. The cells are quickly restored in warm water. If the water is too cool, though, some of the cell contents leak out, which damages both the yeast and the dough. If the water is too hot, the yeast will die.

The water used to dissolve the yeast shouldn't contain much sweetener or any salt because these can also harm the yeast. Once the dough is mixed up, the flour acts as a buffer to protect the yeast.

Why do you make such a big deal over temperature?

Like everyone else, yeast works best within a certain range of temperature, and less well in extremes of heat and cold. A warmer environment speeds up its metabolism so that it raises the dough more quickly. Speed isn't everything, though, and a more leisurely rise usually produces better bread. Your own convenience counts, too: by adjusting the dough's temperature within its "comfort range" you can have it ready for each subsequent step just when you expect and want it to be.

Do I have to add salt?

No, but it's tricky to make bread without it. If you want to try, see page 292.

Salt affects the bread in more ways than taste. By strengthening the gluten, it helps the loaf rise higher; by regulating the activity of the yeast, it makes the dough more manageable and predictable. Without salt, and without special precautions, the dough may rise very fast, and then suddenly stop. Because of its weaker gluten and uncontrolled yeast, a saltless loaf will often overproof and collapse in the pan.

I am used to bread recipes that say to mix the liquids and then add flour as required to make the dough. You add liquids to the flour. What difference does it make?

Our mixing method *is* different: it is designed for whole-grain flours, which vary a lot in the amount of liquid they take up. Basing the mixing on the liquids in the standard way is all right with white flour, which is always the same; with whole wheat, you can keep the balance of ingredients much more dependably if the mixing is based on the flour instead.

Why does whole wheat flour vary so much in how much water it takes to make the dough right?

Any flour that has been stored in a damp place absorbs moisture so that a measured amount will require less water than usual. In a very dry climate flour loses moisture to the atmosphere and requires more water to get the right consistency.

But even more influential than storage conditions are the solids in the flour, gluten most of all. Because it is very absorbent, the more gluten there is in the flour, the more water the flour takes up. The flour's starch can also be more or less absorbent, depending on how much it was damaged in the milling.

Surprisingly, whether the flour is coarse or fine makes very little difference except that coarse flour does take in water more slowly, so when you get partway through kneading you may find that the dough seems to be stiffer than you thought it was going to be. No problem — just work more water into the dough as you knead it, until the consistency is right.

Gluten content, starch damage, coarseness of grind — these are variables only when you are talking about whole-grain flours. White flour mills have laboratories that test the flour for gluten content, enzyme activity, baking quality, and other variables, and they make adjustments either by blending the flour or by treating it in various ways so that it is just the same from bag to bag. Whole wheat flour that comes from the giant white-flour mills may be blended in the same way, but most whole wheat flour is made from one kind (usually one crop) of grain, ground up, period. No blending, no stabilizers, no enzymes, no conditioners. You will see over the years that your flours, like fine wines, vary with the kind of grain, the climate that summer, the storage conditions, and many other things. You will notice differences not only in the amount of water the flour will absorb and in the flour's flavor, but in other baking qualities, as well.

Why knead?

When wheat flour is made into dough and kneaded, certain proteins combine to form gluten, which provides the resilient structure that expands and holds the gas released by the yeast, giving you a high, light loaf.

When the dough is first mixed, the proteins are in big knotted clumps, a little like a tangle of new wool. Kneading breaks up the clumps and straightens out the strands, finally working the proteins into a thin, strong, resilient fabric: the gluten "sheet."

The sheet is of course not flat but three-dimensional, something like a cellulose sponge. The gluten forms the stretchy wall around the thousands of cells where the gas bubbles reside. A sponge is full of holes, but in dough, the cells are sealed by the elastic gluten sheet: the gas generated inside them cannot escape.

Besides developing the gluten, mixing and kneading incorporate air, and therefore oxygen. The tiny trapped air bubbles provide the balloons that the yeast will fill with carbon dioxide, raising the dough. Oxygen helps bond proteins into gluten, "improving" the dough — making it stiffer and stronger.

How much kneading is enough?

With experience and observation, you can learn to see and feel when a dough is stretchy and elastic, its gluten fully developed. Before that, the dough is underkneaded and will tear easily. When the dough is underkneaded, the gluten is not strong enough to keep in the gas and the bread won't rise as high as it could.

Too *much* kneading makes the gluten disintegrate; the dough gets wet and sticky again and can never regain its strength. Don't worry: there's not much chance that you would overknead by hand: you'd have to knead vigorously for more than half an hour to do it, *providing the dough was made with good flour.* (With a food processor, though, overdeveloping the dough is a real possibility. See page 410.)

The 300 strokes or 10 minutes we suggest will not always be just right, but it is a good guideline for one loaf and with reasonably efficient kneading should bring the dough close to perfection.

What if the dough stays a rough and sticky mess?

If you have given the dough a righteous ten minutes and it shows no sign of smoothing out and becoming stretchy, you have got some flour that is old, or just too low in gluten to make yeasted bread. *Bad luck!* Please try again when you can get better flour. Meantime, it might be helpful to refer to pages 365 to 368.

Once it's risen, why do I have to deflate the dough and let it rise again?

The dough stops rising when the yeast's metabolism slows down. Because yeast can't move around in the dough, it eventually uses up the nourishment in its immediate vicinity. Deflating the dough moves the yeast to fresh pastures, putting it in contact with a new supply of food and oxygen. And, in fact, the dough has been *fermenting*, and alcohol has been produced by the yeast as it grows. If the dough is not deflated so that the alcohol can evaporate, it will harm the yeast and damage the dough.

"Fermentation," to a baker, means all the changes that go on in the dough from the time it is mixed until it is baked.

The dough changes with fermentation and it is these changes that make good bread. The yeast, for one thing, takes time to attain its maximum power. For another, only with time do dough enzymes have a chance to develop the subtle flavors we appreciate in bread. Maybe most significant, the gluten in the dough takes a while to mellow, becoming strong and elastic. When the gluten has reached its most resilient state, usually at the end of the second rise, the dough is said to be ripe. Ripe dough makes the best bread.

What is ripe dough?

Bakers say dough is ripe when it is at its most elastic, and can best hold the gas that the yeast is making. If you shape your loaves when the dough is ripe, they will rise their highest, have their best possible flavor, texture, and keeping quality, too.

It is good to learn to look for the characteristic signs: all the stickiness will be gone, and the dough will feel pleasantly dry to touch. You may not even need to use dusting flour to keep it from sticking to the board when you shape the loaf. If the supple dough is torn, the gluten strands will be thin and threadlike, where at the outset they were wet and thick.

When dough is first kneaded, the gluten is strong but not resilient. After some time passes, the dough becomes stretchy, and then elastic: ripe. Dough stays ripe for a shorter or longer period of time, depending mostly on the quality of the flour. If the period of ripeness passes, the gluten will soften and the dough rip easily. Bakers call such dough "old"; it makes grayish bread with poor flavor.

Why be so particular about where and how I proof the bread?

Why do all that work, and then blow it with carelessness at the end? Most kinds of bread do best if the proof temperature is the same or only a little higher than the dough temperature. If cold dough is proofed very warm, the loaf will develop a coarse, open grain on the top and sides but remain dense in the center. If very warm dough is chilled during its final rise, the crust area will be thick and tough, and there may be holes inside because the gluten ruptured.

If you overproof a loaf—and every baker does, sooner or later—don't miss the chance to look closely at what happens. The dough rises up, then stops, and the arched curve of the top begins to flatten out. When you put the bread in the oven, it doesn't rise up but stays the size it was or even settles a little, and the crust may blister. If you cut a slice, it will look open and coarse like a honeycomb at the top, dense at the bottom.

Underproofed bread will be dense and may have holes; if it rises in the oven, it is likely to have a big split along one side.

What is oven spring?

Probably not the first time you bake, but one lovely day soon, every step of your baking will go just right: your dough will be silky smooth; each rising will get exactly the time the dough needs; shaping and proofing, letter perfect. In the oven you get your bonus, the big gold star: about ten minutes into the baking the bread rises dramatically, increasing its volume by as much as a third of the original size. *That* is oven spring. If there were no such thing and you did everything right, your bread would still be great—no doubt about it—but when it happens, it is glorious.

Perfect technique will make any bread spring in the oven, but if you are keen on maximizing the event, choose the highest-gluten flour, use adequate sweetener, and include at least one tablespoon butter or two tablespoons liquid oil per loaf.

Whole-Grain Breads

Making the Bread You Want

The following list groups the breads by their characteristics rather than their ingredients — use it when you're looking for just the loaf for a particular occasion.

GOOD EVERYDAY BREADS

RECIPES FOR BEGINNERS

VERY LIGHT BREADS

VERY GOOD KEEPERS

LONG-FERMENTED & SPONGE RECIPES

Fitting Baking into Your Life

Breadmaking is an ancient art; they say we've been at it for at least 6000 years. I really believe it is in our very bones, for it seems to be something that we somehow remember rather than have to learn. Often, the first time people try to knead bread they act as if the dough is going to bite them; they tell you they're not good at things like this, or that they're afraid they'll only waste the ingredients. Pretty soon, though, a kind of peacefulness sets in, the tension and awkwardness disappear—replaced, I think, by some mysterious harmony with centuries of kneaders working in just this way, preparing similarly this most elemental kind of nourishment.

Still, bread is much more than a groovy experience for the person making it. Breadmaking *can* provide a welcome island of calm in our hectic lives, but if there is no space in your schedule for that, you still need good bread. (Probably you need it even more.) We hope to persuade you that with a little skillful juggling, your bread dough—tolerant, patient stuff— will take what stolen moments you can offer it and give you splendid loaves on nearly any schedule at all.

Breadmaking has been so much a part of the rhythm of my own life for the last many years that it is hard to remember *not* doing it; but like almost everybody, I suspect, the very idea of baking one's own bread was overwhelming and outlandish to me until one rainy day when my first loaf burst fragrant from the oven, and was sliced and eaten. I hadn't read much Tolstoy and didn't have any idea of the noble necessity of bread labor, but I did have the feeling that I was doing something dignified and real. Somehow I found time to bake again, and then another time, and before long, every week.

It was in the sixties, in Berkeley, when my life was most hectic, that the comfort of baking meant most of all. I was working full-time in the Cal Library and going to classes or meetings every night. The week seemed to hurtle by without a moment to slow down, and I couldn't *wait* for Saturday and the quiet of my kitchen, and the giant mustard-colored pottery bowl. It was the still point in a whirlpool, and probably saved my life. I made enormous batches of bread, more than a dozen loaves—the apartment was tiny, but it had a big oven—and gave them to nonbaking friends, some of whom needed the nourishment. I admit that I enjoyed eating the bread myself, heavy and sweet as it was in those days, but sharing its goodness was an essential part of the satisfaction.

If you bake regularly, you will gradually work out a comfortable schedule that is all your own. Breadmaking is in this aspect personal: you learn how to give it your best attention, how to work in friendly harmony with the yeast. When you can give it scope to perform its miracle, the yeast will amaze you with its flexibility in adapting itself to your requirements.

Yeasted dough requires attention only at intervals, as every baker knows. It does most of the work itself while you tend to other things, and can fit itself into the nooks and crannies of a truly jam-packed schedule. One busy lawyer friend who manages this feat is Katie. She likes to make bread with an "overnight sponge" recipe, but she sets it up in the early morning, instead of in the evening. The kneading is done before dinner, and the bread bakes later while dishes are washed, stories told, or writs written.

John and Bethann have improvised another variation of the overnight method. They are neighbors who share baking for their two families. He mixes and kneads the dough in the evening, leaving it on his cool back porch until morning, when Bethann takes over. Their cooperative venture bags them four or six loaves per baking; he is strong enough to knead that much dough and she easily manages the rest, using their households' two ovens.

Probably among my friends, the bakers with the biggest challenges are the ones with small children about. For them, life is full of unpredictable adventures, and so the best bread recipes are those that give most leeway in timing. But it isn't only that; when you bake for school-age brownbaggers, so sensitive to critical eyes in the lunchroom, you can make life a lot easier if your good homemade bread *looks* as though it came straight off the supermarket shelf—even when it is packed with nutrition. Busy People's Bread on page 163 is our nominee for best supporting loaf in cases like this. With it, you can set up your ingredients the night before and mix the sponge in a few stolen moments before breakfast. Later—even if it turns out to be several hours later—when the dust settles, you can make the dough, and count on light, nutritious bread to be out of the oven in short order, maybe even by lunchtime.

Melissa, a truly awesome mom and baker we know, makes bread five days a week. On four of them, she starts when she gets home from work at three-thirty, lets the dough rise during dinner, shapes the loaves and bakes them late in the evening. The day she loves is her full day at home, when she can work along with the children to prepare Flemish Desem, the bread her family likes best, and one that has the long rising periods that allow everybody to fit their other activities around it.

Whatever the undenied challenges, surely it is true that having children to bake for—and with—makes it all the more worthwhile. For one thing, you can be sure that your child's daily bread is wholesome and nutritious—not a small thing. But beyond that, the fact that you care to take the trouble to bake their bread instead of buying it is an expression of love that doesn't go unnoticed, however silent the appreciation may be.

In fact, whether or not there are children to share the fun, and even when the loaves emerge from a really ripsnorting schedule, what seems to happen to a lot of people is that over time they draw more and more satisfaction from their bread-making. As its importance in their lives increases, some com-

peting activities can begin to seem less necessary. Slowly, prior-
ities reorder themselves, and your determination to make your
own bread even on a tight schedule becomes a steady impetus
that leads naturally and mysteriously to a more home-centered
and tranquil life.

A Practical Consideration

For more about yeast and its
ways, see page 377; for
specifics about varying
timings, see page 391.

People with demanding schedules often ask us to give recipes
that make bread really fast. This is not impossible, but there
are other options that may be even easier, and better, too. The
thing to remember is that whether you follow a recipe that
takes three hours or twelve or twenty-four, the actual time *you*
put into it—mixing, kneading, shaping—is the same; and that
is only about a half an hour (or even less if you enlist mechanical help). Most of the work is done by the yeast while you do
other things, and if you make a longer-rising bread, you'll find
the dough is more tolerant when your timing is a little off.

The majority of recipes in this book call for warm risings
that get the bread into the oven in about four hours. On that
schedule, half a day a week, or twice a week, provides bread
conveniently for most families. Bread made this way rises high,
has good flavor, and has reasonable keeping quality. But if you
prefer, you can make these same breads on a more leisurely
schedule, giving the dough a total of six or seven hours to rise
at room temperature instead of warmer. The slower pace gives
your loaves extra goodness, and gives you extra leeway.

Or if you want, you can opt to speed up the whole process
so that you have your bread into the oven in less than three
hours. Such loaves don't have the quality of longer-rising
bread, but they taste good and rise very high.

To combine some of the benefits of both a long rise and a
fast one, part of the dough can be mixed ahead of time; this is
called the "sponge method"; the how-tos are given on pages
401 to 405. Sponges offer a lot of flexibility because they do

not require the same careful timing that normal, straight doughs do.

You can make good bread on many different schedules. The skill comes in adjusting the amount of yeast and the dough's rising temperature so that both the yeast's activity and the elasticity of the dough will reach their peak when you are ready to form the loaves. Dough in this prime condition is not a matter of chance, but is at your command; bakers call it "ripe dough", and whatever timing or ingredients go into making it, the result is excellent bread.

In the pages that follow are recipes with scheduling patterns that work. If you don't find one that suits you, refer to the section beginning on page 391 for an overview of many other possibilities with specific suggestions about how to make each of them work for you.

A full explanation of what ripe dough is, and what to look for at each stage along the way, is presented in A Loaf for Learning, the section that precedes this one.

Rockbottom Essentials

These few things are essential. There is much, much more about each of these ingredients *elsewhere in the book and for more information, refer to the pages noted. But whatever* *recipe you choose in this book, please follow the simple guidelines given here.*

FLOUR

Freshness Whole wheat flour, unlike white flour, is perishable and must be fresh to make good bread. If you buy packaged flour and can't read the "pull date" on it, ask your store-keeper. Don't try to make bread with whole-grain flour that has been on the shelf for more than 2 months. If you are in doubt, taste a pinch. There should be no bitterness. When you get the flour home, refrigerate it, wrapped airtight. The day before you bake, take what you will need out to come to room temperature before you use it.

Type To achieve a light loaf of yeasted bread you need flour that is high in protein. Look for "bread" flour or flour milled from *hard red spring wheat, hard red winter wheat,* or *hard white wheat.* Hard red spring wheat usually makes the lightest loaves. If none of these are on the bag, but there is a nutrition profile, look for a protein content of 14% or more, by weight.

"All purpose" flour and pastry flour make tender quick breads, muffins and pancakes, but they do not have enough gluten protein to make light yeasted breads.

Grind A very fine grind will make the lightest loaves, all other factors being equal, but many people prefer coarser stoneground flour for flavor and texture in some breads. *More about flour and milling on pages 363–376.*

YEAST

We call for active dry yeast because it is available every-where and is reliable. The usual amount called for is two teaspoons, which is one packet. If you prefer moist yeast, one cake is the equivalent of one packet. Moist or dry, if the yeast is not fresh—within its expiration date, and properly stored—it cannot raise your bread.

More about yeast on pages 377–381.

OIL OR BUTTER

Make sure it is fresh: rancid fat will spoil your bread. We strongly recommend storing both oil and butter in the refrigerator.

More about fat in general on page 389. More about butter on page 173.

WATER SALT & SWEETENERS

Any water that is good to drink—not extremely hard or soft—will do fine. Normal table salt is adequate for baking. For sweetening, we usually call for honey, but if you prefer something different there are many possibilities, and within bounds, they will all work.

More about water, salt, and sweeteners on pages 382–388.

Whole Wheat Breads

In areas of the Eastern Hemisphere where wheat will grow, bread has provided the satisfying staff of life for many centuries. Then as now the characteristics of the grain vary with climate and locale, and in response to the qualities of their local wheat people have developed innumerable different kinds of bread, from chapathi to challah, bagels to baguettes.

Europeans coming to America brought their love for bread with them. The new land had vast expanses of good soil perfect for growing wheat, and grow it they did. To deal with all that wheat, the roller mill was invented, and its pure white flour revolutionized breadmaking. In time there were generations of bakers who assumed that their flour would be the same from bag to bag, year to year. From then until now in the United States "flour" meant white flour and bread was white bread — puffy, uniform, undistinguished.

But things are changing. With the new consciousness of the importance of nutrition, with the demand for better cooking and eating, and with the increasing pressures of sheer economics (both personal and global), people are coming to require more from their bread. We celebrate this development; it is the reason for this book.

In the pages that follow you will find recipes for all sorts of whole-grain breads. In this particular section are some good plain breads for everyday eating. These recipes are designed to make delicious, flavorful breads using various strengths of whole wheat flour, even flours that, while they are otherwise good, may have a gluten content too low to produce a fancier bread. In this section you will find ways to make tender, light, moist, and delicious loaves that speak eloquently of the goodness of the wheat itself.

Basic Whole Wheat Bread

2 teaspoons active dry yeast
  (¼ oz or 7 g)
½ cup warm water (120 ml),
  about 110°F

6 cups whole wheat bread
  flour (900 g)
2½ teaspoons salt (14 g)

2¼ cups lukewarm water
  (535 ml)
2 tablespoons honey or
  other sweetener (30 ml)
2 tablespoons oil (30 ml)
  or butter (28 g)
  (optional)

Dissolve the yeast in the ½ cup warm water.

Mix the flour and salt in a large bowl, stirring to make the flour fluffy; make a well in the mixture.

Dissolve the honey in the 2¼ cups water and add the oil if you choose to use it. Pour the liquids and the yeast mixture into the well in the flour. Stirring from the center, first combine the ingredients to make a smooth batter; then fold in the remaining flour from the sides of the bowl, mixing them together into a soft dough. Since coarser flours take a while to absorb water, when using them allow a few minutes for the complete absorption of the water before you evaluate the dough. Add water or flour if more are required.

If you want really great bread—best flavor, best rise, best keeping quality—knead the dough for about 20 minutes, or 600 strokes, without adding more flour. The dough should remain soft, and should become elastic and smooth. Rest whenever you want to, but aim for 600 strokes. This is the most amazing and outrageous requirement, but after many hundreds of loaves, we are convinced that thorough kneading makes the critical difference.

If you have opted to use butter in this bread, work it in after the gluten has really begun to develop—about halfway through kneading. The butter should not melt, but should be worked into the dough while still firm. The French way is to smear the butter on the tabletop and knead in bits of it at a time, and if you are working by hand, this is easy and effective. Cutting the butter into chips with a sharp knife, or grating it and working it into the dough is effective, too, whether you are kneading by hand or by machine.

As you continue to work the dough, toward the end of the kneading, it will become lustrous, utterly supple and elastic. It should actually be white, if you look closely, with brown bran flecks clearly visible against the pale gluten.

Form the dough into a smooth round ball and put it into a big clean bowl to rise. (Do not oil the bowl.) Protect the dough from drying out by putting a platter or a plastic sheet over the top of the bowl, and keep it in a warm, draft-free place to rise.

At about 80°F this will take 1½ to 2 hours, at 70°F, about 2½.

Wet your finger and poke about ½ inch into the dough. If the hole does not fill in, the dough is ready. For best results, do not wait until it sighs deeply when it is poked. Gently press out all the accumulated gas, make the dough into a smooth round again, and put it back in the bowl, cover, and let rise again as before. The second rise will take about half as long as the first, at the same temperature. Use the same finger-poke test to decide when it has finished its second rising.

Turn the dough out onto a lightly floured tabletop or board and, keeping the smooth top surface (gluten film) carefully unbroken, deflate the dough by pressing it with wet or floury hands (or a rolling pin) from one side to the other, expelling the accumulated gas. Cut it in half and form each part gently into a round ball, still preserving the smooth gluten film on the outside. Let the rounded balls rest, covered, until they soften, usually 10 minutes or more.

Shape into loaves, place in two greased 8″ × 4″ loaf pans, and let rise once more. Loaves should take 30 to 45 minutes for their final proof. Preheat the oven to 425°F. When ready for the oven, if all has gone well, the loaves will arch over the tops of the pans, touching the sides all the way up. The dough feels spongy but not soggy, and a gentle indentation from your wetted finger fills in slowly. Place in the hot oven. After 10 minutes, turn the temperature down to 325°F. Bake for about 45 minutes to an hour, or until the bread tests done: the loaves should leave the pans easily and be an even golden brown with no pinkish areas, and if you thump their bottoms with your fingertips, they should sound hollow.

NOTE: You can, if you like, use half of the dough from this recipe to make rolls; 12 to 15 small round rolls fit nicely in a 9″ × 13″ baking pan, or nine medium ones in an 8″ × 8″ pan.

Rolls should have a very full proof: their final rising period should be at least as long as the bread made from the same dough or even as much as half again as long. If you make both a loaf and rolls, shape the rolls before the loaf, or just let them rise an extra half hour or so longer than the bread. Bake them for about half the loaf's baking time—depending on the oven temperature and their size—about 20 to 35 minutes. They are done when they are a pretty golden brown top and bottom. When pulled apart, the place where they touched each other will spring back to light pressure. Brush baked rolls with butter, if you like, and cover them with a thick terry towel to keep them soft and warm until you are ready to serve them.

Variations & Fancies

RAISIN BREAD

To make a quickie version of raisin bread from the basic dough, wait until you are ready to shape the loaf. If your pan is 8″ × 4″, press the dough out into a rectangle about 16″ × 7″. In other words, the short side of the rectangle is slightly shorter than the long side of your pan. Cover the whole surface up to about 2 inches from one of the short ends with ½ cup raisins. Add ¼ to ½ cup chopped walnuts, if you like, or ¼ cup toasted sunflower seeds. Press them all very well into the dough with moistened hands or, better yet, with a rolling pin. Dust with cinnamon if you want—it's a fine touch—but resist the temptation to add sugar or butter at this point, or the bread won't bake nicely.

Roll up the loaf jelly-roll fashion, beginning with the short end that was not left bare. Be fanatically careful to press the loaf closely as you roll it so that no air is captured in the part where the raisins are, or it will separate there, make a big hole, and wreak havoc with your toaster. Pinch the ends and seam well. Roll the loaf under your hands until it is the length of the greased loaf pan and ease it in, seam down. Use your hands to press it down well from the center outwards to be certain you have not trapped any air. Dust with cinnamon, proof, and bake.

This makes a pedestrian but quite acceptable raisin loaf. For a really elegant raisin bread and a fuller discussion, see Fruits, Nuts, and Seeds.

For a beautiful loaf of plain bread, bake it round with steam, and it will bloom into a golden sphere. Here's the easy way to do it. Instead of shaping each piece of dough into an oblong, knead gently into a ball and place seam side down in a greased 2 quart round glass or clay casserole with a domed lid. Cover and allow to rise. Preheat the oven to 450°F. When the bread has risen nicely and the dough returns slowly from a gentle indentation of your finger, pour 2 tablespoons warm water over the loaf. Slash 3 slightly curved lines ½ inch deep across the loaf. Cover and bake in your preheated oven at 450° for 20 minutes, then lower the heat to 350°F for the duration of the baking, another 20 to 30 minutes. For more details about steaming bread, see page 106; about slashing the crust, page 104.

STEAMED HEARTH LOAVES

SESAME BREAD OR ROLLS

One of the easiest and most delightful ways to fancy up the basic bread is to sprinkle toasted sesame seeds on the board when you first flatten the dough for shaping. Some of the seeds will find their way into the loaf, and there will be an abundant sprinkling of them on the crust. Rolls made this way are just great.

A less messy method is to sprinkle the pans before you put in the loaf; this works beautifully and is super-simple. To get the seeds to cling to the top of the loaf is a challenge because if your dough is just right, it won't be at all sticky. Moisten it with water or milk or lightly beaten egg, then sprinkle the seeds over the glaze and pat them gently with a moistened hand.

For a more emphatic sesame flavor, use sesame oil in the dough as part or all of the oil measure. Or you can add tahini (sesame butter)—use up to ¼ cup per loaf—with the liquid ingredients.

Crust Embellishments

Simple breads without added sweetener or milk have pale chewy crusts when they are baked in a modern oven in the normal way. Baked hotter with steam, the same bread develops a thin crispy crust that shines and browns beautifully. For instructions on how to achieve this effect in your home oven, see page 106.

On the other hand, if what you're after is a nice crust without a lot of heat and fuss, there are other ways to go than steaming. Try some of these:

FOR A SHINY CRUST Whichever of these ploys you choose, if you are going to go to the trouble to glaze a crust, be careful to cover the whole exposed surface of the loaf or it can look pretty terrible. The best tool is a really soft, fat brush or a feather brush, but a folded, fringed cloth table napkin works pretty well, too. The stiff-bristle "pastry" brushes can dent and deflate poofy unbaked dough if you aren't inhumanly deft.

EGG WASH The classic bakers' bun-wash, good on breads or buns is a mixture of one egg lightly beaten with the water it takes to fill half the shell. For more color, add a teaspoon of honey or brown sugar. You can use milk instead of water for a slightly tenderer, slightly rosier crust. Apply before, near the end, or just after baking. Less shiny, but very good for color and flavor, is to brush the loaf with butter after it comes out of the oven. This will tenderize the crust, too. You can use oil instead of butter, but it doesn't have the same flavor. If you brush with milk before and with butter after baking you get a glowing warm color and butter's special flavor.

CORNSTARCH GLAZE

This glaze is normally used on rye breads, but it works on any kind of loaf.

Stir ½ teaspoon of cornstarch into ¼ cup cold water. Boil for 5 minutes, or until it clears completely. Since this is tricky in these quantities unless you have a really tiny pan, you can make more and keep it in the refrigerator for a week or longer. Brush the glaze on the loaves at the end of baking, and then return them to the oven for a minute; or brush them halfway through the bake and then again at the end, as described.

GARNISHES

You can fancy up any loaf by sprinkling one of these on the board and rolling the shaped loaf in it:

> *sesame, poppy or other seeds*
> *rolled oats or other rolled cereal grain*
> *very finely chopped nuts*
> *slivered, sautéed onions*

Another topping, crunchy and pretty: Soak rolled oats in milk and press them onto the top of the loaf after you put it into the pan.

❧

Whatever way you treat the crust, it isn't a bad idea to keep in mind what expectations you are establishing. If the loaf looks as if it is going to taste one way and in fact tastes another, the folks will be disappointed even if the bread is actually one of their favorites. For example, if you baked a good hearty rye in an angel-food cake pan and garnished it with slivered almonds, even your biggest rye fans would be all geared up to eat Black Forest Torte when they looked at the masterpiece, and even *they* couldn't help being a little disapointed — to say nothing of the folks who abhor rye. The garnish should suit the loaf.

Slashing

Just before you put the proofed bread in the oven, you can slash the top crust to produce a three-dimensional crunchiness. Loaves that will be steamed are usually slashed because it helps them rise during baking; also, when these loaves contain no milk or sugar, the inside of the slash is pale, while the outside crust browns much more, and this is very pretty. Breads with sweetener and milk, when slashed, brown evenly, all the same color—not so spectacular. But slashing can be functional as well as cosmetic: for example, we almost always slash the loaves we bake in our convection oven, milky or not, to keep them from developing big holes just under their thin crusts, a side effect of the unusually dry heat in that oven.

To make the best slashes, use a very sharp knife. Gourmet books often suggest using a razor blade, but that gives me the willies, and anyway, except in the case of rolls, where you need to maneuver in a small place, no razor blade can compare with a sharp knife (the same kind that is the best for slicing baked bread, by the way—long, thin, narrow, wavy-edged). Please, if you do use a razor blade, plan in advance where you are going to put it, or tie a string to it to make sure it doesn't turn up in someone's food. (Incidentally, slashing bread dulls razor blades mighty quickly.)

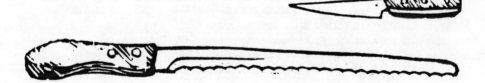

The next thing you need for the best possible slash is daring. Pretend you are Zorro and do it boldly, zip zip. (Next time will be better, I promise.) The bouncier your dough is, the deeper the slash should be—about one inch for the wildly lively ones, ½ inch for normal, good dough. If the dough is flaccid or overproofed, don't try to slash it because the slashes will not open up and the result will be worse than if you'd left well enough alone.

Finally, when making the actual cut, unless you are going straight down the middle of a panned loaf (which is great for breads with a lot of bounce—when you are really sure the loaf will spring in the oven—but a disaster if the loaf is overproofed), don't hold the knife so that it cuts straight down into the dough. Hold it rather at an angle, so that the loaf will open not like a book, but in a sort of Z.

If you are planning to slash a loaf that is glazed, glaze first and slash after, just before putting the proofed loaf into the oven. Rolls can be snipped with scissors to make porcupines.

Molasses Bread

1/4 teaspoon active dry yeast
(not compressed yeast)
(.7 g)
1/2 cup warm water (120 ml)

1/4 cup light molasses —
not raw honey here
(60 ml)
2½ cups cold water (600 ml)

6 cups coarse, stone-ground
flour (900 g) or a
little more
1 tablespoon salt (16.5 g)

2 tablespoons cold butter
(28 g)

Hearty Molasses Bread develops its rich flavor and nutritional value by taking its time. The long, slow fermentation softens the bran particles and gives the dough enzymes a chance to release a wealth of trace minerals. The keeping quality of this bread is outstanding, and the deep, bright flavor of the molasses enhances the flavor of the wheat, making an especially tasty loaf.

FOR A 12-HOUR RISE:

Dissolve the yeast in the warm water; dissolve the molasses in the 2½ cups cold water. Mix the flour and salt in a bowl, and combine all of them to make a dough. The dough should be a little stiffer than usual. Knead about 20 minutes, adding the butter toward the end of the kneading period.

Place the dough, covered, in a cool, draft-free place for up to 10 hours at about 68°F.

In the morning, deflate the dough, which should have risen a lot—as high as it can without collapsing. Place it in a warm spot now—about 90°F. Keep it there, covered, another hour or two until you are sure the dough has thoroughly warmed through.

Deflate the dough, then divide and knead it into rounds; let it rest until softened. Shape into loaves and place in greased pans, letting it rise again at 90° to 100°F. The final proof should take about an hour. Since the bread usually comes up in the oven, don't be dispirited if it has not risen fully beforehand —put it in the preheated oven anyway.

Bake at 350°F for at least an hour. Give this long-rising bread plenty of time to bake, particularly if the loaves aren't very high.

TO MAKE THIS BREAD IN 24 HOURS:

Keep the dough as long as 20 hours in a cool place 55° to 60°F, deflating it at 8-hour intervals (more often when convenient). After that, proceed as above for proofing and baking.

Whole Wheat Sourdough

Sourdough bread, a specialty of Northern California, Eastern Europe, and several points in between, is flavored with a starter — a small amount of dough that's allowed to ferment until it's sour. Since they vary a lot, sourdough starters with especially good flavor are valued highly, and often passed from friend to friend like great treasures. It is in this spirit that we pass Manuel's starter (page 150) on to you.

&

THE STARTER Mix together and keep at about 65°F for 12 to 18 hours. Manuel's starter, kept at room temperature for 12 hours, makes a moderately sour bread that is very light.

THE DOUGH Dissolve the yeast in warm water. Stir the flour and salt together; add the starter mixture and the water and mix them all together to make a soft dough. Knead until supple and elastic.

Form the dough into a ball and place it smooth side up in the bowl. Cover and keep in a warm, draft-free place. After about an hour and a half, gently poke the center of the dough about ½ inch deep with your wet finger. If the hole doesn't fill in at all or if the dough sighs, press flat, form into a smooth round, and let the dough rise once more as before. The second rising will take about half as much time as the first.

Press the dough flat and divide in two. Round it and let it rest until relaxed, then deflate and shape into loaves. Divide into two or three pieces and round them. Let them rest and then shape into loaves: the dough will make two 8″×4″ pan loaves, but it is nicer baked hearth-style on cookie sheets that have been dusted with cornmeal (see page 102.) Make two or three round hearth loaves, or shape into rolls. Let rise in a very warm, draft-free place until the dough slowly returns a gently made fingerprint.

Place in preheated 450°F oven. Follow one of the suggested steaming techniques on page 106. When the crusts show shine and color, turn the heat to 325°F. Continue baking for about 40 minutes for the large loaves, less for the smaller ones, about half an hour for good-sized rolls.

STARTER
INGREDIENTS

¾ cups of Manuel's
  sourdough starter
  (175 ml), or your own

1½ cup whole wheat flour
  (225 g)

¾ cup water, room
  temperature (175 ml)

DOUGH
INGREDIENTS

2 teaspoons active dry yeast
  (¼ oz or 7 g)
½ cup warm water (120 ml)
2 cups whole wheat flour
  (300 g)
2½ teaspoons salt (14 g)

the starter mixture

½ to 1 cup water
  (120–235 ml)
cornmeal for dusting
  (optional)

Scottish Sponge Bread

When the demand for bread exceeds what the usual baking will provide, but kneading up more than a couple of loaves at a time is a bit beyond your endurance, this recipe comes to the rescue. It takes advantage of some shortcuts of old-time Scottish bakers who made large quantities of famous bread without the aid of machines.*

One of the tricks they used was to prepare a portion of the dough—the *sponge*—the night before. This method gives the yeast a head start, so that by the time you're ready to mix the rest of the dough, the yeast will have built its own vigor and also produced the substances that make for good flavor and keeping quality in the final product. An added bonus is that the prior fermentation develops the gluten somewhat so that later on when kneading time comes, there is less work to do. Scottish Sponge is a real old-fashioned baker's sponge—or, in this case, a half sponge, since it contains about half of the dough.

In addition to turning out a relatively easy five loaves, this sponge makes it possible to use lower-gluten flours to good advantage. One practical example: a friend bought a bag of pastry flour by mistake, and with this recipe used it to produce marvelously tasty, light bread.

The sponge offers flexibility, too, because on the second day, if you want, you can divide it into parts, adding different kinds of flour to each part, and so make a variety of breads from the same starter.

*NOTE to owners of dough hooks and food processors: Don't be intimidated—this recipe works beautifully when kneaded by machine, too. In fact it is ideal for making more loaves than yours is designed to knead, because you can mix the sponge the night before, and then make more than one batch out of it on the following morning, completing the kneading of each part separately at that time.

For the first 12 to 16 hours the sponge ferments with no additional attention required; then it is made into the larger dough, which rises twice, for an hour each time. The dough is then divided and shaped, allowed to rise once more, and baked.

We find it helpful to measure out the dough's ingredients and set them aside at the same time we are measuring the sponge ingredients. This makes the dough mixing much simpler, especially if you are on automatic pilot early in the morning.

PREPARING THE SPONGE

When the sponge is to stand for 16 to 18 hours, use the smaller amount of yeast and very cold water (refrigerated or iced, if necessary, to make sure it is 40°F). Use the larger quantity of yeast and cold tap water (about 50°F) when you ferment the sponge for 10 to 12 hours.

≥

Dissolve the yeast in the warm water. Combine the flour and salt. Make a well in the center. Add the cold water, the yeast, and the malt syrup to the well, mixing them all into a medium-stiff dough.

Knead the sponge by hand for 10 minutes only. A sponge needs enough developing to trap the gas, but since it will get more kneading in the full dough, you don't want to develop it fully now.

Place your sponge in a container large enough to hold about three times its bulk. Cover it closely to protect the top from drying out, and place in a cool, reasonably draft-free place. A sponge is ready when it has risen fully and begun to fall back or recede in the bowl. (In fact it looks very spongy.) However, there is a range of several hours during which you can go on to the next step and still get good results.

SPONGE
INGREDIENTS

1 to 2 teaspoons active dry
* yeast (⅛–¼ oz*
* or 3.5–7 g)*
¼ cup warm water (60 ml)

6 cups high-gluten bread
* flour (900 g)*
1 tablespoon salt (16.5 g)

2½ cups cold water
* (600 ml)*
¼ cup malt syrup or
* other sweetener (60ml)*

DOUGH
INGREDIENTS

3½ cups warm water
  (825 ml)
4½ teaspoons salt (25 g)
⅓ cup honey (80 ml)
⅓ cup oil (optional)
  (80 ml)
6 cups whole wheat bread
  flour (900 g)
3 cups whole wheat pastry
  flour (450 g) or
  other low-gluten flour

MIXING THE DOUGH

For one large batch of dough, you will need a giant bowl, about 12 quarts. Put the warm water, salt, honey and oil in the bowl. Break the sponge into little pieces in the liquid, and stir in the flour. Now press the dough hard, first with one fist, then the other to make sure the ingredients are well blended. Feel the dough to evaluate its water content, and if it is too stiff, add water, ½ cup at a time, working it in until the dough reaches the proper consistency. This takes considerable effort, no doubt about it.

Knead the whole dough for 400 strokes or about 20 athletic minutes, until the surface is smooth and shiny. Rest whenever you need to, but if it's easier, divide the dough into more manageable pieces and knead them separately.

Let the dough rise in the bowl for an hour in a warm place, 80° to 85°F. Deflate it, and let it rise again for another 45 minutes to one hour.

If you have not already done so, divide the dough into five pieces, round them, and let them rest, covered, for about 10 minutes, until relaxed; then shape into loaves. Put them in greased 8″ × 4″ pans. If you like, you can make traditional Scottish batch bread: four long loaves (instead of five) baked together in a 10″ × 16″ pan. They will rise to support each other, making the characteristic tall skinny domed loaves. (Butter the sides to make separating them easier.)

Let the loaves rise in a warm place — 85° to 90°F.

If your oven does not hold five loaves at once, put two of them in the refrigerator now in a puffed-up plastic bag. These loaves will rise slowly, and should be ready to bake as soon as the first loaves come out of the oven. Two can bake together in an 8″ × 8″ pan — a little of each method.

Preheat the oven to 375°F. Breads made from long-rising doughs are moister than those from short-rising ones, so they need to bake at a higher temperature or for a longer time. Bake for 50 to 60 minutes for the pan loaves. You may need as much as an hour and a half at 350°F for the batch bread.

VARIATIONS

To prepare different kinds of breads from the one large dough, or to knead each part separately, divide the sponge into five equal parts, and do the same with the dough ingredients. Proceed with each fifth, or with two-fifths or three-fifths, as with the whole dough, kneading until it is fully developed. There are many possibilities, since the pastry flour can be replaced by any low-gluten flour.

Two Great Classics

An artist—poet, sculptor, or cook—may often reach the greatest heights of creativity by not just working within the limitations of the chosen medium but by using the limits themselves as a prod to find new reserves of imagination. In the kitchen, to take the nearest example, turning vegetarian has made great cooks out of middling ones, partly because the challenge casts a new light on everything. The same thing happens sometimes when you have to learn to cook for an allergic family member, or someone who needs to omit fat or sugar: what seems like an obstacle can turn out to be a stepping-stone to something much better, happier, more important, even, than you had suspected.

Medieval village bakers in Europe could not, like modern bakers, load their everyday loaves with milk and butter, sugar and chemical "improvers." They did not have electronically controlled ovens, kneading machines, or even active dry yeast. Their flour was locally grown, and not very high in gluten even in the best years. And so over centuries, limited as they were, these bakers developed a method that makes the simplest wheat-flour dough into truly superb bread. Later, when white flour and commercial yeast came on the scene, the method was adapted to produce what we know today as French bread. It draws much artistry from its ancestry, and makes good use of some modern advantages, too.

In the following pages are two presentations of this classic tradition. The first is our whole wheat version of modern French bread, using active dry yeast along with the traditional timing pattern to make a flavorful, familiar-looking light loaf with the requisite crispy-chewy crust. The second is, to us, the pride of this book: Flemish Desem Bread, the kind of food only a centuries-old tradition can produce. This is, we feel sure, the ancestor of modern French breads, both sweet and sour. The loaves can be as light as yeasted ones, but the leavening comes not from baker's yeast but from a starter born of the wheat itself, and the bread's flavor and keeping quality are unexcelled.

Both breads are delicious and satisfying in spite of the fact that they are made without fat, sugar, or dairy products. They draw their excellence from the marriage of the baker's skill and the natural goodness of the grain.

FRENCH BREAD Perhaps no other nation's people are as serious about bread as the French, and French bread is a triumph of art over circumstance. Even today in France, the law says that daily bread must contain only French flour, plus yeast, water, salt—no additives or adulterants, no imports. French flour is not very high in gluten, but it has excellent flavor. American bakers make their "French" bread from high-gluten American flour, producing quite a different, but also outstanding, bread.

In France daily bread is baked in small shops rather than in the home; it is seldom made in large factories. Bakers in different parts of the country have developed breads with distinct individuality. For example, in some areas, wheat and rye were traditionally sown, grown, and harvested together: in a good year there was plenty of wheat, in a bad year, plenty of rye, always in combination—so the bread is hearty and moist with the flavor and heft of rye.

The recipe we present here translates traditional French techniques into whole grain and home style. The bread is awfully good. The flavor and texture are close to real French French bread (or so we imagine!)—very light, with a velvety crumb and a crispy-crunchy-chewy crust. The bright flavor comes from the wheat itself: the combination of bread flour and a little pastry flour makes a reduced-gluten flour with extra sweetness. The best French bread we ever made came from a gift of winter wheat organically grown in Carissa Plains, California. We used it without pastry flour because its gluten content was a already a little low. The flavor was remarkable—just perfect for French bread.

If, on the other hand, you want your loaf to resemble American French bread—chewy and airy, with the clear ivory flavor of gluten—don't blend flours, but use only bread flour, finely ground. Be sure to knead the dough thoroughly.

A toothsome version of the recipe is achieved by using rough stone-ground flour in place of finely ground. When it is

made with freshly home-ground flour, the bread has to be one of the best in the world. We call it Country French.

Last, for Peasant French, use rye flour in place of the pastry flour. If your flours are freshly ground, you can close your eyes and just about be transported to northern France. This is a good keeper with remarkable flavor.

Whole Wheat French Bread

Getting down to business, there are a few things to remember when you are making this bread: technique, one might say, has to replace the fat and sugar! Most important of all is the one cardinal rule most often ignored (maybe it is just hard to believe): the dough must be kept cool throughout the whole rising period until it goes into the hot oven. If the temperature of the rising dough goes over 70°F, the fermentation changes, and the loaves will simply not have the character, the rise, or the flavor that they should have.

To keep the dough cool, the water used to mix it—except for the yeast-dissolving water—should be quite cold. For hand kneading, cold tap water is usually fine—providing that it *is* cold. In the summer, our own tap water is about 65°F, and by the time the dough is mixed, it is way too warm. Under these circumstances, or if you will be kneading by machine, be sure to refrigerate the water beforehand, or ice it. Machine friction heats the dough 20° to 50°F!

The dough should be kneaded until it is exceptionally silky and elastic. If you use all bread flour, allow longer than usual for the kneading.

Decide before you begin what shapes you will want to make of the risen dough, and how you will bake them. Since this bread is at its best only when it bakes very hot and steamy, check out the steaming methods on page 106 to see which one suits your equipment and the shape you want.

Dissolve the yeast in the warm water.

Stir the flour and salt together. Add the cold water and the yeast and mix together. The dough will be stiff. Add at least half a cup more water by wetting your hands as you knead. Take care to develop the dough very fully; the time that takes will depend on which flours you have used: the high-gluten American version will take *at least* 20 minutes, others somewhat less. The dough should be quite soft when you finish, and silky.

Cover the dough and let it rise in a cool place, never over 70°F at any time. The cool rise makes the splendid flavor of this bread possible; if it is hurried at all by warming the dough, the bread will be astonishingly uninteresting. The first rising period takes about 2½ to 3 hours. If you wish, you may keep the dough cooler, and give it longer, but don't let it go faster. After about 2½ hours, poke a wet fingertip into the dough about ½ inch deep; if the mark stays without filling in at all, the dough is ready to deflate. (If it sighs and collapses slightly, it is too warm. Don't worry, all is not lost, but take steps to make the next two risings cooler.)

Deflate the dough by turning it out onto a lightly floured board and, with wet hands, pressing out all the accumulated gas. Try to handle the dough gently to avoid tearing it. Fold it into itself to make a smooth ball and place the ball again in the bowl to rise. Cover and set it again in a cool place, as before, using the same test to determine when the dough is fully risen. The second rise takes about 2 hours; now it is ready to shape. It should be lively, elastic, not at all sticky on the surface, and still very soft. If the dough still seems a trifle sticky, allow a longer resting period in the next step.

2 teaspoons active dry yeast
(¼ oz or 7 g)
½ cup warm water (120 ml)

5½ cups whole wheat flour,
a combination of:
4 cups bread flour (600 g)
plus
1½ cups pastry flour
(225 g)

2½ teaspoons salt (14 g)

1½ cups cold water (355 ml)
(40° to 50°F)*
more water for kneading

*If you use a food processor
in this recipe, use ice water.

ROUNDING Before shaping the loaves or rolls, you will want to round the dough in loaf-sized pieces; this invigorates the yeast and structures the dough for the best possible rise. If you are making rolls, make one or two rounds. Protect the dough from drafts as you work.

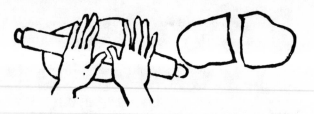

Turn out on floured board and press out gas. Divide and round as shown.

Turn the rounds seam side down and let them rest until they are soft. Use this time to wash the bowl, and to prepare baking pans or whatever other arrangement you will be using to proof the loaves.

Some Possible Shapes

When you consider what shape you want for your French breads, one of the first things to think about is your oven and the utensils you have at hand for baking the bread. Please read the pages on steaming (pages 106 and 107), and plan to start with whatever shapes are likely to work best with your equipment, because the crust of the bread depends on good steaming, and the quality of the bread depends quite a lot on how good the crust is. The traditional shapes we associate with French loaves maximize crust area, and if your equipment and oven can accommodate them, you will have wonderful bread indeed. It is true that the round loaves have less crust, but we like them very much because there is no need to worry about keeping the oven hot enough, or controlling the steam: it is all there in the casserole dish. The bread is plenty pretty, too, and makes great sandwiches.

ROUND HEARTH LOAF

Simple and surefire, and our favorite, is the traditional countryside style round hearth loaf. Round the loaves and let them rest and then, when they get a trifle saggy, round them in the same way *a second time* and place each one in a deep 2½-quart lidded clay or glass casserole, greased and dusted with cornmeal. Alternatively, you can proof them upside down on flour-dusted canvas for later transfer to baking tiles (see page 103) or place them on a baking sheet dusted with cornmeal for proofing and baking.

Shape the rounded loaves into long loaves as shown. Two will fit nicely on a 12″ × 18″ baking sheet. The sheet can be dusted with cornmeal and the loaves placed on them, proofed, and baked on the sheet; or, proof the loaves upside down on canvas and transfer them to tiles (see page 103). (If you choose this option, be sure to make your "peel" a little longer than the loaves will be when they are fully risen.)

Let the rounded loaf rest until it is soft and puffy once again.

Press to 1″ thick. Make an oblong about two-thirds as long as you want the loaf to be.

Fold the sides into the middle and press or roll again to 1″ thick.

Fold lengthwise and seal the edge. Turn the loaf seam-downwards.

Roll back and forth under your palms until it is nearly as long as you want the loaf to be.

This shape is so popular that there are several kinds of rounded pans and long clayware boulanger casseroles especially made for baking it. If you have one of them, follow the instructions for greasing that come with the pan. It may be that your whole wheat dough will rise somewhat less than the white dough the manufacturer expects. If you want your bread to be as big as the pan will accommodate, you can include a little more dough than the pan's instructions suggest. In that case, you will need to increase the baking time, too.

The object of the long thin shape, and of the even thinner versions that follow, is lots of crust. The flavor of any bread derives largely from magical happenings in the complex chemistry of the crust as it bakes. More crust means more flavor, and the crust of French bread *properly baked with steam* is among the best.

These slim long loaves are splendid for picnics, served with soft smelly cheeses — and nothing could be better alongside a hearty soup on a winter evening. Again, it takes a good hot steamy bake to provide the best crust possible. Use either a flat baking sheet or the dippy long baton pans that are sold in every kitchen shop. Shape the loaves like the batards, but use only half as much dough in each one; make each of them as long as your pan, and very skinny.

BAGUETTE

ROLLS You can make them small, for dinner rolls, or larger, for lunches. The traditional shapes are like a batard loaf, only smaller, or round like a tiny hearth loaf. Make six to twelve from half the dough, and treat as you would the loaves except that the smaller the bread, the crustier it will be, and the shorter the time it will take to bake.

About Grease & Cornmeal

When French or other lean breads are to be baked as hearth loaves on a baking sheet, the sheet can be dusted generously with cornmeal and not greased: the loaf will not stick. Note that a really thick layer of cornmeal, say an eighth of an inch, can provide such effective insulation that the oven heat won't reach the bread and its bottom will not bake. A too-thin layer, with much of the pan showing through, of course, can't keep the bread from sticking.

If the bread will touch the sides of the utensil, then that part at least will have to be greased because the cornmeal won't protect it. When grease is used, a dusting of cornmeal is optional, but it does add a nice touch to the finished loaf, and has the virtue of absorbing excess grease in the places the dough doesn't cover, which saves you from having to scrub off burnt grease.

If you don't have cornmeal, other low-protein flours or meals can be used, but corn is best.

Proofing

Whatever the shape, the bread will be ready to bake after about an hour at 70°F. Leave your loaves exposed to the air, but protected from drafts. If necessary, cover them loosely with a big cardboard box, but don't seal the loaves off in a plastic bag. French is the one bread that does *not* want humidity when it is proofing! Be sure that you preheat the oven thoroughly well in advance of the baking so it is plenty hot by the time the bread is ready to go in. When it is ready for the oven, the dough will be spongy and saggy, with a delicate crusty surface.

A professional baker gives his loaves their final rise, or proof, upside down in a cool nonhumid place. Later, when the bread is ready for the oven, it is placed gently on a long-handled wooden paddle, or *peel*, and at that time each loaf is turned over to sit on the firm crust that the air has put on its top-now-bottom. The baker slashes the loaf, and then with a deft push-pull it is made to fly off the peel precisely into its place on the floor of the hot brick oven.

This sounds tricky, but it isn't difficult and home bakers can easily adapt the technique for baking their own French bread on oven tiles or a baking stone. The big advantage is that the top of the loaf (the bottom while it was rising upside down) stays soft, and so continues to rise nicely in the oven.

To proof the loaves upside down, shape them and invert them on a baking sheet or tray lined with heavy cloth and dusted with flour. When the time comes to put them in the hot oven, you will need a rough equivalent of a baker's peel, of a size and shape to suit your loaves and oven. To improvise a peel, try a piece of eight-inch masonite (like a clipboard) or heavy cardboard covered with contact paper, or quarter-inch finished plywood sanded down on one edge. (For round loaves, a thick magazine would work, for that matter.) Your peel should be a little bigger than one loaf and stiff enough to support the loaf if you hold the peel with one hand.

Slashing French Breads

Slash the loaves just before putting them into the oven so that they will have the characteristic open-leaf pattern on their crusty surface. We find that we have the best results of all using our bread-slicing knife for slashing: a long, thin, sharp, wavy-edged blade. For tiny rolls, it is easier to use a very small, extremely sharp, thin-bladed paring knife, or you can snip them with wet scissors—easy and pretty, too. Some gourmet bread books suggest using a razor blade, and it does work, but as we have said elsewhere, for heaven's sake be careful! Razor blades are out of context in the kitchen, easy to forget, and potentially hazardous.

Slash as deep as an inch if the dough seems lively, less if you aren't too sure about it; small rolls take about ½ inch. The slash patterns sketched here give pretty baked results. For the long loaves, make a cut at each end, almost lengthwise, and almost to the middle of the bread. The third long diagonal is in the center. Slash round loaves to suit your fancy—rolls, too.

The prettiest slashes are made by holding the knife so that the blade cuts sideways, almost as if it were peeling the crust, rather than cutting downward into the loaf. Done so, the slashes open upward as the loaf rises during its spectacular spring in the oven. If the cuts are directly downward, the loaf will open out and lie prostrate, not only less beautiful but less tall than it should be.

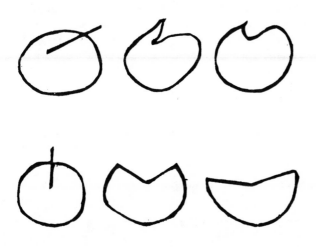

Bake the bread using one of the steaming methods that follow. When the crust begins to color, remove the source of steam and immediately lower the oven heat, because high heat without steam will burn the bread very quickly. When it is golden-brown and beautiful, and hollow-sounding if you thump its bottom with your fingertips, the bread is done. How long that takes depends on the size of the loaves or rolls, and the vagaries of your oven. Generally speaking, this bread bakes in less time than the ones we have described thus far. Giant round loaves, however, can take 45 minutes or more; small thin loaves or rolls may bake in as little as 10 minutes.

Some Methods for Steaming Bread

If French Bread were baked like a normal loaf of bread, its crust would be thick, tough, and pale because bread without added milk protein or sweetener can't brown at moderate oven temperatures. Baked in the traditional way in a brick oven, very hot and steamy, though, the crust becomes beautifully rosy brown, thin and crispy-chewy, and the flavor of the bread is at its best, too. Most of us don't have brick ovens in our kitchens, but a pretty good approximation of their effects can be had with simple everyday equipment—and without endangering life and limb. There are many ways to steam bread but we've found these effective and less hazardous than some other methods.

WETTING THE LOAF

Preheat the oven to 450°F. Spray or paint the proofed bread with warm water, slash it, and put it in the oven quickly so that as little heat escapes as possible. Repeat the painting or spraying every 3 to 5 minutes until the crust begins to brown nicely —this should take about three or four treatments, depending on your oven and your dough. Reduce oven heat to 350°F and bake until the bread is done, as suggested in the recipe.

Advantages of this method: it is very simple and requires no unusual equipment. It can be used with any shape or size of bread. Unfortunately it is effective only in ovens that can recover very quickly the heat lost when the door is open.

STEAMING THE OVEN

Place a small heavy skillet or other pan in the bottom of the oven when you preheat. When you put in the bread, pour one cup of boiling water into the pan, shutting the oven quickly. You can, if you like, use this technique in conjunction with the previous method.

This method is easy, but it works only with a very well-insulated oven—which, unfortunately, most latter-day ovens are not. It can be pretty stressful to the pan you use, too: make sure it is all metal, and one that you don't mind getting warped or rusty.

These two methods will be enhanced if you line your oven with quarry tiles. More about this on page 420. OVEN TILES

Instead of tiles you can use a flat baking stone. Either proof the bread directly on the stone and then put them together into the hot oven, or let the bread rise on floured canvas while the stone preheats along with the oven and them transfer the proofed bread to the stone. With the addition of steam, the home oven comes very close to the traditional brick oven for baking. (Still and all, after many experiments, we find nothing works better than a covered casserole.)

Give the bread its final rise in a covered casserole dish — glass or pottery—which has a tightly fitting domed lid. It should be big enough to allow the dough to do all the rising it wants to, including a good spring in the hot oven: depending on the dough, triple the original size of the dough would not be too much. COVERED CASSEROLE

Ordinary Pyrex covered glass ovenware in the deep 2½-quart size works perfectly for one regular-size (round) loaf. Some of the clay casseroles that can be soaked in water are splendid. The snug domed lid is the crucial thing in whatever you use. Some Corningware lids don't fit tightly enough to hold the steam in, but the casseroles are a good size; if you have one and want to use it, seal around the lid with foil where there are big gaps. Corningware tends to stick, so be sure to grease the dish extra well, and dust it generously with cornmeal.

If you have a heavy metal baking pan, you can bake the bread (on grease and cornmeal) in that, covering it with another similar pan inverted over it. Seal with foil — or just cover it with foil! (Be sure to leave plenty of rising room by ballooning the foil.) We have had splendid French loaves from this method, unorthodox (and easy) as it is.

Let the dough rise in the casserole or pan according to the directions in the recipe. Preheat the oven in plenty of time so that the temperature is at 450°F when the dough has risen. If the casserole is thick clay, there will be a delay while the dish heats up, so put it in the oven a little earlier than you would normally.

Just before you put the bread in the oven, pour 2 to 4

tablespoons of warm water over the loaf. Use the smaller amount with lighter breads, more with the substantial types. This is all absorbed into the top crust, so don't mind that the bread seems to swim at first. Slash, cover, and bake. When the crust is nicely browned, after 20 minutes or so, reduce the oven temperature and finish baking as suggested in the recipe.

This simple, safe, and effective method is our favorite by far. Its only limitation is the shape and size of the pans you can figure out how to cover.

Whatever method you use for steaming, please be careful. The temperatures are high and the presence of steam makes the heat intense. Plan ahead, so that you have the oven racks in place before heating the oven, and so that you know where you are going to put each pan or dish when the time comes.

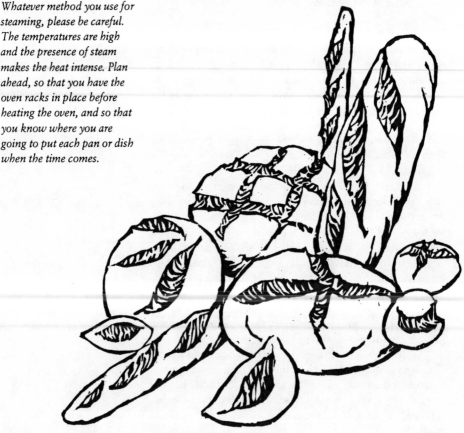

Flemish Desem Bread

Those of us who enjoy it daily think that this is the very best of breads. Its subtle, sophisticated flavor never bores or wearies, but rather draws ever more enthusiastic appreciation; the bread keeps well and digests comfortably. Composed of just a few ingredients—wheat, water, salt—the loaves are light and delicious without sweetener, milk, fat or yeast. Nothing makes better toast, sandwiches or crumbs. To us, this is the perfect Staff of Life.

Making the bread, once you get set up, is easy; getting set up can be fairly challenging. It isn't so much that the procedure is difficult (it isn't), but that the desem, the starter, is a natural (maybe I should say an *old-timey*) creature, who favors rhythms that are slower, ingredients necessarily purer, than we twentieth-century breadbakers are accustomed to provide. The challenge is more to your credulity than to your ingenuity, though both of them may well be tested.

This set of instructions certainly can't be called a recipe in any normal sense, and if you follow it through, you will create much more than a loaf of bread. For us, the desem is a living partner in the twice-weekly adventure of its baking; our affection for it, and our respect, do not easily fall into any normal category; some others who have made desem are less reverent, and refer to their starter as a favorite pet that needs care and attention—but one that has a good deal to give, too. Whatever it means to you, once you succeed in establishing a desem starter, and begin baking the bread, your life will change in a small way: however mundane it may be, something rather wonderful will be yours. This is not a project you would try just once to see how you like it, but it is perfect for serious bread eaters who can bake regularly and who want the best possible bread: simple, flavorful, healthful, satisfying.

Baldwin Hill Bakery

We first learned about desem bread in a tantalizing article in a copy of the *Saturday Evening Post* (January/February 1979), lent to us by a friend who had heard we were setting out to write this book. We had just started working on sourdoughs, and this one sounded really special, but the recipe given in the magazine was disappointingly ordinary. In an adventurous mood, we dialed the Boston information operator, and before long found ourselves talking to baker Hy Lerner himself. He was awfully nice and very generous and patient with help and advice, but more than a little skeptical about our being able to get a real desem starter going.

Hy is a medical doctor with a deep and long-standing interest in the importance of nutrition—not just the "feed 'em and weigh 'em" kind of nutrition, but a respectful understanding of the relevance of people's attitudes toward food and nourishment to their health in the largest sense. He has worked with such diverse lights in the field as Jeremiah Stamler and Michio Kushi, and his pioneering is far from over. The bread is one chapter in the story, and one he gladly shares.

The loaves that come out of the oven at Baldwin Hill Bakery represent the happy culmination of a long odyssey that began over a decade ago when Hy and his wife, Lora, tasted their first slices of a loaf brought to them by a friend. This was real bread, not the health food sort at all, but healthful nonetheless, as well as delicious, and satisfying—the kind of nourishment that ought to be available to everyone. When they could not duplicate the bread in their own kitchens however they tried, Hy and his friend, architect Paul Petrofsky, pooled their savings and went like pilgrims to the Lima Bakery in Belgium, the source of that original marvelous loaf. The Lima Bakery is reputed to be a fortress of closely guarded secrets, but the young Americans were welcomed and housed and taught, and came home determined to produce a similarly perfect product on this side of the Atlantic.

They established the Baldwin Hill Bakery in a beautiful woodland outside Boston where there is plenty of pure water and hard wood to fire the big brick ovens. Now, a decade later, they bake nearly 10,000 loaves a week, distributing them in the area around Boston. Here on the Pacific Coast we have, we think, perfected a home-style version; but we cherish the hope that someday every community will have a Baldwin Hill Bakery so that all those who are unable to bake this bread in their own homes will be able to partake of it.

The Desem

The secret of the chewy-light texture, the full, mellow, tangy flavor, and the extraordinary keeping quality of this bread lie with the *desem*, its unique starter dough. (Desem (day'-zum) is Flemish for "starter.") Microscopic organisms live in the desem, and they leaven and flavor the bread. We would call the bread a sourdough, but in Europe it is called a leavened bread —leavened as opposed to yeasted. The flavor is not all that sour when the bread is properly made: it is much more sophisticated and universal than any rustic sourdough.

Hy speculates that the desem organisms live on organic wheat in the same way that organisms that make wine live naturally on grapes. By providing them with conditions that favor their growth, you can help them to prevail and prosper: that is the object of the method outlined in the following pages.

We have tried many other sourdough starters, but none can hold a candle to either the flavor or leavening power of the desem. The instructions we give here *work*. Following them, we have made many successful desems using different flours and wheats; and friends have proved the formula for us, too. Problems come only when the simple requirements of the desem organisms are neglected through using flour contaminated with pesticide residues or with mold from a dirty mill, or using chlorinated water, or—the easiest pitfall to tumble into (or avoid!)—somewhere along the line, letting the temperatures get too warm or too cold. The desem is *there*: if you follow these instructions it will serve you indefinitely.

What's Going On Here?

Sometimes people (and cookbooks) can make the simplest things seem the most complicated. Surely that is true with Desem Bread—our longest "recipe," and our simplest bread! In a nutshell, here is what the following pages describe.

The bread's unique character and its rise come from the starter—the spirit or soul if you will, that gives life to the dough. The desem *looks* like a little wad of dough—but oh my.

It takes about two weeks to get a desem starter going. The first five days—the desem's infancy, if you like—is spent in a special sort of incubator: a big bag of flour. On the sixth day the desem is moved to the covered crock or jar. You feed it flour and water every day this week and keep it carefully cool.

After two weeks the desem is nearly mature, but not quite. It still needs watching and nurturing until it achieves full vigor.

Once you have a functioning desem you will want to bake with it every week and also to feed it twice a week.

That's the whole idea. The directions that follow are only to explain each part of this process.

What You Need to Have to Start

Starting the desem is so simple that providing for it would have been second nature before the Industrial Revolution: pure water, organic stone-ground wheat, and some time in a cool cellar to bring it to vigorous life. Today, to find unchlorinated pure water is not so easy, and most wheat is treated with chemicals. Not every house has a cellar, and even in the winter it isn't easy to find a place that you can keep at 50° to 65°F. Finally, many of us lead lives sufficiently hectic that making a commitment to the regular care of a starter dough seems like a luxury. But even considering all this, there is no reason to be intimidated; it can be done, it is not all that difficult, and once you get set up, making the bread is simplicity itself.

Pure spring water is best (not distilled: bread dough does better when its water contains minerals). If your tap water is otherwise good, you can dechlorinate it by boiling and leaving it uncovered overnight. Use this water at room temperature or cooler, to feed your desem and make up your dough. If you will be using a dough hook, the water should be cold.

WATER

Coarsely ground and fresh, preferably not more than five days from the milling—that's the ideal. The flour you choose should be milled from hard red winter or hard red spring wheat. (See pages 365–368 for details on selecting flours.) It must not have been treated with pesticides, and it must have been milled cool in a clean mill. Because of these requirements, making a desem can tell you a lot about your flour.

You'll need at least 10 pounds of flour for the desem's incubator, to surround it while it is developing. The desem itself requires about 7 cups of flour in the first five days. Because its freshness is so important, it is well worth the trouble to grind this amount yourself. You can buy wheat berries in your natural food store.

If you use a mill, be sure that it is absolutely clean, or you may share the experience of one friend who had been assured that cleaning a mill wasn't necessary. His fledgling desem grew a "cover crop" of green mold. Another attempt from a dirty

FLOUR

If you find it impossible to find good flour or wheat in your locale, write to one of the suppliers listed on page 427.

mill smelled like rotten meat. (Incidentally, you'll be glad to know that as long as your starter dough maintains its bright, fresh smell, you can be confident that it isn't growing anything harmful.) If you do grind your own flour, when you measure it, tap the sides of the measuring cup to compact the flour because it will be lighter and fluffier than bagged flour.

TEMPERATURE   Find a place that is between 50° and 65°F to keep the desem. This has been the hardest requirement for many people to meet, but temperature really is critical to growing the right organisms in the starter. Above 70°F souring organisms are favored; below 50°F the leavening organisms hibernate. The first time we started a desem it was August, hot inside the house and out. We took the thermometer from our refrigerator and walked all around the house and yard, finally settling on a spot under the house; it was too cold at night so for the first week, we took the desem in at night and out again every morning. It worked.

In the winter a garage or porch that is unheated during the day may be ideal, or sometimes the back corner of a low cupboard has a cool, steady temperature. Spring and autumn may be better for making a desem if the weather is extreme in your area. If you aren't sure, a thermometer is worth getting.

TIME   It takes two weeks to develop a desem. During this period, to help the new starter get going, you need to feed it every day with a small portion of fresh flour and water. You can use your desem to bake with after the first week. Even when the desem is very young, the bread is delicious; in fact, in some ways the flavor is most interesting at this stage.

Making the Desem Starter Dough

10 pounds or more of organic whole wheat flour (to surround the desem)

2 cups (300 g) coarse stone-ground flour to go into the desem (can be part of the 10 pounds)

½ to ¾ cup unchlorinated water (120 to 175 ml) at room temperature, about 65 to 70°F

FIRST DAY: SATURDAY, FOR EXAMPLE

Put your ten pounds of flour in a container that is more or less as deep as it is wide. A very strong brown paper bag of the proper dimensions, an 8 quart bowl, or a bucket all work well.

Take about 2 cups of flour and mix it with ½ cup of water. Add more water (or flour) if necessary to make a dough ball that is stiff but not an absolute brick. Knead it for a few minutes, make it smoothly round, and *bury it* in the flour. It should be completely surrounded by flour at least three or four inches in every direction. Smooth the top of the flour, and cover the container to keep out insects and other intruders. Store at between 50° to 65°F, *not over 70°F at any time,* for about 48 hours.

SECOND DAY: SUNDAY

Maintain the temperature — no need to disturb it today.

THIRD DAY: MONDAY

The top surface of the flour may show a split or crack. Things are happening! Dig out the dough ball and, if there is a dry crust, cut it away with a sharp knife. Then cut away enough more so you're left with half the amount you started with. If no skin has formed, just cut the ball in half — keep one half and throw the other away.

You now have half a ball of the dough. With clean hands slowly work ¼ cup of pure water into the dough to soften it. Knead in one cup of flour and add more water or flour as necessary to restore the ball to its original size and stiffness. Knead it smooth, round it, and bury it again in the container of flour. Smooth and cover the flour, this time for 24 hours at the same cool temperature.

FOURTH DAY: TUESDAY

Repeat what you did yesterday. By now the desem should have a slight fragrance of fermentation to it—fresh—a little like sprouting wheat. If yours doesn't have this aroma, make it somewhat softer this time by adding a little more water.

FIFTH DAY: WEDNESDAY

Repeat what you did yesterday.

SIXTH DAY: THURSDAY

Today, instead of discarding half the desem, soften the whole thing with ⅓ cup of water. Add 1 cup of flour. Add more water or flour as necessary to get the usual consistency. This time do not bury the ball but store it in a closed, nonmetal container. A glazed crock is perfect, but a glass or plastic container will work also. Just make sure there's room for the desem to expand a little. If the container is glass, the lid should not fit airtight.

SEVENTH DAY: FRIDAY

Soften the entire desem with ⅓ cup water and add 1 cup flour to it. Adjust the consistency so that you have a medium stiff dough—slightly softer than on the previous days. Knead about 10 minutes or 300 strokes. Cut the dough into 4 equal parts, rounding one part and returning it to the container in its cool storage place. Combine the other three parts and cover. This combined three-quarters will be the starter for the bread you prepare tomorrow. Leave it to ripen overnight at room temperature, preferably 65°F but not over 70°F. The smaller dough ball is your desem, which will provide the starters for future bakings.

Baking Bread with a New Desem

The proof of the pudding is in the eating, and the proof of the desem is, too. You will want to bake bread after the first week to get an idea how your desem is faring. Even though the bread will not be light yet, its flavor should be wonderful.

When the desem is very young it doesn't have nearly the power that it will later on, and so at first you will need to plan for a longer fermentation time and a larger proportion of desem than you will need later on.

Soften the desem in the 1⅓ cups of water. Stir the salt into the flour. Mix with the water and desem, adding additional water or flour as necessary to make a slightly stiff dough. Allow a few minutes before you make the final adjustment of consistency. The dough should be softer than the desem itself but slightly stiffer than ordinary pan dough, so that when you squeeze it you don't have to strain, but you do feel the muscles in your fingers working.

Knead the dough well, about 20 minutes or 600 strokes by hand, about 10 minutes with a dough hook on slow speed. Continue until the dough becomes stretchy and strong. In our experience it is easy to underknead desem dough by hand, and easy to overknead it with a machine. Notice that desem dough made with coarse flour feels dry to the touch when you first mix it up, but as kneading progresses, it begins to feel sticky: this is somewhat the opposite of what happens with ordinary doughs. After you finish kneading, the surface should be smooth and shiny, slightly sticky to the touch.

Set the dough in a bowl large enough to allow it to expand slightly—about a four-quart capacity would do. Cover the top of the bowl with a platter or plastic, and set it in a draft-free place at cool room temperature, about 65° to 70°F, for eight to ten hours.

2¼ cups desem
(has 3 cups flour)
1⅓ to 1½ cups cool
unchlorinated water
(315 to 355 ml)
3 cups flour (450 g)
2½ teaspoons salt (14 g)

MIXING THE DOUGH

KNEADING

During the eight to ten hours, the desem dough may scarcely rise up—this is quite normal. If convenient, deflate or punch the dough some time around the last hour or so; this invigorates the leavening organisms.

The dough has now finished its cool fermentation and is ready for its warm final rise. During this next stage, the surface will lose its shine and stickiness and become dry to the touch. This is *ripe dough.*

As time passes and your desem grows stronger, you will shorten the rising time until finally it takes just 4 hours for this first, cool part of its rise. You can gauge how much time you need by evaluating the dough for ripeness as described above.

When the rising period is finished, follow the instructions for shaping, proofing, and baking given in the full Desem Bread Recipe on page 125.

TASTE THE BREAD   If the bread you make is as good as it really ought to be, you can be sure it will get more delicious *and lighter* with every baking from now on. But what if it isn't? Maybe your flour is the culprit: a desem can only be as good as the wheat from which it was made. A couple of our testers made desems that were acrid and sour, with no leavening power; we finally traced the problem to their wheat. If the wheat is damaged or has been treated with chemicals, the kind and number of organisms it harbors will be adversely affected. So far as we know, there is no way to find out before you try making the desem. If it tastes really terrible to you and you didn't let the starter get too warm at any stage, the flour was bad, and at this point there's no rescuing the desem because it isn't there. Please do try again with better wheat or flour. Write to one of the sources listed on page 427 if there's no place nearer to home.

The Second Week

At this stage, your desem is a teenager, so to say. It is developing rapidly—young and strong, but not quite what it will become. You can help it to its full potential by giving it new food
every day and keeping it at a steady cool temperature: the leavening organisms will multiply and predominate more and
more. Daily feeding and kneading also prevent the maturing
starter dough from becoming alcoholic, which would reduce
its leavening power.

Assuming that you will want to use your desem to make
bread again at the end of the week, how much flour and water
should you add each day? The desem you're starting out with
contains one cup of flour, and you'll always want to keep that
much desem in the storage place. You need a desem containing
3 cups of flour for one (two-loaf) baking, so measure 3 cups of
flour and put it near your desem. Use ⅓ cup of that flour for
each day's feeding until the last day, when you can use the remaining cup or so.

Each time you feed it, soften the desem in water measuring somewhat less than half the amount of flour you'll add,
then adjust the dough's consistency by adding a little more
flour or water. Knead the whole newly fed desem about 10
minutes, until it begins to be sticky. Set it in its storage container and keep it in its cool place. On the last day, the day
before you will bake again, divide the desem. Three-fourths
will be the starter for the next day's bread (it will have 3 cups of
flour in it); one-fourth of it (with 1 cup of flour), set aside as
your "mother starter" for future bakings. Store both of them at
about 65°F overnight.

To make the bread, follow the recipe on page 117.

Now, about the desem itself: if your starter is making
bread that is as light and fresh-tasting as you want, start storing
it according to the instructions given in Care of the Mature
Desem. If you want it to develop more leavening power than it
has right now, give it another week on the same schedule as the
one you have just completed. If you aren't sure whether your
two-week-old desem is what it should be, here are a few things
to look for.

*It is really interesting to bake
with your desem every day
this week so that you can
watch how its leavening
power develops, and taste the
subtle changes in the flavor of
the bread it produces. For
instructions, see bottom of
next page.*

If your desem has been nurtured under the best conditions, it will probably be able to ripen its dough in 4 hours the first time you change to the regular desem bread recipe on page 124.

Watch the condition of the desem itself. When you open its container on baking day, the first whiff may be alcoholic but that evaporates quickly. The fragrance is not sour but wonderful—pleasantly cidery. Ripe desem looks a little like beige cottage cheese inside. Just as dough ripens, desem too ripens, in its own way. In a ripe desem the gluten is completely digested by microorganisms, so when you soften it in water, it disintegrates completely. You can see this when you mix up the bread dough. If you try the same thing with an ordinary dough, or with unripe desem, white starch will wash into the water, leaving a rubbery, insoluble gluten in your hand.

As the desem gains in power, it will ripen more quickly, gradually coming to the stage where it is at its best about 12 to 14 hours after it has been fed; this seems to be the tempo that gives it its greatest leavening power as well as its best flavor. It may take a few bakings, though, before its forces come into balance.

If you would like to watch your desem grow by baking a loaf every day while it comes to its own, simply double your starter with half a cup of flour each evening. (When the desem is so young, you don't want to increase it by more than double at one time.) Knead well, divide in two; use one of the pieces as your starter the next day. Mix with half a cup of water, one cup of flour, and a scant teaspoon of salt. Proceed as in the newly fed desem recipe, making one small loaf at a time.

Please refer to the feeding schedules on the next pages.

If you have a dependably cool place, and will be very regular in your care, the desem will thrive kept unrefrigerated. The temperature should be steady at between 50° and 55°F. If you are going to be baking every day, this would be the ideal arrangement. There is something wonderfully romantic, not to mention delicious, about keeping your starter dough in a crock in the cellar and bringing it out to bake fresh bread daily. That is essentially the tradition the village baker followed—his desem was never idle. Maybe some small community bakeries will be able to revive this tradition. What a great thing that would be!

But for most people it is a lot more convenient to store the desem in the refrigerator. In its first few days in the cold the desem does lose some of its strength and the dough for the next baking may require a little extra rising time to ripen. But the desem adapts quickly to refrigerated storage and needs only the usual 4-hour fermentation from then on.

Ordinarily there is a bit of alcohol on the surface when you unwrap a desem that has been stored, but it quickly evaporates, and the inside is fresh and sweet. If you let a desem get too warm, though, or don't feed it on schedule, it can get so alcoholic that it loses its leavening strength and smells unpleasantly sour. Bread baked with it is heavy and sour, and most often the crust rips open during the final rise.

Never fear, all is not lost. There is an old saying, "If you give it a chance, the desem always wins out in the end." Help the desem recover by feeding it daily and giving it at least an 8-hour stretch at its favorite temperature each time you feed it. Make the desem fairly stiff and knead it well before you put it away. Keep it tightly wrapped in the cloth. Sour desem, if it is not too awful, can work well in the recipes on pages 130 to 133.

STORING THE DESEM

NURSING A
NEGLECTED DESEM

Two Suggested Schedules

IF YOU BAKE TWICE A WEEK OR OFTENER

START *with your mature desem:*
> It measures about ¾ cup,
> contains 1 cup flour,
> and weighs ½ pound.

FEEDING *About 12 hours before you mix the dough feed your desem:*
> ⅔ to 1 cup water
> 2 cups flour

THE DESEM *Set aside one-third (about ¾ cup) for future bakings.*

THE BREAD STARTER *Round the remaining two-thirds to ripen
> as starter for your bread dough.
> It contains 2 cups flour.*

IF YOU BAKE ONCE A WEEK

START *with ⅓ cup of your mature desem:*
> It contains ½ cup flour,
> and weighs ¼ pound.

FIRST FEEDING *Midweek feed your desem:*
> 3 to 4 tablespoons water
> ½ cup flour

SECOND FEEDING *About 12 hours before you mix the dough feed your desem:*
> ⅔ to ¾ cup water
> 1½ cups flour

THE DESEM *Set aside one-fifth (about ⅓ cup) for future bakings.*

THE BREAD STARTER *Round the rest to ripen as starter for your bread dough.
> It contains about 2 cups flour.*

Feeding Your Mature Desem

From now on, feed the desem about 12 hours before you plan to mix up the dough for baking. The desem does have to be fed twice a week, minimum, to keep its leavening power, whether or not you bake bread with it. We give two plans for feeding, one if you will be baking once a week, and the other if you will bake twice a week or oftener.

Whether you bake once a week or twice, the feeding method is the same—except that you will not take out a part if you are not going to bake.

Dissolve the desem in the water. Add the flour and more water or flour as necessary to make a fairly stiff dough. *Knead 10 minutes.* If you will be baking next day, divide the lump. Round the part you will use to make bread the next day, and keep it in a covered container with a little room to expand; the smaller part is your desem. Round the desem and tie it up snugly in a clean (not bleachy) cloth, and again in a second cloth. Keep it in a tightly closed nonmetal container. Keep both of them at 60° to 70°F for 12 to 14 hours; after that, put the desem in its closed container in the refrigerator, and make bread with the other, larger lump.

If you will not be baking the next day, feed the desem, then wrap and ripen it as described above.

If you want control of the quality of your bread, we really do encourage you to keep track of the amount of flour that is in the desem. If you know that, you can calculate the total quantity of flour in the bread you make, which means you can keep the salt and the starter in proportion. Here is a rough estimate of weights and measures:

Wherever we call for flour, of course, we mean whole wheat bread flour, preferably coarsely ground and fresh.

Water means unchlorinated or dechlorinated pure water, not too hard or soft.

Keep the desem very pure; avoid contaminating it with any extraneous stuff, particularly salt, that would damage its leavening power.

If you have to miss a baking, go ahead and feed the desem as if you were going to bake; either discard the portion of desem you would otherwise use for baking, or use it in one of the recipes at the end of this section.

CALCULATIONS &
MEASUREMENTS

DESEM MEASURING EQUIVALENTS (APPROXIMATE)

Amount of flour	Measure	Weight
½ cup	⅓ cup	¼ lb
1 cup	¾ cup	½ lb
2 cups	1½ cups	1 lb
3 cups	2½ cups	1½ lb
4 cups	3 cups	2 lb

Desem Bread Recipe

4 cups flour (600 g)
2½ teaspoons salt (14 g)

1½ cups desem
1⅓ to 2 cups cool water
    (315 to 475 ml)

MIXING THE DOUGH

With a vigorous desem, ripened for 12 to 14 hours after feeding, this recipe takes about seven hours from beginning to end. It differs from the recipe for making bread with a week-old desem in the timing and also in the proportion of desem used in the dough: once the starter attains its full vigor, the desem makes up only one-third of the dough.

Mix the flour and the salt. Soften the desem in the smaller amount of water, then mix in the flour, adding additional water or flour as necessary to make dough. Wait a few minutes before you adjust the consistency. The dough should be softer than the desem itself but slightly stiffer than ordinary pan dough, so that when you squeeze it you don't have to strain but you do feel the muscles in your fingers working.

Knead the dough well, about 20 minutes or 600 strokes by hand, about 12 minutes with a dough hook on slow speed, until the dough becomes stretchy and strong. We find that desem dough is easy to underknead by hand, easy to overknead with the dough hook; overkneaded loaves tend to rip toward the end of their final rise.

As we have mentioned before, you will notice that desem dough made with coarse flour feels dry to the touch when you first mix it up, but as kneading progresses, it begins to feel sticky—somewhat the opposite of what happens with ordinary doughs. When you finish kneading the dough, the surface should be smooth, shiny, and sticky under your palm.

Set the dough in a bowl large enough to allow it to grow, about a four-quart capacity for this amount of dough. Cover the top of the bowl with a damp cloth or plate and set aside in a draft-free place to rise at room temperature, about 65° to 70°F.

The dough usually takes about four hours to ripen. Deflate it at about the three-hour mark. It will not rise up high like ordinary dough during this time, but if its surface loses its shine and feels unsticky to the touch, then the dough is ripe and ready to shape.

Turn the dough out onto the kneading surface top down, and gently press it to deflate it. The dough is usually not sticky, so additional flour is not needed, but if your dough seems too soft, flour the board lightly before turning the dough onto it. Throughout this part of the process, try to preserve intact the smooth surface that developed on top of the rising dough. This gluten film will make the best top crust for your hearth loaves.

Flatten the dough and divide it in half. With the gluten film downwards, press the dough into flat circles about an inch thick. Fold the edges as shown, pressing with the heel of your hand to seal the "petals" of the flower down, four or more times until a springy ball is formed.

Turn the dough ball over on its side, and rotate it while pressing on the bottom half to make a teardrop shape.

Then, turning the loaf right side up, with a repeated rhythmic motion that is at once downward, inward and rotating, smooth it into a perfect sphere with a little foot on the bottom.

As you turn and round the loaf, the foot should not become a cavern. Turn the loaf over to check the foot until you are sure of it. When done just right, the foot is made of a small amount of dough drawn down from the sides of the ball of dough and pressed together underneath by the edges of the palm and little fingers.

*2 two-quart covered
    casseroles,*
OR
*4 six-inch diameter bowls,
    stainless steel or
    Pyrex,*
OR
1 7″ ×11″ baking dish,
OR
*any similar-size appropriate
    baking dishes*

*a plastic bag (or two)
    large enough to hold
    the container(s)
    comfortably*
a source of warmth
a thermometer

Let the dough rest covered for 15 minutes or more, and then, when it has relaxed and is supple again, flatten and repeat the rounding procedure, then put the loaves to proof. This whole process structures the dough inside the ball and stretches the gluten film tightly over it. This method helps the finished loaves to bake into a high, round shape, and is worth perfecting. The double rounding really does help the bread rise higher, with an evener crumb texture.

Put the loaves, seam side down, in baking dish(es) that have been greased and dusted with a sifting of cornmeal. Proof them (give them their final rise) for 1½ to 2 hours at 95°F and near 100 percent humidity. It is absolutely essential to approximate this temperature and humidity if you want light bread.

Maybe the simplest way to do it is to wet the inside of a plastic bag with water, put the bread in it, puff it up well, and seal it. Keep it in a place warmed by a source of mild heat, like an oven with a pilot or electric light, the door held open a little to get the right temperature. When the time comes to preheat the oven, one possibility is to set the loaves over a pan or sink filled with very hot water. Or use a heating pad on low-medium setting for the whole time. Having a thermometer is most helpful in this department.

Proof the bread until it feels completely spongy to the touch and loses all its firmness; it may even sag just a little.

Desem Bread is a traditional hearth bread, meaning that it is formed into a loaf and baked without a pan, directly on the floor of a steamy brick oven. Baked in round casserole dishes with snug domed lids, however, the loaves nearly duplicate the hearth-baked version. For specifics on this, see the discussion of various steaming methods on page 106.

Preheat the oven in plenty of time to have it up to temperature when the bread is ready to bake. Just before you put the bread into the oven, poke a few ½ inch deep holes in the top of the loaf with a serving fork or skewer. This prevents the crust from pulling away from the loaf. Bake the bread at 450°F with steam until the crust browns nicely, then reduce the heat to 350°F to finish the bake, about an hour in all.

Desem bread is done when it is deep golden or rosy

brown, and sounds hollow when you tap the bottom of the loaf. If you aren't sure, though, take a look at the crumb. If you have baked two loaves next to each other like buns, just break them apart and look there; otherwise, make a small slice in one edge. Press on the bread crumb with a light touch: if it springs back, it is done. But if the fingerprint remains and gloms together, looking very wet, return the bread to the oven for another 15 minutes. Many things can increase the time this bread requires to bake: if your dough was soft, if it fermented extra long, if you bake in glass. If your oven is very hot, if it is well-steamed, if you use metal baking pans, or if the bread rises especially well—these things decrease the baking time.

We are obviously exceedingly fond of this bread and dearly hope that all goes well with you in making it, so that you will be able to enjoy it as much as we do. In the rest of this section are some bits of information that may be of interest to you once you have the fundamentals down pat. There is also a trouble-shooting table to help you pin down any problems you might be having. Everything here is based on our own experiments (which seem endless) and our experience over the last four years of daily or twice-weekly bakings, not only one recipe at a time but also in giant batches of more than 30 loaves, baked on the hearth. Still, it is not unlikely that you will come up with improvements, or perhaps have questions that are not answered here. If so, we would love to hear from you. It seems that every time we bake, someone rhapsodizes, "This is the *best* desem bread we have *ever* had!" May it be so with you, too.

Desem can be formed into standard loaf shapes and baked in loaf pans. To cover them for steamy baking, simply invert a loaf pan and put it on top. You will need 3½ pounds for two 8″×4″ loaf pans—slightly more than the quantities in this recipe yield; maybe generously rounding your cup and spoon measures is the simplest way of increasing the quantity of dough. The dough for pan loaves is best made slacker (with more water), because with the pan to support it, softer dough rises better.

Slash the tops to give them room for rising—three diagonal slashes, holding the knife blade almost parallel to the surface of the loaf. This makes very pretty loaves.

Desem makes fine French-type crusty rolls. Use the dough for one loaf to make half a dozen or more round or torpedo-shaped rolls. Proof and bake as you do the hearth bread, but slash the rolls with a very sharp knife held on the diagonal, just before putting them into the steamy oven. Bake until done, about ½ hour to 45 minutes, depending on their size.

This can be a controversial suggestion, but some think that a few raisins in the desem buns are a delicious addition. Sesame on the outside gives a third alternative. Whatever way you prepare these, providing there is plenty of steam in the oven, they are outrageously delicious, crusty-tender. They're great the next day in the lunchbox, too, particularly if you take care not to overcook them or to let them dry out afterwards.

Desem bread keeps very well: it maintains its fresh flavor for several days stored in a ventilated but closed container like a bread bin. To keep it moist as long as a week, cool the loaves completely and refrigerate them tightly sealed in a plastic bag. Some of our friends who make sandwiches from their desem bread all week prefer to slice and freeze the amount needed for the last few days; some others say that the bread isn't even at its best until it has aged a few days.

You can revive a loaf that has lost the dew of freshness: brush it with water, wrap in foil or brown paper, and put it into a 350°F oven for about ten minutes.

Troubleshooting Desem Bread

If your loaves are dense and heavy:

The desem has become alcoholic (see Nursing a Neglected Desem).

The dough was not kneaded well enough.

The flour you used had a low gluten content.

The proof temperature was too low.

The water was chlorinated.

The flour you have been feeding your desem is poor quality.

The starter was not fully ripened.

You omitted the "round and rest" step.

If the bread tastes sour:

The desem has become alcoholic.

The desem was stored too warm.

The mixing water was too warm.

The dough fermented too warm.

It fermented and/or proofed too long.

The flour or wheat was of poor quality.

If there's a big space just under the top crust ("flying crust"):

You didn't poke it—or poke it enough—with a skewer.

If there are big cracks or splits in the crust:

The dough had not relaxed when the loaf was formed.

The gluten was weakened. Several things can do this:
    using too much starter
    over- or underkneading
    fermenting too long or too warm
    using flour that is too low in gluten or not good quality.

If the crust is thick and tough, or pale:

Most likely there was not enough steam at the beginning of the bake.

Other Uses for Ripe Desem

Suppose you can't bake bread one week. You still have to feed the desem, but do you have to throw out the extra starter? No, no, what a pity to do that, especially when you can use it in one of these scrumptious recipes: crackers that take about 20 minutes; dosas that take maybe half an hour to cook, after standing overnight; and yeasted desem buns that can be on the table in four hours (well, that's less than the desem's seven, and they are good buns).

Desem Crackers

Use a rolling pin to flatten the ripe desem on a well-floured board. Roll as thin as you can; paper thin is best. Sprinkle with salt and use the rolling pin to press the salt into the dough so it will stick; lightly brush with oil if you want. Cut into squares and transfer to a well-oiled cookie sheet. Prick each cracker with a fork.

Bake until delicately brown. Any oven temperature between 275°F and 425°F will do, but watch them—the thinner they are, and the hotter the oven, the more quickly they will be done. Take them out before they are really brown.

These crackers are marvelous with sesame seeds sprinkled on them along with the salt.

You can cut them into circles or any shape, but if the dough will have to be rerolled, using pastry flour on the board will help keep them from getting tough.

They will stay crisp several days if stored airtight.

Yeasted Desem Buns

This recipe makes tasty buns with either prime desem or desem that is somewhat over the hill.

Dissolve the yeast in ¼ cup warm water. Dissolve the desem in the ⅓ cup warm water. Mix the salt and flour, and add the liquids, adjusting with more water or flour as necessary to make a slightly stiff dough.

Knead well. Let dough rise in a warm place, about 80°F. If the dough is not ripe—not dry to the touch—deflate and let rise again. Deflate and cut into thirds, then cut each third into thirds so you have 9 pieces. Round like tiny hearth loaves, and place in a greased and floured 8″×8″ baking dish. Cover well or use your covered casserole. Proof thoroughly, at least one hour in a warm, humid place. A long proof is the secret of getting a light bun.

Preheat the oven to 450°F or as hot as you can. Paint or spray the buns with warm water. Bake covered or in a steamy oven (see page 106) until they begin to brown, about five to ten minutes. Reduce heat to 350°F and bake for another 20 minutes or so, until done.

The dough from this recipe will also make a good hearth loaf, or an 8″×4″ pan loaf. Bake in a steamy oven until the crust browns nicely, then reduce the heat and continue cooking as above until the loaf is done.

½ teaspoon active dry yeast
¼ cup warm water
½ cup desem,
    approximately
⅓ cup warm water
1 teaspoon salt
1⅓ cups of flour
    (fine grind is nice)

Desem Dosas

1½ cup water (355 ml)
1 cup whole wheat flour
  pastry flour is good
  (150 g)
2 tablespoons oil (optional)
  (30 ml)

Dosas (pronounced doh' shez) are paper-thin South Indian pancakes, rather like a tasty, savory crepe. These Desem Dosas are surprisingly reminiscent of the authentically fermented rice-and-gram version—certainly enough like the real thing to serve with chutney, and even with masala potatoes. In fact you can serve them with nearly anything—they are good with saucy marinated tofu, piping hot; with any soft cheese; with cottage cheese and fruit—or just plain.

Stir the desem into the water, mix in the flour and oil and let stand at least half an hour. It can stay as long as two days in the refrigerator. If you like extra zip, you can mince a teaspoon of fresh ginger and onion and even a bit of fresh garlic (cut all of them *tiny!*) and add them to the batter. Chopped coriander leaves are good too, though none of the above make cooking the dosas any easier.

When you are ready to cook, add more water to make a *very* thin batter—a little thinner than a good crepe batter. Pour onto a hot seasoned or lightly oiled skillet or griddle, tilting the griddle so that the batter spreads evenly, and as thin as possible, exactly as if you were making a crepe. It should cover the pan with a hundred tiny lacy holes. Turn and brown lightly on the other side. These are tricky to do—be prepared to mess up a couple.

If you are familiar with classical dosas and want to make them more like they do in Kerala, prepare the batter with whole wheat pastry flour. Let it stand overnight. Put a spoonful of batter in the middle of a slightly cooler than medium-hot griddle, and use the back of the spoon to spread the batter thin in a clockwise spiral.

If the batter picks up—comes away from the griddle following your spoon—lower the heat a little. Use another spoon or your spatula to scatter a few drops of oil on the top of the dosa, and at any edge that threatens to stick. As soon as the dosa pulls away from the pan, it is ready to turn over. Cook on both sides until crispy.

Dosas can be good either thin and crisp or a little thicker and soft. They are cooked through if there's no sizzling sound when you press them with the back of the spatula.

Makes 8 to 12 12-inch dosas.

By the way, if you are tempted to try to make these into thick American-style pancakes, be advised: the desem will not let itself become caky in this form. If you like hefty, moist, chewy pancakes in the sourdough tradition, however, they are perfect.

Rye Bread

Winter-hardy and willing to thrive in sandy soils of low fertility, rye is grown all over the world, from Tanzania to Argentina. But it is the Eastern and Northern European countries that we have to thank for the great classic rye breads. Each region has, over centuries, developed its own traditional specialties, and the variety is impressive, with flavors ranging from sweet to sour to spiced; textures range everywhere from dense and hearty to light and airy; shapes and sizes can be round and square, gargantuan and minuscule.

In recent decades, in many of these places, people have begun to abandon their traditional local breads in favor of American-style refined wheat products, so that ancient methods are being forgotten. Baking with rye is an art quite different from, and more demanding than, baking with wheat. The collection of recipes we offer in this section is a good one, but it can give only the barest hint of the magic that centuries of artistry have coaxed out of this difficult grain; so far as we have been able to find out, very few recipes for the really genuine regional breads exist: rye bread is a living tradition — and, except for a few specialties, maybe an endangered species.

Nutritionally, wheat and rye are remarkably similar, but when rye flour is added to dough, the bread is denser, moister, darker, and better-keeping than an all-wheat bread. The baker accustomed to high-gluten wheat flour will find that rye offers challenges: the dough can be sticky, tough — difficult to handle and to bake. We consulted Manuel Freedman, master wholefoods baker, about rye problems, and he shared some of his secrets with us. The mixing and kneading procedure outlined in this section is our own adaptation of his professional techniques.

ABOUT RYE FLOURS There are at present no U.S. government standards for what the term rye flour means. If it comes from a large commercial mill, though, it is almost sure to have had the bran and germ removed. "Rye meal" and "pumpernickel flour" are sometimes whole-grain, but you can't count on it. Probably most reliable is stone-ground whole rye flour from a reputable local miller. That may be hard to come by! If you are fond of rye breads and don't find flour you like close to home, it might be worth grinding your own, because whole rye flour needs to be fresh. Once ground, rye deteriorates even faster than whole wheat; buy or grind just what you can use in five to six weeks, and store it in the refrigerator. Like wheat, rye flour should come to room temperature before it is mixed into dough.

When one of our dedicated bread testers was getting ready to bake rye, she went to the store and selected "medium rye flour," thinking that a medium grind would be quite nice. As it happens this is a term for one of three commercial varieties of "white" rye flour, the other two being "light" and "dark." The terms lead you to think that you are buying refined, less refined, and whole-grain flours, but actually they are all refined flours. Light rye flour is the whitest, most powdery-fine, and it has more starch and less protein than dark rye flour, which is the white rye flour left over after the light rye has been extracted. All but the tiniest bits of bran and germ have been removed from dark rye, though characteristically it is coarser. Our friend's medium rye flour was a blend of light and dark. Although we tested our recipes with stone-ground whole rye flour, if you can't get it, don't let that stop you from making the breads. They'll work well anyway.

Rye has a talent for fermentation. Rye sours have a long tradition: not only do they impart unequaled fragrance and a savory tang to the finished bread but they also condition the dough. Without them, rye dough, particularly whole-grain rye dough, tends to be alkaline. The acid quality of a sour, and also its fermenting organisms, keep the bread from being wet and gummy. Rye recipes without sourdoughs usually include some acid ingredient to achieve the same effect.

RYE SOURS
& ACID INGREDIENTS

A recipe which contains almost all wheat flour with a little added rye can be mixed in the usual way, but when the proportion of rye increases beyond about one-sixth, the bread will be better if the dough has special handling. Slow, gentle mixing, with a more gradual addition of liquid ingredients, gives rye the best chance of success. The dough should be soft and smooth, and not sticky.

The main character in the drama of wheat breadmaking is clearly the gluten protein, which determines wheat's baking quality: resilient, flexible, structure-building—definitely hero material. Rye contains some proteins that could make gluten, but more significant are the cereal gums called pentosans: slimy characters, with a tendency to viscosity. If you give them a chance they will greedily slurp up the water before the potential gluten can form, making the dough sticky and weak. If the mixing is too rough as well as too fast, they will make the dough bucky also—brittle, and likely to rip.

To mix a rye-wheat dough, slowly stir just enough liquid into the flour to bring a stiff dough together. In our experience, it takes about two-thirds of the recipe's wet ingredients. Keep the remaining water in a separate bowl and wet your hands and the table from it as you work. Use the water more generously the first ten minutes because during this period the dough should get soft (but not sticky). Use it more cautiously the last ten minutes. Knead 15 to 20 minutes, if possible, but stop when the dough feels sticky even if that happens before the time is up.

Mixing rye with a food processor is not impossible. One good friend of ours makes his staff of life every week in his Cuisinart, and his only problem has been to keep the bread from being too light. He has perfected his method, tailoring his bread to suit his taste. So can you. Allow yourself a little room for experimentation, though, while you learn to control the development of rye dough in your food processor, because with rye especially, the terrific speed of the machine requires extra alertness to avoid overmixing.

The principles, however, are the same: first add enough of the wet ingredients to bring the dough together. (Make sure your liquids are cool—except the water for dissolving the yeast

—because the machine heats up the dough so much.) Add additional water as needed to make a soft dough. Needless to say, rye doughs will be at their best many revolutions sooner than high-gluten wheat doughs.

By hand or by machine, the trick is to get the liquid in, and the dough soft and smooth, before the dough gets unreasonably sticky. (Special instructions for making rye doughs using a dough hook, page 415.)

Rye, like any whole-grain flour, will vary in the amount of liquid it absorbs. Watch the character of the dough rather than try to keep to an exact liquid measure. The important thing is to add the water gradually, carefully watching the dough's consistency.

The larger the proportion of rye to wheat in a recipe, the more liquid it will take to get the dough to come together. A 100 percent rye dough requires most of the recipe's liquid at the outset, asking only a little more water and a short kneading thereafter to make the dough smooth.

FERMENTATION OR RISING PERIOD

Rye has a knack for fermenting, and if you want to keep your doughs from getting away from you, make them cool—about 72° to 80°F. Should the dough overferment, the loaves are likely to rip open while they proof. To help control the fermentation, before you shape rye dough either let it rise twice at room temperature, *or once in a warmer place,* but not twice in a very warm place (90°F). Deflate the dough when your gentle, wet finger makes a ½ inch hole that does not fill in. Try not to let the dough go so long that it sighs deeply around the finger-poke.

Because rye ferments so enthusiastically, we don't really recommend making a "fast" dough with extra yeast. If you want to hurry your rye bread, give it just one rise in a very warm place.

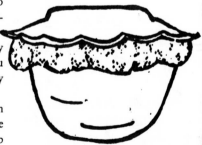

The gluten in rye dough is fragile, and may tear when handled. To help overcome this problem while shaping the loaves, use a little water rather than a dusting of flour to keep the dough from sticking to hands and table.

Proof the dough long enough with a gentle heat (80° to 90°F) to let it warm through and, if it contains wheat, rise well. Even so, few part-rye breads will rise quite as high as their whole wheat cousins. Without letting them overproof, allow enough time before you put the loaves to bake so that the dough feels spongy. If they are neither overproofed nor under-proofed, there is a good chance that they will spring in the oven — the cardinal sign that everything all along the way, from mixing through proofing, has gone as it should. The crumb of a rye that has sprung up well is truly superior, but even loaves that aren't so high have the full rye flavor, and are just as delicious.

BAKING For centuries, earthy, traditional rye breads have been baked in brick ovens with high initial heat and then a long bake at descending temperatures; much of the appeal of these classic breads develops in the oven, so proper baking makes a big difference with old-fashioned ryes. Whatever kind of rye bread you make, though, be sure to bake it thoroughly — underbaked rye leaves a wet-pinky-woolly taste on the back of your front teeth, quite unpleasant.

With high temperatures in the oven, the problem of flashing — the fluctuation of heat as the flame goes on and off with the oven thermostat — and of hot spots is intensified. The bake is much better in an oven that can hold a steady, even heat. (See our suggestions for using quarry tiles or oven stones to even out the heat, and the pages on steaming breads for good ways to bake lean ryes — pages 420 and 106, respectively.) A simpler and entirely adequate method for making a pretty, shiny dark crust is painting the loaf with the following cornstarch glaze.

Glaze

Steaming encourages the highest rise and the best flavor, but any loaf will be plenty pretty if you give it a dark, shiny crust with this simple and effective glaze.

¼ cup cold water
½ teaspoon cornstarch
1 teaspoon honey
*   or molasses (optional)*

ॐ

Mix the ingredients and cook together about 5 minutes until clear. Brush on the loaf about 1 minute before it comes out of the oven, being sure to cover all of the exposed surface. For a darker, shinier crust, brush the mixture on during the baking period as well—about halfway through or so, but not before that.

Making "Black" Breads

To darken the color of any bread, include a *little* carob flour, Postum or other cereal beverage, or cocoa. You can use dark liquids like coffee or prune juice, or the broth left after you steam raisins. Other ingredients that will darken bread: boiled, blended raisins, cooked black beans, black molasses. Carob, like any of the others, can shout if you don't use a light hand, and weigh down the loaf as well. Just a little, though, as in the recipe that follows, will do a great job of darkening the dough.

We were interested to learn that the traditional "black" breads were really brown, taking their color from the whole-grain flours of which they were made—rye or buckwheat, for example. In preindustrial days, oftentimes whole wheat flour was bolted to extract white flour for the upper classes, and then the poor folks' "black" bread was dark because it included extra bran and wheat germ.

Dark Rye Bread

2 teaspoons active dry yeast
(¼ oz or 7 g)
1 cup warm water (235 ml)

3 cups whole rye flour (385 g)
4 cups whole wheat bread
flour (600 g)
2 tablespoons carob powder
(18 g)
2½ teaspoons salt (14 g)
½ teaspoon caraway seeds

1 cup tepid water (235 ml)
2 tablespoons honey (30 ml)
2 tablespoons cider
vinegar (30 ml)
2 tablespoons oil (30 ml)

1 cup more tepid water
to knead (235 ml)

Tender and caky with the oil, slightly chewy without it—no one will guess that the rich color and round flavor come from carob. A good all-around loaf for sandwiches of any kind, this is a light bread, and a good keeper.

੩

Dissolve the yeast in the warm water. Mix the flours, carob, salt, and seeds. Mix the liquid ingredients, except for the last cup of water.

Stir the yeast, then the vinegar mixture, into the flours gradually, using enough liquid to make a very stiff dough. Add any remaining liquid, and then the cup of water as you knead, making the stiff dough gradually soft.

Form the dough into a ball and put it smooth side up in the bowl. Let it rise in a draft-free place until a ½-inch poke from your wet finger does not fill in. Press flat, form again into a smooth round, and let rise again as before. The second rising will take about half as long as the first.

Deflate the dough and form into two 8″ × 4″ pan loaves, or three hearth loaves. Let them rise in a warm place until the dough slowly returns a gently made indentation of your wet finger. Put the loaves into a preheated 350°F oven for about 50 minutes. This bread does better if you do not slash the loaves; it is a good candidate for the cornstarch glaze.

Sour Corn Rye

A delicious bread: the flavor delights, almost surprises and delights, with every bite. Outstanding sandwich bread, scrumptious toasted — and it keeps well, too.

❧

Stir the cornmeal into the boiling water and set aside, covered.

Dissolve the yeast in the warm water. Mix the flours, seeds, and salt in a bowl.

Mix the yogurt, vinegar, oil, and honey into the corn mixture, stirring until smooth.

Stir the cornmeal mixture into the flours, then stir in the yeast. Use your hands to work the ingredients together into dough, adding more water if required. The dough should be quite stiff. Knead for about 5 minutes, dipping your hand every 10 strokes or so into the extra ½ cup of water so that you gradually work it into the dough. The dough will become quite soft: stop kneading when it gets dramatically sticky. This should take about 15 minutes, but whatever the timing, once the dough gets sticky, stop kneading.

Form the dough into a ball and place it smooth side up in the bowl. Cover and keep in a warm, draft-free place. After about an hour and a half, gently poke the center of the dough about ½ inch deep with your wet finger. If the hole doesn't fill in at all or if the dough sighs, it is ready for the next step. Press flat, form into a smooth round, and let the dough rise once more as before. The second rising will take about half as much time as the first.

Press the dough flat and divide in two. Round it and let it rest until relaxed, then form into round or oblong hearth loaves or into 8"×4" pan loaves. Dust the baking utensil with cornmeal after greasing it, and place the shaped loaves on or in it. Let them rise in a warm, draft-free place until the dough slowly returns a gently made fingerprint. Place in a preheated 400°F oven. After 10 minutes turn the heat to 350°F and continue to bake about 50 minutes more. This bread has a wonderful rise and a warm deep-red crust with bright golden "break" on the sides — extraordinarily pretty.

¾ cup cornmeal (90 g)
¾ cup boiling water (175 ml)

2 teaspoons active dry yeast (¼ oz or 7 g)
¼ cup warm water (60 ml)

3½ cups whole wheat bread flour (525 g)
2 cups whole rye flour (255 g)
2 tablespoons caraway seeds (16 g)
2½ teaspoons salt (14 g)

1½ cups yogurt (350 ml)
2 tablespoons cider vinegar (30 ml)
¼ cup oil (60 ml)
2 tablespoons honey (30 ml)

½ cup water (120 ml)

Peasant's Hearty Rye

2 teaspoons active dry yeast
  (¼ oz or 7 g)
1½ cups warm water
  (355 ml)

4 cups whole rye flour
  (coarse, freshly home-
  ground) (520 g)
3 cups whole wheat bread
  flour (450 g)
2½ teaspoons salt (14 g)
1 teaspoon caraway seeds

1 tablespoon molasses
  (15 ml)
2 tablespoons cider
  vinegar (30 ml)

1 to 1½ cups more water
  (350 or more ml)

This bread rises surprisingly well, though its crumb is dark and tender. The flavor is richly rye, full and wholesome. A very big hit with old-fashioned rye fans, who compare it to what they used to get in the old days in New York or Los Angeles (depending). An especially good sandwich bread because it is not at all sweet. Good toast, and a very good keeper.

❧

Dissolve the yeast in the warm water. Stir the dry ingredients together.

Mix the molasses and vinegar. Gradually work the yeast mixture, then the molasses-vinegar mixture into the dry ingredients, using more water as necessary to make the dough come together. It will be very stiff. Knead it, working in as much of the 1½ cups of water as the dough requires to become soft and supple (10 to 20 minutes of kneading time.)

Form the dough into a ball and place it smooth side up in the bowl. Cover and keep in a warm, draft-free place. After about an hour and a half, gently poke the center of the dough about ½ inch deep with your wet finger. If the hole doesn't fill in at all or if the dough sighs, it is ready for the next step. Press flat, form into a smooth round, and let the dough rise once more as before. The second rising will take about half as much time as the first.

Press the dough flat and divide in two. Round it and let it rest until relaxed, then deflate and shape into loaves. Let them rise in a warm, draft-free place until the dough slowly returns a gently made fingerprint. Bake in a preheated 450°F oven for ten minutes, then lower the heat to 325°F and continue baking until done, about an hour in all.

Apply the cornstarch glaze (page 139) to the baked loaves, returning them to the oven for two minutes.

Petaluma Rye

Light and airy, with an enthusiastically full rye taste in spite of the relatively small measure of rye in the dough. A fine balance of flavors that makes good sandwiches or toothsome toast.

Since there is only ½ cup rye flour per loaf in this recipe, there is no need to use the special rye mixing method.

ಈ

Dissolve the yeast in the warm water.

Stir the dry ingredients together in a bowl, making a well in the center.

Mix the hot water and the honey, and add the buttermilk, oil, and lemon juice. To protect the yeast from these acidic ingredients, pour them into the well in the flour, stirring to pancake-batter consistency before you add the yeast. Fold in the remaining flour and check the dough for wetness, adding more flour or water if necessary.

Knead the dough until it is smooth and almost silky though gently slubbed, of course, with caraway. The dough will be ragged and unpromising for nearly 20 minutes, but will become really smooth at last. Form the dough into a ball and place it smooth side up in its bowl.

Cover and keep in a warm, draft-free place. After about an hour and a half, gently poke the center of the dough about ½ inch deep with your wet finger. If the hole doesn't fill in at all or if the dough sighs, it is ready for the next step. Press flat, form into a smooth round, and let the dough rise once more as before. The second rising will take about half as much time as the first.

Press the dough flat and divide in two. Round it and let it rest until relaxed, then deflate and shape into loaves. Let them rise in a warm, draft-free place until the dough slowly returns a gently made fingerprint. Bake about 45 minutes at 350°F.

2 teaspoons active dry yeast (¼ oz or 7 g)
½ cup warm water (120 ml)

5 cups whole wheat bread flour, preferably finely ground (750 g)
1 cup rye flour (130 g)
1 tablespoon caraway seed (or use less, or omit)
2½ teaspoons salt (14 g)

¾ cup water, very hot (175 ml)
2 tablespoons honey (30 ml)
1¼ cup buttermilk (300 ml)
2 tablespoons oil (30 ml)
2 tablespoons lemon juice (30 ml)

Orange Rye

1 tablespoon dried rose-hip
    pieces (7 g)
1 cup water (235 ml)

2 teaspoons active dry yeast
    (¼ oz or 7 g)
¼ cup warm water (60 ml)

3 tablespoons honey (45 ml)
1 cup cold buttermilk
    (235 ml)

4½ cups whole wheat
    bread flour (675 g),
    finely ground
2 cups whole rye flour
    (255 g)
2 teaspoons salt (11 g)
grated peel of 2 oranges
1 tablespoon anise seed

½ cup tepid water,
    or as required
2 tablespoons butter (28 g)

Marvelously perfumey, delicately flavored, feather-light.

Simmer the rose hips in 1 cup of water for 5 minutes, until the liquid is a light reddish-brown; strain, reserving the tea.

Dissolve the yeast in ¼ cup warm water.

Dissolve the honey in the rose-hip tea, and add the buttermilk. Combine the flours, salt, peel and seeds. Stir in the yeast mixture and buttermilk mixture. The dough should be somewhat stiff, but not too stiff—add more water if necessary. Knead in the remaining ½ cup of water, adding it generously the first 10 minutes. Knead the butter into the dough now, and add more water cautiously thereafter until the dough softens. Stop if the dough becomes sticky.

Place in a covered bowl to rise at warm room temperature, until the dough feels spongy and a ½-inch finger-poke fills in slowly, about 1½ hours. Deflate and let rise once again about 45 to 60 minutes. Divide in half and round. Let the dough relax.

Shape into regular loaves, or rounds to bake in pie tins, or make rolls—all these work beautifully with this bread. Place in greased pans and keep in a warm place for the final rise, 85° to 90°F. Let the dough rise until spongy to the touch, when a fingerprint fills in slowly, even if it takes an hour to get there—this one should be *light*. Bake at 350°F about 45 minutes. When done, brush the crust with melted butter.

Raisin Rye

One of our most popular and toothsome ryes, this is a mildly sweet, all-occasion bread that makes outstanding rolls as well.

ટ્

Cook the raisins for 5 minutes in 1 cup water. Drain, reserving the liquid to use as a part of the water measure.

Dissolve the yeast in the ½ cup warm water.

Stir the dry ingredients in a mixing bowl. Combine the molasses, cider vinegar, oil, and raisin water in a 2-cup measure and add enough cold water to total 2 cups. Mix the yeast and the other liquids into the flour to make a somewhat stiff dough.

Knead well, using water on the table and on your hands to soften the dough. After about 10 minutes, before the dough becomes sticky, flatten it out on the board, spread the raisins on it, fold it up, and knead the raisins in. Stop kneading when the dough shows signs of becoming sticky.

Form the dough into a ball and place it smooth side up in the bowl. Cover and keep at warm room temperature in a draft-free place. After about an hour and a half, gently poke the center of the dough about ½ inch deep with your wet finger. If the hole doesn't fill in at all or if the dough sighs, it is ready for the next step. Press flat, form into a smooth round, and let the dough rise once more as before. The second rising will take about half as much time as the first.

Press the dough flat and divide in two. Round it and let it rest until relaxed, then deflate and shape into loaves. Let them rise in a warm, draft-free place until the dough slowly returns a gently made fingerprint. Bake about an hour at 350°F. Cornstarch glaze (page 139) makes this bread as pretty as it is tasty.

1 cup raisins (145 g)
1 cup water (235 ml)

2 teaspoons active dry yeast
  (¼ oz or 7 g)
½ cup warm water (120 ml)

3 cups whole rye flour (385 g)
4 cups whole wheat flour
  (600 g)
1 teaspoon salt (16.5 g)
½ teaspoon caraway seeds

3 tablespoons molasses
  (45 ml)
2 tablespoons cider
  vinegar (30 ml)
2 tablespoons oil (30 ml)
raisin water plus
  additional water
  if needed

water as required for
  kneading, about ½ cup
  (120 ml)

Ukrainian Black Bread

1 teaspoon active dry yeast
    (⅛ oz or 3.5 g)
¼ cup warm water (60 ml)

1 cup strong coffee (235 ml)
1 teaspoon blackstrap
    molasses (5 ml)
    (optional)

3 cups whole rye flour
    (385 g)
⅓ cup whole buckwheat
    flour (42 g)
1¼ teaspoon salt (7 g)

This is not like store-bought Russian rye but dense and intense. The bread is indescribably tasty. This amount makes one long skinny loaf, or 2 shorter ones. Slice cracker-thin.

૱

Dissolve the yeast in warm water. If you are making fresh coffee for the purpose, make it double strength using boiling water; allow to cool until warm. Stir in the molasses.

Combine the dry ingredients. Add the yeast solution and ¾ cup of the sweetened coffee. If required, add the rest of the coffee to bring the dough together. Knead until soft and smooth, using a little water on your hands and the board, but not so much as to let the dough get very sticky. Knead 5 to 10 minutes.

Cover and let rest for 2 hours at room temperature. Using a generous amount of water on your hands, knead briefly and shape into a round ball. Let it rest for 30 minutes more, covered with a damp cloth. Rolling the dough back and forth under your palms, shape it into a long, skinny loaf or two, about 2 inches in diameter. Again, use plenty of water so the surface of the dough doesn't crack.

Grease either a cookie sheet or a French baton pan and place the shaped dough on it. Proof in a warm and humid place, around 85°F, until the dough is soft—approximately 45 minutes. Don't expect it to rise very much: it won't. Bake in a hot and steamy oven (see page 106) for 20 minutes, then without steam at 375°F for another half-hour or so. Check while baking to make sure the loaf is browning evenly on the top and bottom, repositioning the bread in the oven if necessary.

Vollkornbrot

We were determined to find out how to make classic dark Pumpernickel for this book, but after three years of fruitlessly scouring American and German books on bread, writing to German friends of friends, and so on, we had really given up on it—until our own neighbor magically turned up with an authentic loaf and this recipe, which he now happily makes every week. For a description, I don't think I can improve on the note he included with that first gift loaf:

> Laurel,
> I am willing to bet my soul and its overcoat that
> you never before held a loaf of bread of this size that
> weighed more than three pounds. If you were to drop it
> on your floor, it would break a tile. I am very pleased
> with this result. It is nice and chewy and it has a
> crust worthy of being called a crust. . . .
>
> You will note that it takes six days from the
> initial preparation of the Starter to the climactic
> consumption of the first thin slice. A fellow could
> starve in the meanwhile if it weren't for an
> occasional loaf of Holsum from Diekmann's. . . .

This recipe makes three regular-size loaves. The bread bakes nicely in covered casserole dishes or clay pots that mimic the old-fashioned brick oven, but it does even better in three normal-sized loaf pans, each one wrapped in aluminum foil for the first three hours of baking. The loaf is about 3 inches high, and should be sliced, according to tradition, about ⅛ inch thick.

1½ teaspoons active dry yeast
(5 g)
3 tablespoons warm water
(45 ml)
¼ cup fine whole wheat
flour, about (30–40 g)

Step one: Dissolve the yeast in the warm water and add enough flour to make a soft dough. Keep in a loosely covered glass or clay container at about 85°F, 15 to 24 hours. Do not let the dough dry out.

STEP TWO

Step two: Mix the additional flour and warm water into the first starter, making a firmer dough this time. Cover and let ferment until it has doubled or tripled and looks spongy. This takes about 5 hours at 85°F or about 24 hours at 70°F.

½ cup fine whole wheat
flour, about (70–80 g)
¼ cup water (60 ml)

You now have a starter that can be stored in the refrigerator for several months; keep in a tightly covered jar that is not more than three-fourths full.

PRELIMINARY DOUGH

1½ teaspoons active dry yeast
(5 g)
6 cups water (1½ l)
2 tablespoons Starter
(30 ml)
6¼ cups rye flour (800 g),
finely ground
1 pound wheat berries
(whole grains) (450 g)

Prepare the evening before baking day.

Dissolve the yeast in a cup or so of the water at 110°F. Stir in the starter, then alternately another 2¼ cups warm water and the rye flour. Let the mixture stand 12 to 14 hours at room temperature.

Rinse the wheat berries in warm water. Bring 2¾ cup water to a boil. Turn off the heat, add the wheat berries, and let them sit overnight. By morning the berries should have burst open; if they don't, bring them to a boil again and cook until they burst. Let them cool to warm-room temperature.

MAIN DOUGH

1½ tablespoons salt (25 g)
2 generous tablespoons each,
ground caraway seeds
and ground coriander
6⅔ cups rye flour (850 g)

Stir the salt into the wheat mixture.

Mix the ground seeds into the rye flour. Pour half of this mixture into the preliminary dough and stir in the wheat berries. Work in the remaining flour, adding more water if necessary. Cover with a platter or plastic sheet and let the dough rise for about three hours in a warm place, until it is soft and quite spongy.

When the dough is ready to shape, grease the casserole or whatever pans you are going to use. Dust them with sifted bran or sesame seeds.

Press the dough into the pans, smoothing the surface with a wet spoon. Cover the pans and let the bread rise for 1 to 2 hours until small rifts appear in the top. Place covered breads on the lowest shelf of a cold oven and bake 1 hour at 425°F, then 2 hours at 215°F. Remove the covers or foil and bake another hour (longer in clay!), again at 425°F.

If you bake in three normal pans covered with aluminum foil and your oven is reliable, you can follow our baking timings with confidence. But if you use a covered casserole, especially a clay one that is soaked in water before baking, or one with wider dimensions, more baking time will be required. If you have a scale and want to be really sure when the bread is done, you can weigh the loaves both before and after baking. The bread will lose 12 percent of its weight in baking, so, for example, if your loaf weighs 3 pounds 4 ounces before baking, it will be done when it weighs 2 pounds 14 ounces.

Let the baked loaves cool on cake racks for half an hour to an hour; turn them out of the forms, and let them rest two days in a cool, airy place before slicing. Slice very, very thin.

NOTE: *If you grind your own rye flour, the seeds can be ground along with the rye berries — or grind them in the blender if you can't find them already ground. Coriander is hard to grind fine: a light toasting beforehand helps a lot.*

Making Sourdough Ryes

Manuel's Rye Sour

With its genius for fermentation, rye makes a super sourdough starter, much better both for rye and for wheat sourdough breads than any wheat starter we have come across (except, of course, desem, if you can count that as *sour*). This sort of starter is added for flavor and for its conditioning effect rather than to leaven the dough—yeast does that—so the sour is easy to store and maintain. No doubt it passes through stages when it has plenty of leavening power, but none of our recipes depends on that.

This recipe came to us from master whole-foods baker Manuel Freedman, and following his instructions we made good starters over and over. Still, we couldn't quite believe that the tiny amounts of milk and yeast were necessary until we tried making starters a few times without them: mysteriously enough, they really do make a difference.

TO MAKE THE SOUR

Mix together the flour, water, milk, and seed grain of yeast until smooth — the mixture should be the consistency of pancake batter. Keep at warm room temperature, anywhere from 65°F to 80°F, in a nonmetal container that is covered to keep out intruders. Let stand for 3 to 5 days, stirring twice a day, until pungently fragrant. If the odor becomes unpleasantly sour, you have let it get too warm and should begin again.

1 cup rye berries,
*   freshly ground*
O R
1½ cups whole rye
*   flour (175 g)*
1½ cups water (375 ml)
½ teaspoon milk
1 grain (one granule) yeast

TO STORE THE SOUR

Store undisturbed in the refrigerator in an airtight nonmetal container. It will keep much longer than anyone would think — we have used ours after as much as two months of total neglect, and found it sleepy but alive. A black, watery liquid will usually collect on the top. Don't panic, it is merely oxidation, like potatoes turning dark after they are cut. Just stir the black stuff back into the brew.

If your sour has been dormant in the refrigerator and you are in doubt as to whether to use it, bring it to room temperature and double its volume with flour and water. Allow it to sit out at room temperature, stirring twice daily, until it bubbles up. Stir, and take a whiff — if the fragrance pleases you, it will certainly be good in the bread.

TO USE THE SOUR

When you want to use the sour in dough, let it come to room temperature and give it a chance to bubble up, if it will — allow the better part of a day. Replace what you remove with fresh flour and water before refrigerating the sour again. For example, if you take out ¾ cup, mix in ¾ cup flour and ¾ cup water, maintaining the pancake-batter consistency.

Roberta's Sourdough Rye

¾ cup Manuel's Rye Sour
¾ cup warm water (175 ml)
2 cups rye flour (255 g)
¼ onion, separated into
   pieces

Splendid sourdough rye, bright, tangy, with no off-flavor; the bread is amazingly light.

ᐓ

The night before baking day mix starter, water, and flour, and spread the onion over the top of the mixture, pushing it down lightly into the dough. Cover tightly and leave 12 to 15 hours or more at room temperature.

4 teaspoons active dry yeast
   (½ oz or 14 g)
⅔ cup warm water (160 ml)

starter mixture from above

3½ cups whole wheat flour
   (525 g)
2½ teaspoons salt (14 g)
1 tablespoon caraway seeds

⅓ cup warm water
   (80 ml), about

In the morning dissolve the yeast in the warm water. Remove the onions from the starter mixture.

Stir the flour, salt, and seeds together and then mix in the yeast and starter mixtures, squeezing with your fingers until the dough comes together. Knead about 15 minutes; wet your hands with the remaining ⅓ cup of water from time to time until it is all used up and the dough becomes soft and begins to feel sticky. Ideally, these things should happen at about the same time, in 15 to 20 minutes, but they may not. Add the water very slowly; stop kneading when the dough is soft or begins to be unpleasantly sticky.

Put dough in clean bowl, cover, and let rise once, at about 80°F, for approximately 1½ hours. Divide into two or three small pieces, round, and let rest for 15 minutes or so, covered. Shape into hearth-style loaves and place on a greased baking sheet that has been dusted with cornmeal. Let rise again in a warm place until the dough slowly returns a gently made fingerprint.

Slash the loaves in a tic-tac-toe pattern and place them in a preheated oven (450°F). Bake with steam for 10 minutes (see page 106); reduce the heat and finish baking without steam at 325°F for 40 to 50 minutes, or until done.

German Sourdough Rye

A classic, old-fashioned bakery rye: mild in flavor, substantial, satisfying. Beginning with a very small sour starter, the baker builds the dough for this bread in three stages. Since the timing is unusual, it may fit into a schedule that ordinary breads do not: the *basic sour* ferments overnight, then is mixed into a larger sponge, the *full sour*. After around four more hours of fermentation, the dough is mixed and shaped, and goes into the oven within an hour. The final loaves are large hefty rounds with thick, burnished crusts.

ક

BASIC SOUR Combine the starter with the rye flour and add enough water to make a stiff dough. Keep at room temperature overnight, about 12 hours at 70°F.

FULL SOUR To make the full sour, soften the basic sour in 1 cup water. Combine with the flour and add just enough water to get the mixture to come together in a very stiff, claylike dough. Knead it, working in another 2 to 4 tablespoons water to soften the dough, but not so much that it gets sticky. Let it stand covered in the bowl at room temperature, around 4 hours.

DOUGH Dissolve the yeast in the warm water and combine with the remaining ingredients, including the full sour, to make a stiff dough. Knead in another 1½ cups of warm water, or whatever is necessary to make the dough soft but not sticky. Let it rest for 10 minutes, then divide it in two and shape it into round loaves, using water liberally on the dough surface so it won't tear. Let rise in greased round 2½-quart bowls, preferably glass casseroles with lids. Keep in a warm place, 85° to 90°F, until the dough becomes soft. This usually takes 30 to 45 minutes, never more than an hour.

Preheat the oven to 450°F, allowing it plenty of time to reach temperature. Pour ¼ cup warm water over each loaf, cover, and bake in the hot oven. After 20 minutes reduce the temperature to 400°F and bake for another hour until done. These loaves are large so they take a long, hot bake.

BASIC SOUR

⅓ cup Manuel's Rye Sour
   (90 ml)
   OR
¼ pound of Flemish
   Desem starter (115 g)

1 cup whole rye flour (130 g)
¼ cup tepid water (60 ml),
   approximately

FULL SOUR

basic sour from above
1 cup tepid water
2 cups whole rye flour (255 g)

DOUGH

4 teaspoons active dry yeast
   (½ oz or 14 g)
1½ cup warm water (350 ml)
full sour from above
3 cups whole rye flour (385 g)
3 cups whole wheat flour
   (450 g)
3¾ teaspoons salt (21 g)
½ teaspoon caraway seed

Using the Bean

Homemade, fragrant, hot from the oven—bread offers a natural way to help smooth and encourage the transition to a more healthful diet. Try to include certain other wholesome foods, though, and sometimes a wall of resistance goes up. It's one thing when we ourselves find new items strange and unsatisfying at first; but when our family's health is at issue, and logic, persuasion and the nutrition charts don't seem to carry much weight, it's time to call upon art, and maybe even a little sleight of hand, to keep everybody in harmony.

The recipes in this section definitely fall into the sleight-of-hand category. They are not meant for people who can happily sit down to enjoy a hearty meal of good plain bread and beans; they are designed for those who, while acknowledging the fine nutritional contribution of legumes, would just as soon not take them neat. They are for moms who want to give their kids a more nutritious diet despite their resistance to it, and for people on the go who are likely to make a meal of toast. Above all, they are meant to address situations where the taste buds are more convincing than any nutrition chart: "I don't *care* if it is good for me, I *don't* LIKE *it!*"

These breads are good nutrition, and good eating, too; the recipes are original and reliable. They show that you can incorporate an impressive amount of legume protein into bread without compromising its natural appeal—and there is a broad spectrum represented here, too. We hope that the recipes serve you well, and that the guidelines we have worked out will enable you to design your own bean breads, perfectly tailored to your needs and taste.

SOME CONSIDERATIONS WHEN BAKING WITH BEANS

Most of these recipes call for either soy or garbanzo beans. Other kinds will work, but for our money, their flavors and their nutritional contribution just don't compare. The noble Black Turtle Bean stands as the remarkable exception.

Big Daddy Soy, of course, is a bean unto itself. No other boasts the protein or the range of vitamins and minerals, and few can match the cooked beans' modest, sweetly self-effacing flavor either, for that matter. For the baker, though, soy presents interesting complexities and challenges.

For one thing, soy protein has a binding effect on bread dough, actually tying up the gluten so that the loaf is unable to rise very well. Learning this tidbit nearly knocked us over, because for years our daily loaf—a hefty one—was loaded with cooked, mashed soybeans. During that period we completely forgot that bread could spring up while it baked. Our research for this book revealed the reason and, happily, the remedy, too: 1 tablespoon of shortening or 2 tablespoons of oil mixed into each loaf will lubricate the gluten sufficiently to overcome soy's binding effect. Taking this into account, all our soy recipes call for a conditioning amount of oil or butter, and if you want light bread, don't leave it out. Soy affects dough in other ways, too, which we will discuss in the next pages.

Garbanzo and black turtle beans are not so concentrated nutritionally as soy, but they are nevertheless quite nourishing. Because they are easier on the dough, you can add a larger amount, and come out about even in protein—and perhaps ahead in flavor—after all. These two have the further advantage of making good bread without added fat.

COOKED BEANS
Probably our favorite way to use beans in bread is to cook them, mash them, and work them into the dough. Breads made this way are mild in flavor and have a moist crumb that stays soft for days—this is particularly true with soybeans.

Coarsely cracked soy grits offer an easy alternative to whole beans, because they cook so quickly and don't bind the gluten as much as the other soy products. Don't use the small crack grits, though: they make the dough heavy and crumbly. Soy grits have a nutty flavor and are easy to find in natural foods stores. To us, raw grits have a subtler flavor than toasted—but whichever you get, do steam and cool them before you add them to your dough, as suggested in Health Nut Bread, page 166.

BEAN FLOURS
Soy and garbanzo flours are available in natural foods markets, or you can grind them fresh at home if you have one of the powerful grinders. Garbanzo flour—try ¼ cup per loaf—pretty much disappears in bread; bakers have used it for centuries. Soy flour is more demanding.

We generally choose full-fat soy flour for baking; deep yellow in color, it contains all the original fat-soluble nutrients of the whole bean. When you buy full-fat soy flour, be sure it is fresh, because bread made with even a little bit of rancid soy flour will neither rise well nor taste good.

Defatted and partially defatted flours are less perishable. Commercial bakers generally prefer the defatted kind because it is less expensive and does not go rancid. The fat has been removed with a solvent, and the flour lightly toasted to destroy enzyme activity. A grayish beige color, it is sometimes called soy powder.

Raw soy flour contains many active enzymes including lipox-
idase, which even in small amounts bleaches flour, and conditions dough so that the bread made with it rises higher. The
"improving" amount is about one tablespoon of soy flour per
two-loaf recipe calling for two pounds of wheat flour. You can
add this amount of soy flour to any recipe for its conditioning
effect, but don't expect miracles; it will be very subtle. In these
amounts soy's gluten-binding activity is negligible.

We suggest limiting the amount of soy flour to one-third
cup in a two-loaf recipe, maximum. Beyond that, it seems to
us, the flavor of the soy flour—which is pretty awful—takes
over. Also, even at this level, the conditioning effect is so powerful that the dough ripens extremely fast. Let such doughs rise
only once before shaping—or better yet, let them rise once
before you add the soy flour, and then once again before you
shape the loaves. Some techniques for doing this are included
in our recipes for Busy People's Bread and Famous Captain
Carob Bread.

Incidentally, any raw soy product, including flour, contains substances called soybean trypsin inhibitors (SBTI) that
get in the way of protein digestion. Soybeans in any form
should be eaten only after they are cooked enough to inactivate
this substance. Baking soy flour in bread is sufficient to do this,
in the opinion of scientists who work in the field.

If you drink soymilk, maybe you have already discovered the
secret of baking any that is left over into delicious, featherlight
loaves. Soymilk bread is quite a lot like a dairy bread, pale inside, with a glossy dark crust—sometimes people mistake it
for egg bread. If the soymilk is not first-day fresh, however, it
can make a truly weighty loaf, because even in the refrigerator
the brew develops a lively population of bacteria. To subdue
them, bring the soymilk to a boil, and then cool it before you
use it in the dough.

If you make your own soymilk you might wonder about
baking your okara (the leftover soy fiber) into your bread. Our
advice is don't. True, okara has a respectable nutrition quo-
tient and should not be wasted; so far as we could tell, though,
after many imaginative experiments, bread dough is not the

place to use it unless you are fond of heavy, wet, bland loaves, more or less indigestible.

Finally, it was suggested to us with great enthusiasm that we make sure to have a Tofu Bread in our book. We really did try, but incorporating tofu in the dough invariably made heavy, lackluster loaves, at least for us. There are so many good ways to use tofu *on* bread, why put it inside? We were saved at the last, when our friends Bill Shurtleff and Akiko Aoyagi sent us a recipe for a very tasty tofu-applesauce quick bread. After some further testing, we are delighted to say that you can put as much as a whole cup of grated tofu into almost any flavorful *quick* bread (see pages 309 to 337 for our quick bread recipes) without noticeably reducing its appeal. You add a gram per slice of high-quality protein, a good bargain in a quick bread.

The bean breads that follow are real staff-of-life recipes based on whole foods. Each one is rich in nutrient value and, when well made, light enough to please the finickiest child or the most discerning adult.

Mediterranean Garbanzo Bread

Garbanzos, also known as chickpeas, are not quite such nutritional powerhouses as soybeans, but they provide very respectable nourishment, and they work well in bread. Milder in flavor and easier to cook and mash than soy, they also demand less added sweetener, are easier on the dough, and, unlike soy, do not prevent the bread from rising if you omit the oil or butter. Cook them ahead of time so they will be ready just before you need them. Stored even a short time, they ferment slightly, and that can keep the dough from rising high.

This recipe makes a plain, mild bread, scarcely sweet, with a firm crumb. It keeps very well; a good everyday bread for sandwiches and toast, and a good springboard for your own imaginative variations.

ⅺ

Cook the garbanzo beans in a quart of water for 3 hours, or until soft. Use a pot that is plenty big, because they will double in size as they cook. Drain, reserving the broth; mash and cool the beans.

Dissolve the yeast in the warm water.

Combine the flour and salt, the dimalt flour, if used, and the mashed garbanzo beans. Dissolve the honey (if used) in the 2 cups of liquid. Pour that and the yeast solution into a well in the center of the flour and gradually mix together, adding more water or flour as necessary to make a soft dough. Knead well, about 20 minutes, until smooth.

Form the dough into a ball and place it in the bowl. Cover and keep in a warm, draft-free place. After about an hour and a half, gently poke the center of the dough about ½ inch deep with your wet finger. If the hole doesn't fill in at all, or if the dough sighs, it is ready for the next step. Press flat, form into a smooth round, and let the dough rise once more. The second rising will take about half as much time as the first.

Press the dough flat and divide in two. Round and let relax, then deflate and shape into loaves. Let them rise in a warm place until the dough slowly returns a gently made fingerprint. Bake 45 minutes to an hour at 350°F.

1 cup dry garbanzo beans (200 g) (2 cups cooked)

2 teaspoons active dry yeast (¼ oz or 7 g)
½ cup warm water (120 ml)

5 cups whole wheat bread flour (750 g)
2½ teaspoons salt (14 g)
½ teaspoon dimalt
OR
2 tablespoons honey (30 ml)
garbanzo bean cooking juice plus cold water to make 2 cups (475 ml) liquid, about 70°F
¼ cup olive oil (60 ml) (optional)

Soybean Bread

We made soy bread for many years, cooking the beans overnight before baking day in a crockpot set on high. We never
dreamed that the loaves could be as light as this recipe makes
them—a big improvement over the version in *Laurel's Kitchen*.
Soybean Bread is admired for its spectacular nutrition and its
warmth of flavor; the cooked beans help the bread stay moist
for a long time.

There are a few small challenges to preparing this bread,
not the least of which is getting the beans cooked and ready
when you want them. They do, alas, need to be freshly cooked.
Even one night in the refrigerator and they may ferment
enough to affect the bread's rise.

You can simmer them overnight, in a crockpot or some
other way. The heat should be high enough to keep them
dancing—preferably, though, not all over the stove, which is
one of the less fragrant likelihoods in this process. To prevent
their boiling over, cover the pot only partially, and keep the
flame low enough for just a slow boil. (Use a flame-tamer, if
that helps.) The pesky critters will also try to boil dry, so use a
big pot and plenty of water. Well, that's the worst of it.

Soft-cooked, drained soybeans are easy to mash with a
potato masher while they are hot. Or if you prefer, cook them
only about 4 hours, in which case they will mash a little short
of satiny smooth, and the bread will have little nubbets in it,
which some people consider the last word in textural delight.
You can, of course, use a grinder or food processor instead of a
potato masher.

The thick stock from the beans is wonderful, *not* in the
bread but for making Soy Gravy: Sauté chopped onion and
garlic in 3 tablespoons oil, add 2 to 3 tablespoons lightly
toasted whole wheat flour, and stir and cook gently for 2
minutes. Add a cup of soy stock and bring to a boil; season
with salt and pepper. If you want to be fancy, add sautéed
mushrooms and a pinch of marjoram. The gravy is so
delicious, it's worth cooking the beans just for that, but then
it's worth cooking them just for this, too:

Cook the beans. Mash in time to add their warm pulp to the dough just before its second rise.

Dissolve the yeast in the warm water.

Mix the flour and salt in a bowl, making a well in the center. Stir the honey into the water, add the oil, and then mix the liquids and yeast into the dry ingredients, making a dough that is quite soft. Knead for 5 to 10 minutes, long enough to give it the strength to hold in the gas but not until the gluten is fully developed because you will be doing more kneading later on. Put the dough in a clean bowl, cover and set in a warm place to rise.

Check after an hour or an hour and a half to see if the dough is ready to deflate. Use the finger-poke test—make a hole about half an inch deep in the middle of the dough using your wet finger. If the hole remains without filling in, deflate the dough. If the hole fills in, more time is required; if the dough sighs and collapses, it has been kept too warm, or let go too long to be at its best, so in the next rise watch it more closely to be sure to take it up in time.

Turn the risen dough out on a lightly floured board and flatten it out. Spread the warm mashed or ground bean pulp on the dough. Fold or roll up, and then knead together for 10 to 15 minutes, until the dough is really elastic. Let it rise again in a warm place as before.

Flatten the dough on a lightly floured board. Divide in two, and working carefully, knead into rounds. Let these rest covered until relaxed, and then, taking care not to tear the dough, shape into loaves. Just before you press the dough out for the final part of the shaping, sprinkle the board with the sesame seeds so that the loaf will pick them up. Place in greased 8″×4″ loaf pans and keep in a warm, moderately humid place for the final rise. The loaves should come up very well: when they arch above the tops of the pans, and the risen dough returns slowly from a gentle indentation of the finger, put them into a preheated oven and bake at 350°F for about 45 minutes—longer if the rise was not so high.

¾ cup raw soybeans (150 g), about 2 cups cooked

2 teaspoons active dry yeast (¼ oz or 7 g)
½ cup warm water (120 ml)

5 cups whole wheat flour (750 g)
2½ teaspoons salt (14 g)

3 tablespoons honey (45ml)
1¾ to 2 cups lukewarm water (475 ml)

¼ cup fresh unrefined sesame oil (60 ml)

2 tablespoons lightly toasted sesame seeds (18 g) (optional)

(If you are not keen on the flavor of sesame, use another oil or butter, and omit the seeds on the crust.)

Soymilk Bread

2½ cups soymilk,
   unflavored (600 ml)
2 tablespoons honey (30 ml)

2 teaspoons active dry yeast
   (¼ oz or 7 g)
½ cup warm water (120 ml)

6 cups whole wheat flour
   (900 g)
2½ teaspoons salt (14 g)

3 tablespoons butter (42 g)
   OR
6 tablespoons oil (90 ml)

This is often mistaken for an egg bread because it rises beautifully to give a perfect, airy slice that has good flavor and a slightly chewy, thin, dark crust. It is just right for toasting and for sandwiches.

੨੦

If the soymilk is not first-day fresh, bring it to a boil, then cool to lukewarm. To cool it quickly, place the pan in a sink or dishpan partly filled with cold water, and stir the soymilk occasionally. Stir the honey into the soymilk. (If you choose to use oil and not butter, add the oil, too.)

Dissolve the yeast in the warm water.

Combine the flour and salt in a mixing bowl and make a well in the center. Pour in the soymilk and yeast mixtures and stir all together, adding more water or flour as required to make a soft dough. Knead very well, about 20 minutes vigorously. If you are using butter, add it toward the end of the kneading time without melting, working small pieces into the dough until it is smooth and lustrous.

Because of the ripening influence of the soy, allow this dough to rise only once in a warm place, about 80°F, before shaping. Apply the usual test to see if the dough is ready: poke gently with your wet finger, about ½ inch in the center of the dough. If the dough sighs or if the hole does not fill in at all, flatten the dough and divide it, forming two rounds. Let them rest, and then shape into loaves. Let rise in two greased 8″×4″ loaf pans at a slightly warmer temperature, 85° to 90°F. When they are ready for the oven, slash with three diagonal lines for a pretty crust and higher rise in the oven. Bake about 45 minutes at 350°F.

GOOD VARIATIONS

੨੦ Add sunflower seeds—about ¼ cup per loaf—while you shape the dough.

੨੦ Roll the loaf in poppy seeds.

੨੦ Add raisins—⅓ cup per loaf—when shaping the bread.

Busy People's Bread

The recipe on the following pages makes really good bread, but there is more to it than that: you can use these timing alternatives to help fit many other bread recipes into your schedule. The bread is delicious. We probably adjusted the ingredients and tested the recipe a hundred times, determined to achieve just this: a bread that will please the pickiest children while satisfying the most diligently nutrition-conscious parents. For the children, the bread looks professional—even store-bought —with a high, airy, pale slice spiked with raisins. But there's a bonus: the ingredients provide power-packed nutrition, and the recipe offers unusual flexibility, which is especially note-worthy in a soy bread.

The recipe contains soy flour, and so requires only one rising after the sponge is mixed into dough, before the loaves are shaped. You can substitute garbanzo flour for the soy, or use this recipe to adapt other, non-soy recipes to the Busy People's pattern. When you use a recipe that does not include soy, the dough will ripen more slowly, so your bread will be better if you let the full dough rise a second time in the bowl before you shape the loaves.

As everyone knows, it is much easier to measure out ingredients when you have some peace and quiet and can concentrate on what you're doing. We like to set up all the ingredients the night before, so that mixing can be on automatic pilot, so to say, first thing in the morning. That way you never forget the salt, and the raisins are cool when you need them.

The slow option takes from 3 to 5 hours in the sponge, and about 1½ hours to rise once the dough is mixed, with a final proof time of approximately 45 minutes. The fast option takes about 1½ hours in the sponge and about 1 hour once the dough is mixed. Its proof time is a little shorter, too; either option can be speeded up in the last stages if you want to do that; both take a little less than an hour to bake. Which timing you choose depends on your own schedule, but the more leisurely rise gives the bread better flavor and keeping quality, and is more forgiving if your own timing is off a little.

Busy People's Bread Recipe

SLOW OPTION

Sponge: 3 hours
Dough: 1½ hours to rise
  ¾ hour to proof

SPONGE

2 teaspoons active dry yeast
  (¼ oz or 7 g)
½ cup warm water (120 ml)

3 tablespoons honey (45 ml)
1¼ cups tepid water (300 ml)

4½ cups whole wheat
  bread flour (675 g)
6 tablespoons milk powder
  (45 g)

DOUGH

1 cup warm water (235 ml)
1 cup whole wheat flour
  (150 g)
⅓ cup soy flour (23 g)
1 tablespoon salt (16.5 g)
2 tablespoons butter (28 g)
1 cup raisins (145 g)

TO MAKE THE SPONGE

Using the sponge ingredients from either the fast or slow options, dissolve the yeast in the warm water, and the honey in the other water measure. Stir the flour and milk powder together and then add the liquids, mixing to make a stiff dough for the slow sponge, a soft dough for the fast sponge. Knead briefly, about 5 minutes—long enough so the dough has the strength to hold in the gas, but not so long that the gluten is fully developed. Put the slow sponge in a cool place to rise, about 70°F, the fast sponge in a warm place, 80°F.

Steam the raisins about 5 minutes, allowing them an hour or more to cool before you add them to the full dough.

TO MAKE THE DOUGH

Soften the risen sponge in the dough water measure. Combine the remaining whole wheat flour, bean flour, and the salt if you haven't added it already. Work this mixture into the sponge; an efficient way to do this is to squeeze them together with your fingers. Add water or flour as required to make the dough soft, but not excessively soft, and continue kneading to make a smooth, elastic dough. Before the dough is fully developed, knead in the butter, then the raisins.

Form the dough into a ball and place it smooth side up in the bowl. Cover and keep in a warm, draft-free place. After about an hour and a half, gently poke the center of the dough about ½ inch deep with your wet finger. If the hole doesn't fill in at all or if the dough sighs, it is ready for the next step.

Press the dough flat and divide in two. Round it and let it rest until relaxed, then deflate and shape into loaves. Place in greased 8″ × 4″ loaf pans and let rise in a warm, draft-free place until they arch over the tops of the pans and the dough slowly returns a gently made fingerprint. Bake about an hour at 350°F.

The loaves will have a rich-colored crust and a pale, raisin-studded inside. Let them cool before slicing, as the bread is quite soft.

TIMING FLEXIBILITY

The slow sponge takes about 3 hours at 70°F; if you would like it to take 4 or 5 hours, add the salt to the sponge rather than when you make the full dough.

If you would like to speed the final rising stages of either option, dissolve another 1 teaspoon active dry yeast (3½ g) in the dough water measure. Keep the dough in a warmer place, about 90°F, and although it may take 45 minutes to an hour to rise fully, the shaped loaves will come up in the pan in as little as 20 minutes.

VARIATION

You can substitute garbanzo flour for the soy flour. If there is no soy in the bread, the butter is optional; without soy, you will need to allow the full dough to rise twice before you shape the loaves.

FAST OPTION

Sponge: 1½ hours
Dough: 1 hour to rise
½ hour to proof

SPONGE

2 teaspoons active dry yeast
(¼ oz or 7 g)
½ cup warm water (120 ml)

3 tablespoons honey (45 ml)
1½ cups warm water
(350 ml)

4 cups whole wheat bread
flour (600 g)
6 tablespoons milk powder
(45 g)

DOUGH

¾ cup warm water (175 ml)
1½ cups whole wheat
flour (225 g)
⅓ cup soy flour (23 g)
1 tablespoon salt (16.5 g)
2 tablespoons butter (28 g)
1 cup raisins (145 g)

Health Nut Bread

Not all health nuts are nuts—here they are soy grits, acting nutty in one of the most popular breads we made while working on this book. All the versions tested were well received, even including a couple of early experiments that could in truth only be called duds.

When you add soy grits to bread, as we have previously bleated, if you have a choice in the matter, go for raw rather than toasted—and for the biggest ones you can find; don't even bother trying the fine-crack type unless you crave bricks. Whatever grit you get, simmer and cool before kneading into the bread; otherwise they'll rip up the dough.

Along with the nutty grits, you'll be adding pieces of dried fruit. Our local rancher's dried apricots are like mahogany chips, dark and hard. *That* kind has to precede its appearance in the bread with a brief hot-water bath: afterwards it is tender and wonderfully flavorful. (The yeast appreciates the bathwater enormously.) Fruit that is very soft will disappear into the dough, even if you don't steam or soak it. The best treatment for that sort, so far as we have discovered one, is to cut the fruit into raisin-sized pieces (with wet scissors or knife), spread it out on racks on a baking sheet, and bake in a 200°F oven until it becomes firm—about half an hour. Even if the color darkens, the flavor is improved. Since this fruit can't take stewing, use apple juice or plain water in the dough instead of the fruit broth. If you use water, the bread will be much less sweet, but good anyway.

Choose the intensely flavorful fruits: apricots and raisins, certainly; peaches, prunes, currants; probably not dates in this one, or figs.

Simmer the soy grits in water in a small, heavy saucepan for 15 minutes, covered. Keep the fire low so the grits don't burn, and check them a couple of times, adding a few tablespoons of water, if necessary. You want to come out with nicely cooked, unburned soy grits and no extra liquid. Keep the grits covered in their pan while you make the dough.

⅓ cup large-crack raw soy grits (51 g)
½ cup boiling water (120 ml)

Prepare the fruit by boiling, baking, or just cutting up, so that it is firm but not hard. If simmered, drain well and cool the liquid to use in the bread. Set the fruit aside.

1 cup assorted dried fruits (140 g)

Dissolve the yeast in the ½ cup warm water.

2 teaspoons active dry yeast (¼ oz or 7 g)
½ cup warm water (120 ml)

Mix together the yogurt, oil, and fruit broth, water, or juice. Add cold or warm water to make 2¼ cups of lukewarm liquid. Mix the flour and salt in a bowl and add the liquid ingredients and the yeast, mixing well. Knead for about 15 minutes. The dough should be elastic and supple, but not quite to the silky stage. Cover and let rise in a warm place. How long will depend on how warm it is and whether you have used the fruit broth, bottled juice, or water; but rise it will. It is ready when your wet finger makes a ½-inch hole in the dough that does not fill in.

½ cup yogurt (120 ml)
3 tablespoons vegetable oil (45 ml)
1½ cups fruit broth, apple juice, and/or water (350 ml)

Turn the risen dough out on a lightly floured board and gently press into a big, very thin oblong. Spread the grits, the fruit, and the seeds on the surface of the dough, and fold it up, pressing the dough to compact it and expel any trapped air. Round it, smoothing the top, and let rise again. The second rising will take about half as long as the first.

5½ cups whole wheat flour (830 g)
2½ teaspoons salt (14 g)

Turn out and press flat. Divide in two, form rounds that are as smooth as possible, and cover them. Let the dough rest until its suppleness returns, which may take 15 to 20 minutes. Shape into loaves for two 8″×4″ pans, or make round loaves: this bread is particularly nice baked in pie tins, in glass or crockery bowls, or as one big round on a clay pizza stone. Let rise again, and then place the loaves in a preheated 350°F oven, baking about an hour, or until done. The big loaf will take longer, of course; if it rises well it should be done in an hour and a half. The dough has a lot going on in it, and should you find that it doesn't rise as well as it ought to, do allow extra baking time. The flavor will be fine.

¼ cup toasted sunflower seeds (14 g)

Famous Captain Carob Bread

2 teaspoons active dry yeast
  (¼ oz or 7 g)
2½ cups warm water
  (590 ml)

5 cups whole wheat flour
  (750 g)
2½ teaspoons salt (14 g)
6 tablespoons milk powder
  (43 g)
⅓ cup carob powder (23 g)

2 tablespoons butter (28 g)
¼ cup honey (60 ml)
¼ cup soy flour (14 g)

This bread is favored even by those who profess to scorn carob. A light, moist, close-textured, very nutritious bread, it is popular with children nonetheless. It tastes a little strange with savory sandwich fillings, but it's a natural with peanut butter and nut and date butters, or with any mild cheese. Keeps well, makes great toast.

❧

Dissolve the yeast in the warm water.

Mix the wheat flour, salt, milk powder, and carob in a big bowl. Combine with the yeast, mixing to make a slightly stiff dough. Knead for about 10 minutes, but not more.

Form the dough into a ball and place it smooth side up in the bowl. Cover and keep in a warm, draft-free place. After about an hour and a half, gently poke the center of the dough about ½ inch deep with your wet finger. If the hole doesn't fill in at all or if the dough sighs, it is ready for the next step.

Use an eggbeater or fork to cream the butter and honey until they are smooth and fluffy. Work the soy flour into this, mixing until smooth. Turn the dough out onto the lightly floured surface, and press it flat. Spread the soy butter on the dough, fold or roll up, and knead until smooth and supple, about 10 more minutes. Keep in its warm spot to rise again.

Deflate the dough, divide in two, and gently form into rounds. Allow to rest for about 10 minutes, then shape into two loaves and place in greased 8″ × 4″ pans. Let rise again as before, until the dough returns a gently made fingerprint slowly. Bake in preheated 350°F oven for about 50 minutes.

CAPTAIN CAROB CHIPPERS

Add ½ cup (80 g) unsweetened carob chips to one loaf's worth of dough before shaping. Divide into twelve pieces and make little rounds, placing them in a greased muffin tin. The chipper rolls bake in about half an hour, and dusted with powdered sugar they could *almost* pass for cupcakes. This dough also makes a wonderful, strange loaf baked in a pie tin (or loaf pan). Some people hoot "Outrageous," but I don't notice them hanging back when the slicing begins.

Black Turtle's Raisin Bread

This hefty cakelike bread would be worth making even if it were not so nutritious. Cooking the turtle beans in an iron pot makes them very black, which gives the bread its most distinctive appearance; it also adds a significant amount of iron to an already impressive array of nutrients. Black turtle beans are a gold mine of protein (45 grams in that one cup), iron, calcium, phosphorus, potassium, and B vitamins.

What amazing bread this is! The flavor is quite special. Good hot from the oven, good for egg salad or tofu sandwiches, good with pale cheeses, good toasted, and a good keeper.

🍂

Cook the beans. Drain them, reserving the liquid.

Add cold water to the bean liquid, or pour some of it off, to bring the measure to 2 cups. Either mash the beans with a potato masher and then combine them with the 2 cups liquid, or blend beans and liquid together in an electric blender or food processor until nearly smooth. Cool the mixture to about 100°F. Add molasses and oil. The total measure should be about 1 quart.

Dissolve the yeast in the ¼ cup warm water.

Mix the flour and salt in a bowl. Add the bean mixture and the yeast to the flour to make a soft dough. Knead very well, about 20 minutes. Add the raisins toward the end of kneading. Cover the dough and let it rise very warm, about 95°F.

After about 45 minutes, gently poke the center of the spongy dough about ½ inch deep with your wet finger. If the hole doesn't fill in at all, or if the dough sighs, press it flat, form again into a smooth round, and let it rise once more as before. The second rising will take about half as long as the first.

Press the dough flat, divide in two, and form rounds. Let it rest until it is soft again, which won't take long. Gently form into fat round hearth loaves or regular pan loaves (8″ × 4″); either shape will work very well. Let them rise about half an hour. Don't slash the crust. Bake in a preheated oven at 350°F for about an hour.

1 cup raw black turtle beans (200 g) — scant 2 cups cooked

2 cups of liquid from cooking the beans (475 ml)
¼ cup blackstrap molasses (60 ml)
2 tablespoons oil (30 ml)

4 teaspoons active dry yeast (½ oz or 14 g)
¼ cup warm water (60 ml)

5 cups whole wheat bread flour (750 g)
1 tablespoon salt (16.5 g)

1 cup raisins (145 g), steamed 5 minutes and drained

Breads with Milk & Eggs

Milk is not a necessity in breadmaking, and the traditional breads of Europe attain their impressive spectrum of distinguished flavors and textures without it. Europeans save the butter and cheese to put on top. But on this side of the Atlantic, bakers have generally welcomed the contributions milk makes to the quality of dough, and to the bread it becomes. In this section we explore some ways of using dairy products to make loaves that are more nutritious, longer-keeping, lighter, more interesting.

On the nutrition score, adding milk to bread significantly increases its protein and mineral content. Milk also improves bread's keeping quality and makes the crumb texture tender as well. Loaves made with milk have a subtle sweetness, a close, delicate texture, and a richly colored crust. Whole wheat breads with milk taste softer, less wheaty, than those mixed with water.

Doughs made with milk tend to be a trifle sticky, but even so, when used properly, milk makes life easier for the baker because it increases the length of time that the dough is ready to shape and bake, giving more leeway in timing. In addition, yeast is stimulated by milk, and one of milk's proteins, casein, strengthens the gluten so the bread can rise higher. It's important, though, to scald fresh milk because that protects the dough from two other milk proteins that would otherwise inhibit its rise.

Pasteurized milk has been heated already, it's true, but this low-temperature process is not enough to denature the gluten-weakening proteins. When you scald milk, skin forming on top signals that it has reached the required temperature: it is then ready to cool and use in your bread. (Scalding is not so important when the proportion of milk to other liquids in the recipe is half or less.)

DRY MILK Supermarket powdered milk is produced by a low-temperature process to protect its flavor, and it is not ideal for use in baking, at least in sizable amounts, unless it is first reconstituted and scalded. As with fresh milk, though, if the proportion of powdered milk used is small, no more than ¼ cup non-instant powder per two-loaf recipe, usually the effect on the bread is not detrimental.

In developing and testing our recipes, we have used non-instant nonfat powdered milk. Low-fat and whole powdered milk are also available; since these products can become rancid, taste them before using if there is any doubt about their freshness: rancid fat can spoil your bread.

Yogurt and buttermilk add a rich flavor and tenderness. As with fresh milk, you will want to keep the quantity you use below half the amount of liquid in the recipe. The other liquid will usually be water. We find, in fact, that this works out in other respects: too much yogurt makes the bread taste yogurty (rather than marvelous), and too much buttermilk makes it so tender that the dough can just fall apart. How much is too much? It depends on your yogurt, but ⅓ cup per loaf is a good amount. Buttermilk is subtler, and can make up as much as half the liquid in any bread.

It is especially important that the the cultured products you use in your bread taste fresh, because if the flavor is off, likely enough the culprit is alive and active, and quite capable of sabotaging your bread dough.

CULTURED MILK PRODUCTS

In times past, buttermilk was what was left over from making butter. Nowadays, commercial buttermilk is cultured from lowfat or nonfat milk, usually, and varies a lot in flavor from brand to brand both in consistency and tartness. If you make your own butter, you know how good buttermilk can be, but when we call for buttermilk in this book, we mean the com-

BUTTERMILK

mercial kind. Since it is almost always salted, the quantity of added salt in these recipes is low. If you have unsalted butter-milk, ¼ teaspoon salt per cup of milk will bring the dough to the saltiness intended in the recipe.

YOGURT Yogurt gives bread tenderness, a fine texture, and a unique richness of flavor that is fuller and tangier than that you get from buttermilk. Be most particular about the freshness of the yogurt you use in baking: a lot of fellow travelers can set up housekeeping in a batch of yogurt, and some of them make the bread taste weird. We have friends who cultivate their yogurt with an expansive "let it be" policy about protecting the starter from outside influences. The yogurt is pretty interesting stuff, with a kind of ripeness you might look for in Camembert or an old Gorgonzola. When one of these was used in A Loaf for Learning, the normally light, subtly flavorful bread emerged dense and bluish-gray, with a strange beerish flavor.

COTTAGE CHEESE Cottage cheese plays the part of a liquid in bread, providing impressive amounts of protein and calcium and extra rising power, too. Bread made with cottage cheese is usually very light and moist. For all its advantages, though, these days a cup of cottage cheese can more than double the price of a loaf of homemade bread, so unless you are looking for a way to sneak a lot of protein and calcium into someone's diet, it's a pricey option.

CHEESE From Tillamook to Gruyère, cheese is even more expensive. Delicious *on* whole wheat bread, cheese just doesn't make much of a show *in* it, unless you use a powerful lot. But if you have an occasion that merits really sensational cheesy rolls or loaves, it can be done, for sure. Choose any plain light bread recipe, like Fresh Milk Bread, for example. Add at least a cup of grated sharp cheese to the dough for each loaf's worth of bread, working the grated cheese into the dough after the kneading is nearly completed. To help the flavor sing, include some complementary spice or herb: for example, a tablespoon of dill weed with Swiss, or a teaspoon of chili powder with cheddar. The milk protein and the added fat from the cheese will enhance the rise, so the bread should be light and airy. Be careful not to overbake cheesy rolls or breadsticks, or they may become dry.

Butter is the only fat we use that can be called shortening, meaning that it gives the bread crumb the velvety-soft quality called short. Because it can stay unmelted in the dough, butter actually lubricates the gluten, making the loaf noticeably higher. (You have to use at least twice as much liquid oil to get a similar effect.)

If you want the butter you use to do all it can for you, add it cool, rather than melted. The French method is to smear the butter onto the board after the kneading is nearly done, working it into the dough until it disappears and the dough is smooth and lustrous. You can also cut (or grate) cold butter into tiny pieces and knead it in — again, after the gluten has had a chance to develop. In either case, the lubricating effect is unmistakable. It may seem like a time-saver to melt the butter, but though you get the flavor that way, you don't get the extra rise.

As to the flavor of butter — well, what could be more delectable? And yet with whole grains, which have their own character and are not merely backdrop like white flour, butter's taste plays a supporting role: very good indeed, but subtler than the flavor of the grain itself.

Note here that we use ordinary butter in our recipes; if you use sweet butter you may want to increase the salt by a pinch. Salt is added to butter as a preservative, and it does help prevent it from going rancid: sweet butter keeps much less well. Sweet or salted, don't be tempted to use up rancid butter in your baking. Rancid fat is not only unhealthful but can spoil the bread.

Fresh Milk Bread

"Drink this now," Jo Anne said, blue eyes ablaze, handing over the steaming mug. "Not since I was a girl in Scotland have I tasted *this*."

I drank obediently. "Is it—milk?" I really wasn't sure. It tasted like liquid flowers.

"Fresh from the cow. You never get this nowadays." Jo-Anne had been visiting a neighbor who has a small dairy farm. His cows were giving more than he could process and we were the beneficiaries.

"*Do you realize* that the milk from our local dairies goes all the way to Sacramento for processing? Most of its goodness is gone by the time it comes all the way back in a paper carton. And before long, the way things are going, all you will see on the supermarket shelves is sterilized milk months old, from 6,000-cow milk factories a thousand miles away. If *we* had a cow . . ."

When Jo Anne takes a decision, nothing will stop her, and this morning from my window I can see a pretty little Jersey heifer across the way, graceful as a deer. Soon enough she will give us fresh milk every day too. Meantime, what a beautiful, gentle, sweet creature! She has charmed all of us—and those *eyes!* Her name is Shoba, which means the "bright one," and her friend and custodian is Jo Anne's daughter Julia.

Well, besides drinking it and making unimaginably good yogurt with it, what do you do when the spring makes the bucket overflow with liquid flowers? When our neighbors sent their extra milk our way, we put some in our bread, and it was sensational. The recipe works just fine with any fresh whole milk, even if it isn't from your local cow.

Scald the milk and cool to lukewarm. To cool it quickly, put the pan of hot scalded milk in a dishpan of cold water, and stir the milk until it cools. Stir the honey into the milk.

Dissolve the yeast in the warm water.

Measure the flour and salt into a large bowl and stir lightly. Make a well in the flour and pour the milk and the dissolved yeast into it. Stir from the center outward, until all the flour is mixed in, making a stiff dough. Knead vigorously for about 15 minutes without adding more flour. Use the extra water on your hands to keep the dough from sticking, working in as much as you need of the ½ cup (or even more) to make a soft, elastic dough. Now knead in the butter in bits, continuing to work the dough until it is silky.

Form the dough into a ball and place it smooth side up in the bowl. Cover and keep in a warm, draft-free place. After about an hour and a half, gently poke the center of the dough about ½ inch deep with your wet finger. If the hole doesn't fill in at all or if the dough sighs, it is ready for the next step. Press flat, form into a smooth round, and let the dough rise once more as before. The second rising will take about half as much time as the first.

Press the dough flat and divide it in two. Round and let relax, then deflate and shape into loaves. Place in greased 8" × 4" loaf pans and let rise in a warm place until the dough slowly returns a gently made fingerprint. The loaves should arch beautifully over their pans.

Place in a preheated oven (350°F) and bake about 40 minutes, or until done. For a less deeply colored crust, turn the heat down to 325°F after 15 minutes and bake about 50 to 60 minutes in all. If the occasion merits, brush the crust with butter. Cool this bread before you slice it.

You can also make excellent rolls with this recipe. Bake them about fifteen to twenty minutes at 400°F after the bread comes out of the oven. If you want, bake them along with the bread at 325°F; they will be paler and less moist inside, and they'll take about half an hour to bake. A sprinkle of poppy seeds is pretty. Brush the rolls with butter and serve them piping hot.

2 cups fresh whole milk (475 ml)
¼ cup honey (60 ml)

2 teaspoons active dry yeast (¼ oz or 7 g)
½ cup warm water (120 ml)

6 cups stone-ground whole wheat flour (900 g)
2½ teaspoons salt (14 g)

½ cup more water (120 ml)
2 tablespoons cool butter (28 g)

Buttermilk Bread

This is one of our most beloved recipes. Tender, featherlight, bright-tasting bread that is somehow perfect with any sandwich filling, and devastating (in its subtle way) as toast. It keeps exceptionally well, too, when hidden. The bread may be slightly extravagant for everyday, but it makes an occasion of any simple dinner.

For the lightest, most delicate version, use very finely ground spring wheat flour. Coarsely stone-ground flour makes an earthier, tenderer bread. For rolls that are light as a feather, include the larger amount of butter in the dough; for bread, the smaller measure is plenty. Well-kneaded dough made with bread flour will give airy, chewy rolls; if you prefer soft rolls, use a cup of whole wheat pastry flour in place of one cup of the bread flour.

The buttermilk conditions the dough to give the bread its special tenderness. Because of this conditioning, or mellowing, of the gluten, be careful not to overwork the dough, particularly if you are kneading by machine. Be careful, too, not to let it rise too long at each stage or else the loaves may tear in the final proof.

Dissolve the yeast in the warm water.

Mix the hot water with the honey and add the buttermilk. The temperature should be just slightly warm.

Stir the flour and salt together, making a well in the center. Pour the yeast and buttermilk mixture into the well, and stir from the center outwards, incorporating all the flour. Test the dough to see whether more flour or more water is needed and adjust accordingly. The bread is lightest if the dough is slightly soft. For rolls, it should be quite soft. Knead about 20 minutes, adding the butter in cold bits at the end of the kneading time.

Form the dough into a ball and place it smooth side up in the bowl. Cover and keep in a warm, draft-free place. After about an hour and a half, gently poke the center of the dough about ½ inch deep with your wet finger. If the hole doesn't fill in at all or if the dough sighs, it is ready for the next step. Press flat, form into a smooth round, and let the dough rise once more as before. The second rising will take about half as much time as the first.

Press the dough flat and divide in two. Round it and let it rest until relaxed, then deflate and shape into loaves or rolls. The recipe makes two loaves for 8″ × 4″ pans. Or shape the dough into rounds, flattening them slightly, and place in pie tins. Bake a little less time than loaves. These rounds, cut into wedges, make really good dinner bread. For rolls, one loaf's worth of dough makes 9 large or 15 small dinner rolls in 8″ × 8″ or 9″ × 13″ pans, respectively. Sesame seeds complement the flavor perfectly, though they are not at all required.

Place the shaped dough in greased pans and let rise in a warm place until the dough slowly returns a gentle fingerprint. This dough makes a very high loaf when properly kneaded, so be a little bold about giving it time. Bake the bread in a preheated 325°F oven for nearly an hour. Rolls take 15 to 20 minutes, depending on their size, at 400°F. Brush the rolls with butter when they come out of the oven (the bread, too, if you feel fancy).

*2 teaspoons active dry yeast
(¼ oz or 7 g)*
½ cup warm water (120 ml)

*¾ cup very hot water
(175 ml)*
¼ cup honey (60 ml)
*1¼ cups cold buttermilk
(300 ml)*

*5½ cups whole wheat
flour (830 g)*
2 teaspoons salt (11 g)

*2 to 4 tablespoons butter
(28–56 g)*

Yogurt Bread

This delicious bread is the one we feature in A Loaf for Learning. In this version, the recipe is adapted to the sponge pattern. Making part of the dough ahead lets you prepare the rest on a faster schedule than normal, without sacrificing the quality of the bread. (It also makes it even more important to use yogurt that is *fresh*.) The timing and measurements here are for a sponge that ferments for 6 to 10 hours; for other sponge timings, see page 405.

SPONGE INGREDIENTS

1 teaspoon active dry yeast
(3.5 g)
¼ cup warm water (60 ml)

3 cups whole wheat
bread flour (450 g)
2 teaspoons salt (11 g)

3 tablespoons honey*
(45 ml)
⅔ cup yogurt (160 ml)
⅓ cup cold water (80 ml)

*For the highest bread, do
not use raw honey in a long
fermentation like this one.
Use pasteurized honey, or else
a refined sweetener like brown
sugar.

TO MAKE THE SPONGE

Dissolve the yeast in the ¼ cup warm water. Mix the flour and salt in a bowl; add the honey, yogurt, cold water, and dissolved yeast, making a *stiff* dough. Knead about 5 minutes, and set aside in a cool place, snugly covered to keep the dough from drying out, but with plenty of room in its container for the sponge to rise. Keep at room temperature for the shorter period, or in a very cool place if it will stand a full ten hours.

When you mix the sponge into dough, once again you have the choice whether to let it rise more or less quickly, depending on how warm the mixing water is and how warm you keep the dough. For dissolving the yeast, though, use warm water always.

TO MAKE THE DOUGH

Dissolve the yeast in the warm water. Soften the sponge with the liquids and work in the rest of the flour measure, adjusting the consistency as required. Knead until silky, about 15 minutes.

Form the dough into a ball and place it smooth side up in the bowl. Cover and keep in a warm, draft-free place. After about an hour check to see whether the dough is ready. Gently poke your wet finger about ½ inch deep into the center of the dough. If the hole doesn't fill in at all or if the dough sighs, it is ready for the next step. Press flat, form into a smooth round, and let rise once more as before. The second rising will take about half as much time as the first.

Press the dough flat and divide in two. Round it and let it rest until relaxed, then deflate and shape into loaves. Place in greased 8″ × 4″ loaf pans and let rise in a warm, draft-free place until the dough slowly returns a gently made fingerprint. If the dough rises nicely, slashing the loaves can be very pretty. We like to make one long vertical cut, about ¾ inch deep, in Yogurt Bread. Bake 45 minutes to an hour at 350°F.

DOUGH INGREDIENTS

1 teaspoon active dry yeast
    (⅛ oz or 3.5 g)
1 ½ cups warm water (350 ml)

the sponge from above
¼ cup oil (60 ml)

3 cups whole wheat flour
    (450 ml)

Overnight Started Bread

This is one of our standbys. A good all-purpose bread for sandwiches and toast, it is flavorful and dependable. Because the sponge ferments overnight, the bread has some of the qualities of a long-rising dough: warm flavor and good keeping quality. The addition of fresh ingredients in the morning provides characteristics you would expect from a fast dough: energetic yeast activity and a high, speedy rise.

The composition of the sponge, incidentally, is not arbitrary. Much testing and tasting—and some research, too—have gone into balancing the ingredients. There is just enough salt, for example, to control the fermentation for the long rise; and including the milk from the beginning, rather than adding it with the dough ingredients, significantly improves the flavor of the bread. If you use this recipe as a pattern for adapting other recipes to the sponge method of mixing, you'll want to experiment for a couple of bakings to decide just which ingredients should be included in the sponge, and which later, in the full dough.

SPONGE INGREDIENTS

¼ teaspoon active dry yeast
  (1 g)
¼ cup warm water (60 ml)

2 cups whole wheat flour
  (300 g)
6 tablespoons powdered
  milk (45 g)
½ teaspoon salt (1.75 g)

¾ cup cold water (175 ml)

TO MAKE THE SPONGE

Dissolve the yeast in the warm water. Combine the flour, powdered milk, and salt, stirring well to keep the milk powder from lumping. Add the softened yeast and the cold water and mix vigorously for about 5 minutes.

Cover and leave in a cool room until you are ready to make the bread, 12 to 18 hours. If you will be leaving it for 18 hours, use very cold water, and keep the sponge in a place that is quite cool.

TO MAKE THE DOUGH

Dissolve the yeast in the ½ cup warm water. Dissolve the honey separately in the 1 cup of water. Mix the sponge and sweetened water together. Your fingers do the best job, though it *is* messy. Next, incorporate the yeast into the mixture.

Mix the salt and flour, and make a well in the center. Pour the sponge mixture into the well, and fold in the flour. Mix all the flour into the sponge, squeezing it with your fingers to make sure it is uniform. Is there enough water in it? This will depend on the flour, the timing of the sponge, and other variables. If it seems a little stiff, wet your hands and knead in more water, as much as half a cup, whatever's needed. All that stirring and squeezing may have been a lot of trouble, but both develop the gluten in the dough and cut down on kneading time. Knead the dough, working in the butter toward the end of the kneading time. Keep kneading until it is all absorbed and the dough is smooth and silky. Whether you add the butter or not—it does make a spectacular difference in the bread—the dough should take only about 10 minutes of efficient kneading to attain supple perfection.

Form the dough into a ball and place it smooth side up in the bowl. Cover and keep in a warm, draft-free place. After about an hour and a half, gently poke the center of the dough about ½ inch deep with your wet finger. If the hole doesn't fill in at all or if the dough sighs, it is ready for the next step. Press flat, form into a smooth round, and let the dough rise once more as before. The second rising will take about half as much time as the first.

Press the dough flat and divide in two. Round and let relax, then deflate and shape. The bread is good in standard loaves, hearth-style rounds, French batons, or big hard rolls. Proof about 45 minutes in a very warm place.

This bread benefits very much from high initial heat and a a steamy oven (see page 106) though a standard bake is plenty good. Baking times will vary according to the shapes you have chosen, from 25 minutes for rolls to almost an hour for bread, at 350°F. If you steam the rolls or the bread, reduce the total baking time by about ten minutes.

DOUGH INGREDIENTS

1¾ teaspoons active dry yeast (6 g)
½ cup warm water (120 ml)

2 tablespoons honey (30 ml)
1 cup warm water (235 ml)

2 teaspoons salt (11 g)
4 cups whole wheat flour (600 g)

more water as needed

3 tablespoons butter (42 g) (optional)

Lemony Loaves

2 teaspoons active dry yeast
  (¼ oz or 7 g)
½ cup warm water
  (120 ml)

5½ cups finely ground
  whole wheat flour
  (825 g)
2 teaspoons salt (11 g)
¼ cup wheat germ, toasted
  (28 g)
peel of one lemon, grated
  (about 1 tablespoon)

1¼ cups cottage cheese
  (300 ml)
¾ cup water, nearly
  boiling (175 ml)
2 tablespoons honey (30 ml)

2 tablespoons cool butter
  (28 g)

A bright, full-flavored bread that is very light and nutritious.
This recipe makes excellent rolls.

‰

Dissolve the yeast in the ½ cup warm water.

Stir the dry ingredients, including the lemon peel,
together, and mix the cottage cheese, hot water and honey
separately; combine all the ingredients except the butter.
Knead about 20 minutes, incorporating the cool butter
towards the end of the kneading time.

Cover and let rise in a warm place, being careful not to let
the dough go longer than necessary each time. This is quite important. After about an hour and a half, gently poke the center
of the dough about ½ inch deep with your wet finger. If the
hole doesn't fill in at all or if the dough sighs, it is ready for the
next step. Press flat, form into a smooth round, and let the
dough rise once more as before. The second rising will take
about half as much time as the first.

Press the dough flat and divide in two. Round it and let it
rest until relaxed, then deflate and shape into loaves. Place in
greased 8″ × 4″ loaf pans and let rise in a warm, draft-free
place until the dough slowly returns a gently made fingerprint.

Place in preheated oven and bake at 325°F 40 minutes or
so, until done. This bread makes delightful rolls; make any
fancy shape, or cloverleaf rolls with poppy seeds. You can also
just divide one loaf into 12 rounds and fill the greased cups of a
muffin tin. Give them a full proof, and bake about 15 minutes
at 425°F (or longer at 325°F along with the bread). Brush
with butter.

Eggs

Eggs add protein and make the bread richer and higher-rising. Since bread with egg tends to dry out rapidly, most recipes call for extra fat to counteract this. Often, too, for greater tenderness the sweetener is increased; and if you use a lot of egg, more salt is needed to keep the bread from being too bland.

Adding eggs to whole wheat, we think, does make a bread rather less interesting in flavor, and so when we include them, it is most often in recipes that get their sparkle from some other source (raisins, for example). Relatively simple egg breads like Vienna or Challah draw their elegance from their baker's careful attention to making a flavor-rich crust. Vienna bread is baked hot with plenty of steam at the outset; Challah is "washed;" both are shaped to increase the amount of crust surface and thereby enhance the flavor of the loaf.

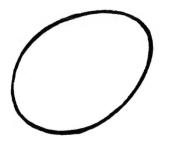

Whole Wheat Egg Bread

6 cups finely ground whole
  wheat flour (900 g)
1 tablespoon salt (16.5 g)

2 teaspoons active dry yeast
  (¼ oz or 7 g)
½ cup warm water (120 ml)

4 eggs, plus water to make
  2¾ cups (650 ml)
¼ cup oil (60 ml)
3 tablespoons honey (45 ml)

1 egg for glazing, and
  poppy or sesame seeds
  if desired.

Whole grain flour produces bread of an earthier mood than the white flour with which Challah is usually made. The recipe is therefore not an exact translation, but it is as authentic as we could make it—and very good. Some people like to add raisins; if you are one of them, use about 1 cup per recipe. Steam the raisins to soften them, then cool; work gently into the dough toward the end of the kneading period.

❧

Stir the flour and salt together in a bowl. Make a well in the center.

Dissolve the yeast in the warm water, and set it aside while you mix the other liquids.

Break the eggs into a quart measuring cup. Add enough tepid water to make 2¾ cups; then add the oil and honey, and beat until smooth. Add this mixture and the yeast to the well in the flour, and stir together. Knead the dough until it is silky and supple, adding water by wetting your hands, as necessary. The dough should be soft, but not flabby; the important thing is the kneading: for the very best and highest bread, an efficient kneader will require about 20 minutes to develop the dough to its springiest.

Form the dough into a ball and place it smooth side up in the bowl. Cover and keep in a warm, draft-free place. After about an hour and a half, gently poke the center of the dough about ½ inch deep with your wet finger. If the hole doesn't fill in at all, it is ready for the next step. Press flat, form into a smooth round, and let the dough rise once more as before. The second rising will take about half as much time as the first. Keep your eye on the dough, and don't let it go so long that it sighs when you poke it. Egg-rich doughs like this benefit from a slightly shorter rising, particularly if you will be spending extra time shaping the bread (not unlikely with this one).

There are many ways to shape this dough, the classic being to braid it. For two good sized plump and pretty braids, flatten the dough out on your table, making an oblong about 12 inches by 18 inches. Cut it in half lengthwise and then cut each half in thirds, making each piece the same size. Form *smooth* balls out of the pieces, and cover with a thick damp cloth or an inverted bowl to keep them from drying out while you work.

When the rounded dough softens, roll three of the balls into snakes about 18 inches long, working each of them back and forth under your palms, from the center toward the ends. Try to keep them smooth and even: don't rush. Professional bakers use fine rye flour to dust the snakes, which prevents them from *bleeding*, or pulling into each other, during their final rise. If you have no rye flour handy, any kind will do.

Braid from the center toward each end—this is strange but helpful. For the best final result, keep the braid somewhat loose; don't stretch or pull the strands. When you have your braid, place it in a greased loaf pan or on a greased baking sheet, dusted with seeds if you wish. Repeat the whole process with the other 3 pieces of dough. Let them rise in a warm humid place until the soft dough returns a gently made fingerprint (wet finger) slowly.

If you know how to braid 4 strands instead of 3, the loaf will be higher. Here is a fast way to braid a pretty braid with only *one* strand: it takes a little practice, but works not only for loaves but for rolls as well. Incidentally, this recipe makes good, very light rolls, providing they are not allowed to dry out at any time.

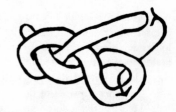

1

2

3

4

Brush the braids with an egg wash made of one egg plus the amount of water that will fill half the shell. Use a soft paint-brush, a feather brush, or a fringed cloth napkin for this: those stiff commercial pastry brushes can be hard on the dough. Cover the whole exposed surface carefully, but don't let the egg wash collect in the valleys. Sprinkle with seeds, if you choose, and place the masterpiece in a preheated 350°F oven. Bake until nicely browned, about 35 minutes for a long thin braid, or 45 minutes for a fat one; in loaf pans, allow at least 45 minutes, unless the bread is fantastically light.

NOTE: If the smell of the baking egg wash is obnoxious to you, next time wash the bread just after it comes out of the oven, instead of just before it goes in. The effect is nearly the same, and the heat of the bread cooks the egg to a respectable shine without added time in the oven.

SOME TIPS If you want really high slices—not at all necessary for dinner bread, but convenient for sandwiches—make a braid that you twist only three times, so that it is very short and fat. For the highest slices of all, put this loaf in a regular 8″×4″ pan. These fatter breads will take a little longer to cook, and need to cool before slicing.

A very long, skinny braid made with long, thin snakes can be formed into a circle on the baking sheet and is quite spectacular served hot from the oven. It will bake much faster, and in fact you can bake it at a higher temperature *much* faster if it is very thin indeed.

Featherpuff Bread

1½ cups cottage cheese
(355 ml)
2 eggs, slightly beaten
¼ cup honey (60 ml)
½ cup water (120 ml)

2 teaspoons active dry yeast
(¼ oz or 7 g)
½ cup warm water (120 ml)

5 cups whole wheat flour,
finely ground (750 g)
½ cup powdered milk
(60 g)
1½ teaspoons salt
(8.25 g)

2 tablespoons butter, in
cold chips (28 g)

This is not an inexpensive bread, but it is packed with protein, and much loved. Probably you could say it represents some outside limit of what a dairy bread can be, both in ingredients, and in the bread itself: tender, exceptionally light, pale and rather sweet, with a very dark crust. It is hard to believe that a single bread can incorporate so much milk and eggs, but it does, and gracefully.

&

Warm the cottage cheese gently in a saucepan. Remove from heat and mix in the eggs, honey, and water, taking care that the cottage cheese is not so warm that it cooks the eggs. The final mixture should be about 80°F.

Dissolve the yeast in the warm water.

Mix the flour, powdered milk, and salt thoroughly, making a well in them and adding the liquids. Mix to make a dough, and test for consistency, adding water or flour if needed. The dough should be very soft, and it will be sticky to work with, but if you add too much flour at this stage, the dough will be dry later on and the bread not so high as it should be.

For the lightest bread—and this one can be outrageously light—knead very well. Knead at least 15 minutes; then add the butter little by little, and knead again until quite silky.

Because it contains so many eggs, this dough rises rather slowly. Even so, be careful not to wait too long. When it has risen well, gently poke its center with your wet finger, applying the usual test to see if it is ready to deflate. The dough should not sigh, but is ready as soon as the hole you have made remains without filling in. Press the dough flat and shape it again into a smooth ball. Let it rise again as before.

Divide in two and form smooth rounds. Protect the rounds from drafts, letting them rest until the dough regains its suppleness. Shape carefully, and place in greased 8″ × 4″ pans for the final rise. When spongy and quite high, put in preheated 325°F oven and bake for about an hour—check at 45 minutes, though; if the bread is exceptionally light, it will bake faster. The bread is prettiest brushed with butter when it comes out of the oven.

Do, please, let this one cool completely before you try to slice it, or it will squash.

Cinnamon Rolls

Featherpuff bread is light and rich-tasting, so it makes good rolls. If you are fond of breakfasting on cinnamon rolls, we suggest using this dough for making them, not only because they will be light and tasty, but because this recipe is protein and calcium-rich, and rolls from it make a more complete meal than those from a plainer dough.

When shaping the bread, roll one loaf's worth into a big rectangle. Brush with softened butter and sprinkle generously with brown sugar and cinnamon—chopped walnuts, too, and a few raisins if you like. Roll up jelly-roll fashion, sealing the end well. Now, using a loop of strong thread or light cord, cut the roll into slices as illustrated. Arrange comfortably close together on a greased baking pan, and let rise in a warm place until very soft. Bake along with the bread (or slightly warmer) until nicely brown—about 20 minutes for smallish, thin rolls, or 40 minutes for big puffy ones.

The richness of the roll, how many coils the spiral has, how big it is, and how many you get—all these depend on your whim. If you roll the dough very thin and use lots of goodies, you can rapidly approach candy. Big tender light rolls with a single graceful swirl of cinnamon may be just as appealing at the breakfast table, and a whole lot less reprehensible nutritionally.

Cottage Herb Loaf

¼ cup minced onion (60 ml)
2 tablespoons oil (30 ml)

2 teaspoons active dry yeast
 (¼ oz or 7 g)
½ cup warm water (120 ml)

1 cup cottage cheese (235 ml)
½ cup finely chopped
 parsley (120 ml)
1 tablespoon dill weed

1½ tablespoons honey
 (22 ml)
1 egg, beaten

1½ teaspoons salt (8.25 g)
2½ cups whole wheat flour
 (375 g)

Just a handful of dough makes a big round herbed dinner loaf, at once light and nourishing.

Sauté onion in oil.

Dissolve yeast in water, and set it aside.

Add cottage cheese, parsley, and dill weed to onions and heat gently to warm them. Stir together cottage cheese mixture, honey, and egg.

Mix salt with 2½ cups flour; add yeast and cottage cheese mixture. Turn dough onto floured surface and knead until supple. Cover and let rise in a very warm place, about 90°F. The dough will come up very quickly—in about 45 minutes!—so don't let it get away from you. Check by poking the center with your wet finger. If the hole you make remains without filling in at all, press the dough flat, shape it into a smooth round once more, and let rise again as before. The second rise will take about 25 minutes. Apply the same test to see if it is ready to shape.

Deflate the dough and shape it once more into a smooth round. Press seam side down into a greased round casserole or pie dish, and let it rise in the same warm place until it is high and spongy-feeling. The last rise will take only about 15 minutes if the dough is warm enough.

Meantime, preheat oven to 350°F. Brush top of loaf with oil; bake for 45 minutes. Cool, if you have time, then cut into wedges and serve.

Vienna Bread

Vienna put itself emphatically on the breadmaking map around the turn of the century with its remarkable white bread. Our version is an equally remarkable whole wheat bread, simple in its ingredients, delicate yet flavorful, tender and bright; a surprisingly good keeper. To look authentic, the loaf should be a pointy, ruddy version of the classic French bread shape. Vienna bread requires steaming to give it a good crust, because the flavor otherwise is so delicate as to be underwhelming.

ᐒ

Dissolve the yeast in water. Combine the flour and salt. Mix the egg, oil, honey, and 2 cups of water. Mix the liquids and the yeast into a well in the flour. The dough should be just a little stiffer than usual; add more of the water if you need too, though, by wetting your hands as you knead the dough very well. Allow 20 minutes by hand.

Let rise in a warm place (80°F) about an hour and a quarter. Deflate and let rise again, about 45 minutes or so; test as usual by poking the dough about ½ inch deep with your wet finger: it is ready for the next step if the hole does not fill in at all. Be sure that you take up the dough each time before it has reached the point where the circumference of the finger-poke sighs—this will protect the flavor of your bread.

Divide the dough into two or three pieces. Shape rounds, and let them rest until they regain their suppleness. Dust a baking sheet generously with cornmeal. Shape the loaves as for French bread, except make the ends more pointy and the middle plumper.

Place loaves side by side on the dusted baking sheet; let them rise again warm, without humidity. Toward the end of the proofing period, preheat the oven very well, to 450°F. Slash the loaves just before you place them in the hot oven; make long, parallel horizontal slashes—as deep as an inch if the dough seems very bouncy and resilient.

It is essential to steam the bread liberally during the first 15 minutes of baking, until the crust shows good color (see page 106): then reduce the oven temperature to 325°F. (Leave

2 teaspoons active dry yeast
    (¼ oz or 7 g)
½ cup warm water (120 ml)

6 cups whole wheat flour,
    finely ground (900 g)
2½ teaspoons salt (14 g)

1 egg
2 tablespoons oil (30 ml)
1 tablespoon honey (15 ml)
2 to 2¼ cups warm water
    (475 to 530 ml)

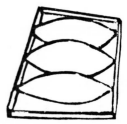

the oven door open briefly if necessary to get the heat down.) Bake until done, up to half an hour more. This bread is best when it is not overbaked, so be vigilant. How fat you make the loaves, how much they rise, and how close they are together on the baking sheet all influence the amount of time the bread takes to bake.

Try using the dough from this recipe for the Kaiser rolls that follow. They are good eating, and fun to make.

Kaiser Rolls

These spectacular rolls are, admittedly, a little tricky to shape, but even though our own early experiments were far from bakery-perfect, there was never a scrap left over. When properly made, the rolls are very beautiful; properly made or not, they are large, tender-crusty, delicious. The recipe makes 16 rolls.

Prepare the dough for the Vienna Bread recipe, using 2½ cups of water so that the dough is soft. Follow the directions for mixing and rising.

Divide the risen dough into four pieces, shaping them into smooth rounds. Cover them snugly. When the first one relaxes, press it flat with your palms and cut it into four equal pieces. Round each one of these into a ball.

To shape the rolls, wait until each small ball is slightly relaxed. Flatten it with your hand to about ⅜ inch thick. Gently press the thumb of the left hand into the center of the disc. Use the left index finger to lift up a section of the dough, bringing it over the thumb. With the side of the right hand, hit the dough against your thumb firmly. Repeat this action clockwise five times, but don't hit the last section, just twist it and press it into the center of the roll where your thumb was. All this may sound unlikely, but it is most satisfying to figure out. When you complete the last roll, you'll wish you had more dough.

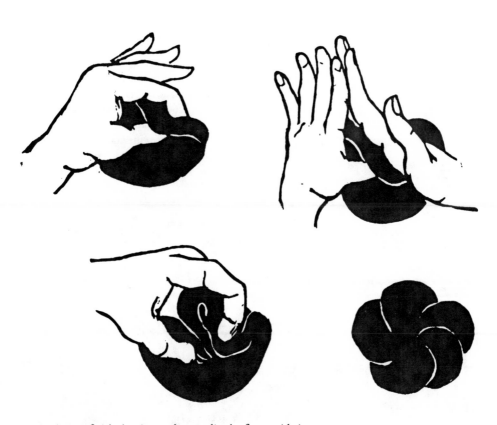

As you finish shaping each one, dip the flower side into a dish of poppy seeds and place it upside down on a greased baking sheet, with enough room so that the rolls won't touch each other when they rise. You can get about 8 on a 12″ × 18″ baking sheet. Allow them a good hour to proof, in a warm, dry place — then pick up each one and very gently turn it right side up on the baking sheet. Pop them into a very hot oven: for best results, preheat the oven to 450°F and steam it (see page 106) for 10 to 15 minutes. Turn the oven down and bake the rolls for about 15 minutes more at 350°F. They are done when crispy brown all over. If possible, bake them near the top of the oven. If you bake on the bottom rack, put an extra baking sheet under the pan on the bottom so that the rolls don't burn.

With the Grains

Here converge two opposing schools of breadbaking. On the one hand is the crowd who will add nearly anything—certainly any leftover cereal—to bread dough: the motive can be earnest Thrift; sometimes it's a kind of unabashed bravado. These good folks are genuinely fond of their inevitably hearty loaves, and even when some of their friends don't share their enthusiasm, it turns out all right because a bread that has a lot of cooked grain in it will not stale quickly.

In the second school, rather more button-down, are those who admire the featherlight commercial "honey-wheatberry" bread and long for a recipe that will enable them to make such loaves In Their Own Kitchens: they want to reproduce the pale, airy, sweet, tender loaves, luscious with soft nuggets of Real Wheat strewn throughout. Alas, careful reading of the fine print on the wrapper reveals that the first (hence, the most plentiful) ingredient is white flour—cunningly called "wheat" flour, but *not* "whole wheat." Very few home bakers would be able to replicate that bread with whole wheat flour; now you are one of them, should you be so inclined.

Whichever school you favor, and even if you are not ready to join either, this section will be useful if you are interested in including whole and cracked grains, and grains other than wheat, in your breads. Generally, these are not recipes for beginners: quirks and pitfalls lurk here, which is why we have gone into such detail on the grains.

WHEAT   Here, we are talking about wheat that isn't ground into flour — about whole berries or berries that have been cracked, and about bulgur wheat, a special kind of cracked wheat that is particularly good for baking.

Cracked Wheat   You can make nubbly, pretty bread with ordinary cracked wheat, but it takes some doing. For one thing, it is the same color as the dough, and so tends to be invisible. (We suggest a remedy for that in the recipe on page 203.) The other problem with cracked wheat is that it is often too finely ground. When you buy it, or if you grind your own, try to get a crack that is nearly half of a wheat berry—very large. Most we've seen on store shelves is really sort of a wheat meal, and when added to bread it does nothing more than make it heavy and crumbly. If you mill your own, it is worth sifting out the smaller particles.

Bulgur wheat is the sort of cracked wheat we like best for adding to bread. Use the coarsest size. It keeps its shape with noble persistence, and is different enough in color to show up against wheat dough. Natural foods stores often sell bulgur in bulk, or you may find it on the supermarket shelf.

You can soften grain for using in your dough in several ways. Probably the easiest is to rinse a cup of grain and stir in a cup of boiling water, letting it stand, covered, until the water is absorbed. If you use more water, as you would if you were cooking the wheat for normal eating, it will be too fluffy and tender to keep its shape in the dough.

Wheat berries from red wheat, sprouted two or three days, make a very good show in a whole wheat loaf. Knead them, about half a cupful per loaf, into any bouncy plain bread dough. Slightly less wonderful but plenty good are unsprouted whole berries cooked chewy-tender, kneaded into the dough in the same proportion.

OATS

Oats give whole wheat a subtle sweetness and a little extra chew. The flavor of oats blends well with wheat, mellowing it and making it taste richer. You can use rolled oats uncooked in bread but it won't be any lighter for their presence. On the other hand, if you use porridge made from rolled oats to replace most of the liquid in bread dough, the result is an exceptionally light and chewy-tender loaf.

Steel-cut oats or oat groats must be cooked. Bread using their porridge makes a slightly heavier, moister loaf, but one with outstanding eating quality that keeps very well.

For a very pretty crust on dark breads especially, or on any bread with oats inside, coat the loaf with rolled oats after shaping. Either spread the oats on the table and roll the loaf in them, or just sprinkle them in the greased pan before you put the bread into it; for the top, brush with milk or water and dust with oats just before putting the bread in the oven. Hearth loaves can be baked on a rolled-oat-strewn baking sheet, but strew with a light hand: too thick a layer will keep the loaf from cooking on the bottom.

BARLEY

Ordinary barley has tough, sharp hulls that adhere so tightly that the grain must be milled many times—"pearled"—to get them off; the germ and the useful bran layers are lost in the milling, needless to say, along with the indigestible hull. We can't recommend using pearl barley. But recently a naturally hull-less barley has become available in some places. We are told it's an ancient grain, probably originally from Tibet. If you can get it, you will enjoy making porridge from it, and using the porridge in your bread, as we describe in the oatmeal section.

CORN Nearly everybody likes the sweet flavor of corn and its sunny color. In yeasted bread, corn poses unique problems and takes a little extra care to achieve a light loaf.

The most cornmeal you can just plunk into a normal two-loaf whole wheat bread recipe is about ½ cup, substituted for that much wheat flour. The bread may be a little dense, but it should be tasty. It is much better to cook the corn first, and then add it to well-kneaded dough made with finely ground high gluten flour. Even then, corn softens the wheat gluten and you may begin to think you will have to *pour* the dough into the pan—but if you follow the method described in the Ana-dama recipe on page 210, you can have light, delicious bread in a very corny mood.

Generally choose cornmeal that is as coarsely ground as possible. Your loaves will be lighter and the corn will show up better.

Cook the cornmeal before you add it to the kneaded dough, using as little water as possible. If your recipe calls for oil, stir it into the cooled corn mush before adding it to the dough.

A final word on corn: once ground, it turns rancid rapidly. This is a phenomenon of recent years, a side effect of breeding corn for very high-yield crops. Maybe in the near future breeders will be able to correct the problem, but in the meantime virtually all the cornmeal—degermed or not—and other corn products that are sold commercially are a little rancid, a little bitter. Cornmeal that is really fresh—homeground, most likely, and stored (in the refrigerator) for less than five days —is sweet sweet sweet, an astonishing difference no one can fail to celebrate.

MILLET Millet sold for human consumption is hulled, and its tiny spheres are unusually clean. It can be added just as is to bread dough, and will give crunch (but not tooth-breaking crunch) and a pretty dotted-swiss look to the slice. The flavor is very subtle, but for visual and textural effect, one-fourth cup of millet per loaf makes a good show. To bring out its delicate flavor, rinse the grain and heat it dry (stirring all the while) in a big heavy pan until it just begins to brown.

For less crunch, cook the millet in water. You can add a cup per loaf or more; if the grain is well cooked you won't see it in the slice. The loaf will very likely be a little heavy, but it will be moist and will have millet's sunshiny warmth of flavor. For a very good millet bread, add cooked millet as part of the water measure in a light plain recipe like Buttermilk Bread, page 176.

Kasha, as the Russians call it, or whole groats have every advantage in breadmaking over the flour ground from them. The flour is heavy; even a little bit makes bread grayish and dense. The groats, however, properly prepared, can flavor the loaf without weighing it down.

BUCKWHEAT GROATS

Rinse the grain and heat and stir in a heavy pan until lightly toasted and fragrant. Mixing a beaten egg into a cup of groats before toasting is traditional and does help to keep the grains whole and separate; if you don't have a nonstick pan, a little oil helps prevent sticking. After toasting, you can either cool the groats and add them as is to the dry ingredients for the recipe, or knead them in later. Or you can soften them a little, and instead of white sparkling crunchies in the slice, you will have soft taupe nubbets. To soften, pour boiling water over the hot toasted grain. Use water to equal only *half* the measure of the groats: stir it in, and cover tightly until the water is absorbed and the grain cool. If you are tempted to use leftover kasha (cooked groats, that is) or to cook the grain in the amount of water for normal eating, it will turn mushy and disappear into the dough. This does not make for light bread. Raisins and sunflower seeds are good with buckwheat.

It is sometimes suggested that leftover rice (brown rice, of course) be added to wheat dough. Add one cup to a plain, light loaf's worth of dough, and you will have a chewy, rather flat-tasting bread with rice grains showing throughout. A more interesting approach is to use rice in one of the "naturally fermented" breads. Their fuller flavor and greater density accommodate rice's subtlety very well. See page 215.

RICE

RYE & TRITICALE   Either of these is good to use like wheat, cracked or whole, as described 2 pages back. Both are also useful ground into flour, as we will see in the pages that follow.

SOY GRITS   Soy grits—the largest crack possible—make a very successful cracked "grain" in bread, with a nutritional plus. Be sure to precook them, even the toasted ones, for 15 minutes or more in an equal quantity of boiling water; otherwise, they can rip up your dough. About ⅓ cup of cooked grits per loaf is a reasonable amount. For the best flavor, sweeter and not so beany, choose untoasted grits.

MIXED GRAIN CEREALS IN BREAD   There is a large natural foods firm in these parts that sells a nine-grain bread; for a commercially produced loaf, it is excellent. We buy and enjoy their nine-grain cereal, and so decided to try to make up our own version of the bread. For starters, we just added leftover cooked cereal to dough, as we have done successfully with oatmeal—but what a disaster!

The cereal contains wheat, rye, barley, triticale, corn, oats, millet, flax, and soy grits—an innocent list, but somewhere in there was dynamite for the dough. (Another time we put the uncooked cereal, which is quite finely ground, into rolls. Added along with some sautéed onions and Parmesan cheese to well-kneaded dough made with strong coarse flour, it made big light soft rough-hewn "Raggedy Rolls": *they* were great.) But why tell you all this? I think it is by way of saying that someone else's mix of grains may not be just what you would want, and there are more reliable ways of coming up with a good mixed-grain bread than adding a cereal.*

One simple and effective way is just to add half a cup of sprouted grains or the same amount of whole or *coarsely* cracked grains (steamed chewy-tender, drained and cooled) to the well-kneaded, elastic dough for any normal, high-rising whole wheat loaf. There will be flavor and nubble aplenty, and the bread will look pretty too.

*That delicious nine-grain bread, by the way, turns out to be made from sprouts! If you want to try it, see our suggestions for making sprout breads, page 278.

Using Non-Wheat Flours

Another sort of mixed-grain bread simply includes a little of each of several kinds of grain flours along with the wheat. If you want to try this you can keep your loaf light by following the example of commercial bakeries: add only a tiny amount of each non-wheat flour. A very good kneader using super high-gluten wheat flour could include as much as ⅔ cup *total* of non-wheat flours as part of the 6 cups in a normal plain bread recipe. Even then, remember, you have reduced your margin for error, so be careful to knead and ferment the dough just right.

One consideration here is that most other grains are blander-tasting than wheat. When you include them in whole wheat bread, they generally do little more than make the loaf heavier and less flavorful. Three exceptions:

Rye flour, added in amounts up to ½ cup per loaf in place of an equal quantity of wheat flour, enriches the flavor of the bread and makes a moister, heartier loaf. Expect the dough to be a little bit on the sticky side. If you want the bread to *taste* like rye, add a spoonful of caraway seeds. Breads with a larger proportion of rye flour succeed best with a different mixing technique; see the Rye Breads section for much more about all this, pages 134 to 169.

Buckwheat flour is strong-flavored and very heavy. Use it in small quantities — ¼ to ⅓ cup per loaf will make a hefty buckwheat flavor. The loaf will have a warm fragrance and the characteristic blue-gray color. Sunflower seeds and raisins both complement buckwheat's rather strident flavor beautifully. (For a very tasty recipe including buckwheat flour check the Saltless Bread section, page 294. Add 2½ teaspoons of salt to the flours listed in the recipe, if you aren't going salt-free.)

Triticale flour (trit'-ih-*kay*'-lee) is a newcomer among grains. A cross between wheat and rye, it was developed for hardiness and high protein content. Unfortunately, depending on where the grain was grown, and which of hundreds of strains it came from, it may have considerable gluten content or very little. We have made high, sweet-flavored loaves with 100 percent triticale flour, and then with another batch of flour have not been able to get much rise at all. If you want to try, we suggest beginning with half wheat and half triticale, to see how it goes. Be careful not to overknead. We suggest doubling the honey in the recipe. If you are buying grain to grind yourself, plump grains will be high in starch, slim ones higher in protein, as a rule.

With the exception of these three, we find that chunky grains (either sprouts or coarsely cracked, lightly cooked cereals) work better than flours. Perhaps because the dough can support a larger amount of grain than of flour, the grains give more flavor and character to the bread; its appearance and keeping quality benefit as well.

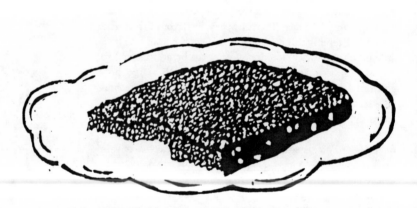

NOTE: Here's a problem we haven't solved: the grains on the outside of the crust will bake into hard nuggets. We have never found a way around this, though we have tried. Chew circumspectly, and let us know if you come up with a solution.

Cracked Wheat Breads

Cracked Wheat Bread I is the nearest thing to the popular commercial honey-wheatberry bread. It is light, pale, pretty, delicious — far better in every way than its store-bought counterpart. Cracked Wheat Bread II is a very different loaf: hefty, tender, with a rich full flavor that comes from the happy combination of wheat and dates. The wheat sings out because the bread has no dairy products to mellow its flavor; dates, with their natural fruity sugar, sweeten the loaf.

Cracked Wheat Bread I

TO USE CRACKED WHEAT

The night before, mix the wheat, molasses, and cool water. The water should cover the grain when you start; add more if necessary. Let stand in a cool place until morning.

⅓ cup coarse cracked
    wheat (55 g),
    OR
¾ cup bulgur wheat (128 g)
2 tablespoons molasses
    (30 ml)
water to cover, ¾ cup

TO USE BULGUR WHEAT

Just before you dissolve the yeast and begin to mix the dough, boil ¾ cup water. Mix the bulgur, molasses, and water in a heavy saucepan. Bring them to a boil, stirring, and cover, removing from heat. Set aside.

2 teaspoons active dry yeast
    (¼ oz or 7 g)
½ cup warm water (120 ml)

❧

Dissolve the yeast in the ½ cup warm water.

Dissolve the honey in the hot water and add the buttermilk.

Stir the flour and salt together in a mixing bowl and make a well in the middle. Add the buttermilk mixture and the yeast, combining them to make a dough. Knead partway, for about 10 minutes only, then let rise in a warm place about an hour and a half. Test to see whether it is ready to deflate: wet your finger and poke the center of the dough about ½ inch deep. If the hole does not fill in at all or if the dough sighs, go on to the next step. Otherwise, allow a little more time.

Drain any excess water from the wheat. Spread the butter on the kneading surface and turn the dough out onto it, flattening the dough to a large oblong. Spread the grain out on the

2 tablespoons honey (30 ml)
¾ cup boiling water (175 ml)
1¼ cup cold buttermilk
    (300 ml)

5½ cups finely ground
    high-gluten whole wheat
    flour (830 g)
2½ teaspoons salt (14 g)

2 tablespoons butter (28 g)

dough and fold them together. Knead the grain and the butter into the dough, and keep working them together until the dough is silky and lustrous, stretchy and even—except for the brown grains, of course. This will take about 10 minutes. Let the dough rise again as before; this time it will take about half as long.

As soon as the dough tests ready, turn it out onto the tabletop and press to deflate. Cut in half and round each part. Cover and allow to relax very well—this may take 15 minutes unless your dough is quite soft. Use flour on the board when you shape the loaves, and be very gentle to keep the gluten film from tearing. This dough makes very fine hearth loaves, splendid buns or rolls, and big spectacular pan loaves (two loaves, 8" × 4" pans).

The shaped dough should rise quite high before you put it into the preheated oven. It does best in a place that is warm and not too humid. Have the oven ready a little early, and if the tops of the loaves begin to rip from the stress of the wheat, get them into the oven. Usually they won't rip if you have kneaded well, but whether they do or not, their crusts will be pretty if you slash them. If there is a rip, slash so as to make it look intentional—if no rip, three diagonal cuts made with the knife held at an angle let the loaf rise maximally in the oven and look its spiffy best, too. Hearth loaves take as well to this pattern as the panned kind.

Put the loaves into a preheated oven as soon as you finish slashing them. Start the oven at 400°F; after 10 minutes turn the heat down to 325°F and bake for almost an hour. When the loaves come out of the oven, brush the tops with butter.

Cracked Wheat Bread II

This bread is wonderful made with a roughly stone-ground high-gluten wheat, but any good strong flour will do the trick. It is not a beginner's loaf: there are lots of challenges to the strength of the dough here, and though the bread can be high and light under skilled hands, novices might expect a smaller loaf than otherwise—it's delicious anyhow for sure.

Stir the wheat into the boiling water and let stand, covered, while you measure the other ingredients. The grain should cool to lukewarm by the time you are ready to add it to the dough.

Simmer the dates in ¾ cup boiling water for about ten minutes, stirring to be sure they don't stick. Usually they lose their shape while they simmer; if yours don't, mash 'em. Add ¾ cup cold water and cool to lukewarm; add the lemon juice and oil, and stir in the bulgur wheat.

Dissolve the yeast in the ½ cup warm water.

Stir the flour and salt together, fluffing the flour. Make a well in the center of the flour mixture, and add the cooled date/wheat liquid and the yeast. Mix them together, and adjust to make a dough that is soft but workable; knead it for about 20 minutes.

Form the dough into a ball and place it smooth side up in the bowl. Cover and keep in a warm, draft-free place. After about an hour and a half, gently poke the center of the dough about ½ inch deep with your wet finger. If the hole doesn't fill in at all or if the dough sighs, it is ready for the next step. Press flat, form into a smooth round, and let the dough rise once more as before. The second rising will take about half as much time as the first.

Press the dough flat and divide in two. Round it and let it rest until relaxed; this will help in the shaping, since the relaxed dough is less likely to tear, which this dough does tend to do. Shape the loaves carefully, forming either round hearth loaves or standard pan loaves. Should the dough tear while you are shaping the loaves, press it back together with wet fingers.

For the best rise, keep the dough in a warm, only slightly humid place. If, when it is ready to go into the oven, you find that it has torn on the top, use a sharp knife to slash the loaf artfully, guided by the tears.

Bake in a preheated oven, 350°F, for about 45 minutes or a little longer.

⅔ cup large-crack bulgur wheat (112 g)
¾ cup boiling water (350 ml)

¾ cup pitted dates (135 g)
¾ cup hot water (175 ml)
¾ cup cold water (175 ml)
2 tablespoons lemon juice (30 ml)
2 tablespoons oil (30 ml) (optional)

2 teaspoons active dry yeast (¼ oz or 7 g)
½ cup warm water (120 ml)

5½ cups whole wheat flour (830 g)
2½ teaspoons salt (14 g)

Oatmeal Bread

1⅓ cups raw old-fashioned
   rolled oats,
   OR
⅔ cup raw steel-cut oats
   (both weigh 106 g)*
2 cups boiling water (475 ml)
1 tablespoon salt (16.5 g)*

2 teaspoons active dry yeast
   (¼ oz or 7 g)
½ cup warm water (120 ml)

3 tablespoons honey (45 ml)
¼ cup oil (60 ml) (optional)

5 cups finely ground whole
   wheat bread flour
   (750 g)

*If you have leftover oatmeal
porridge, you can use 2 cups,
and 2¾ teaspoons salt

Cooked oatmeal makes up the liquid in this recipe, and the result is an outstanding loaf, very different from, and totally superior to, bread made by adding raw oats. When the porridge is made with rolled oats, the bread is light and bright; it has a rich creamy flavor—very subtle, but with great warmth. When you use steel-cut oats instead, the loaves are not so spectacularly high, but the flavor is even better, and the bread has outstanding keeping qualities. Either way you get bread good for toast, good for any kind of sandwich. We consider this one of the best basic breads for everyday eating.

ã

Cook the oatmeal in the water until it begins to thicken; add the salt and set aside for several hours or overnight. If you use leftover oatmeal, bring it to room temperature.

Dissolve the yeast in the ½ cup water.

Mix the honey and oil into the oatmeal, and add it and the yeast to the flour. Even if the dough seems very stiff, don't add more water just yet: the flour will absorb water from the oatmeal very slowly, so the dough softens as you work. Knead the somewhat stiff dough for about ten minutes, and if it still seems stiff then, add water gradually by wetting your hands and kneading until the dough has taken in as much water as it requires to become soft and supple. If you use leftover oatmeal that is fairly thin, you may find that you need to add flour on the board instead of water.

Form the dough into a ball and place it smooth side up in the bowl. Cover and keep in a warm, draft-free place. After about an hour and a half, gently poke the center of the dough about ½ inch deep with your wet finger. If the hole doesn't fill in at all or if the dough sighs, it is ready for the next step. Press flat, form into a smooth round, and let the dough rise once more as before. The second rising will take about half as much time as the first.

Press the dough flat and divide in two. Shape it into balls and let them rest, covered, until very much softer. Shape gently into hearth-style or standard 8″ × 4″ pan loaves. Sprinkle a greased baking sheet, pie tins, or loaf pans with rolled oats before placing the shaped loaf on or in them. For a fancy touch, brush the tops of the loaves with warm milk, and then sprinkle with more rolled oats that have been soaked in the warm milk.

Let rise once more in a warm place, and bake about 45 minutes at 350°F.

৯

These are special; they take the basic mellow-creamy oatmeal bread flavor and complement it perfectly, achieving a happy wedding of flavors that is dressy enough for a special occasion or for gifting, but not so flashy that the bread is useless for everyday purposes.

WALNUT-OATMEAL BREAD

Add about ⅓ cup chopped walnuts—lightly toasted, if you will—to each loaf. For best results, add them at the time of shaping, because the walnuts give the dough a lavender tint otherwise. (Not to hint that there is anything wrong with lavender bread, of course.) After dividing the dough, roll one loaf's worth at a time into a good-sized rectangle on a lightly floured board. Spread the nuts out on top, and press them down into the surface of the dough. Fold or roll the dough up, aiming to have an even distribution of nuts and a smooth surface on the top when you are through. Let this dough rest, covered, until it relaxes; this will take longer than it would have if the dough had not been exercised by the incorporation of the nuts. Shape into hearth or pan loaves, taking care to press out all the gas and trying to avoid tearing the gluten film. If you like, include finely chopped nuts along with the oats on the crust, a nice touch.

SUNFLOWER-OATMEAL BREAD

Add 2 to 4 tablespoons toasted sunflower seeds to each loaf just as you would walnuts in the above instructions—or, for a completely different effect, also very good, add the same amount of *raw* seeds to the oatmeal when you put it on to cook. Their flavor is sweet, subtle, and pervasive when the seeds are cooked this way.

WITH THE GRAINS 207

Barley Bread

Substitute a generous ⅓ cup of cracked barley for the oat measure. Cook the barley for at least half an hour. Let it stand overnight if possible; if you don't, the bread will be less fine-textured, more like a cracked-grain bread than otherwise, but plenty good, too.

SESAME-BARLEY BREAD

Substitute barley malt extract for half the honey measure, and use sesame oil. Roll the loaf in seeds before baking. A dramatically flavorful loaf.

Honeybutter Oat Bread

Soft and sweet, with the richness of butter and honey and the mellowness of oats, this is probably a bread for company, though if there are any leftovers, they'll keep for days. You can make pretty, dark-crusted hearth loaves or very fine-textured pan bread.

If you are looking for a very light oat bread, try Oatmeal Bread. This recipe *can* make light loaves if your kneading is really good, but that is demanding because the dough is sticky and has to start out extra soft because the oats take in water as the bread rises. We recommend the one-hand-and-a-scraper method of kneading for this bread. It is definitely worth the trouble, however.

Dissolve the yeast in the ½ cup warm water.

Combine the dry ingredients in one bowl, and mix the milk, yogurt, and honey in another. Make a well in the dry ingredients, and pour the yeast and the milk mixture into the well. Mix into dough and knead very well, until it is smooth and elastic. Toward the end of the kneading time, incorporate the butter, and knead until all the dough is exceptionally silky. At the beginning of the kneading period this dough will be extremely soft and sticky. Don't succumb to the temptation to add flour or it will become hard and dry as the oats take in the extra water over the next few hours.

Form the dough into a ball and place it smooth side up in the bowl. Cover and keep in a warm, draft-free place. After about an hour and a half, gently poke the center of the dough about ½ inch deep with your wet finger. If the hole doesn't fill in at all or if the dough sighs, it is ready for the next step. Press flat, form into a smooth round, and let the dough rise once more as before. The second rising will take about half as much time as the first.

Press the dough flat and divide in two. Round it and let it rest until relaxed, then deflate and shape into either hearth or pan loaves. Sprinkle the greased baking utensil with rolled oats before placing the shaped loaves in or on them. If desired, use the milk and oat topping described in the Oatmeal Bread recipe. Let rise once more in a warm, draft-free place until the dough slowly returns a gently made fingerprint. Bake the loaves in a preheated 325°F oven for about one hour, or until done.

2 teaspoons active dry yeast
(¼ oz or 7 g)
½ cup warm water (120 ml)

5 cups finely ground whole
wheat bread flour (750 g)
⅔ cup rolled oats (raw)
(53 g)
2½ teaspoons salt (14 g)

1½ cups scalded whole
fresh milk, cooled
to lukewarm (350 ml)
½ cup yogurt (120 ml)
5 tablespoons honey (75 ml)

3 tablespoons cool butter
(42 g)

Anadama

1 cup boiling water (235 ml)
1 cup coarsely ground
    cornmeal (122 g)

2 teaspoons active dry yeast
    (1/4 oz or 7 g)
1 2/3 cups warm water (395 ml)

4 cups finely ground whole
    wheat bread flour (600 g)
1 tablespoon salt (16.5 g)

1/3 cup molasses (80 ml)
1/4 cup oil (60 ml)

We simply can't believe the scurrilous story about the irate backwoodsman and his lazy wife, Anna. This fine combination could never have been born of anger; it is just too good. A sweetly delicious golden bread with a deep brown crust, Anadama keeps well and makes grand toast.

We call for coarsely ground cornmeal. If you use finely ground cornmeal you will have a smaller loaf, but a tasty one.

This is a bread we make often; we are inordinately fond of its chewy texture and full, satisfying flavor. Still, this is a demanding recipe, and the instructions are not to be taken lightly unless you want bread that is as dense as it is tasty.

≥≈

Boil the water in a heavy saucepan and stir in the cornmeal. When the mixture is smooth, cover and cook gently for a few minutes—just until the corn begins to crackle. Remove from the heat and set aside, still covered, to cool slowly. It is a good idea to do this the night before, particularly with the coarse cornmeal. If you are using finer cornmeal, you can let it sit for

as short a time as 15 minutes, and then spread out on a platter to cool quickly. If you are in doubt, bite a tiny bit of the corn; if it is still hard, give it more time.

When the corn is approaching room temperature, dissolve the yeast in the warm water.

Mix the flour and salt, and add the dissolved yeast. Stir together and then knead the dough, developing it very well but being careful, especially with mechanical help, not to over-knead. It will have to be very strong to carry so much corn.

Use a fork or your fingers to stir the molasses and oil into the corn, working out all the lumps. Press or roll the kneaded wheat dough out on a tabletop, making a large rectangle. Spread the corn mixture onto the dough, and fold or roll it up. Now, with patience, humor, and determination, knead the corn into the dough. It will be a mess for a while but finally a bumpy dough will form. The dough will become softer as the corn begins acting on the gluten of the wheat, but resist the temptation to add more flour at this point, as the dough will stiffen up in the final stages of rising. Amazing stuff.

Cover the dough and let it rise in a warm place (80°F), for an hour and a half or so, until a ½ inch deep hole made by your *wet* finger does not fill in at all. With *wet hands* deflate the dough and let it rise in its warm place once more, this time for about 45 minues. Turn the dough out onto a floured board and deflate; divide into two lumps and gently shape them into rounds. Let them rest until they are quite saggy, then form carefully into loaves.

This bread is really at its prettiest baked in greased 1½ quart bowls, dusted with fine cornmeal before the rounded loaf is put inside. For best effect, choose a bowl with a round bottom; glass or stainless steel or pottery all work fine. The bread does beautifully, too, baked in standard-size 8" × 4" loaf pans, and it's probably easier to handle if you will be making it into sandwiches. It is generally far too soft for a successful freestanding hearth loaf.

Let the shaped loaves rise in a warm place for about 45 minutes or until a gentle indentation of the finger fills in very slowly.

Place in a preheated 350°F oven; bake about an hour.

Kasha Bread

1 cup raisins (145 g)
1½ cups water (350 ml)
2 tablespoons oil (30 ml)

2 teaspoons active dry yeast
   (¼ oz or 7 g)
½ cup warm water (120 ml)

¾ cup buckwheat groats
   (122 g)

2½ teaspoons salt (14 g)
5½ cups whole wheat
   bread flour (830 g)

Even those who usually don't favor the outspoken Russian grain often do like this bread — and buckwheat fans are crazy about it. The hearth loaf is like a big taupe soccer ball, very pretty. Good hot from the oven with Better-Butter* or soft white cheese; great with saucy tofu, or peanut butter; especially fine as an accompaniment to a hearty winter soup.

❧

Bring the raisins and the water to a boil in a saucepan, and simmer until the fruit is soft. Remove from heat and blend raisins and water in blender or food processor, or force through a sieve, making a thin, smooth paste. Add cold water or ice to the blended raisins to make 2½ cups of liquid. Cool to lukewarm, and add the oil.

Stir the yeast into the ½ cup warm water. Rinse the buckwheat groats well in warm water, drain, and put in a broad skillet. Heat, stirring constantly, until the grain is dry, turns reddish brown, and smells good. (See page 199 for some variations on this.) Mix the roasted groats, the salt, and the flour together. Make a well in the center and add all the liquid ingredients, blending them into a bumpy dough. Adjust the water and then knead extra well — 25 minutes for light bread! Because of the kasha, the gluten will have a lot of work to do. The dough starts out warm, and the yeast responds enthusiastically to the fruit sugar, so the bread rises quickly. Form the dough into a ball and place it smooth side up in the bowl. Cover and keep in a warm, draft-free place. After a little less than an hour and a half, gently poke the center of the dough about ½ inch deep with your wet finger. If the hole doesn't fill in at all or if the dough sighs, it is ready for the next step. Press flat, form into a smooth round, and let the dough rise once

*BETTER-BUTTER is an easy-spreading mixture of butter and oil, a favorite recipe from *Laurel's Kitchen*. Blend 1 cup oil with 1 cup soft butter; to keep it firm longer at room temperature, include 2 tablespoons each, water and non-instant milk powder, and ¼ teaspoon lecithin; ½ teaspoon salt is optional.

more as before. The second rising will take about half as much time as the first.

Divide in two, handling the dough very gently from here on. Round the loaves, letting them rest until they are really relaxed, being careful to cover them to prevent their surfaces from drying out. For hearth loaves, round the dough again — the double rounding does make the loaves rise higher — and place on greased baking sheet to rise, again in a warm place. Instead of rounding the second time, you can shape the dough into loaves for standard 8″ × 4″ pans.

Let rise once more, about 30 to 45 minutes, until the touch of your moistened finger makes a dent that fills in slowly. Pan loaves should rise up nicely if you have done your kneading, arching over the top of the pan when they are ready to bake.

Whether you have made hearth or pan loaves, they will benefit from being slashed before you put them in the oven. We show patterns we like below. The pan loaves may rip on the surface during the proof, and if they do, just make the best of whatever rips there may be when you do your slashing.

Put the proofed breads in a 400°F oven, and after ten minutes turn the heat down to 350°F, baking the bread about 50 minutes in all. It may take a little longer, but the loaf is done when it sounds hollow if thumped on the bottom.

Crunchy Millet Bread

2 teaspoons active dry yeast
  (¼ oz or 7 g)
½ cup warm water (120 ml)

2 tablespoons honey (30 ml)
1 cup cottage cheese (235 ml)
1¼ cup hot water (300 ml)

½ cup millet (100 g)
5 cups whole wheat flour
  (750 g)
2½ teaspoons salt (14 g)

2 tablespoons butter (28 g),
  OR
¼ cup oil

This is a pretty, polka-dotted loaf, high in protein and calcium. When the slices are toasted, the little millet dots look like stars in the sky. Finely ground bread flour has the edge over coarser grinds in this one: the pale millet shows up better.

For the warmest flavor and crunchiest crunch, rinse and pan-toast the millet before you start, but if you choose to use the millet untoasted, it works fine.

❧

Dissolve the yeast in the warm water.

Stir together the honey, cottage cheese, hot water, and, if you use it, the oil. Mix the millet, flour and salt together, making a well in the middle; pour in the yeast and the cottage cheese mixture. Adjust as required to make a soft dough by adding either flour or water. Knead until very elastic, about 20 minutes.

Form the dough into a smooth ball, cover it, and let it rise *once* in a warm place. Divide in two, and gently form into smooth balls—smooth except for the millet! Let the balls rest covered until they regain their suppleness, about 15 minutes; if the dough is soft, you are less likely to rip the gluten. Shape the loaves carefully, dusting the board with flour to help prevent the dough from tearing. The recipe makes two high, light 8″ × 4″ loaves, two very pretty hearth-style loaves baked in pie tins to cut into wedges for dinner, or a couple dozen dotty rolls.

Proof in a warm place, giving the round loaves and the rolls a very full proof. The pan loaves should arch beautifully above the sides of the pans. The bread is ready to pop into a preheated 400°F oven when a gentle indentation from your wetted finger fills in slowly. After baking about ten minutes, reduce heat to 325°F and continue until done, about 45 minutes in all—longer if the bread is not so light as it should be.

Corn-Rice Bread

Some people feel strongly that bread is much better—both more healthful and more flavorful—when it is made without adding yeast but by letting the dough mature and ripen slowly by itself over a longer period of time. Organisms similar to those that would make a desem starter do begin to thrive in such doughs, and even though there is no *added* yeast, there is considerable biological activity in the dough during the long fermentation due to so-called wild yeasts and dough enzymes; their by-products produce a loaf that is almost always exceptionally flavorful. The bread will not rise very much, though it may spring a little in the oven from the expansion of steam.

There are several unyeasted breads in this book. The present recipe is the kind gift of Marcia Miller from the Bexley Natural Food Co-op in Columbus, Ohio; it is one of the best we have tasted. As you might expect from the modest salt measure, the bread's flavor is subtle; but before you increase the salt, try it as is, sliced very thin, with a miso-tahini spread.

2 cups cornmeal (244 g)
4 cups whole wheat bread flour (600 g)
2 tablespoons corn or sesame oil (30 ml)
3–4 cups cooled, cooked brown rice (about 700 g)
1¼ teaspoons salt (7 g)
1½ cups water, or more (355 ml)

ॐ

Mix the cornmeal and flour and rub the oil in with your fingers. Mix in the rice, working it until the grains are all separate. Add the salt and enough water to make a pliable, kneadable dough; how much water you need will depend on the wetness of the rice; if your rice is on the chewy side, you may want as much as 3 cups. Knead the sticky dough until elastic, about 15 minutes.

The bread can be shaped at once and baked, but it is at its best (and lightest) if you let it stand, covered, 12 to 16 hours at a cool room temperature, then shape into two round hearth loaves and put them on a cornmeal-dusted baking sheet. Place in a cold oven, turn to 350°F, and bake about an hour.

Cool completely before slicing, and slice very thin.

VARIATION

Add sesame seeds or sunflower seeds, about 1 tablespoonful per loaf.

Fruits, Nuts & Seeds

No one needs to be told that raisins and walnuts and caraway seeds have a special place in the world of breads. Every homeland and almost every holiday boasts some particularly wonderful fruited or seeded or nutted bread all its own, with the fragrance of tradition to enhance the enjoyment of every bite. We have not attempted to include many such recipes—the best of them are your own family secrets—but if you are longing to make a wonderful bread that has form in your mind, but no name (and no recipe), a dozen fancy books of recipes will never supply it as readily as the application of your imagination and experience can; and if you're a little short on that, this section hopes to fill you in.

Making breads that are laced with fruits is a sure way to win high marks with the eaters, but it can be tricky, and what promises opulence, if not glory, can betray you with a weighty, gooey, or holey loaf—not at all what you had in mind. We hope that the tips in this section will help you produce exactly the bread you *did* have in mind, or at least one that pleases as much as it surprises you.

This writing is just now being haunted by a tiny strawberry-blond fairy-godmother figure named Joan, a friend in the old days in Berkeley. She fell into breadmaking with vast enthusiasm, following no rules whatever, and was delighted with the results whatever they were. Her loaves were always freestanding, free-form, unutterably dense, and so packed with fruits and seeds and other marvelous things that when she pressed a chunk (there was no question of *slicing*) into your hand and asked with shining eyes if this wasn't the most *incredible* bread you'd ever eaten, you had to agree.

There is a bit of Joan in most of us, thank goodness, but there's a prudent streak too, and in these days of soaring prices and shrinking hours, usually we would rather make sure the loaves we lavish our time and money on are going to be light as well as tasty, edible as well as incredible, free from holes and goo, and sliceable, even toasterable and sandwichable — though none the less special for that when there are raisins and nuts on the scene.

We are veterans of literally hundreds of loaves of raisin bread, and have done a bit of research, too, to try to understand and explain some of the quirks as well as some of the special talents of natural fruits, nuts, and seeds. In this section we talk about how to use them to their best advantage, giving recipes we have developed and like very much, to serve both as examples and as springboards to your own creations. The section groups fruits with nuts and seeds not because they have much in common as ingredients but because they complement each other so beautifully. When one is included, adding another is simply the logical thing to do.

ONE WORD ABOUT CINNAMON

(Which is not a fruit, not a nut, not a seed.)

Though it is probably the favorite of all the sweet spices, cinnamon is after all made of ground-up tree bark, so don't add it to dough along with the flour, or it can tear up the gluten and reduce the bread's rise. In addition, cinnamon reacts with yeast dough in a mysterious way, producing a metallic flavor that is extremely unpleasant to those who are sensitive to it. As you'll see, we like to add cinnamon when the loaf is being shaped, either as a dusting on the crust, or rolled into the loaf in a delicate swirl.

Fruits

When we think of fruit in bread, raisins come instantly to mind, and in fact they are hard to beat. Other very flavorful fruits shine, too: dates, of course, apricots, prunes and currants. Fruits with subtler flavors like apple or pear can make a less showy but very good contribution when as juice or stew they provide the bread's liquid measure and its sweetener, naturally. Any addition of fruit improves the keeping quality of the bread.

If you have experimented much baking with fruits you will have observed that sometimes they seem to interfere with the normal rise of yeasted bread. We don't know of research that pinpoints the exact reasons, but it is not unlikely that fruits contain acids, active enzymes, and reducing sugars, any one of which could affect the quality of your dough. It is hard to generalize, but there are a few tricks that can help insure good results.

If you are baking with a new fruit whose effects on the dough you don't know, take a few precautions. Later, when you are familiar with its ways, you may decide that this fruit doesn't hurt the dough and so abandon these techniques with that particular fruit.

The fruit should have about the same moisture content as the dough, or be just a little drier, to prevent its juice from being drawn into the dough. For raisins and currants that are tender but not so soft they fall apart, steam or simmer for a few minutes, drain immediately, and let them cool before using. (When you don't mind darkening the color of the bread, use the broth as a part of the liquid in the recipe.) Cooking the fruit also deactivates stray enzymes in the fruit that could affect the dough.

Currants need to be washed. Prunes and dates need to be pitted, unless you buy them so; this is easy to forget. We find that there is more variation in the flavor of prunes than in most fruits, by the way, and the good ones are better than you could think. Pitted dates should be checked for inhabitants.

Unsulfured dried fruit is dark brown, tart, and often leathery: it needs to be steamed briefly—but not too soft,

please. As we've mentioned elsewhere, soft apricots can disappear into the dough and make the bread unpleasantly tart. If the fruit you buy is already quite soft, it is worth *baking* it a half an hour or more in the oven on low heat, so that it can develop the toughness required to stand up and be noticed when the bread's eating time arrives. Even if the exterior becomes somewhat crusty in the process of drying out in the oven, the flavor improves.

There's another view on making fruited breads that holds that the best time to add the fruit is *after* the bread is sliced. Stew apricots, for example, in orange or pineapple juice to make a thick, tangy jam, and spread it on your toast. If the bread is plain, you are then free to use soy spread and tomato or cheddar and pickles on your sandwiches, and not have the challenge of tailoring all the week's lunches to those succulent bits of apricot in the bread. Still, apricotty bread with peanut butter or almond butter or cream cheese is a real knockout— not to mention that fruit breads make a most welcome gift.

GLOOM ON THE DRIED FRUIT FRONT

It is no secret that bright-colored dried fruits get that way because some form of sulfur has been used to preserve them. Grave questions are being raised about the safety of this ancient technique, and more information seems to be coming every day. Some people are allergic to sulfur, and they shouldn't have these fruits at all. The rest of us might do well— especially if we eat a lot of dried fruit—to choose the less colorful, unsulfured kind until more research has been done and we know more about the long-term effects of the residues left by this kind of processing.

Most of these recipes direct you to add dried fruit to the dough just at the end of the kneading period. The advantage is that there is minimal wear and tear on the dough that way, the fruit is evenly distributed, and you don't have to fuss with it again.

On the other hand, if the raisins are too hot from steaming to add them at the beginning, or you want to add them to only one of the two loaves you are making, there's no law that says you have to add them in the first stage. For example, you can fold fruit (and nuts) into the dough after the first rise, when you deflate the dough. Press it flat, spread the fruit, fold it up, and let rise again.

Another alternative is to add the fruit when shaping the dough. Instead of shaping in the usual way, roll it into a rectangle using many *light* strokes of the rolling pin. Use as little flour on the board as you can get away with. For a regular loaf pan, the rectangle should be about seven inches wide (just shorter than the length of the pan), and about two feet long. Cover the surface of the dough with about ½ cup of dry raisin-sized pieces of fruits and/or about ¼ cup of chopped nuts. Leave about 2 inches free at the far end so that you will be able to seal the loaf. Lightly press the pieces into the dough with your rolling pin so that the dotted surface is nearly smooth, and then roll the dough up tightly, being fanatically careful not to incorporate any air into the roll at all. End up with the bare two inches and seal very well by pinching. Place the seam downwards and run the rolling pin gently lengthwise over the loaf to expel any air that might have sneaked in. Put the loaf in a greased pan as usual. Dust the top with cinnamon for extra pizzazz.

Because of all the pushing around, the loaf may want some extra rising time, but if you have done this perfectly, you will have a swirl of fruit and the sliced bread will not separate along the swirl, wreaking havoc in your toaster. If the fruit is wet—stewed prunes, for an extreme example—or if there is too much, or if you succumb to the temptation to add sugar and butter, the swirl will separate perforce. The wet fruit probably will also prevent the dough from cooking. (That can wreak havoc with your digestion.)

An elegant way to use fruit in bread is to let it provide both the liquid and the sweetener, producing a flavorful and long-keeping loaf. Stew and puree any very sweet fruit. Use the fruit and its broth, blended together and cooled, in place of part of the liquid in any fairly basic recipe. With applesauce, the fruit can make up all the liquid in the dough, except what is required to dissolve the yeast, of course. The bread will be light and will keep well; but in spite of the quantity of fruit, it won't be distinctly appley in flavor. (The applesauce should be reasonably sweet, please.) You can also use apple juice in your dough as sweetening liquid. One cup of apple juice is about as sweet as 1 tablespoon of honey: it makes a loaf that rises well and has good color, though the keeping quality of the bread is not enhanced as it would be by the use of whole fruit.

Peaches, pears, prunes—any sweet fruit simmered and pureed can sweeten bread for you. Often you won't need quite so much as with apple. For example, used in this way, ½ cup per loaf of raisins does the trick; dates, a little less. But don't expect their flavors to sing out solo so much as to form part of a duet with the heartiness of the whole grain. (It is bread, after all, not cake or jam!) Apricots, sour plums, fresh pineapple, tart grapes—fruits that aren't sweet themselves obviously can't be called on to sweeten your loaf. Any fruit that is very acid, even if it is cooked, will damage the yeast.

Orange and lemon peel give a happy zip to the things that they're put into, but we can't really bring ourselves to tell you to use them *unless* you are lucky enough to get them unsprayed, or at least undyed. There really is no way to wash the pesticides or chemical dye off the skins. For your consideration, here is what we have been able to find out about the chemicals used in California, where the regulations are more stringent than in most other places. Of course, the fruit in your own market may come from California or from other citrus-growing areas at different times of year. Try to find out where the fruit comes from and don't use the peel if there's a chance it was dyed.

In California it is illegal to dye fruit, and dyed fruit that is brought in from other states has to be labeled "color added." The labeling used to have to be on the orange, but now it can be just on the box, a problem when the fruit is not sold to the consumer from its carton. The dye used, citrus red number 2, has caused cancer in animals. Efforts to ban its use have failed because "nobody eats orange peels"! (Do we even want it in our compost pile?)

With regard to pesticides, the law prohibits spraying orange trees for a specified number of days before the fruit is picked, and the pesticides on them are supposed to have degraded by that time. The law is for the safety of the pickers, as well as the consumer.

When the fruit is packed, smelly sheets of paper impregnated with fungicides are put into the carton. Currently, the fungicides used are diphenyl-o-phenylphenate and thiabendazole. The first is often incorporated in a wax and used to coat a whole panoply of fruits and vegetables, from apples to bell peppers. There have been tests on citrus peel itself, and the levels of the chemical have been well below FDA tolerance levels. O-phenylphenate, by the way, is the active ingredient in household disinfectants like Lysol, and is officially thought to be one of the safer poisons around (if there is such a thing.)

Thiabendazole, the second antifungal in the citrus papers, turns out to be what you give your cow or dog or, (if you run the zoo), your giraffe to rid it of intestinal worms. It has been extensively tested on mammals, to say the least, and is considered very safe.

If you think that no poison is safe and you can't get untreated citrus peel, none of the recipes here will fail if the peel is omitted.

Nuts

Whether your style is Old-fashioned or Health Food, gourmet or homegrown, nuts probably rate pretty high on the list of goodies for making meals and treats more appealing. They contain substantial amounts of unsaturated fat, and so become rancid before long, if they are exposed to air or warmth. Keep nuts in the shell in a cool place, protected from damp; without shells, they need to be in the refrigerator, airtight; chopped—use them as soon as you can. Freezing is most effective, though it does destroy their natural vitamin E.

In bread, so it seems to me, pecans rate the very highest marks for their unmistakable sweet sparkle. They keep their individuality, don't become soggy, flavor the whole loaf, don't weigh it down, and are universally appreciated. But who these days can afford them? If you can, just add ¼ to ½ cup chopped pecans to any plain or raisiny loaf. Terrific.

PECANS

Walnuts are a pretty good second, but since rather than sweet they are pleasantly bitter, they require extra sweetener to balance their flavor. (An unsweetened walnut loaf is vehemently nonsweet, but good in its own way.) The bitterness of walnuts can be reduced if the nuts are toasted slightly and cooled before using. Toasting helps prevent them from getting soft in yeasted doughs as the raw ones will, when they are there from beginning to end; but toasted or not, they do tend to color the dough a sort of lavender-gray, unless you add them just before shaping. Walnuts provide a natural flavor balance to sweet fruits, particularly raisins, and they are outstanding with oatmeal.

WALNUTS

ALMONDS Last year a friend gave us some tiny almonds that had been grown on an organic farm: they had three times the flavor of larger almonds from the store, and when toasted, made a terrifically flavorful addition to bread. Normal almonds, even if they are toasted—and it helps—don't always have enough oomph to make much of a show in a loaf of bread. If you think your almonds are pretty blah and don't consider it cheating, you can spike them with a teaspoonful of almond extract— (but you can spike soy grits with almond extract and get nearly the same effect, with some other advantages).

CASHEWS, BRAZILS, & FILBERTS Cashews are even subtler than almonds in yeasted breads, but not brazil nuts. If you add a half-cup of chopped brazils to any loaf, the flavor is unmistakable, and the nuts keep their crunch to the last—it is a crispy crunch, almost more like raw celery than like a nut, but the flavor is there, singing out. Filberts too keep their splendid pungent sweetness, and give a lot of flavor. They are a fine choice to use along with fruits for really fancy fare. Toast them lightly.

PEANUTS If we can dignify peanuts by considering them in the nut section (they are of course really beans—nothing wrong with beans, mind you), we find them pretty awful in breads, quite rubbery even when toasted and added at the last, before shaping the loaf. A very peanutty flavored loaf can be achieved, however, by including ¼ cup or more of peanut butter in the dough, and the bread's texture will be very good (that is a lot of fat). Put the chopped peanuts on the crust.

PINE NUTS Last, should you come into an independent fortune—or have your own piñon trees and *lots* of time—pine nuts are wonderful. Try the pine nut pinwheels from *Laurel's Kitchen*. We haven't included a recipe in this book because since *Laurel's Kitchen*, alas, the price of pine nuts has shot into the empyrean.

Seeds

Some people think of Seeds as a little weird and health-foody, but when it comes down to it, they are old favorites ready for renewed interest: sesame, poppy, sunflower seeds, caraway, fennel, anise. Since it is impossible to generalize, let's look at them as the individuals they are:

In this book we always mean the unhulled variety called SESAME "natural" or "brown" in the store. The kind you buy at the supermarket in tiny packages for a minor fortune are hulled and bleached. See if you can't find the unhulled ones sold in bulk at a more reasonable price: not surprisingly, those hulls are loaded with essential minerals and B vitamins too.

Sesame seeds have a delightful warm, deep brown flavor familiar to nearly everyone. Their size and shape make them easy to use on and in bread — to embellish a crust, usually all you need to do is roll the dough in the seeds as you shape it. For the very best flavor, toast them lightly beforehand in the oven or on the stove top in a heavy pan (no oil required). As they toast, they pop, so use a deep pan like a Dutch oven on top of the stove if you don't want them all over the place. Stir for even toasting.

Much of the flavor of any bread comes from its crust, so when bakers want bagels or rolls flavored with sesame, onion, garlic, poppy, or caraway, they use plain dough and put the flavoring on the crust. It permeates! This is true with loaves as well as rolls, though since there is proportionately less crust, the effect is subtler. For a nicely sesame flavor, all that is necessary is seeds on the crust. Sesame enthusiasts who want more emphatic flavor may want to use fresh unrefined sesame oil when mixing up the bread.

You can add toasted seeds to the dough, too, though it won't make the bread any lighter. Ground toasted seeds add less flavor than you would expect, and definitely make a denser loaf; similarly with tahini, the flavorful sesame butter available in every natural foods store nowadays, often in raw, toasted, and in-between versions.

When you buy sesame seeds, try to get them American-grown. For years ours came from Mexico, but more and more often they were seriously dirty—full of sticks, rocks, and mouse droppings. Since that time we have also learned that controls on the use of pesticides outside the U.S. are nonexistent, with American corporations exporting to Latin America tons of toxic agricultural chemicals that are banned here. As we go to print, we cannot really recommend buying any food product from south of the border. Things improve when people are concerned enough; I would like to think that the situation will soon change completely.

POPPY SEEDS Poppy seeds are usually more for sparkle than for flavor, though if used in sufficient quantity they certainly do have their own distinct taste. With poppy seeds, very little makes a wonderful show: just 1 or 2 tablespoons on a loaf's worth will make an unmistakably poppy-seeded bread; a tablespoon sprinkled on a baking pan turns ordinary rolls into something special.

Don't get white poppy seeds by accident—people will think it is sand or, worse, mold. The black ones are called blue when you order them in bulk.

SUNFLOWER SEEDS Sunflower seeds are so nutritious, so nutty, so easy to grow right here at home. Why don't we love them more? I think it is because for years, when you visited any natural foods restaurant, you could count on finding the poor innocent seeds sprinkled in and on everything, often as not having been substituted for more expensive "real" nuts; and there'd always be a few, raw and soggy, in the bottom of the bowl when you finished your salad.

Fortunately, our children are untouned by these experiences, and they are crazy about them. Furthermore, almost anyone enjoys them when their flavor sings along with raisins and buckwheat—natural complements, since the little seeds are favorites in Russia, where kasha originated.

Unlike sesame, sunflower seeds do not have much natural antioxidant and so become rancid quickly once the seed itself is broken. For this reason they are not so practical to grind for butter or meal. Sort through the seeds you buy to remove any that are discolored or moldy or whose shells have stuck to them — these make poor eating and may well be responsible for some of the Enemies of the Seed. Sunseeds are eminently nutritious, full of vitamins and minerals and fine quality protein.

Toasted sunflower seeds are good in or on breads; about ¼ cup is plenty for including in the loaf. They are at their nuttiest when toasted; the flavor of the raw ones is milder, sweeter. Sunflower seeds are good not only with buckwheat but with oatmeal, and with any dried fruit.

Caraway, fennel, and anise, three cousins, are sometimes confused one with another.

CARAWAY, FENNEL & ANISE

Anise is the strongest of the lot, on the sweet side with its licoricey fullness of flavor. Fennel is more herby (it provides the characteristic flavor of pepperoni sausage — or soy-sage — and authentic Italian tomato sauces). With a bright pungent flavor in a lighter mood, fennel brings just the right sweet piquancy to make Lemony-Fennelly Bread extra-special. Caraway is the most familiar of the three, putting in its appearance in rye breads, on bagels, and in some English sweet buns. Most of all though, caraway has come to mean *rye* — so much so that if you make a whole wheat bread and put caraway in it, several people will assume it is rye; and conversely, very few will recognize rye bread without the seeds.

The three can be exchanged one for the other when someone has a strong antipathy to one, but the results will be a little different. How to say? Fennel is treble, caraway tenor, and anise bass. Or fennel is chartreuse, caraway purple, and anise dark gray in flavor.

Cumin is actually a member in this family too, more exotic perhaps, certainly less familiar in the United States as a seed than as the ground spice that gives character to Mexican foods. The whole seeds look very much like caraway, but cumin is not like anything else. Added to bread, it has a roguish red chili flavor much loved by some. Use with caution — the first time, anyhow.

CUMIN

Deluxe Raisin Bread

1 cup raisins (145 g)
1½ cups water (355 ml)

2 teaspoons active dry yeast
   (¼ oz or 7 g)
½ cup warm water (120 ml)

¼ cup oil (60 ml)
2 tablespoons honey (30 ml)
1 egg, beaten slightly
   OR
¼ cup water (60 ml)

5¼ cups finely ground
   whole wheat bread flour
   (790 g)
2½ teaspoons salt (14 g)

¾ cup chopped walnuts,
   (90 g) (optional)

Deluxe Raisin is one of our earliest recipes, and though others go in and out of vogue, this one has never fallen out of favor at all. It is an utterly dependable, delicious light bread, just sweet enough. It behaves just as you hope it will in the toaster or in the lunchbox.

ત

Rinse the raisins to remove any dirt. Cover them with the 1½ cups of water and bring to a boil. Reduce flame and simmer for 5 minutes. Drain, reserving the liquid, and set the raisins aside.

Add cold water to the liquid from the raisins to bring it to 1½ cups again. Let it cool to lukewarm.

Dissolve the yeast in ½ cup warm water.

Mix the raisin water with the oil, honey and the egg.

Measure the flour and salt into a large bowl. Make a well in the center of the flour and pour the liquid ingredients into it. Stir from the center outward to form a smooth batter, then fold and stir the rest of the flour into the liquid. Check to see if the dough needs more water or flour and add as necessary. Turn the dough out onto the table and knead until elastic. Don't be stingy with the kneading: even with the extra weight of the fruit, this bread can be exceedingly light. Stop before you would ordinarily consider the dough perfect, though, especially if you have been kneading with mechanical help; otherwise the next step can be too much.

Flatten the kneaded dough out on the tabletop and distribute the raisins and nuts, if used, on the top. Roll up and gently knead in the fruit. This takes doing, but eventually they will all be worked in.

Cover the dough and place it in a warm, draft-free place to rise. It will take from 1½ to 2 hours to rise fully; test by making a ½-inch hole in the dough with a wet fingertip: if the hole fills in slightly, give more time; if it remains, or remains and the dough sighs, deflate and let rise again, which will take about an hour.

Divide the dough and shape it for loaves. Of course, with the raisins poking through, it is not possible to keep a perfect gluten film, but do the best you can. This is a light, high-rising dough and will overcome the sweet little obstacles very nicely. Remove the raisins that pop out of the finished loaf, though, because they can burn in the oven and make the pan hard to clean. Sprinkle the loaves with cinnamon if you like.

Place the shaped bread in a warm, humid place to rise. It should double in an hour or less—check it after half an hour.

Bake at 325° to 350°F for 45 minutes to an hour—high-rising loaves will take the least time. Let the bread cool before slicing or you may find your airy loaf has become a misshapen pancake!

Since this is a great gifting bread, here are a few ways to make it fancier:

ᴈ• Bake hearth-style in a pie tin.

ᴈ• Put a shine on the crust, either with an egg wash or by brushing with butter after the loaf comes out of the oven.

ᴈ• Use the dough to make round dinner rolls in a baking pan or in muffin tins.

A Few Words About Giving Bread

No one need be told that a hot loaf of bread fresh from the oven makes a wonderful present, both for giving and for receiving. If the loaf has to wait a day or even more, choose bread that keeps especially well, and store it carefully. If possible, you could refresh it by wrapping in a damp towel and warming it briefly before you hand it over. We keep a supply of new, clean paper bags for wrapping fresh gift bread, because if a hot loaf is put in plastic, the bread will "sweat" and be soggy, or worse, moldy, when the otherwise lucky receiver goes to eat it.

Fruited Loaves

1 cup chopped dried
   apricots (130 g)
⅔ cup pitted, chopped
   prunes (112 g)

2 teaspoons active dry yeast
   (¼ oz or 7 g)
½ cup warm water (120 ml)

5½ cups whole wheat flour
   (830 g)
1 tablespoon salt (16.5 g)
grated peel of one lemon

2½ cups liquid—
   include prune and
   apricot broth (590 ml)
2 tablespoons honey (30 ml)

½ cup toasted, chopped
   almonds (71 g)

2 tablespoons butter (28 g)
   O R
¼ cup oil (60 ml)

A very light bread, exceptionally tasty. The combination of nuts and fruit here is quite special and harmonious. The bread keeps well—though not of course for weeks like a traditional fruitcake! Because the little nubbets of apricot and prune are part of the charm of this bread, be sure to keep the fruit firm as described on page 218.

ॐ

Prepare the fruit and set aside.

Dissolve the yeast in the warm water.

Measure the flour, salt, and lemon peel into a bowl. Stir lightly and make a well in the center.

If you stewed the fruit, measure the liquid and add the honey plus water to make a lukewarm 2½ cups. Add the oil now, if used.

Pour the liquid mixture into the well in the flour and stir them together from the center to make dough the consistency of pancake batter in the middle of the flour. Now add the yeast and continue to stir and fold until all the flour is incorporated. The object here is to buffer the acidity of the fruit juice with flour before exposing the yeast to it.

Knead until the dough is smooth and well-developed. Toward the end of the kneading, after about 15 minutes, smear the butter on the tabletop in the French manner and work it into the dough. Add the fruit and nuts little by little until the dough is uniform, with the bits of fruit and nuts throughout.

Form the dough into a ball and place it smooth side up in the bowl. Cover and keep in a warm, draft-free place. After about an hour and a half, gently poke the center of the dough about ½ inch deep with your wet finger. If the hole doesn't fill in at all or if the dough sighs, it is ready for the next step. Press flat, form into a smooth round, and let the dough rise once more as before. The second rising will take about half as much time as the first.

Press the dough flat and divide in two. Round it and let it rest until relaxed, then deflate and shape into loaves. Place in greased 8″ × 4″ loaf pans or round again to make hearth-style loaves on a baking sheet or in pie tins. Let the loaves rise in a warm, draft-free place until the dough slowly returns a gently made fingerprint. If you did your job on the kneading table, and all has gone well, the loaves will rise exceptionally high. Bake at 325°F for about 50 to 60 minutes.

For special occasions, brush the finished loaves with butter, or a glaze (¼ teaspoon cornstarch plus ¼ cup cold water and ¼ teaspoon honey, simmered five minutes). Glaze the baked loaves and return them to the oven for 1 minute.

The dough makes wonderful rolls. Bake 15 small ones in a 9″×13″ pan (or 9 large ones in an 8″×8″ pan), using one loaf's worth of dough.

Apricot-Sesame Bread

Prepare Whole Wheat Bread (page 80), using 3 tablespoons of honey and 3 tablespoons of good, fresh sesame oil per 2 loaves. Knead 1 cup diced apricot pieces into the dough toward the end of the kneading period, or add them when you shape the loaf. Roll the shaped loaves in sesame seeds before putting them in pans. This is a subtle, not-too-sweet loaf, flavorful, light, and chewy.

Deep Dark Date Bread

2 teaspoons active dry yeast
  (¼ oz or 7 g)
1 cup warm water (235 ml)

5 cups whole wheat flour
  (750 g)
1 tablespoon salt (16.5 g)
¼ cup carob powder (17.5 g)

2 tablespoons molasses
  (30 ml)
1½ to 2 cups water (475 ml)
¼ cup oil (60 ml)

½ cup chopped dates (90 g)
½ cup chopped walnuts
  (60 g)

A caky, very sweet-tasting bread even though it has only a little sweetener. No one will guess there is carob in it unless you tell the secret.

When walnuts are three dollars a pound, we make this bread without them, and there have been no complaints. If you put them in, they are at their best if lightly toasted beforehand.

❧

Dissolve the yeast in the warm water.

Mix the flour, salt, and carob powder in a big bowl. Mix the molasses, water, and oil together and add them and the dissolved yeast to the flour mixture to make a soft dough.

Knead until very well developed, springy, and elastic, and then add the dates and walnuts and continue to knead until they are evenly distributed in the dough.

Form the dough into a ball and place it smooth side up in the bowl. Cover and keep in a warm, draft-free place. After about an hour and a half, gently poke the center of the dough about ½ inch deep with your wet finger. If the hole doesn't fill in at all or if the dough sighs, it is ready for the next step. Press flat, form into a smooth round, and let the dough rise once more as before. The second rising will take about half as much time as the first.

Press the dough flat and divide in two. Round it and let it rest until relaxed, then deflate and shape into regular or hearth loaves. Place in greased 8″ × 4″ loaf pans or in pie tins or on a baking sheet, and let rise in a warm, draft-free place until the dough slowly returns a gently made fingerprint. Bake in a pre-heated 325°F oven for about an hour.

Golden Date Bread

In this loaf, dates are the only sweetener, disappearing into a beautiful fawn-colored slice, soft and medium light, that keeps very well. The happy consumers can't tell you *what* is in the bread, but "it's really good!"

&

Simmer the dates in 1 cup water until they are soft. Use cold water to bring the total measure to 3 cups of warm datey goo, and let stand until cool enough not to harm the yeast.

Dissolve the yeast in warm water.

Mix the flour and salt, and add the liquids and yeast to make a soft dough, adjusting with more water as needed. Knead until the dates have nearly disappeared and the dough is soft, smooth, and elastic (about 20 minutes), adding the butter toward the end of the kneading period in cold bits, and working the dough until it is silky and lustrous.

Form the dough into a ball and place it smooth side up in the bowl. Cover and keep in a warm, draft-free place. After about an hour and a half, gently poke the center of the dough about ½ inch deep with your wet finger. If the hole doesn't fill in at all or if the dough sighs, it is ready for the next step. Press flat, form into a smooth round, and let the dough rise once more as before. The second rising will take about half as much time as the first.

Press the dough flat and divide in two. Round it and let it rest until relaxed, then deflate and shape into loaves. Place in greased 8″ × 4″ loaf pans and let rise in a warm, draft-free place until the dough slowly returns a gently made fingerprint. Bake in a preheated 325°F oven about an hour.

For a very good loaf that is less sweet, reduce the dates to ½ cup.

1 cup pitted dates (178 g)
1 cup water (235 ml)

2 teaspoons active dry yeast
(¼ oz or 7 g)
½ cup warm water (120 ml)

6 cups stone-ground whole
wheat flour (900 g)
2½ teaspoons salt (14 g)

2 tablespoons butter,
cool (28 g)
additional water,
if required

Substitute ¼ cup sesame oil for all of the butter in this recipe, adding it with the liquids. Roll the dough on sesame seeds while shaping, incorporating the seeds into the loaf and onto the crust. Proof and bake as above. Dates are dynamite with sesame, naturally.

DATE-SESAME BREAD

Spicy Currant Bread

For a pretty and impressive holiday loaf, bake this bread—the whole dough—in an angel food cake tin. Serve with soft cream cheese and ripe pears.

It *is* truly delicious bread, but notice that there is quite a lot of bran in it. It would make an especially good gift loaf for someone who uses bran, but *not* for someone accustomed to a low-fiber diet.

We like the allspice, but the bread is also good with cloves, which give it a very distinctive flavor, with a clean nip to it. Or use a blend of cinnamon, cloves, and nutmeg, or simmer a big tablespoonful of minced fresh or crystallized ginger with the currants and apple juice: zippy and wonderful.

If you start the night before, the bran has a chance to soften and absorb water, which makes the bread soft and helps it keep very well. If you find yourself without the time to do it that way, soak the bran as long as is convenient for you. If there is not even time to let the apple juice mixture cool by itself, speed the cooling by putting the bottom of the saucepan in a tub of cold water until lukewarm. Unless you purposely speed it up, (see page 393), this is not a fast rising bread, but it rises high.

ôà

The night (or several hours) before: rinse the currants to remove any dirt, cover them with the apple juice in a saucepan and simmer together for five minutes. Drain the currants and measure the juice: add water to restore the measure to 2 cups. Stir in the bran and spice. Cover and set aside in a cool place. Note that if you soak the bran overnight, it takes up more liquid than if you soak it a shorter time. The dough will therefore require more added water because the bran won't give that liquid back to the dough.

Dissolve the yeast in the warm water.

Stir the oil and molasses into the apple juice. Mix the flour and salt in a bowl; make a well and add the yeast and the apple juice mixture. Mix thoroughly and knead to make a supple dough, adjusting the liquid or flour as necessary. Knead for 15 minutes or so, then work in the currants, kneading until they are evenly distributed in the dough.

Form the dough into a ball and place it smooth side up in the bowl. Cover and keep in a warm, draft-free place. After about an hour and a half, gently poke the center of the dough about ½ inch deep with your wet finger. If the hole doesn't fill in at all or if the dough sighs, it is ready for the next step. Press flat, form into a smooth round, and let the dough rise once more as before. The second rising will take about half as much time as the first.

Round the dough in a loaf-sized piece or pieces, and let rest until soft. The recipe makes enough dough for two high 8″ × 4″ pan loaves, or you can make one large ring. For the ring, round the whole dough and let it rest until it relaxes, then press from one side to the other to deflate. Use your thumb to make a hole in the center. Gently enlarge the hole to about 5 inches without tearing the dough. Place in a greased angel food cake pan, tucking the outside edges under if necessary, to make the top smooth and nicely rounded. If you are deft and can shape the loaf just right before putting it in the pan, dust the pan with poppy seeds. Or, dust cinnamon on top of the crust after forming the ring. This shape also works beautifully on a big cookie sheet, without the angel food cake pan, though the bread is flatter. Don't skip the hole in the middle, or the big loaf won't bake through.

You can also make smaller rounds with or without the hole. Bake them on pie tins, or two or more rounds per cookie sheet. Or make big, pretty muffins, 12 to one loaf's worth (half the recipe).

Let the shaped dough rise once more, until it slowly returns the indentation made with your wet finger. Place in preheated 350°F oven. The baking time will vary with the size and thickness of the dough: in the tube pan it will take almost an hour; the muffin-sized breads, about 25 minutes.

1 cup currants (140 g)
2 cups apple juice (475 ml)
⅓ cup miller's bran (17 g)
1 teaspoon allspice

2 teaspoons active dry yeast
 (¼ oz or 7 g)
½ cup warm water (120 ml)

¼ cup oil (60 ml)
2 tablespoons molasses
 (30 ml)

5½ cups whole wheat
 flour (830 g)
2½ teaspoons salt (14 g)

more juice or water
 if required

Applesauce Walnut Bread

1 cup applesauce (235 ml)
3 tablespoons oil (45 ml)
1 cup buttermilk (235 ml)

2 teaspoons active dry yeast
(¼ oz or 7 g)
1 cup warm water (235 ml)

5½ cups whole wheat
flour (830 g)
2½ teaspoons salt (14 g)

⅔ cup walnuts (80 g),
toasted and chopped

A moist and long-keeping bread, just sweet enough for good eating, but not too sweet for any kind of sandwich. The flavor of the walnuts comes forth and the apple plays a quiet supporting role.

❧

Heat the applesauce until it is quite warm. Slowly stir in the oil and the cold buttermilk.

Dissolve the yeast in the water.

Blend the flour and salt in a large bowl. Make a well in them and add the liquids. Stir from the center to mix, folding in the rest of the flour and combining to make a medium-soft dough. Add more water or flour if required. Knead very well; toward the end of the kneading, work in the walnuts.

Form the dough into a ball and place it smooth side up in the bowl. Cover and keep in a warm, draft-free place. After about an hour and a half, gently poke the center of the dough about ½ inch deep with your wet finger. If the hole doesn't fill in at all or if the dough sighs, it is ready for the next step. Press flat, form into a smooth round, and let the dough rise once more as before. The second rising will take about half as much time as the first.

Press the dough flat and divide in two. Round it and let it rest until relaxed, then deflate and shape into loaves. Place in greased 8″ × 4″ loaf pans and let rise in a warm, draft-free place until the dough slowly returns a gently made fingerprint. Bake about an hour at 350°F, though if the bread rises as well as it can, the loaves may take less time in the oven.

Wheat-Nut Anise Bread

Light, sweet, nubbly, with the perfume of anise, this bread comes into its fullest appeal on the second day.

ॐ

Cover grain and seeds with cold water and let stand overnight; or pour boiling water over them, and let stand for ten minutes in mixing bowl. The wheat may not cook or absorb all the water; that's okay. Cool to lukewarm.

Dissolve the yeast in the cup of warm water.

Mix oil and honey well, and add eggs. Add to the bulgur mixture. Mix the flour and salt in a bowl, and add the liquids. Feel the dough to see whether it needs more water, and if so, add the water by wetting your hands and working it in as you knead. It may require as much as a cup. The dough will be sticky, but knead it well so it can carry the bulgur. The dough should be soft because the wheat will continue to absorb water, particularly if you did not soak it overnight.

Form the dough into a ball and place it smooth side up in the bowl. Cover and keep in a warm, draft-free place. After about an hour and a half, gently poke the center of the dough about ½ inch deep with your wet finger. If the hole doesn't fill in at all or if the dough sighs, it is ready for the next step. Press flat, form into a smooth round, and let the dough rise once more as before.

Press the dough flat, cut in two, and shape into rounds. Let them rest until well softened, then form the loaves carefully to avoid tearing the smooth surface; a judicious dusting of flour on the board helps. Place the shaped loaves in greased 8″×4″ pans, or make round hearth loaves in pie tins or on a cookie sheet. Proof in a warm, slightly humid place until very high. They are ready for the oven when the dough slowly returns a wet fingerprint. It may happen that because of the roughness of the dough, the surface of the loaf tears. If it does, then just before putting it in the oven, slash the top with a serrated knife in an artistic way so the spontaneous rip looks intentional.

Place the risen loaves in a well-preheated oven, 350°F, for 45 to 50 minutes.

¾ cup coarse bulgur wheat (128 g)
2 teaspoons anise seed
1 cup water (235 ml)

2 teaspoons active dry yeast (¼ oz or 7 g)
1 cup warm water (235 ml)

2 tablespoons oil (30 ml) (optional)
¼ cup honey (60 ml)
2 eggs, slightly beaten

5 cups finely ground whole wheat flour (750 g)
1 tablespoon salt (16.5 g)

Manuel's Seed Bread

3 cups whole wheat
bread flour (450 g)
1¼ teaspoons salt (7 g)
1 tablespoon sesame seeds
(9 g)
2 teaspoons poppy seeds (7 g)
3 tablespoons sunflower
seeds (10 g)
1½ cups water, tepid
(375 ml)

This naturally leavened bread has a wonderful taste and dense but bready texture. It won't rise much in the bowl as it ferments, but it may surprise you by springing in the oven. The fermentation time is 12 to 18 hours at room temperature, but on a cold winter day it may take longer.

❧

Combine all the ingredients except the water. Make a well in the center, pour in the water, and mix into a slightly stiff dough, adding more water or flour if necessary. Knead well. Keep the dough in a covered container to protect it from invading critters, and in a reasonably cool place, about 70°F. Let it ferment for 12 to 18 hours, kneading it about two-thirds of the way through the rising time to refresh the dough.

When the dough feels dry (unsticky) and elastic, divide it in two and knead gently into rounds. Let it rest protected from drafts for another 30 minutes to soften, then form into 2 small round loaves. Sprinkle poppy seeds on the table and roll the loaf tops on them.

Place in two greased 1-quart bowls or on a greased cookie sheet. Put the shaped loaves into an oven preheated to 350°F without further rising, and bake until done, about 1 hour and 15 minutes. The wheat-colored crust will brown lightly. Allow to cool completely; slice thin.

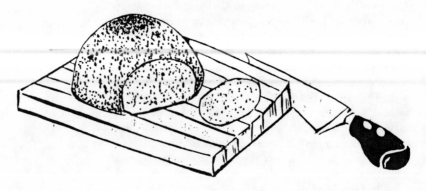

Lemony-Fennelly Bread

The lemon and fennel combination make a delicate, buttery, light and tender loaf. If you aren't keen on fennel, the bread is good without it, but it does add a distinct gourmet touch. If you want to omit the fennel, poppy seeds are pretty and harmonize nicely—or go seedless.

2 teaspoons active dry yeast (¼ oz or 7 g)
½ cup warm water (120 ml)

5½ cups finely ground whole wheat flour (830 g)
1½ teaspoon fennel seeds
2½ teaspoons salt (14 g)
1 tablespoon freshly grated lemon peel

1 cup warm buttermilk (235 ml)
¼ cup honey (60 ml)
juice of one lemon (30 ml)
1 cup water (235 ml)

2 tablespoons butter (28 g)

Dissolve the yeast in the warm water.

Mix the dry ingredients, including the lemon peel, in a large bowl.

Mix the buttermilk and honey and add them to the dry ingredients, then stir until partially mixed. Stir the lemon juice and the water together and then add, mixing the whole together. Finally, add the yeast mixture and combine to make a soft dough. This sequence may seem complicated, but it protects the yeast.

Knead very well, adding the butter in tiny cold chips after the dough has become supple and elastic. Knead until completely absorbed.

Form the dough into a ball and place it smooth side up in the bowl. Cover and keep in a warm, draft-free place. After about an hour and a half, gently poke the center of the dough about ½ inch deep with your wet finger. If the hole doesn't fill in at all or if the dough sighs, it is ready for the next step. Press flat, form into a smooth round, and let the dough rise once more as before. The second rising will take about half as much time as the first.

Press the dough flat and divide in two. Round it and let it rest until relaxed, then deflate and shape into loaves. Place in greased 8″×4″ loaf pans and let rise in a warm, draft-free place until the dough slowly returns a gently made fingerprint. Bake about 50 minutes at 350°F.

My Heart's Brown Stollen

4 teaspoons active dry yeast
   (½ oz or 14 g)
½ cup warm water (120 ml)

7 cups finely ground whole
   wheat bread flour
   (1650 g)
2 cups whole wheat
   pastry flour (300 g)
2 teaspoons salt (11 g)
1 cup small curd cottage
   cheese (235 ml)
2 cups hot water (475 ml)
¾ cup honey (175 ml)
¼ cup rum (60 ml)
3 eggs

¾ cup butter (170 g)

There are perhaps as many traditional recipes for stollen as there are bakers of it. Ours is a new tradition, as good as the old ones but not so wildly rich. The rum is optional, but it does provide a heady dash. (If you prefer a boozier stollen, soak the dried fruit in rum overnight before you proceed.) The cottage cheese makes the bread at once tenderer and a little less reprehensible nutritionally, and is quite traditional in some parts of Germany.

This recipe makes two large stollen or several small ones. It keeps well for over a week, but store in the freezer if you want to keep it longer. It is truly special sliced super thin and served for Christmas tea.

A note here on the baking: Try to use heavy cookie sheets, and keep the bread away from the bottom of the oven if yours tends to overheat there, as most do. It may help to put a second cookie sheet under the first one, especially on the bottom rack. Turn and reverse the loaves halfway through if they are not baking evenly.

ₔ

Dissolve the yeast in the ½ cup water.

Stir the flours and the salt together. Mix the cottage cheese, hot water, honey, and rum together well, then add the eggs. Add to flour mixture. Mix the dough and knead about 10 minutes, then work in the butter. Stop kneading when the butter is all incorporated; you will be working the dough more when you add the fruits and nuts.

Cover the dough and let it rise in a warm place. Deflate it after an hour and a half or more, when your wet finger makes a hole in the center of the dough that does not fill in. Return the dough to its warm place to rise again. Meantime, prepare the fruit.

Chop all of the fruit so that it is about the size of raisins. If your apricots or peaches are very leathery, pour boiling water over them and let them stand until they are softer, but not mushy! All the fruit for this bread should be firm in texture so it doesn't get lost in the dough as you knead it in. If your almonds are not very tasty, toast them quite well and sprinkle a tablespoon of almond extract over the nuts when they are chopped.

Work the fruit into the dough on a large surface in a place you can protect from drafts. Flour the surface and turn the twice-risen dough onto it. Press the dough flat, and then with a rolling pin very gently roll it as large as it will tolerate without tearing. Don't be rough.

Cover the dough and let it rest about 10 minutes. Mix the fruits and nuts together and turn onto the dough. Roll or fold them together and in a leisurely way knead in the goodies so that the dough incorporates them uniformly. Divide and round the dough — make one round for each loaf you want to make — and let it rest again, covered, for at least 15 minutes. The dough will rise amazingly considering all it has been through. You can make two large stollen or as many smaller ones as you like.

To shape, press or roll each of the rounds into a long oval. Then fold it over lengthwise, not quite in half, as shown in the illustration.

Place the shaped stollen on greased cookie sheets and let them rise again in a humid, warm place until the dough slowly returns a gently made finger-print. Bake in a preheated oven (325°F) for about an hour for the large ones, proportionately less for the smaller. Allow plenty of time for cooking, since the fruit holds moisture, but watch closely so that it does not over-bake. When cool, dust with confectioner's sugar.

grated peel of 2 lemons,
about 2 tablespoons
grated peel of 2 oranges,
about ¼ cup
1 pound raisins (454 g),
about 3 cups
1 pound other dried fruits
(454 g), about 3 cups
(include a good amount
of apricot plus currants,
peaches, pineapple,
prunes — or more
raisins!)
1½ cup toasted almonds
(213 g), chopped coarsely

melted butter, about ¼ cup
(60 ml)
confectioner's sugar,
about ½ cup (60 g)

Lynne's Holiday Loaves

1 cup walnuts, chopped
    (120 g)
1 cup raisins (145 g)
1 cup boiling water (235 ml)

¼ cup honey (60 ml)
1 cup orange juice (235 ml)
2 tablespoons oil (30 ml)

2 teaspoons active dry yeast
    (¼ oz or 7 g)
½ cup warm water (120 ml)

5½ cups finely ground
    whole wheat flour
    (830 g)
2½ teaspoons salt (14 g)
2 tablespoons grated orange
    peel (peel of
    2 or 3 oranges)

Chewy and dark with exceptional flavor, this bread has no dairy products—unusual for holiday baking. It keeps very well, retaining its goodness as long as a week under good storage conditions.

Please note! When people have trouble with this recipe it is because they alter the order of mixing and damage the yeast with the acidic liquids. Do follow the directions closely for this one, because it makes wonderful bread given the chance.

❧

Prepare the walnuts by toasting slightly in the oven.

Rinse the raisins and pour the boiling water over them in a pan. Simmer for five minutes. Drain immediately, setting aside the raisins and bringing the measure of the water back to 1 cup.

Dissolve the yeast in the ½ cup warm water. Separately mix honey, orange juice, oil, and raisin water.

Mix the flour, salt, and orange peel in a large bowl. Make a well in the center of the flour and pour in the orange juice mixture. Combine these until they are nearly mixed, and then add the yeast. Mix to form a dough, and knead *five to ten minutes only.* Cover and set aside to rise in a warm place.

When the dough has risen until your ½-inch fingerprint remains without filling in, knead about 10 minutes more, gradually adding the raisins and walnuts as you knead. Let rise again.

Divide in two. Round them and let them rest, covered, until relaxed. Make pretty round hearth loaves, or two 8"×4" pan loaves. Set them in their warm place to rise again, and then bake in a preheated 350°F oven for about 55 minutes, or until done. Small hearth loaves will take less baking time.

Small Wonders

This is a kind of patchwork section, each bread special in its own way, and quite different from all the others; what they have in common is that they are good eating, and not loaves. The recipes vary a lot, too, in how demanding they are: making breadsticks, for example, is easy—kid stuff for sure—and anyone with even a little chutzpah can make our bagels. (Even so, just see whether they aren't the best you've ever tasted.) Ah, but dinner rolls—*there's* a challenge worthy of a baker's steel: high, light, tasty, tender delicacies that demonstrate your consummate mastery of breadmaking. (Won by faithfully following through A Loaf for Learning twelve times, and making perfect bread eleven times.)

Making Soft Dinner Rolls

When you have built up a solid reputation as a breadbaker, the time will come when Aunt Agatha (who has never until now acknowledged the existence of brown flour) approaches you and announces, "You may make the rolls for the Family Reunion Thanksgiving Dinner. Make them soft and tasty—and *light*, not like those rocks you served when we had dinner at your house."

Well, maybe your aunt is more diplomatic, but the implication is there. It is a challenge—one of the more interesting challenges in breadmaking, because you want to take the hot rolls out of the oven at the last minute so that they are fresh and soft and the kitchen and dining room are full of their fragrance. If the dears don't work, there is nowhere to hide. But if they do work, the critics are *really* impressed. "These rolls taste just like you hope the ones they serve in a nice restaurant will taste, only they never do." Ah, glory.

GENERAL SUGGESTIONS   The instructions that follow should guide an experienced baker to make choices that will produce very beautiful results, but if there is more in this section than you ever wanted to know about making rolls, ignore the excruciating detail. Just form a loaf's worth of any light dough into smooth balls, let them rise, and bake them. Served hot from the oven, your rolls will be delicious, and probably just as welcome to their eaters as they would be if they were made using every trick in the book. That said, here are the fine points (for Aunt Agatha's kin).

FLOUR   If the occasion is a dressy one, choose very finely ground flour. For less formal times, coarse stone-ground flour makes wonderfully "country" rolls, tender and flaky. If you want them chewy, go for the highest-gluten hard spring wheat flour you can find. For the melt-in-your-mouth variety, a slightly lower gluten content is called for—for example, a reasonable winter wheat flour of medium strength. Or use your high-gluten flour, substituting whole wheat pastry flour for one cup of it.

FOR SOFTNESS   Including the softer flour will help give a tenderer roll. Chief among the professional baker's tricks is using *lots* of fat. We would go so far as to double the amount of butter in the recipe for a special occasion, and enhance its effect by using buttermilk, for example, which helps give a very tender crumb texture when it is used as part of the liquid measure of the dough.

EGGS   Since their yolks lend richness and tenderness, and their whites give a higher rise, eggs are often included in roll dough. Their presence doesn't improve the flavor of the roll much, though, when you are using whole wheat. If you want to include eggs, be extra careful not to let the rolls dry out in the proofing, and be sure not to overbake them, or they will be dry and horrid. Our Challah recipe makes good eggy rolls if you follow these suggestions. For best results, proof in a humid place and bake with a little steam at the outset.

Whether or not you include eggs, your rolls will achieve their best flavor and highest rise only if you knead the dough until the gluten is completely developed, and keep the consistency quite soft. Also, be careful not to let the dough ferment too long, particularly if you are going to take the extra time to make fancy shapes. If you are not an old hand at shaping rolls and think you might need some leeway, you can let half the dough rise its second time in a cooler spot so that it is not ready to shape until you have finished with the first half. This is also a useful ploy if your oven space is limited: you can arrange for the second pan of rolls to be ready to begin its final rise just when the first pan goes into the oven.

Part of the charm of rolls is that you can use your imagination to make fanciful shapes that delight the eye. On the following pages we have sketched some classic shapes that work well — that is, they are simple to do, bake evenly and look beautiful.

At the other end of the spectrum, quite a few connoisseurs hold that for sheer eating quality, the plain cushion-shaped roll, whose soft sides have been supported by its neighbors', is the very best: and plenty pretty, at that.

The last secret for making your rolls featherlight is to allow plenty of time for the final rise after shaping. We would go so far as to say that rolls should be slightly overproofed, so long as the dough has not gotten old already from too much rising in earlier stages, or too much time spent in the shaping.

Whatever the shape, if you want the crust to glow with a soft luster, brush the tops of the rolls with melted butter after baking. For a shinier finish, brush with bun wash: one egg beaten lightly with the amount of water it takes to fill half of its shell. Brush on immediately *before* baking, or just when the rolls come out of the oven; their heat will cook the egg and the surface will glisten. (The egg does tend to slide down and burn on the cookie sheet.) For shine and softness, wash before baking, and brush with butter after.

Use a soft brush, a feather brush, or a fringed napkin for glazing unbaked dough; a stiff brush can undo all your good work by squashing the airy delicacies at their weakest moment. And please, if you are going to go to the trouble, take care to cover the whole exposed surface evenly. A messy washing doesn't make any big improvement in the rolls' appearance. Butter looks best, incidentally, if the coating is thin.

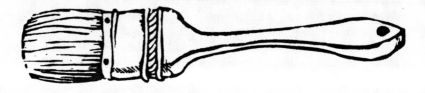

Best Soft Dinner Rolls

One recipe of Buttermilk Bread will make two 9″ × 13″ pans of terrific rolls — either 12 or 15 rolls to the pan, or as many clover-leaf, bowknot, palmleaf, swirl, fan-tan, etc, rolls, on a baking sheet.

For best flavor, start the dough cool, gradually warming it from rise to proof. Mix a 70°F dough; first rise slow, 70°F; second rise, 80°F; proof 90–95°F, for example. If you follow this pattern, the first rise will take about 2½ hours; the second, about an hour, or a little more, and the proof, about 45 minutes. However you schedule your risings, though — fast, slow, or accelerating — be careful not to let the dough rise longer than it needs to (not so long that it sighs when you poke it after each rising), because shaping rolls takes extra time, and you don't want to spoil the flavor by letting the dough get old.

SHAPING CUSHION
STYLE PAN ROLLS

Flour the board lightly. Flatten the dough and divide it in two or three pieces, rounding each one. Let them relax, covered, to protect them from drafts. Uncover one round and press it flat. Divide into three even parts, cover two, and then make four or five rounds out of each piece.

Try to keep the smooth gluten film intact on each roll. Sprinkle the greased pan with sesame or poppy seeds if you wish, and then place the rounds in the pan. The rolls should be no more than ½ inch apart. They will move closer as they rise, finally supporting each other and making the pale, soft sides characteristic of dinner rolls of this type. The object now is to have them just the right distance apart so that the risen roll is a nicely domed cube when it is finished rising and baking. Placed too close together, the rolls will be tall and narrow, and probably hard to separate. If they are too far apart, their sides won't rise together, and the rolls will be flattish and crusty. When you make larger rolls, they will do best spaced slightly farther apart; for smaller rolls, place them closer together. Smaller rolls, since they don't rise as much, take proportionately more pan space. Nine large rolls fill an 8″ × 8″ inch pan with one loaf's worth of dough; fifteen smaller ones are just right in a 9″ × 13″ pan, from the same amount of dough. For other shapes, see the next pages.

Let rise in a warm, humid place, 95°F, being careful not to expose the rolls to drafts. They should have a full proof. Since they are smaller than a loaf of bread and well-supported, they won't fall and can tolerate a much fuller proof than loaf bread can, and still rise in the oven.

PROOFING

A most annoying problem in baking rolls is to have them get too hard on the bottom from uneven heat in the oven. Most often you can avoid this by using thick, shiny pans and not putting them on the bottom rack. Also helpful is to protect the rolls by putting a second baking sheet underneath the one the rolls are on. Be sure to take a peek after about 15 minutes so that you can reverse or rotate the pans if necessary (or maybe even take the rolls out, if they have baked in that short time).

BAKING

The object is to have the rolls brown nicely without drying out. The two-ounce rolls we have described will bake in about 20 minutes in a preheated 400°F oven, but especially if they are exceptionally light, they may be ready sooner, so keep an eye on them. Smaller rolls, or fancy shapes that are spread out on their baking sheet, also take less time — and a slightly higher oven heat as well. The bigger the roll, the longer the bake and the lower the temperature.

Making Fancy Shapes

For other shapes, follow the suggestions for washing and buttering the crusts that were given above. We don't use the egg wash on fancy shapes, as a general rule, just brush them with butter; if they are fragile, brush them only *after* baking.

THINGS TO WATCH Small, thin parts bake more quickly than thick parts; keep the sizes even for each roll and pan of rolls so you can avoid burning part while trying to get the rest cooked through. When baking a great artistic masterpiece worked in dough or little creatures shaped by a child, tiny parts can be protected to some extent by foil once they are brown.

Be careful, whatever the nature of your rolls, not to overbake them. Overbaking is the easiest pitfall with rolls, and what a pity to ruin them at the last, after all that work.

CLOVERLEAF The simplest and maybe the most surefire. Grease a muffin tin and into each cup drop three smooth one-inch balls of dough. These can be decorated with poppy or sesame seeds.

FAN-TANS Probably too rich for anyone's good. Roll the dough thin (⅜ inch), brush with softened butter, and cut into 1¾-inch strips. Pile the strips on top of each other about 5 high and cut into squares. Place on edge in muffin pans. When they have risen, they will be the shape of a muffin with the shadow of five buttery slices. This one is tricky, but even if they aren't perfect, they will be gone in no time. Chill dough before shaping if you're serious about elegant results.

The following shapes start with a snake of dough. For the smoothest snakes and the best final results, begin with a ball of dough larger than a golf ball and smaller than a tennis ball. Roll it on a lightly floured board under first one and then both palms, working from the center outward to the ends, over and over. Don't let the dough fold or twist, and try not to let it dry out or tear, either.

BOWKNOTS Roll each portion of dough into a smooth snake about ¾ inch thick and about 10 inches long. Flour the board to keep the dough from sticking to itself. Tie in a simple knot, loosely, and place on a greased sheet. Fast, easy, and pretty.

SNAILS Roll the snake into a pinwheel.

BRAIDS Use the method on page 186 to make a tidy braid out of one snake about 18 inches long, or braid three thin strands and tuck the ends under.

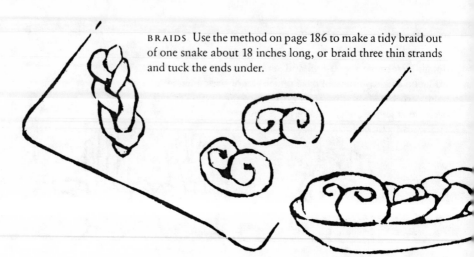

PALMLEAF Roll the 18-inch snake halfway, and begin from the other end to meet halfway. This is traditional, but I can't imagine why they call them palmleaves. (In New York, they're called butterflies—a little more descriptive.)

Use your imagination. Any shape is viable so long as there is not too much difference between the thin part and the thick part.

Breadsticks, etc.

If you can give up a small wad of your dough when you are shaping, any kid from the toddler stage on up will love making a shape to bake, be inordinately proud of the result—and delighted to eat it, too. When baking such works of art, keep in mind that the tiny thin parts will tend to burn, while large lumps take much longer to bake. You can shield small parts with foil once they brown, to protect them from burning.

Even when they can't have a direct part in the process, grade schoolers are thrilled to come home to your bready rendering of their initials, or a favorite animal you've softly sculptured and baked especially for them. On a more mundane and practical level, the manageability of small soft-crusty breads makes life easier for very young ones whose tiny hands are relatively new to the eating game. (Eaters who have been at it for many years also appreciate breadsticks, incidentally, especially alongside a hearty minestrone soup.)

You can make 12 soft foot-long breadsticks out of a loaf's worth of risen dough. Rolled in sesame or poppy seeds, they provide a chewy, toothsome accent to a light meal. If sesame and poppy are getting ho hum, try caraway or fennel, or, more daring, whole cumin seeds, spicy-hot.

To shape, divide the dough into 12 parts, form balls and roll into snakes. Place side by side on a greased cookie sheet, allowing room for them to double in girth. Let rise until a gentle touch makes an indentation that fills in slowly; bake at 325°F until lightly brown, usually about ½ hour, preferably not near the bottom of the oven. Let them cool somewhat before removing from the sheet. For crisper breadsticks, roll them thinner and bake at very low heat for as long as an hour.

Dinner Rolls for Aunt Agatha

2 teaspoons active dry yeast
    (¼ oz or 7 g)
1 cup warm water (235 ml)

3 tablespoons honey (45 ml)
1 cup buttermilk (235 ml)
1 egg

5 cups finely ground
    whole wheat bread flour
    (750 g)
1 cup whole wheat pastry
    flour (150 g)
2 teaspoons salt (11 g)

¼ cup cool butter (56 g)

Dissolve the yeast in the warm water.

Mix the honey, buttermilk, and egg, stirring until smooth.

Stir the flours and salt together in a bowl, making a well in the center. Add the yeast and the other liquids, mixing from the center to make the dough. Knead about 12 minutes, until the dough is smooth and supple. If necessary, add water by moistening your hands as you knead—the dough should be very soft. Press the butter into a smear on the tabletop, and gradually knead it in, working until the dough is lustrous and utterly silky.

Let rise in a covered container at warm-room temperature for about 2 hours, or until your wetted finger makes a hole that does not fill in. Deflate the dough carefully, keeping the smooth top surface intact. Let rise again, perhaps a little warmer, for about 1 hour, until the dough once again does not fill in your test poke-hole.

Turn out on a lightly floured kneading surface, and deflate. If you will be making all the dough into rolls, divide it into four equal pieces. (If you don't need so many rolls, half of the recipe can be rounded and then shaped into a regular loaf.) Form the dough into balls, keeping the gluten film, the smooth surface, unbroken.

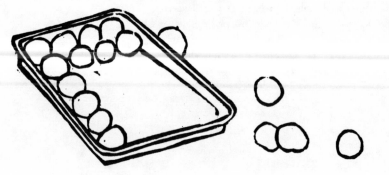

Cover the rounded pieces of dough with an inverted bowl or damp cloth to prevent them from drying out while you work. Let the dough rest until the first ball is relaxed, soft and pliable — this step is especially important here. Gently press the soft dough flat; cut in half, then in threes. Form one round roll out of each piece, trying hard to keep the smooth surface intact. Repeat the process with all the rest of the dough, placing the rolls in greased muffin cups, or about ½ inch apart in a greased baking dish.

Ideally, you would want a shiny thick aluminum bun pan measuring 11″×16″ to fit 24 such rolls — but two Pyrex dishes (8″×8″ and 9″×13″) would be fine, or a large cookie sheet. If you have extra space on your pan, rather than spread the rolls out, cluster them the suggested ½ inch apart so that they will rise and bake properly. Prevent the grease on the unused space on the pan from burning by dusting it generously with cornmeal or rolled oats or flour.

Cover and let the shaped rolls rise in a very warm place. To prevent them from drying out and forming a tough top crust that can't bake nicely, keep a pan of hot water near them while they rise, or seal the rising rolls in a puffed-up plastic bag that has been rinsed out with hot water. Let them have plenty of time to rise: as much as 45 minutes or an hour, even, until they show slight signs of sagging, then pop them in a preheated 400°F oven for about 20 minutes — just until they are beautifully brown. If the rolls have risen particularly well, they may bake even faster. Brush them with melted butter, just after baking.

If you can't plan to serve them immediately, let the rolls cool, seal tight, and store them in the refrigerator. Warm them for 15 to 20 minutes before serving, wrapped lightly in a damp towel so that they won't dry out. An alternative is to make a brown-and-serve version: bake the rolls the first time for half an hour at 275°F so that they cook but do not brown. To serve, preheat the oven to 450°F and bake the rolls about 15 minutes, or just until nicely brown. Be careful (yawn) not to overbake.

Buns

For making buns, any high-rising bread dough will do, but preferably not one that has a fermentation longer than the normal 4-hour dough. Basic Bread (page 80), Buttermilk Bread (page 176), Egg Bread (page 184), Featherpuff (page 188), Brian's Bread (page 282), or Soymilk Bread (page 162) would all be good choices. If convenient, use no more than 1 tablespoon of sweetener per loaf unless you like really sweet buns. Prepare the dough as usual, covering and letting it rise twice, then rounding it into loaf-sized balls to rest before shaping.

As soon as one of the big balls has relaxed, press it out into an oblong about one inch thick. Cut this into six pieces as equal as possible, and round each of them into a little ball. Work on the balls one after another in order, covering them with a damp towel or an inverted bowl to prevent their drying out while they are resting. Use a little flour on the board as necessary to keep the dough from sticking.

If you were making rolls, you would simply set the balls to rise, and when they were baked, they would be round, even vaguely spherical, puffs — at once too tall and too small to put around a soyburger! To render these round rolls into proper buns, all that is necessary is to press the shaped dough flat with a rolling pin (or your hand) *so that they are as big around as you want the finished bun to be: they will rise up, but not out.* Work quickly but gently, being careful not to tear the smooth surface of the dough as you roll it out; aim to flatten but *not squash* the dough. If you want seeds on the buns, sprinkle the tabletop with the seed of your choice before you start rolling each one, and turn it once in the rolling process.

When you have them all lined up on their greased baking sheet, ready to rise for the last time, they will look fairly unpromising, flat as pancakes and nearly the same size. Still, have faith. Cover and put them in a warm humid place to rise, and give them plenty of time: they can proof until they feel very spongy, and a gently made indentation doesn't fill in at all.

Preheat the oven so that when they are ready, it will be ready too, at 400°F, if possible. (If you have a loaf of bread to bake at the same time, the bread's temperature will do well

enough for the buns, but they'll take a little longer, and be a little drier.) Bake the buns in the top half of the oven so that they will stay soft on the bottom.

Put a small pan of boiling water in the bottom of the oven for the first ten minutes. Bake until the buns are a pretty golden brown all over, about 20 minutes. (If you want to bake two pans at a time, on two racks, place a third cookie sheet under the pan on the lower rack to help protect it from too much bottom heat. Even so, you may want to reverse them midway.)

These buns are substantial, each one containing about as much bread as two slices of loaf bread. As your technique improves, you may want to include less dough in each bun: in that case, they will be flatter than pancakes when rolled out, and only your perfected technique will insure that they will attain a wonderful puffy lightness when finished. Still, given that we are home bakers and don't have the sophisticated equipment of the factory that makes supermarket buns, ours may not be quite so high or so fluffy as the supermarket variety. They will more than make up for it in flavor, though, that's for sure.

Hot Cross Buns

2 cups raisins (300 g)
1 cup dried apricots (130 g)
1 cup walnuts (120 g),
  or use filberts or
  other flavorful nuts,
  chopped

2 teaspoons active dry yeast
  (¼ oz or 7 g)
½ cup warm water (120 ml)

6 cups finely ground
  whole wheat bread flour
  (900 g)
2 teaspoons salt (11 g)

2 large eggs, beaten
  (some set aside)
3 tablespoons honey (45 ml)
1 cup water, very hot
  (235 ml)
1 cup cold buttermilk
  (235 ml)

more water as required
¼ cup butter (56 g),
  room temperature

We love to serve these Easter breakfast, when there is a vast crowd of people to please, because the pleasing is certain, and there is not much fuss that morning—just warming the buns and maybe making a splendid fruit salad.

As usual, we have substituted natural ingredients for the traditional candied fruits, with results that to us seem far superior both in taste and appeal.

❧

Prepare the fruit: steam the raisins briefly, drain and cool. Either steam or bake the dried apricots so that they are about as soft-firm as the raisins. Chop apricots to the size of raisins. Toast the nuts lightly and chop them into similarly raisin-sized pieces.

Dissolve the yeast in the warm water and set aside. Mix the flour and the salt in a bowl, making a well in the center.

Break the eggs into a small bowl and beat them slightly, setting aside about three tablespoons to use for egg wash later. (If you forget to save some out, or someone gives it to the cat, just use another egg for the wash.) In a separate bowl, mix the honey and the hot water and add the buttermilk; stir in the beaten eggs.

Pour the liquids and the yeast into the well in the flour and mix, then knead. Keep your hands wet as you work the stiff, sticky dough, letting it take in as much water as it requires to become soft and supple. When the dough is silky and elastic, add the butter in the French manner by smearing it on the tabletop and kneading until all the butter has been incorporated. Gently knead in the fruits and nuts a handful at a time.

Form the dough into a ball and place it smooth side up in the bowl. Cover and keep in a warm, draft-free place. After about an hour and a half check the dough to see how it is doing. Gently poke the center of the dough about ½ inch deep with your wet finger. If the hole doesn't fill in at all, the dough is ready to deflate. Because of the weight of the rich ingredients, it may rise more slowly than you expect, so be prepared to give it a little extra time. This dough should rise very well indeed, but do keep an eye on it, and go on to the next step before the pressure of your finger-poke makes the dough sigh. Press out the accumulated gas, carefully shape the smooth round again, and let the dough rise once more, as before. The second rising time will be about half as long as the first.

While the dough is rising, plan your baking strategy. The dough for one recipe will make about 30 big buns, and will fill two 12″ × 18″ inch cookie sheets, three across, five down. Not everybody can claim two such pans or the oven space to bake them together: you may need to bake in two stages — for example, to fill two 9″ × 13″ pans twice. Also, should you want to make smaller rolls (the recipe makes 60, very dainty) — you will need not only more pan space, since little ones take more room, but also more shaping time. For staggered bakings, and/or extra shaping time, you can refrigerate the portion of the dough that you will not be able to shape within half an hour or so. If you have a scale, you can calculate all this very accurately, but whether you do or not, the dough is amazingly tolerant, and there is a lot of leeway.

For estimating, the big buns weigh about 2¾ ounces each, and are a little larger than a golf ball when formed. It is useful to make the buns in straight rows, by the way, because if you do, making the crosses is lots easier.

We have not included cinnamon and other spices in the dough because they can damage the gluten and impede the rise; but traditionally, hot cross buns are flavored with a blend of winter spices. In this recipe the glaze is spiked with cinnamon and provides a mild spiciness, but if you would like more, sprinkle spices on the greased baking pans before putting the buns on them to proof. A tablespoon of cinnamon, ½ teaspoon nutmeg, ¼ teaspoon cloves, plus cardamom and ginger, make a good mix. Put them in a shaker and use that to dust the pans lightly after they are greased.

Shape the dough into smooth balls and arrange them in rows on the pan. The large ones should be about an inch apart; the small ones, half an inch. *After* shaping, let the rolls rest until the dough relaxes, about 10 minutes, and then flatten them slightly with the bottom of a quart jar or with your palm. They don't need to be pancake flat like a regular bun, but if you don't

GLAZE:

3 tablespoons honey (45 ml)
1 tablespoon butter (14 g)
½ teaspoon cinnamon

White frosting, about 1 cup:
  optional (use any
  simple powdered-sugar
  type frosting)*

*If you want to avoid using
the white sugar, many possi-
bilities exist for substitutes:
one would be to use ricotta or
cream cheese sweetened with
pale honey, applying it just
before you serve the buns.

press them down a little, they will be like little globes—less than ideal in this case.

Let the buns rise in a warm, humid place for half an hour or more. Preheat the oven to 375°F. Make the egg wash: use the reserved egg plus 1½ tablespoons of water (or one egg plus the water it takes to fill half the shell); beat until smooth but not frothy. Just before the buns are ready to go into the oven, when gentle pressure of your wet finger fills in slowly, take a spatula or dough cutter and mark each bun with an indented cross, pressing down about halfway into the dough (pressing but *not* cutting.) Brush with egg wash. Let the dough recover for a few minutes and then put the buns into the hot oven.

Make the glaze by bringing its ingredients to a boil; remove from the heat.

Check to make sure the buns are not burning on the bottom. If necessary, move the baking sheets around in the oven to insure an even bake.

Immediately after taking them out of the oven, brush the buns with the cinnamon-honey glaze, making sure to cover the whole surface of each one. After they cool, mark the cross again, this time with the white frosting.

The buns are splendid warmed up. The white frosting keeps itself together quite well through the rewarming, which is nice. This recipe is one of the all-time most acclaimed of our Fancy Traditionals, partly because it is so much fun to do, especially with two or more people working together.

English Muffins

There are many legends about these favorites. A lot of people will tell you that they aren't English at all, that they are as American as French fries—but anyone who has dipped into Elizabeth David's fascinating *English Breads and Yeast Cookery* knows that they *were* made in England, even if they are no longer. Ms. David gives formulas down the centuries, and includes an old engraving of a gigantic griddle that was used to bake them in times past.

We have tried dozens of recipes, used rings, no rings; baked on griddles and in the oven—and feel pretty sure now that what follows is the best collection of secrets of success you can get, whichever flavor or style English muffin you want.

There is a vast array of English muffins on the market now in our part of the country. Only a few years ago, there was just one that was the real thing. In the old days, if you found yourself hungry in San Francisco with only a couple of coins, you could drop into the steamy warmth of any Foster's coffee shop and for a quarter get a cup of coffee and the best English muffin in the world. It would be chewy, with big holes everywhere, toasted and dripping with butter. The flavor was a little sour, but not too sour, and very rich. It was everything you could want if you were really into English muffins.

The popularity of Foster's muffins grew and grew and—so the legend goes—the company at last moved out of its little dark bakery in the basement of an old building in the city into a spiffy new place with all shiny new stainless-steel equipment Up To Code. The trouble was the tiny little guys, the unique yeasts and who-knows-what that made the muffins what they were didn't go along. They were left behind, and lost forever. Wonderful Foster's is no more.

No, alas, we can't summon them back. But we can tell you how to make holey, moist, chewy muffins out of whatever bread dough you think would make your ideal muffin. Our favorite is Desem bread, but Sprout Bread, Overnight Starter Bread, or almost any recipe with character will do very nicely.

After you knead the dough to perfection according to the recipe you choose, you can divide it and set aside half for mak-

Follow these instructions to make English Muffins from your favorite bread recipe. Most any dough with character will do; these work beautifully:

French Bread
Flemish Desem Bread
Overnight Started Bread
Yeasted Sprout Bread

ing regular loaf bread, if you want to. In that case, with one loaf's worth of dough, you can make eight muffins. The muffin dough must be slightly overkneaded, and much wetter than regular bread dough, so keep wetting your hands as you work, and knead in as much water as you can. Stop when the dough is so soft that it is almost runny, and before the gluten falls apart. Finally, cover and set the dough to rise, following the instructions for whatever bread recipe you are making. The muffin dough will rise more quickly than its stiffer bread counterpart, however, because it is so wet.

Divide each loaf's worth into eight equal pieces, and form each piece into as smooth a round as possible. Put the rounds on a very generously *floured* baking sheet, cover, and set it to proof in a warm place. The round balls of dough will have sagged down to about one inch high when they're ready. Heat your griddle now. If the recipe you are using calls for more than a very little sweetener, the griddle should be only moderately hot, much cooler than you would use for pancakes, for example. Even with Desem or French or any other unsweetened dough, the griddle should be just about medium heat. If the griddle is too cool, all that will happen is that your muffins will have an extra-chewy crust, and take a little longer to cook. Unless the griddle is hopelessly unseasoned you shouldn't need to grease it.

With a wide pancake turner and a magician's sleight of hand, pick up the muffins one at time and place them flour-side down on the hot griddle. Turn them after about 5 minutes, when they are brown on the bottom; turn them again when they are brown, and keep turning them at about 5-minute intervals to keep the crusts from burning. They are done when the sides, which will not brown, of course, are springy. If in doubt, split one open with a fork and eat it. Good, no? Traditional to toast them, of course, split (not cut) in half.

Troubleshooting English Muffins

The next day the muffin will be rather dramatically smaller than it was when you took it off the heat. We allowed enough dough for really big muffins, so the shrinkage shouldn't be a problem, but if all else is fine, and you want them bigger, next time make seven.

If there aren't enough holes, and they aren't big enough for you, next time knead longer and add more water. If your dough was not kneaded fully in the first place, it may not have gotten *overkneaded*, as it has to, during the second kneading. If all this seems a bit much, you can use a cup of pastry or rye flour in place of a cup of bread flour when you mix up the dough; this will require less kneading to develop its gluten fully. Or if you like sourdough muffins, use a sourdough recipe; the sour will break down the gluten too.

If the inside looks a tad gray, the dough fermented too long. Next time take it up sooner. Wet dough ferments faster than proper bread dough.

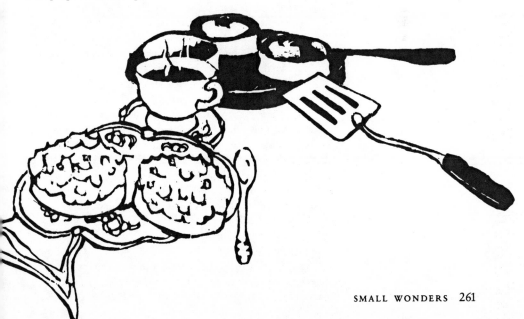

Chapathis

3 cups whole wheat flour,
preferably freshly
stone-ground (450 g)

1 teaspoon salt (5.5 g)

1½ cups warm water
(350 ml)

USEFUL EQUIPMENT:

a rolling pin
a griddle
long thick oven mitts

a dish towel or other
cloth, white linen
or muslin
OR
long-handled tongs
that are not sharp

These wheaten breads are served all over India, particularly in the North—but they can be enjoyed anywhere in the world. For best flavor, make the dough with fresh stone-ground flour and give it some time to itself before it is cooked; but if need be, the breads can be prepared with whatever whole grain flour you have, and very quickly. Even considering their perhaps unfamiliar shape, they are the best fast bread we know.

Serve with curries or with peanut butter and honey or cheese and tomato or simply butter. Super!

❧

Mix the flour and salt in a bowl. Slowly add the water, working it into the flour until the dough comes together. It should not be wet, but it should be soft. You can make it slightly stiff at first, then add water as required while you work the dough. Knead until very soft and silky, about 20 minutes. If possible, let the dough rest at room temperature for 4 hours or overnight; if you are in a hurry, make the chapathis right away.

Pinch the dough into about 12 balls, golf-ball size. Keep them covered with a damp cloth while you first round each one smooth, and then, one at a time, flatten them with a rolling pin on a floured board, making them approximately 7 inches across. Don't roll the pin off the edge of the round or the chapathi's rim will get too thin. Shape them all, and stack with a little flour and waxed paper between. When you have only a couple to go, heat the griddle. It should be about pancake hot, a medium-high heat. If it is too hot, the chapathis will burn, but if too low, they won't puff up. Best of all is to work together with a friend, one rolling and the other baking.

Keep an inverted bowl over the uncooked breads while you bake them one by one so that they don't dry out.

If your griddle is not well-seasoned, put a thin film of oil on it to keep each chapathi from sticking. The chapathis leave flour on the griddle that will burn, so wipe it off as you go along. You will use the dish towel for pressing on the chapathi to encourage them to puff up, and if it is white it stays cooler; form it into a smooth wad that is easy to hold.

Place the first chapathi on the hot griddle and let it sit there for one second, then turn it over. Use the cloth to apply gentle but firm pressure to the top of the cooking chapathi. Concentrate most of your pressing on the area just inside, but not on, the edge. Press down hard, but don't let the cloth stick to the dough. The object is to help the chapathi form steam pockets; ideally it puffs up like a balloon, filled with its own steam. At first the bread may blister in just a few places. By pressing, you can enlarge these small bubbles. Turn the chapathi over as soon as the bottom browns lightly. It won't brown evenly, especially if it has made the steam pockets, but will be a pretty pattern of brown and beige. It is done when it is brown nicely on both sides, with no wet-pinkish areas.

If you have a gas stove that has a high flame, you could try a second cooking method that works better for some people. Instead of pressing the dough on the griddle, let the chapathi cook a few seconds on each side to set the surfaces, and then with tongs pick up the chapathi and hold it over the high open flame. If you are deft, it will balloon without burning.

These wonderful breads are best served immediately, but you can wrap them in towels and keep them warm in the oven until time to eat; don't let them dry out, though.

Roberta's Incredible Bagels

2 teaspoons active dry yeast
(¼ oz or 7 g)
¼ cup warm water (60 ml)

2 tablespoons non-diastatic
malt syrup (30 ml)
1 cup water (235 ml)

5 cups whole wheat flour
(730 g)
2¼ teaspoons salt (12 g)

1¼ cup water (300 ml)

⅓ cup malt syrup (80 ml)
1 gallon boiling water (4 l)

Fun to make, good to eat.

Soften the yeast in the warm water.

Dissolve the 2 tablespoons of malt syrup in 1 cup of water.

Mix the flour and salt. Add the yeast mixture and the malt mixture, and enough of the additional 1¼ cup water to make a fairly stiff dough.

Let this dough rise until double, covered to protect it from drying out. Put the water on to boil and dissolve the ⅓ cup malt in it.

Grease a 12″ × 18″ cookie sheet, or 2 smaller ones.

Form the risen dough into three big balls. Round each one, and let it rest until relaxed. Shape into bagels by this easy but very untraditional method.

Flatten the balls one by one, and cut into four pieces. Shape each piece into a ball (round it by rolling under your cupped hand). Let the balls rest briefly and then poke your thumb through their middles, twirling each new bagel on your thumb to enlarge the hole until it (the hole) is about 1½ inches in diameter. Preheat the oven to 425°F.

Let each bagel rest for about 5 minutes, then place it in the boiling malted water. Cook 2 or 3 at a time, and adjust the heat so that the water is simmering all the time. The bagels will sink, then rise in a few seconds—if they don't sink, they rested too long. No harm done, just turn over so that both sides get wet. After a minute in the water, remove them with a slotted spoon and place them an inch apart on a greased cookie sheet.

Bake at once, about 35 minutes, turning the bagels over at the halfway point if they haven't browned evenly.

FANCY BAGELS: use sesame seeds, poppy seeds, sautéed minced onion (with or without garlic), caraway seeds. Either dip the boiled but unbaked bagel in the topping and place on cookie sheet with the coated side down or wash the tops of the bagels before baking with a mixture of ½ beaten egg and 2 tablespoons water, then sprinkle with the chosen garnish. The wash makes even ungarnished bagels shiny and pretty.

Pocket Bread (Pita)

In the last few years these nifty little breads have become a staple item, and they are available nearly everywhere. A balloon of crispy-soft bread, they are good for filling with anything to make a sandwich, whether it is the traditional falafel and sliced cucumbers, or more mundane things like soyspread and sprouts. Pita is tasty and doesn't get soggy, and furthermore, as our favorite two-year-old said the first time his sandwich came to him in a pocket, "Mommy! It didn't fall apart!"

Almost any plain bread dough can be used to make these, but we offer this recipe, which has been very reliable for us. Make it as it is written, or with twice the yeast and warmer water for a very fast rise. (If you go this route, you can easily have them on the table in 2½ hours. Keep the rising dough at 90°F.

SHAPING

Once the dough has risen, the rolling and shaping are easy; the trick is in getting the baking just right. The breads actually cook inside from the steam they generate as they puff in the oven, so they don't brown much on top. Depending on your oven, it may take a little experimentation to adjust the heat and paraphernalia to make sure that the pockets get enough bottom heat that they puff, but not so much that they burn.

BAKING

If you have a gas stove, you can bake pita on the floor of the oven or on a heavy cookie sheet (not Teflon) on the oven floor. Preheat the cookie sheet along with the oven. Electric stoves are trickier. It's best to heat the oven from the bottom only, so in *Laurel's Kitchen* we suggested snapping the top heating element out. Then we received an angry letter from a woman who had been making the bread for her dinner party, and in snapping out the top element, had blown out her stove's electrical system. If your top element is not made to snap out, *leave it in.* Try shielding the baking pockets from top heat by putting another cookie sheet on the very top rack under the top element. A well-heated oven stone or tiles can give the immediate bottom heat that is the secret of puffy pockets.

Pocket Bread Recipe

2 teaspoons active dry yeast
  (¼ oz or 7 g)
½ cup warm water (120 ml)

6 cups whole wheat bread
  flour (900 g)
2½ teaspoons salt (14 g)

2½ cups water (590 ml)

OPTIONAL:

1 tablespoon honey (15 ml)
2 tablespoons non-diastatic
  malt syrup (30 ml)
¼ cup sesame oil (60 ml)

Dissolve the yeast in the warm water.

Mix the flour and the salt and make a well in the center. If you are using the sweeteners and oil, stir them into the 2½ cups water; pour the liquids and yeast into the well in the flour, and stir from the center outward, making a smooth batter. Fold in the rest of the flour and mix thoroughly. Check to see whether the dough requires more water or flour, and add what is needed to make a soft dough. Knead very well.

Form the dough into a ball and place it smooth side up in the bowl. Cover and keep in a warm, draft-free place. After about an hour and a half gently poke the center of the dough about ½ inch deep with your wet finger. If the hole doesn't fill in at all or if the dough sighs, it is ready for the next step. Press flat, form into a smooth round, and let the dough rise once more as before. The second rising will take about half as much time as the first.

Preheat the oven to 450°F when the second rising time is nearly finished. Turn out the risen dough and press flat on the board. Divide it into 20 to 24 pieces and shape them into smooth rounds. This will make pockets about six inches across; you can make them larger or smaller, of course. Let the rounds rest ten minutes or longer until they are quite soft. Protect them from drafts to keep the surface of the dough from drying out. *This is essential.*

Use as much flour on the board as you need to keep the dough from sticking. Roll about five of the rounds into flat circles about as thick as a heavy wool blanket and six inches across. If they are too thick, they will make nice buns but they won't puff; if they are too thin, or if you are too rough with the rolling pin, they will puff in places, but won't balloon up. Put the rolled breads on the floor of the hot oven, or on the cookie sheet or tiles or what have you, and close the door.

Start rolling out a few more, but don't get distracted: check the breads in the oven in three minutes. They should have puffed by then, and may have browned a little on the bottom. If so, open one and check to see if the insides are done. They will be moist, but shouldn't look shiny-wet. If you think they need a little more time, you can bake them a bit more on the top rack while the next batch bakes on the bottom of the oven. Don't let them get crisp, though, or brown, because they will break when you fill them. The steam inside them bakes them extremely fast, and they will stay soft and flexible when cool. From here on out, work as efficiently as you can. The trickiest part is not to let the breads burn. Adjust your oven heat up and down as necessary.

NOTE: The honey, malt syrup, and oil are included for flavor only, and breads made without any of them puff at least as well as those made with them—maybe better.

Sicilian Pizza

BREAD

1 teaspoon honey (5 ml)
2½ cups warm water
  (590 ml)
2 teaspoons active dry yeast
  (¼ oz or 7 g)
1 tablespoon salt (16.5 g)

6 cups whole wheat flour
  (900 g)
2 tablespoons olive oil
  (30 ml)

½ cup warm water (120 ml)

This is a dinner bread rather than pizza as we usually think of it. The piquant sauce makes added cheese or butter quite superfluous.

ઽ

Dissolve the honey in the 2½ cups warm water, and stir in the yeast.

Stir the salt into the flour. Make a well in the center, and pour the oil and the yeast mixture into the well. Starting from the center, stir with a spoon or with your hand until the dough incorporates all the flour.

Turn the dough out on the table and put about a half cup of warm water in the mixing bowl. Use this water instead of flour to keep the dough from sticking to your hands and the table while you knead. You will probably be able to use up the water, ending with a soft, pliable dough that's very elastic. For best and lightest results, knead very well, about 20 minutes.

Form the dough into a ball and place it smooth side up in the bowl. Cover and keep in a warm, draft-free place. After about an hour and a half, gently poke the center of the dough about ½ inch deep with your wet finger. If the hole doesn't fill in at all or if the dough sighs, it is ready for the next step. Press flat, form into a smooth round, and let the dough rise once more as before. The second rising will take about half as much time as the first.

Turn the dough out on a lightly floured board. Shape it into a smooth round (or rounds, if you are going to make two) and let it rest until quite soft. With floured or wet hands, pat it from one side to the other to press out all the accumulated gas. Keep patting and pressing—or flinging and twirling—being careful not to tear the dough, until it is the size and shape you need. The dough fills one large or two small pizza pans, or a 12″ × 18″ cookie sheet. Pull a little extra dough up around the edge to keep the sauce from spilling over; if the dough is too elastic for this, let it rest a few minutes, and try again. After it relaxes, it will stretch more easily.

Mix sauce ingredients in blender or food processor or hand food mill until smooth.

Spread on the sauce, and let the bread rise again in a warm place for about half an hour, or until it is soft and spongy. Bake about 25 minutes in a well-preheated oven, 375°F.

SAUCE

2 tablespoons olive oil
½ onion, coarsely chopped
1 clove garlic
3 tablespoons tomato paste
⅔ cup chopped tomatoes,
    fresh or canned
½ teaspoon salt
½ teaspoon each,
    oregano and basil
¼ teaspoon pepper

Cheesy Pizza

Use this recipe to make normal pizzas: they can be as authentic or homey as your mood dictates. Roll the dough thinner, making two rounds about 14 inches across. Brush with olive oil, and spread with tomato sauce. (If you like plenty of sauce, you will need about two cups, twice as much as the above recipe provides.) Add olives, green peppers, mushrooms, or what have you, and top with grated cheese. Mozzarella, about 1 cup grated cheese per pizza, plus grated Parmesan, is traditional, but if there is none on hand, jack (or cheddar even) will fill the bill for most occasions.

Sour Cream Biscuits

2 teaspoons active dry yeast
  (¼ oz or 7 g)
¼ cup warm water (60 ml)

3 cups whole wheat flour
  (450 g)
1 teaspoon salt (5.6 g)
1½ teaspoon baking powder
  (4.5 g)
½ teaspoon baking soda
  (1.5 g)

1 egg
1¼ cups mock sour cream*
  (300 ml)
1 teaspoon honey, optional
  (5 ml)

These are real biscuits with extraordinary flavor, very light because they rise not only from the usual baking powder and soda but from yeast as well. No one who's not in the know ever suspects that you can make such tender, tasty biscuits with so little fat. For best tenderness, use a medium-gluten flour, or part bread flour and part pastry flour.

≈

Dissolve the yeast in the warm water.

Sift together the dry ingredients, returning any bran that stays in the sifter back into the mixture.

Beat the egg and mix it with the mock sour cream and the honey, if used. Add them and the yeast mixture to the dry ingredients, stirring as well as possible, and then kneading briefly until the dough sticks together.

Turn out on a lightly floured board. Roll with rolling pin to thickness of about ½ inch. Cut with 3-inch biscuit cutter, dipping it in flour between biscuits.

Set the biscuits on an ungreased baking sheet and leave them for an hour at room temperature; or at least three hours, or overnight, in the refrigerator. Cover them to prevent their drying out.

Before baking, preheat the oven thoroughly, to 450°F. Bake 12 to 15 minutes, until delicately brown. Serve hot.

*If you already have *Laurel's Kitchen,* you probably know about Mock Sour Cream, but if not just blend these ingredients well: 1 cup low fat cottage cheese, 2 tablespoons lemon juice, 3 tablespoons mayonnaise, ¼ cup buttermilk. Makes about 1½ cups.

Sprouts & Spuds

SOME NATURAL DOUGH CONDITIONERS

In our search for ways to make the home baker's job easier, we looked for natural equivalents for the dozens of chemicals bakers use, figuring that if professionals resort to such aids, surely there must be a few innocent additives that would be helpful in the home kitchen. We tried a lot of things that we read about, including ginger, garlic, crushed vitamin C tablets, slippery elm bark, and rose hip tea. None of them made much difference so far as we could tell, though we did produce some pretty flavorful loaves. Some time later, our cereal scientist friends told us that even many commercial additives don't have much effect when used with whole wheat.

In our researching attempts, some of the most interesting information we came across was in old books written for bakers — books published around 1920, when the local bakery still might or might not have a kneading machine. For example, one book suggested that adding a tiny amount of wheat germ to your white flour had an improving effect on the dough. The amount suggested was not too different from the amount that occurs naturally in whole wheat flour. The one additive that all the old books praised was potatoes, and of the things you can add to bread, we too like potatoes best. Potato bread recipes, and information about using potatoes, appear in the pages that follow. (By the way, we did finally include the rose hip tea; its fruitiness brightens and warms — and who knows? perhaps lightens — our Orange Rye Bread. See page 144.)

The additive you most often find listed on the side of white flour sacks is malted barley flour. It is incorporated when the flour has been found to be deficient in diastatic enzymes.

Whole wheat flour is seldom supplemented in this way. If you would like to use dimalt (that is, diastatic malt flour) in your bread for sweetness, and you don't like the fancy prices they charge for it in the health food store, you can make your own; it is simple to do, as we explain in the pages that follow.

Some other ingredients that are an integral part of many recipes — soy flour, for example, or milk products — do condition and improve the dough; we have discussed their talents in their respective sections. The Great Granddaddy of all dough conditioners, of course, and a high-tech one at that, is yeast. But aside from lively yeast, the two essentials for light bread are basic: fresh high-gluten flour and plenty of kneading.

About Sprouting & Malting

In the following pages, wheat is sprouted three different lengths of time to produce three very distinct kinds of sprouts. *They are not interchangeable.* If the grain is sprouted only a little, it can be ground into dough to make airy yeasted bread. Sprouted longer before grinding, it will make a dense, caky loaf. Sprouted still longer, until enzyme activity is at its peak, the grain, ground and dried, becomes malt flour, or dimalt.

The crucial element here is the timing. So much is going on so fast in those tiny powerhouses we call sprouting grains that there is very little leeway for using them in the recipes: one talent develops, peaks and fades, and another appears, only to have its brief flowering and also pass away. If your sprouts are at their best when you aren't, or vice-versa, put them in the refrigerator to use later in casseroles or salads; they are delicious. And by all means try again.

HOW TO SPROUT WHEAT

Rinse the grain and cover with tepid water, letting it stand 12 to 18 hours at room temperature. Allow the longer period in cooler weather, the shorter period in warm.

Drain off the liquid, rinse the grain with fresh, tepid water, and store in a dark place with a damp cloth over the top of the container. Rinse at least every 12 hours for as many days as is specified in the recipe you are following, checking carefully on the progress of the sprouts themselves.

GRINDERS

For making malt flour, any grain grinder that you would use for dry grains will work, providing it does not heat the flour above 120°F.

If you want to use your sprouts without first drying them, you can chop them fine or coarse with a knife, blender, or food processor, or in a meat grinder. Do not try to grind sprouts that are not completely dried in a grain grinder or stone mill that is not designed for wet grinding.

For the sprout breads use a food processor, a Corona-type mill that can accommodate wet grains, or a meat grinder.

Malt

The sugar most abundantly produced in sprouting grains—with the help of an enzyme called diastase—is maltose. The flavor is our familiar malt. Commercial malt is almost always made from barley, but wheat, rice, and other grains can make malt too, though in smaller amounts.

Added in tiny quantities to bread dough, *diastatic* malt provides an abundant supply of fuel sugar to the growing yeast, with some to spare. It helps the bread rise nicely, taste sweet, and brown well in the oven, just as if there had been a small amount of sweetener added to the dough. All of this makes *dimalt* as it is called, a great boon to people who want to get away from the use of refined sugar.

In scientific texts you will see the diastatic enzymes referred to as amylases.

Be careful though: if the quantity of dimalt added is too large, the bread turns into a gooey mess that will not rise or bake properly. There is a wide range of enzyme activity in the various kinds of malt. Our own, made from wheat berries, is a low-medium activity malt, but even so we would hesitate to add more than ¼ teaspoon per loaf's worth of dough. This amount gives roughly the sweetness you would expect from a teaspoon or two of honey. When you experiment with your own malt, start with ¼ teaspoon, and if you want to increase it, go gradually until you notice that your bread is gummy—then go back one step, and use a little less. Since the enzymes keep working throughout the rising times, use less dimalt for longer-fermented breads. We do not recommend dimalt for extremely long-rising doughs.

Our recipe for homemade dimalt calls for wheat because wheat is easy to get and barley is not. If you can get whole hull-less barley, it does sprout wonderfully and of course makes excellent malt. Be sure to rinse sprouting barley faithfully three or four times daily, as it tends to mold quickly. We don't recommend trying to use regular barley that has its hulls clinging to its sides because we know of no way short of commercial milling (which would remove the germ too) to get the hulls off, and they are truly unpleasant and indigestible.

To make dimalt: sprout the grain, dry it out, grind it up, and *voilà!* Here are the particulars.

TO MAKE DIASTATIC MALT FLOUR (DIMALT)

Prepare sprouts as described on page 273, letting them grow a total of about three days, until the sprout of the little plant—not the thinner rootlets, which appear first—is nearly as long as the grain itself.

Rinse and drain well, and dry very gently on a towel. Spread the sprouts on a baking sheet and keep them in a warm, dry, well-ventilated place at about 120°F until the grains are completely dehydrated. This may take a day or two. To test them, chew one: it should be brittle, with no toughness.

Use a grain grinder to mill the dried sprouts into flour, taking care not to let them get hot as they grind or the enzymes will be destroyed. Store cool and airtight. One cupful of grain will yield about 2 to 3 cups of malted flour.

DIMALT WITHOUT FLOUR

If you don't have a grain mill, you can use the sprouts—undried—to good effect. In an ordinary blender, puree ¼ cup sprouts with part of the liquid for a 2-loaf recipe. Alternatively, towel off the sprouts and use them whole or chopped as a sort of cracked wheat. In that case, since much of the enzyme will stay in the sprout and not enter the dough, you can use as much as a full cup per loaf of whole sprouts; ¼ cup chopped. The longer they are in the dough, the greater the effect on it, so gauge your timing to the quantity of sprouts you have in the bread. (By the way, when you eat bread made with whole sprouts, be wary of the ones on the crust: they will bake hard.)

NON-DIASTATIC MALT

Ordinary (non-diastatic) malt syrup, the kind we call for in some of our recipes, is used only as a flavoring and sweetener, not for any enzyme activity. Should you inadvertently overheat your sprouts so that their enzymes are destroyed—this happens at about 140°F—they can still flavor bread or hot cereal in a malty way that is quite delicious.

Unyeasted Sprout Bread

This "simplest of breads" contains *only* sprouted wheat: nothing else. The commercial versions sold under the brand names Essene and Wayfarer's Bread (and perhaps others) have been very popular, but making them at home is pretty challenging: but here it is, a recipe that *does* work. If your first try is off in some way, either bland-tasting or else too wet, next time pay more attention to the timing of the sprouts, because that is the crux of it. The finished bread should be moist, flaky, dark, a little sweet—dense without being heavy. Its devotees consider it the purest of breads, and since it has no flour, no yeast, no salt, sweetener, fat, or dairy products, who can argue?

Use about a pound of wheat per loaf. Start with 2 to 3 pounds, about 6 cups of wheat: that will make three good-sized loaves. Choose hard spring or winter wheat. Soak it in warm-room-temperature water for 18 hours, then keep it covered in a dark place, rinsing it three times a day until the little sprout is one-third the length of the grain. This will take about 36 to 48 hours, maximum. If you fear that the sprouts may get away from you before you can grind them up, slow them down by putting them in the refrigerator toward the end of the time.

If the sprouts are too young, the bread will not be sweet; if too old, the bread will be gooey and will never bake out.

Remove the excess moisture from the sprouts by patting them with a terry towel. Grind them with a Corona-type mill or a meat grinder, or about 2 cups at a time in your food processor, using the regular steel blade. Make them as smooth as possible. What results from the grinding is sticky, but knead it very well, nonetheless. For this, mechanical help is welcome, and if you ground the sprouts in your food processor, just keep processing each 2 cups for about 3 minutes in all, stopping just before the dough ball falls apart. How long this takes will depend on the kind of wheat you use: watch carefully.

By hand or with a dough hook knead until the gluten is developed, somewhat longer than you would do with a normal dough. If you are kneading by hand, keep the dough in a bowl and use a hefty wooden spoon or dough knob unless you want to abandon yourself to the ancient mud-pie method of squeezing it between your fingers until the gluten gets going and the going gets easier.

Whatever method you have used to get to this point, cover the dough and let it rest for about an hour or so, then shape it into smallish oblong loaves and place on a *well*-greased baking sheet. Bake slowly, not over 325°F for 2½ hours or until nicely browned. (The bread does well in a solar oven, if you have one.)

Cool the loaves and wrap them in a towel. Put them in plastic or brown paper bags, and set aside in a cool place or in the refrigerator for a day or two. This softens the leathery crust and gives the insides time to attain their moist flaky perfection.

VARIATION (and a big improvement): Grind ½ cup of dates along with each pound of sprouted wheat. Other dried fruits can work well, too, but we like dates best by far. Raisins make a very sticky, very black loaf; it is too sweet unless you reduce the measure by half.

Yeasted Sprout Bread

To make this bread using your food processor, turn the page.

This is a distinctive bread with lots of chew, lots of character, lots of appeal. We suspect that we should credit some of the goodness of our own version to the inefficiency of the third-hand (reformed) meat grinder that we use to grind the sprouts. It simply will not grind very fine, so the bread is quite coarse and flecked with the bran. We like it that way, but if you can grind the sprouts really fine, you can make extremely fine-textured light bread.

In developing this recipe, we had help from Al Giusto, who has been making sprouted wheat bread for the natural foods market in the San Francisco Bay Area for thirty years. His bread is featherlight, velvet-textured, excellent. For him, the secret is the extremely fine grind. Coarse or fine, though, the bread is good.

In this recipe the trick is to sprout the grain just until the tiny sprout is barely beginning to show and the grain itself is tender — about 48 hours. If the grain is not tender, your grinder will heat up, making the dough too hot. But if the sprout develops long enough for diastatic enzymes to get going, you will have very gooey bread that will never bake through. It is because the grain is not sprouted long enough to develop the enzymes and be sweetened by them that the recipe calls for a generous amount of honey. Without it, the bread simply doesn't taste very good.

This recipe, as we mention above, is based on what we can make with our grinder or food processor. If you have equipment that can produce a really smooth grind with only tiny bran particles, the resulting dough will make lighter bread and so probably be more than enough for two loaves. You can either make a few rolls or buns with the extra, or reduce the quantities to what you would use for two normal loaves: 2 pounds of wheat, ¼ cup honey, 2½ teaspoons salt, 2 teaspoons yeast.

Sprout the wheat berries as described above, drain them very well, and cool them in the refrigerator for several hours.

Dissolve the yeast in the warm water.

Add the honey, salt, and yeast to the ground sprouts and mix together well. The dough will feel sticky but stiff. Add water if needed to soften the dough, but be cautious, it should be just right without it. Knead well. This is not so easy as with a normal dough, particularly if the grain is coarsely ground; it takes plenty of work to develop the gluten fully. Knead until the dough is really elastic, considerably longer than the usual amount of time.

Form the dough into a ball and place it smooth side up in the bowl. Cover and keep in a warm draft-free place. After about an hour and a half, gently poke the center of the dough about ½ inch deep with your wet finger. If the hole doesn't fill in at all or if the dough sighs, it is ready for the next step. Press flat, form into a smooth round, and let the dough rise once more as before. If the dough is cold, which it may be unless your grinder warmed it up, the first rise will be fairly slow, but as the dough warms up, the rising will telescope.

Divide in half and gently knead into rounds. Use water on your hands to prevent sticking, and keep the balls as smooth as possible. Let them rest until they regain their suppleness while you grease two standard 8″ × 4″ loaf pans, or pie tins, or a cookie sheet. Press the dough flat and divide in two. Round it and let it rest until relaxed, then deflate and shape into loaves. Place in greased loaf pans and let rise in a warm, draft-free place until the dough slowly returns a gently made fingerprint. Bake about an hour at 350°F, though if your bread rises very high, it will take less than that.

6 cups hard spring or winter wheat berries, (2½ lb or 1135 g), a little more than 3 quarts sprouted, weighing about 4 lb (2 k)

2 teaspoons active dry yeast (¼ oz or 7 g)
¼ cup warm water (60 ml)

⅓ cup honey (80 ml)
4 teaspoons salt (22 g)

FOR ONE LOAF

*3 cups hard spring
 wheat berries
 (1¼ lb or 575 g),
 (about 6 cups
 sprouted)*

*1 teaspoon active dry yeast
 (⅛ oz or 3.5 g)*
*2 tablespoons warm water
 (30 ml)*

2 teaspoons salt (11 g)
*3 scant tablespoons
 honey (40 ml)*

Sprout bread makes excellent use of the talents of food processors. The steel blade grinds the sprouts and kneads the
dough too — a big contribution with this bread, which is hard
to knead by hand. The result is a flaky-textured bread with incomparable flavor, easy as pie.

The honey and the water with the yeast make just enough
liquid for the processor to work the grain into dough.

&

Sprout the wheat berries as described, then refrigerate until
they are cool, overnight or longer (but since they still grow in
the refrigerator, not more than a day or two.)

Dissolve the yeast in the warm water.

Put the regular double stainless steel blade, *not* the dough
blade, in a standard-size processor and measure just over 2
cups of the sprouted wheat, a third of the total, into the bowl.
Pour about 2 teaspoons of the dissolved yeast liquid, a scant
tablespoon of honey, and about ⅔ teaspoon of salt over the
wheat in the bowl. To protect the yeast, use separate measuring
spoons for each of the ingredients.

Process until the ground wheat forms a ball, about one
minute. Scrape the sides of the bowl, and process about two
more minutes. Stop processing before the ball completely falls
apart; if your wheat is not exceptionally high in protein a
minute and a half might be all it can handle. If it falls apart,
check the time, and with the next two batches, stop a little
sooner.

Repeat with the remaining two-thirds of the ingredients,
in two parts. Knead the three dough balls together.

For the rising and baking, proceed as with the recipe on
the previous page.

Once you have perfected this bread, you may want to vary it by including another grain, or several grains, along with the wheat when you sprout it. If you want *light* bread, be sure that the mixture stays at least three-quarters spring wheat. Other grains will be available at your natural foods store: triticale, barley, rye, corn, buckwheat. Use a light hand with the last two.

If you like, you can also sprout lentils, limas, soybeans, garbanzos, or any other bean along with the wheat. Again, start with a small spoonful, and work up from there. If you include more than just a few soybeans, add 2 tablespoons oil or 1 tablespoon butter per loaf when you mix the dough.

BASIC WHOLE WHEAT BREAD WITH SPROUTS

Knead ½ to 1 cup of sprouted grain about three days sprouted into any good strong plain whole wheat dough. The sweetness of the sprouts makes additional honey or other sweetener unnecessary, and they hold moisture too, so the bread is plenty moist without oil, and keeps well. It will be a little dense but amazingly flavorful. Allow extra baking time—more sprouts, more time. For best results, pat the sprouts dry on a towel before adding; for lightest bread, add them after the second rise.

This bread is to be chewed with circumspection. The grains on the outside of the loaf will be fairly crunchy, and the ones that failed to sprout will be tough, whether inside the loaf or out. Watch out for them lest you damage a tooth.

Brian's Bread

4 teaspoons active dry yeast
  (½ oz or 14 g)
½ cup warm water
  (120 ml)

6 cups finely ground
  whole wheat bread
  flour (900 g)
¼ cup full-fat soy flour,
  very fresh (14 g)
¼ teaspoon dimalt*
2 teaspoons salt (11 g)

¼ cup orange juice (60 ml)

3 tablespoons honey (45 ml)
1½ cups warm water
  (355 ml)

2 tablespoons cool butter
  (28 g)

*You can use ¼ cup fresh
sprouts (3 days) instead of
dimalt. Add to the orange
juice, and blend smooth in
blender.

Our friend Brian, the dashing nutritionist and savant, developed this recipe from a commercial bakery formula, using natural equivalents for their chemical additives. It makes a high, light bread that tastes like commercial bakery bread— only better.

The recipe is ideal for making buns.

ϡ

Dissolve the yeast in the ½ cup water.

Mix the flours, dimalt, and salt in a large bowl, making a well in the center.

Mix orange juice, honey, and warm water, and stir into the well in the flour, mixing first in the center until you have a smooth batter; add the yeast to this and continue mixing until a supple dough is formed. Add more water or flour if necessary, but keep the dough soft.

Knead 20 minutes by hand, or until the dough is extremely stretchy. It should remain soft. Toward the end of the kneading, add the butter in cold bits, then continue kneading until the dough becomes lustrous, soft, and silky.

Form the dough into a ball and place it smooth side up in the bowl. Being sure that there is plenty of room for the dough to expand (even triple), cover, and keep in a very warm (90°F), draft-free place. After about an hour gently poke the center of the dough about ½ inch deep with your wet finger. If the hole doesn't fill in at all or if the dough sighs, it is ready for the next step. Press flat, form into a smooth round, and let the dough rise once more as before. The second rising will take about half as much time as the first.

Divide the dough into two, and using a rolling pin, gently press out all the gas. Round the halves and let them rest, covered, until they relax before you shape them into loaves. Try to avoid using much dusting flour on the board. Place the shaped loaves in greased 8″ × 4″ loaf pans, and set in a very warm place (90 to 95°F) to rise. Protect the loaves from drafts and provide some humidity if possible, either by putting the loaves in a puffed-up plastic bag with a spoonful of hot water in it, or by putting a pan of hot water near the loaves as they rise. Proof the loaves until the dough returns slowly from a gentle touch of your wet finger.

Bake in a preheated 350°F oven for about 45 minutes, or a little longer. *Cool before slicing*—this one is far too poufy to slice before it is cool.

Sea Biscuits

These are delicious crackers, with a flavor similar to commercial Rykrisp, only better. The recipe was developed by our good friend Alan Scott when he was a shipboard chef, but it's tasty under any circumstances.

½ cup wheat berries
1 tablespoon oil
½ teaspoon salt
½ teaspoon baking soda
1 teaspoon caraway seeds
¾ cup rye flour, about

ঌ

Sprout the wheat for 2 to 4 days but not so long that there is any green in the shoots. Grind fairly fine. Mix in the oil, salt, soda, seeds, and enough rye flour to make a stiff dough. Form into golf-ball-sized rounds, then roll out on a well-floured board as thin as possible, not thicker than ¼ inch. Bake on a dry griddle on low heat for about 5 minutes on each side, or in a medium-low oven, until very slightly brown.

Potatoes in Bread & Other Topics

In its 6,000-year history, bread has been adulterated in unnumbered ways because good strong clean wheat flour is a treasure that is really quite rare. When potatoes came to Europe from the New World, canny bakers recognized in them great possibilities for stretching their dough to make more loaves. Incredibly, unlike the usual more dubious additives, a little potato actually made the bread better—lighter, sweeter, better keeping —and potatoes have been used that way ever since.

The only small caution here has to do with a fascinating and somewhat awful little organism called Rope (*Bacillus mesentericus*). "Ropy" bread was the bane of the old-time bakeries because it would appear without warning and make whole batches of bread useless. The loaves would come out of the oven looking beautiful, and no one would suspect a thing until one was sliced—and had nearly no insides! Just a gooey hole that smelled like an overripe cantaloupe. This has happened in our century, even, and to someone we know.

The villain here is a kind of mold that, although it meets its doom in the oven, produces spores that survive the baking heat. When the loaf begins to cool, the spores grow wildly, with the bread for food. They multiply rapidly inside the loaf —with the results we have described.

Rope contamination of wheat or flour is rare these days. (Our friend's ropy bread *was* from bad flour—white flour, lest you think otherwise.) Potatoes, though, can harbor spores on the skin and especially around the eyes, and that is why we suggest that you peel them carefully and remove all questionable parts, then rinse them under running water before cooking to use in bread. An added safety in many of our recipes is the use of cultured milk, which makes the dough a little acid: molds don't thrive in acid media. (In fact, the old bakery manuals say that to get rid of rope you have to remove every speck of flour and scrub the whole place with distilled vinegar.)

These days, the phenomenon is exceedingly rare: we have never had rope in any of our kitchens. Don't let the possibility deter you from trying what are surely some of the finest of breads.

Potato breads are bright-tasting, the potato lending a subtle round sweetness. The slice is airy and moist, slightly chewy —perfect for toast and sandwiches. With whole wheat flour, the potato flavor seems to benefit from the mellowing addition of milk, and, except for Murphy's Bread on page 290, the potato recipes in this section do include dairy products.

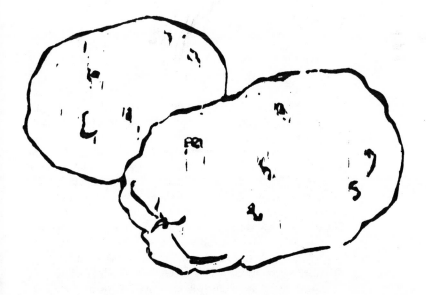

Potato Bread

1 medium-large potato,
   about ½ lb (225 g)

2 teaspoons active dry yeast
   (¼ oz or 7 g)
¼ cup warm water (60 ml)

1 cup fresh yogurt or
   buttermilk (235 ml)
1 cup hot potato water
   (235 ml)
2 tablespoons honey (30 ml)
2 tablespoons oil (30 ml)
   (optional)

6 cups whole wheat bread
   flour (900 g)
2½ teaspoons salt (14 g)

In spite of the extra time it takes to boil and mash the potatoes, we find ourselves making this bread frequently because it is such good eating.

≈

Peel the potato and trim off eyes and dark spots. Rinse under running water, cut into quarters, and boil until tender. Drain, reserving the water.

Dissolve the yeast in warm water.

Blend the liquids and the potato together. If you don't have a blender, just mash your potato and mix it in.

Combine the flour and salt, and mix them thoroughly.

Combine the liquids and drys. The dough will probably be a little bit stiff; depending on how much water your potato contained, it might be quite stiff. Add water on your hands as you knead for about 20 minutes, so that you end with a supple, soft, very bouncy dough.

Form the dough into a ball and place it smooth side up in the bowl. Cover and keep in a warm, draft-free place. After about an hour and a half, gently poke the center of the dough about ½ inch deep with your wet finger. If the hole doesn't fill in at all or if the dough sighs, it is ready for the next step. Press flat, form into a smooth round, and let the dough rise once more as before. The second rising will take about half as much time as the first.

Divide into two loaves, though if you have added extra potato or if your flour is very good or if you are a super kneader, there may be more dough than you require for two normal loaf pans. (If you have a scale, each loaf should weigh 1¾ lb, 800 g, or a little more.) Make hearth loaves — this dough makes wonderful hearth loaves — or just form the usual two loaves, plus a few rolls or buns.

Let the loaves rise in a warm, humid place until a gentle indentation of your wetted finger fills in slowly. Traditionally, potato bread has a dusty, floury crust. To achieve this effect, dust the loaf lightly with fine flour — pastry flour is best — just before baking. The flour will stick if the bread has been proofed in a humid place; otherwise, spray the crust lightly with warm water before dusting the loaf.

If you make hearth loaves, slash them before putting them in the oven; the tic-tac-toe pattern, or just three parallels, work well. We usually slash the loaves in pans, too, because this bread almost always rises very well in the oven.

Bake in preheated 350°F oven for nearly an hour.

OPTIONS

੨ If you have leftover mashed potatoes, you can use them in the bread. Use 1 to 1½ cups per recipe. If there is milk, salt, and butter in the mashed potatoes, you will probably want to reduce the bread's salt measure slightly. Leftovers may hold extra liquid, so be alert to that.

੨ For richer flavor and a little more rise, include an egg as part of the liquid measure. Beat it into the yogurt or buttermilk before adding the water.

੨ For a close-textured crumb, particularly pale and milk-sweet, stir six tablespoons of powdered milk into the dry ingredients. This amount of milk exceeds the maximum we generally suggest for unscalded milk or milk powder, but the conditioning effect of the potato counteracts the effect of the milk proteins, and the bread is light, airy, and delicious.

SESAME-POTATO BREAD

Use sesame oil for the oil measure in the bread. Roll the dough in sesame seeds after shaping the loaf. This is particularly delicious bread.

Potato Rye Bread

1 good-sized potato,
about ½ lb (225 g),
pared and cooked
cooking water from
the potato

½ cup yogurt (120 ml)
2 tablespoons oil (30 ml)
or butter (optional)

2 teaspoons active dry yeast
(¼ oz or 7 g)
½ cup warm water (120 ml)

3 cups whole rye flour
(385 g)
4 cups whole wheat flour
(600 g)
2½ teaspoons salt (14 g)
½ teaspoon fennel seeds

additional water, about
1 cup (235 ml)

Rye, wheat, potatoes, and fennel give this long-keeping bread a sophisticated European mood.

ɞ

Mash the potato. Add enough additional water to the potato water to make 1½ cups. Mix together the potato, yogurt, and oil (if used).

Dissolve the yeast in ½ cup warm water.

Mix the flours, salt, and seeds, then stir in the potato mixture and the yeast. Use some of the additional water also, if necessary, to make a very stiff dough. Knead the dough for about 20 minutes, incorporating the extra 1 cup water (or more potato water) gradually as you go along, until the dough is soft, supple, and smooth.

Form the dough into a ball and place it smooth side up in the bowl. Cover and keep in a warm, draft-free place. After about an hour and a half, gently poke the center of the dough about ½ inch deep with your wet finger. If the hole doesn't fill in at all or if the dough sighs, it is ready for the next step. Press flat, form into a smooth round, and let the dough rise once more as before. The second rising will take about half as much time as the first.

Press the dough flat and divide in two. Round it and let it rest until relaxed, then deflate and shape into pan or hearth loaves. Place in greased 8″ × 4″ loaf pans, or on a baking sheet dusted with corn meal. Let rise in a warm, humid, draft-free place until the dough slowly returns a gently made fingerprint. Bake about an hour at 350°F.

Blustery Buns

Chop and sauté the onion and garlic in the oil, cooking very gently so that they turn golden without browning. Add the honey and continue to cook for another couple of minutes.

Let this mixture cool and knead it into the dough for Potato Rye. One medium onion and a small clove of garlic is plenty for some people for two loaves, but if you really like this sort of thing, you could use all the onion in one loaf's worth of rolls (phew!). In either case, for decorative effect, keep a tiny bit of the onion to smear on the top of the rolls, after shaping. Makes 24 small or 12 giant buns, if you use two loaves' worth of dough.

1 onion
1 clove garlic
2 tablespoons oil (30 ml)
  (olive is good, or
  any cooking oil)
1 tablespoon honey (15 ml)

½ or 1 recipe
  Potato Rye Bread

Murphy's Bread

1 cup soymilk (235 ml)
2 tablespoons honey (30 ml)

2 teaspoons lemon juice
   (10 ml)
1 cup potato water and/or
   tap water (235 ml)

2 teaspoons active dry yeast
   (¼ oz or 7 g)
½ cup warm water (120 ml)

5½ cups whole wheat flour
   (825 g)
2½ teaspoons salt (14 g)

1 cup cooked mashed potato
   (235 ml)

This non-dairy potato bread is named for the Irish—who take their potatoes neat.

෨

Scald the soymilk and mix in the honey; set aside to cool. Mix lemon juice, potato water, if any, and tap water to bring the quantity to one cup.

Dissolve the yeast in warm water. Mix together the flour and salt, then rub the potato in with your fingers. Pour the liquids into a well in the center and stir the flour gradually into it. Add more water or flour as necessary to make a soft dough. Turn out on the board and knead thoroughly.

Form the dough into a ball and place it smooth side up in the bowl. Cover and keep in a warm, draft-free place. After about an hour and a half, gently poke the center of the dough about ½ inch deep with your wet finger. If the hole doesn't fill in at all or if the dough sighs, it is ready to shape. Since there is soy in the recipe, the dough should be ripe and ready to shape after only one rise.

Press flat and divide in two. Round and let rest until relaxed, then deflate and shape into loaves. Place in greased 8″ × 4″ loaf pans and let rise again in a warm, draft-free place until the dough slowly returns a gently made fingerprint. Slash the tops and bake in an oven preheated to 350°F for about 45 minutes, until done.

Herbed Dinner Loaf

The herbs are subtle, and the bread very moist: great for lunch the next day, toasted, alongside a bowl of tomato soup.

☙

Dissolve the yeast in the warm water.

Mix all the other ingredients together and then add the yeast. Knead until springy, about 10 minutes; the dough should be quite soft. If it seems too stiff, wet your hands as you knead to incorporate more water.

Cover the dough and let it rise in a very warm place for about an hour, or a little less. To check, poke your wet finger into the middle of the dough about ½ inch deep; if the hole does not fill in at all or if the dough sighs, you can deflate it and set it to rise again. The second rise should take less than half an hour if it has been kept warm enough.

Press flat, shape into a smooth round, place in a well-greased casserole dish or in a greased loaf pan, and let rise again as before. It should be ready for the oven in less than half an hour. Preheat well, to 350°F; bake for about 45 minutes.

2 teaspoons active dry yeast
(¼ oz or 7 g)
½ cup warm water (120 ml)
(can be potato
cooking water)

⅔ cup cooked mashed
potatoes (160 ml)
½ cup cottage cheese
(120 ml)
½ cup hot potato or
tap water (120 ml)
1 tablespoon oil (15 ml)
1 ½ teaspoons salt (8.25 g)
1 teaspoon dill weed
or parsley
1 teaspoon chopped
celery leaves
¼ teaspoon thyme

3 cups whole wheat flour
(450 g)

Saltless Breads

Who these days hasn't heard about the dangers of too much salt? Is there one among us who can down even a small bag of pretzels (much less potato chips) without a nervous twitch, a pang of guilt? But *bread* is not a salty food, so why this section?

All true, and unless you are on a sodium-restricted diet — or are one of the people who actually prefer bread without added salt — bread is one of the last places you would want to cut back: a little salt goes a long way in bread, not only transforming the flavor but strengthening the dough to make a lighter loaf. Even so, it can be done, and the saltless bread that tastes so blah at first gradually begins to taste just right if you are persistent and dedicated to reeducating your palate to a saltless regime.

And so if it is saltless loaves you want, tasty and light as they can be, we offer in this section some hints and also some really excellent recipes. Other breads in this book can be made without added salt, following the guidelines here. In general, look for recipes with a lot of flavor interest: the ryes and the sourdoughs, for example, will be most successful. Most of our recipes call for 2½ teaspoons of salt for two loaves; such breads do not depend wholly on salt for their flavor, but the ones that do call for a full tablespoon of salt are apt to need it.

If you are on a salt-restricted diet and have made an honest but futile attempt to get to like saltless bread, try using just 1 teaspoon in each of the following recipes, which is only ½ teaspoon per loaf — a third of what would be in a store-bought loaf of bread. Unless you eat a whole loaf in a day, you won't be getting a lot of salt from it.

When you make bread without salt you will find that the dough rises quickly, so watch it carefully to make sure that it doesn't overferment. To help control the fermentation, try making the dough with cool rather than warm water and letting it rise at room temperature. Keep the dough on the stiff side, and most important, don't let the shaped loaves rise too long in the pan, but put them in the oven a little before you think they are ready; otherwise they can collapse.

Though a saltless loaf rises faster, it will never be so high as the same bread made with salt. Since denser loaves are more flavorful, this is a natural compensation for the absence of salt. Nonetheless, you do want the bread to rise, so be sure to knead your dough as well as you can, letting the gluten develop as much strength as possible. If kneading is difficult for you and making saltless bread important to your health, it would be worth investing in a kneading machine, either a dough hook or food processor, to do the muscle work for you.

Incidentally, making rolls out of all or part of the dough has special advantages when you bake salt-free. Rolls can rise longer than loaves without danger of collapsing, and the increased crust area gives extra flavor and appeal—especially when poppy or sesame seeds add their cheery zest. Turn to Small Wonders, page 243, for shaping suggestions.

For information about low-sodium leavenings for quick breads please refer to page 311.

Saltless Variety Breads

¼ cup raisins (35 g)
2 cups water (475 ml)

2 teaspoons active dry yeast
   (¼ oz or 7 g)
½ cup warm water (120 ml)

5 cups whole wheat flour
   (750 g)
¼ cup skim milk powder
   (30 g)
½ cup sunflower seeds,
   chopped (28 g)
1 cup buckwheat, rye,
   or triticale flour,
   O R
2 cups rolled oats (150 g)

This bread is tasty, nutritious, satisfying. If you knead with a food processor, the first step of the recipe should be done in advance, either several hours ahead or the day before, so that the raisins and water can be chilled. Otherwise the dough will be far too warm to make good bread.

              🌭

Simmer the raisins in the water for 5 minutes, then blend smooth in blender or processor (or chop fine by hand). Set mixture aside to cool.

Dissolve the yeast in warm water. Mix the dry ingredients in a bowl, make a well in the center and pour in the liquids. Stir from the center out to make a slightly stiff dough, adding more water or flour if necessary. Knead well, a full 20 minutes by hand, until the dough is supple.

Cover the dough in the bowl to protect it from drafts and let it rise at room temperature until a gentle finger-poke about ½ inch deep—wet your finger first!—leaves a hole that does not fill in *or fills in very slowly:* about 1½ hours. Deflate the dough and let it rise again, about 45 to 60 minutes.

Divide the dough in two and knead gently into rounds, being careful not to rip the smooth top surface. Use dusting flour lightly as necessary. Let the rounds rest until they soften, about 15 minutes, then shape the loaves for loaf pans or round 2 quart casseroles with lids. Roll in oats for an attractive touch. Let rise again in a warm place until spongy, but be careful not to overproof—a fingerprint indentation should not remain in the dough but should fill in slowly. Preheat the oven to 425°F in time for it to be up to temperature when the bread is ready to go in.

If you bake the loaves in covered casseroles, pour 2 tablespoons warm water over each one before covering and baking. Bake for 20 minutes, then lower the oven temperature to 350°F and bake until done, another 20 or 30 minutes.

If you bake in loaf pans, paint the loaves with warm water, place in the hot oven, and immediately turn the heat down to 350°F. Bake for nearly an hour.

Slightly Sourdough

We tried making this bread in two versions: without salt, and with a teaspoonful per loaf. We tested it on friends who like to go light on the salt, and to our surprise they all preferred it saltless. In their opinion, if you add salt to this bread you detract from the earthy, whole-grain flavor.

If you do not have a sourdough starter already, it takes a few days to make one; follow the recipe for Manuel's Rye Sour on page 150. The day ahead, bring the starter out of the refrigerator, double it, and let it bubble up in a warm place. Measure out the 1½ cups and return the rest to the refrigerator.

ৼ

Dissolve the yeast in warm water. Make a well in the center of the flour and add the starter and the yeast mixure. Mix into a dough, adding enough additional water to make it soft, but not too soft. Knead thoroughly, about 20 minutes. The dough will be quite sticky due to the starter, so maybe you'll want to use a spatula or dough cutter in one hand to lift and turn the dough.

Keep in the bowl to rise, covered and protected from drafts, at room temperature. When you can poke your finger into the dough and the center of the hole does not fill in, probably about 1 to 1½ hours, deflate the dough and let it rise again. The timings are variable because the rye sour may add yeast activity of its own. The second rising will probably take about 30 to 45 minutes.

Divide the dough in half and knead gently into balls, then let them rest until they soften. Using plenty of dusting flour, shape into round loaves and roll the tops in poppy seeds. These bake very nicely in two 1½-quart stainless steel bowls, covered, or in one 2- to 2½-quart covered round casserole. Let rise again in a warm place, 90°F, until the dough warms up and feels spongy to the touch. Pour 3 tablespoons of warm water over the top of each loaf, cover and bake in an oven preheated to 375°F for 50 to 60 minutes until done.

2 teaspoons active dry yeast
(¼ oz or 7 g)
1 cup warm water (235 ml)

1½ cups sourdough starter
(375 ml)
5 cups whole wheat bread
flour (750 g)
½ cup additional warm
water, more or less
(120 ml)

poppy seeds

Bron's Wonder Loaves

1 medium raw potato
(1 cup cooked
and mashed)

1 cup water (235 ml)

1 cup skim milk (235ml)

2 teaspoons active dry yeast
(¼ oz or 7 g)
½ cup warm water (120 ml)

6 cups whole wheat bread
flour (900 g)
½ teaspoon diastatic
malt flour

4 teaspoons sesame seeds
(12 g)

This bread is remarkably light and tasty. Made from fresh, simple ingredients, it fits gracefully into the most rigorously healthful diet. The diastatic malt flour (dimalt) is available in most health food stores, or you can make your own (see page 274).

❧

If you are cooking the potato from scratch, scrub, peel, and cut it into chunks. Cook in one cup water until soft. Using real potato rather than instant, and fresh milk rather than powdered, makes an enormous difference in this recipe.

Scald the skim milk and set it aside to cool.

Dissolve the yeast in the warm water.

Drain the cooked potato and mash it. Combine the potato water with the skim milk and add water of a suitable temperature to bring the liquid measure to 2 cups, body heat.

Combine the whole wheat and malt flours. Rub the mashed potatoes into them. Make a well in the center and pour in the liquids, including the yeast solution. Mix the flour gradually into the liquids to make a dough that is soft, but not *too* soft—it should have some substance to it. Add more flour or water as necessary.

Let the dough rise covered in its bowl, in a warm place, about 80°F. Meanwhile, toast the sesame seeds by stirring briefly in a skillet (no oil is necessary). After about an hour make a ½-inch hole in the center of the dough with your wet finger. If the hole does not fill in at all or if the dough sighs, press it flat and round it again, putting it in its warm place to rise again. The second rising will take about half as long as the first.

Deflate the dough and divide in two, forming smooth balls. Let them rest until the dough softens. Sprinkle the sesame seeds on the table and press the smooth top of each piece of dough on the seeds. Roll into a circle and shape as usual. Place in two 8″ × 4″ loaf pans and keep in the same warm place to rise again, until the dough feels spongy. Bake in an oven preheated to 425°F for 20 minutes, then reduce the heat to 350°F for another 25 minutes or until done.

Rice Breads

For those who cannot eat wheat, a whole-foods diet that is not centered around meat poses challenges. Of course there are many, many interesting grain dishes, especially when you look to the cuisines of the East. But for a Western palate, nothing can quite take the place of bread, and nothing is so convenient or so comfortingly familiar — sandwiches and toast, how could we get along without them? In this chapter we offer a selection of breads and other good foods that will be useful to those who may be allergic to wheat, rye, oats, barley, and other grains, and to milk and eggs as well. The recipes presented here are good but they only suggest the wide range of possibilities.

We recommend using short- or medium-grain brown rice. Flour made from long-grain rice makes bread with a sandy texture. You may run across something called "glutinous rice." Don't worry, there's no gluten in it: it just gets sticky when cooked, a quality required in certain recipes — not, however, those in this book. Plain ordinary short- or medium-grain brown rice is fine.

Rice flour, like cornmeal, performs much better in every way when it is freshly ground; this is true even if your grinder, like ours, can't make it into a fine powder.

About Yeasted Rice Breads

*Corn may be tolerated also. When you see references to "corn gluten," it is corn protein that is meant, not gluten in the allergic sense. Our recipe for Basic Corn-bread on page 328 is glutenfree.

It is probably impossible to imagine how convenient bread is unless you are one of those rare people who are allergic to gluten and can tolerate no grain at all except rice.* If you are allergic to gluten you are probably not a vegetarian — or you are very thin. Maybe we can help change that.

Our yeasted rice breads are based on the dedicated work of two women who were determined to find a way to provide real yeast-raised bread for people whose diets are limited in this way. Maura Bean and Kazuko Nishita of the USDA Western Regional Research Laboratory in Berkeley tested every available natural and synthetic gum, trying to find one that could do what gluten does. They came up with methylcellulose, not what you might call a natural food for sure, but it works. The gum is extracted from cellulose fiber, and is impressively non-toxic.†

Our own version of their work uses brown rice flour instead of white, and includes a long fermentation period to improve both the flavor and keeping quality of the bread. There are three variations: Brown Rice Bread, which tastes like — rice; Garbanzo Rice Bread, with a mellow flavor and the advantage of added legume nutrients; and Soy-Raisin Rice bread, cakier, and sweet. Whichever version you make, be sure that your brown rice flour is really fresh and that it was ground from short- or medium-grain rice, not long-grain.

Your local health food store may be able to get methocel for you. Otherwise it can be ordered by mail, but it is expensive, $7 for half a pound as we go to press. Half a pound will be enough for 24 loaves. To order by mail write to:

Ener-G Foods, Inc.
P.O. 24723, Seattle, Washington 98124-0723

Ask for Methocel K4M (90 HG 4000). Ask for a copy of their product list too. This company sells a variety of products for people with severe food allergy.

†"Evaluation of the health aspects of cellulose and certain cellulose derivatives as food ingredients." FASEB/SCOGS Report 25 (NTIS PB 274–667) 1974; cited in The Food Additives Book, Willis A. Gortner and Nicholas Freydberg, Bantam 1982, page 508.

Brown Rice Bread

The flour in this bread must be from short- or medium-grain rice, not long-grain rice. Start this bread 12 to 18 hours before you want to bake.

6 cups brown rice flour (900 g)

1 tablespoon salt (16.5 g)

2⅔ cup tepid water (635 ml)

≈

Mix the rice flour and the salt, and make a well in the middle. Pour in the water, mixing gradually from the center outward. Beat vigorously for ten minutes either by hand, with a wooden spoon, or with an electric beater at medium speed, to smooth and aerate the batter.

4 teaspoons active dry yeast (½ oz or 14 g)

½ cup warm water (120 ml)

Let the mixture stand at room temperature for 12 to 18 hours.

2 tablespoons honey (30 ml)

¼ cup oil (60 g)

Dissolve the yeast in warm water. Stir the yeast solution, then the honey and oil into the grain mixture and mix thoroughly by hand or machine until completely smooth and uniform. Add the methocel and mix thoroughly again; the dough will become very stiff. (See the tips below.)

¼ cup methocel (28 g)

Spoon into three well-greased 8″ × 4″ loaf pans. Wet your fingers with water or oil and smooth the tops. Keep the loaves in a warm (80°F) and humid place to rise, until the batter reaches the top of the pans. Watch the surface of the dough and be ready to put the bread into a preheated oven as soon as the first tiny pinholes appear on the top. Bake at 350°F for about 45 minutes, or until done. Allow to cool thoroughly before slicing.

SOME TIPS If the dough was too stiff, its surface will be full of holes before it can rise, and the bread will be dense. If it is too wet, it will rise up in a big arch like wheat bread, but it will collapse. With a little practice you will get a feeling for the proper consistency.

≈ Don't try to substitute butter or shortening for the oil in this recipe because they will affect the methocel function.

≈ Store the bread in a plastic bag in the refrigerator, and freeze the extra two loaves until you need them, as the bread tends to stale quickly.

Garbanzo Rice Bread

5½ cups brown rice flour
   (830 g)
½ cup garbanzo flour (70 g)
1 tablespoon salt (16.5 g)
2⅔ cups tepid water (635 ml)

4 teaspoons active dry yeast
   (½ oz or 14 g)
½ cup warm water (120 ml)

2 tablespoons honey (30 ml)
¼ cup oil (60 ml)

¼ cup methocel (28 g)

This bread has a mellower flavor and keeps better than the plain Brown Rice Bread.

❧

Follow the mixing and rising instructions for Brown Rice Bread. Use only two loaf pans and bake slightly longer, about 50 minutes to an hour.

Soy-Raisin Rice Bread

6 cups brown rice flour
   (600 g)
2 tablespoons soy flour
   (7 g)
1 tablespoon salt (16.5 g)
2⅔ cups tepid water (635 ml)

4 teaspoons active dry yeast
   (½ oz or 14 g)
½ cup warm water (120 ml)

⅓ cup honey (80 ml)
¼ cup oil (60 ml)
½ cup raisins (70 g)

¼ cup methocel (28 g)

Denser, cakier, more filling, this bread adds variety and interest. The slice is golden in color and soft, almost like pound cake.

❧

Mix and let rise like Brown Rice Bread, incorporating the soy flour into the first mixing and the raisins along with the honey. Divide the dough into two loaves only, and bake cooler and longer, at 325°F for 50 to 60 minutes, or until done.

Iddlis

In South India, breakfast often means iddlis with chutney or the spicy stew called Sambar. Iddlis are made from simple ingredients, but their preparation calls for considerable artistry, and their flavor is a subtle, sophisticated one that speaks of the ancient heritage from which they come. We include them here because to us they are the very most wonderful of rice foods; and with their breadlike texture (never gummy, please), they provide at least as much satisfaction when buttered and eaten for breakfast as our own toast. They are feathery-light when properly prepared, slightly chewy, with a full, tangy flavor.

Indian cooks make iddlis from a special kind of rice and a legume called urid dal, or black gram. The rice and dal are soaked and wet-ground separately, then mixed together with salt and fermented for about 24 hours. When the batter is just right, it is cooked in a special utensil.

Our friend Madhuri Thathachari, a most charming and accomplished South Indian lady, has helped us to develop the recipe that follows. To achieve best results, we call for parboiling short-grain rice, which prevents the iddlis from getting gummy. Don't try to use long-grain rice because it makes iddlis that are heavy and wet.

If you can get it, use urid dal from an Indian specialty shop—the split hulled kind are easiest to use. Ordinary garbanzo beans also work very well. Their flavors are different, but both are delicious: iddlis made with urid dal are tangy and sophisticated, the garbanzo iddlis are mellower and more familiar to the Western palate.

If you want to use unhulled dal as they do in South India, wash it well after the first soaking period, flooding the dal and letting the hulls float off the top as you swish the beans with your hand. Be thorough: the black hulls change the color of the iddlis from snowy white to gray, with black specks. Iddlis made with garbanzo beans are creamy white perforce.

EQUIPMENT You will need a blender for grinding and either a real iddli pan or a covered skillet with an egg poacher. The real iddli pan will hold 12 or more at once, a much more practical number for serious iddli fans. Since the iddlis will be steamed, the egg poacher or iddli pan must have a tight-fitting lid. Note that the rice and beans need to set for 6 to 8 hours before you begin and the batter needs to ferment for 24 to 30 hours.

&

1 cup short- or medium-grain brown rice (200 g)
½ cup split black gram or garbanzo beans (100 g)
1 cup water, for grinding (235 ml)
½ teaspoon salt (2.75 g)

Wash the rice and pick over the beans and wash them separately. Pour the rice into about a quart of vigorously boiling water and let it cook exactly three minutes, then remove and drain immediately. The rice will swell a little, but it should not become soft or white.

Soak the parboiled rice and the dal separately in tepid water for 6 to 8 hours at warm room temperature. Drain, but do not rinse.

To blend the legumes a mortar and pestle are used in India. Here put enough in the blender or processor to cover the blades and add tepid water to nearly, but not quite, cover. Blend to a smooth, medium-thick paste; the garbanzo paste will be a little less smooth than that made from the dal. Repeat as necessary until all the beans are blended.

Measure the rice and water into the blender in the same way. Blend, but before the mixture loses its granular quality, stop and feel its consistency with your fingers. *Do not let it become completely smooth.* It should feel like a thick paste with many grains of sand scattered throughout.

Combine the rice and legume pastes, and add the salt. Use your clean hands to stir the mixture vigorously for seven to ten minutes: this step is essential. It incorporates air into the mixture so that it changes from a heavy paste to a light batter. Hand-mixing may also help to set up the right fermentation, but we have also used an electric mixer at medium speed and have had good results. The batter should be thick, of dropping consistency. If yours is too thin, make Dosas instead of iddlis this time: see the recipe on page 304.

Set the iddli batter aside to ferment in a covered container, like a glass baking dish. The batter is ready when it rises up in the bowl and looks bubbly on the surface. If you keep it at room temperature, from 70° to 80°F, it will take 24 to 30 hours to ferment properly. Kept warmer than 90°F it will lose its delicate mild flavor and become fiercely sour. If your house is too cool, keep the batter in the oven with the pilot or light bulb on, holding the door partway open with a rolled-up towel, or else find a place where you can maintain a 70° to 80°F temperature.

Traditionally the cups for cooking the iddli are greased with ghee, a specially prepared sort of clarified butter; but regular butter or any semisolid shortening will do. Spoon about three tablespoons of batter into each cup. Since poached-egg containers are a little deeper than iddli cups, they should be only about two-thirds full. Steam over boiling water in a tightly covered pan for about 20 to 25 minutes, or until a toothpick inserted in the center comes out clean. They should rise beautifully and be light and fluffy, gently rounded on the top.

Remove the pan from the steam and let the iddli stand in their cups for a minute, then scoop them out with a table knife. They should come out easily. Butter and serve hot. The batter can be kept for one day in the refrigerator, then brought to room temperature, and steamed.

Makes about 12 iddlis.

Dosas

If you have more than enough iddli batter for one meal, you can thin it out and use it to make dosas, a crepe-thin pancake. Thin with water to the consistency of crepe batter and pour and turn it in a skillet as you would a crepe. For a more authentic and crisper version, spoon a slightly thicker batter into the center of a griddle heated slightly less than for pancakes. Use the back of a large spoon to spread the batter thin in a clockwise spiral. Turn when slightly brown and pulling away from the pan.

Eat dosas as you would a savory crepe, or serve them with this delicious chutney.

Meera's Chutney

¾ cup shredded coconut
2 tablespoons oil
1 chopped onion
2 cloves garlic

4 ripe tomatoes, chopped
1 tablespoon minced fresh
   ginger
½ teaspoon salt
1 green chili (optional)

1 tablespoon oil
¼ teaspoon black
   mustard seeds

If you are using dried coconut, pour over it just enough hot water to cover, and let stand for an hour or more.

Sauté the onion and garlic until soft. Add tomato, ginger, salt, and chili, if used. Cook until the tomatoes are soft. Add coconut and purée in blender, processor, or food mill.

Heat the tablespoon of oil in a tiny, heavy pan. Add the mustard seed and allow it to pop, then *immediately* turn the seeds into the tomato mixture. Stir together, and taste for salt.

Make the chutney quite thick when you will serve it with dosas. For iddli, it should be more soupy, so add tomato juice or water as needed.

VARIATIONS When puréeing the tomato, you can add a handful of either fresh coriander leaves, or several very tender small lemon leaves.

Rice Waffles

This recipe is adapted from the one in *Oats, Peas, Beans & Barley Cookbook* by Edyth Cottrell. Note that both the rice and beans must be soaked for 24 hours before using.

❧

Soak the rice 24 hours in 3 cups water. Drain, reserving 1½ cups water. At the same time, soak the soybeans separately for 24 hours. Drain, discarding the water.

Put all ingredients in blender or food processor and blend until light and fluffy. Let stand at least while waffle iron heats, a half hour if convenient. Blend again briefly just before using.

Grease the hot waffle iron lightly with a brush, using a solid shortening or an oil and lecithin mixture (See page 390). Usually the iron need be greased only for the first waffle. Pour in ½ cup of the batter or more, depending on the size of your iron. Bake for 8 minutes; do not open the waffle iron before 8 minutes are up. Really, don't.

This recipe makes about half a dozen waffles, depending on the size of your iron.

1½ cups raw brown rice
1½ cups water from soaking the rice
½ cup raw soybeans

½ teaspoon salt
1 tablespoon oil
a few drops of lecithin

VARIATIONS Substitute garbanzo beans for the soybeans.

❧ Substitute ⅓ cup raw cashews, almonds, sunflower or sesame seeds for the soybeans. They don't need to be soaked.

❧ Sprinkle sesame or poppy seeds on the waffle before closing the top down.

Quick Rice Breads

These tasty breads will be useful to people who can tolerate dairy products. Bread needs *something* to hold it together; these breads depend on eggs.

Cranberry Rice Bread

¾ cup coarsely chopped
    fresh cranberries
½ cup chopped raisins
OR
use all raisins

⅓ cup chopped walnuts
1 tablespoon undyed
    orange rind

1¾ cups brown rice flour
½ cup potato flour
1½ teaspoons baking powder
½ teaspoon soda
½ teaspoon salt

3 tablespoons honey
2 tablespoons butter or oil
2 eggs, slightly beaten
½ cup orange juice
2 tablespoons lemon juice

A pretty, tart, and holiday-festive loaf, good for breakfast or tea time. When made with only raisins, it misses the colorful sparkle of the cranberries, and is much sweeter.

❧

Preheat the oven to 350°F. Grease an 8″ × 4″ loaf pan.

Stir together berries, raisins, nuts, and orange rind. Sift the flours, baking powder, soda, and salt into the bowl and stir all of them together.

Beat the honey with the butter or oil, then add the eggs and orange and lemon juices, stirring as you add them. Mix until smooth. Add the dry ingredients, mixing just enough to moisten.

Bake about 45 minutes; cool before slicing.

Banana Rice Bread

This is a small loaf, more desserty.

ᴥ

Preheat the oven to 350°F and grease a small-sized loaf pan.

Sift the dry ingredients together, except the tapioca and the nuts. Now stir in tapioca and the nuts if you use them.

Blend the remaining ingredients together and then add the dry ingredients to them. Mix well and pour into the loaf pan. Bake about 50 minutes, or until the bread tests done with a toothpick or small sharp knife. Allow it to stay in the pan for 10 minutes before removing, and then let it cool completely before slicing.

1½ cups brown rice flour
2 tablespoons potato flour
2 teaspoons baking powder
½ teaspoon salt
½ teaspoon baking soda
2 tablespoons tapioca
   (quick-cooking)
½ cup chopped walnuts,
   (optional)

2 tablespoons butter or oil
3 tablespoons honey
¼ cup buttermilk
2 medium-sized bananas,
   mashed
2 eggs, slightly beaten

Basic Rice Quick Bread

A plain, pretty loaf, somewhere on the pound-cake side of bread, but not too sweet for many kinds of sandwiches.

ᴥ

Preheat oven to 350°F. Grease an 8″ × 4″ loaf pan.

Sift together rice flour, potato flour, cornstarch, baking powder, and salt.

If you use butter, cream the honey and butter and then beat in the milk and eggs; if you use oil, simply mix them all together, then combine the wet and dry ingredients quickly and turn into the greased pan.

Bake about 45 minutes or a little longer. Let cool ten minutes, then tip the loaf out of the pan. Cool on rack for at least half an hour before cutting.

2½ cups brown rice flour
⅓ cup potato flour
⅓ cup cornstarch
2 tablespoons baking powder
¾ teaspoon salt

3 tablespoons oil or butter
2 tablespoons honey
1⅔ cups milk
2 eggs, slightly beaten

Rice-Sesame Crackers

3 cups water
1 cup brown rice
½ teaspoon salt
3 tablespoons sesame seeds

This recipe is from *The Good Goodies* by Stan and Floss Dworkin (Rodale, 1974). The crackers are much better than the store-bought kind and are simple and easy to make once you get the hang of it.

જી

Boil the water and add the rice and salt. Bring back to full boil, then cover and simmer over low flame for 45 minutes. Remove from heat. Stir in the sesame seeds. Mash using a potato masher; be pretty vigorous about this.

When cool enough to handle, form the rice into two flat discs, pressing and squeezing to get the rice to stick together. Oil two baking sheets generously. Put one disc in the center of each sheet, then pat and press it into a flat rectangle, keeping the sides tidy. Cover with a sheet of waxed paper as big as the baking sheet, and roll with a rolling pin until it is as thin as possible; patching is quite legal. (Anyhow, the crumbles are as delicious as the crackers.) Remove the waxed paper and cut the dough into whatever size and shape please you.

Bake at 325°F for about 20 to 25 minutes, or until crisp; the edges usually lift off the baking sheet at this stage, and when you pull a piece off, it breaks quite crisply. The crackers will not brown very much.

Quick Breads & Muffins

For rounding out a simple dinner when time is short, or making *Lunch* out of lunch, a batch of muffins or a spicy loaf of Persimmon Bread can be just the thing. Quick breads offer variety, interest, and flexibility, complementing rather than competing with the long-rising breads that are our staff of life.

Without the fermentation period that gives yeasted breads their fullness of flavor, quick breads depend solely on their ingredients to give them pizzazz. Most quick bread recipes that we have seen roaming at large in the world call for a humongous amount of fat and, often, of sugar too. They are in fact not breads at all, but greasy cakes, hiding behind the unassuming innocence of names like "Wheat Germ Zucchini Loaf." Tasty, but good grief! A whole cup of oil, and two of sugar in *one* loaf?

The breads in this section are lean by comparison to such delicacies, but they are just as delicious. Natural ingredients like fruits, vegetables, nuts, seeds, herbs, and spices supply their full, satisfying flavors. The recipes call for a minimum of fat and sweetener to make the breads tender and tasty. We have included flours and grains other than wheat here and there, and have tried to describe some of their possiblities and limitations. We who eat wheat bread every day welcome the variety the other grains offer. Since quick breads do not depend completely on gluten for their rise and cohesiveness (particularly if the recipe calls for egg) some, or even all, of their flour can come from oats, rye, corn, or rice.

Leavenings for Quick Breads

BAKING POWDER   Ordinary double-acting baking powders are effective, and of the several kinds of baking powder, they are the least bitter. If you prefer to avoid the aluminum salts that these products contain, the old-fashioned cream of tartar baking powders—either made at home or bought in natural foods stores—work perfectly well. To make your own, use ⅝ teaspoon cream of tartar plus ¼ teaspoon bicarbonate of soda per cup of flour; this is the equivalent of a teaspoon of single-acting baking powder. Make it fresh each time, or make extra and store it airtight, but only for short periods.

If quick breads appear often on your table, the sodium content of these products and their destruction of thiamine may be more significant considerations than whether or not they contain aluminum.

One teaspoon of baking soda contains 1360 mg of sodium; commercial soda-based baking powders vary, ranging from those made with cream of tartar, with 200 mg, to the double-acting kind, with 330 mg sodium per teaspoon. Those who need to limit their sodium intake carefully can look for potassium bicarbonate baking powder at the health food store, or even in some supermarkets. If your pharmacist will order potassium bicarbonate for you, you can use it in recipes that call for baking soda, and you can make your own sodium-free baking powder at home: 2 cups arrowroot, 2 cups cream of tartar, 1 cup potassium bicarbonate. Store airtight; use an amount equivalent to normal baking powder. Some people find potassium baking powders slightly more bitter than ordinary powders; if you do, probably you will have the best results using them in the more highly flavored or very sweet breads and muffins.

Sodium and aluminum aside, chemical leavenings always generate an alkaline pH and this destroys the B vitamin thiamine, which you would expect to be plentiful in a whole-grain product.

For good rising power with a minimum of baking powder, we suggest using 1 teaspoon per cup of flour.

In batters with a lot of acid ingredients, baking soda can be used by itself (or in combination with baking powder) to get a good rise without the addition of extra acid salts. The quantities are already worked out in the recipes, of course, but if you need to substitute or are making up your own recipe, here are some equivalents. The amounts are approximate because many of these ingredients vary in their acidity from one time to the next, and other ingredients in the batter act as buffers, too. Nevertheless, here is a rough guideline to use for balancing.

½ teaspoon soda PLUS
1 cup fully soured milk or buttermilk

¼ teaspoon soda PLUS
1 teaspoon vinegar or lemon juice

¼ teaspoon soda PLUS
¼ to ½ cup molasses or honey

(To sour milk: 1 tablespoon vinegar or lemon juice or 1¾ teaspoons cream of tartar plus milk to make 1 cup. Let stand five minutes.)

NOTE There is close to ¼ teaspoon baking soda in each teaspoon of baking powder.

Don't mix soda and acid liquids together. Sift the soda (and cream of tartar) along with the dry ingredients, and measure the liquids with the liquid measure.

Always sift dry leavenings with the flour because if there are even small lumps, the final product will have little dark brown places that are impressively bitter.

Adding an egg or two to a quick bread makes it lighter, and its flavor subtler—one reason that breads with more eggs often have more sugar and flavorings, too. In addition, eggs act as binders, making the texture less crumbly; but if wheat flour is included, eggs are not necessary.

Egg can provide enough leavening in a simple recipe—one that is not heavily laden with fruit, for example—so that you need no baking powder or soda at all. Use one egg per cup of flour, beating the yolks separately into the combined fat and sweetener, folding the stiffly beaten whites into the batter as the last step. Reduce the liquid measure by about 2 tablespoons for each egg you add to the recipe.

Because they do not depend entirely on gluten for rising, quick breads and muffins can make good use of flours other than wheat, especially if the recipe includes some wheat flour or an egg or two. They'll make a bread heavier than you'd get with wheat, though rolled oats — not really a flour, of course — can make astonishingly light, very pretty breads and muffins. For one cup wheat flour, you can substitute about:

> 1 cup rye flour or cornmeal
> ¾ cup buckwheat, rice, or barley flour
> 1¼ cup bean flour
> 1¼ cup rolled oats

Keep the flavor and the mood of your proposed substitute in mind when you plan your bread. None of these characters is a straight-across double for wheat; each has its own personality. Most perform better supported by wheat flour.

On the other hand, to use bread flour as the *only* flour, especially in plain loaves or muffins, makes for a flat flavor, and if the vigor of your mixing develops the gluten, the bread will be chewy where it should be tender. Most of the recipes for quick loaves call for a combination of bread and pastry flours, but if all-purpose whole wheat flour is available in your area, and convenient in your kitchen, you could use it instead of the combined bread- and pastry-flour measures. Muffins, and even loaves without the extra burden of fruits and nuts, are perhaps best with whole wheat pastry flour only.

ੋ

WHEAT GERM Wheat germ can add a lot to quick breads, both in flavor and texture, and many of our recipes call for it. We prefer toasted to raw. Wheat germ goes rancid very fast, so don't buy it in large quantities and do store it in the refrigerator.

Liquids, Fats, Sweeteners, Tidbits

WATER; any form of milk; potato cooking broth; fruit juice; crushed, stewed, blended, grated raw fruits; zucchini (as if I had to tell you) — any of these can provide acceptable "wet" ingredients for a quick bread. As a rule of thumb, use about ½ to ⅔ cup liquid for each cup of flour. Of course this will vary with both the nature of the liquid and the type of flour. If you are adding cooked beans or grains, reduce the liquid measure by about ⅔ cup for each cup of beans or cereal you add. We have tried to include recipes that exemplify many of these options so that you can use them as guidelines in devising your own.

FAT in quick breads may be oil or butter or a combination. You can use sesame butter, peanut or other nut or seed butters. If the recipe is plain, choosing dairy butter over oil may make a difference, but if the other ingredients provide interesting flavor, the bread may be just as tasty if you use plain oil. If you do opt for butter, cream it with the sweetener until the mixture is fluffy. The addition of fat in some form contributes tenderness, a soft, moist crumb, and fullness of flavor; we have not found any way to make good quick breads with none at all.

SWEETENERS tenderize the crumb, too, and help the bread cook properly, though if you use enough sweet fruit — bananas, for example, or dates — you actually can make a passable sweet-flavored loaf or muffin without adding the likes of honey or molasses. More practical, though, it seems to us, is to use a little bit of sweetener and have a better-textured as well as a tastier bread.

TIDBITS — chopped dried fruits, nuts, seeds, sprouted grains — can be folded in when you're combining the wet and dry ingredients. If it's protein you're after, you can incorporate as much as a cup of grated tofu or ½ cup cooked soy grits in a quick loaf. Choose a recipe that has plenty of flavor, like Mince Spice Loaf on page 321 or Applesauce Bread on 323. The soy will make the bread's flavor blander.

Nearly everyone has tried the standard zucchini loaves by now, and if you have gotten this far with us, you already know how we feel about them, too. But our own experiments with using zucchini in quick breads have been pretty rewarding, and a few have been good enough to include in this collection. We prefer to add zucchini to herby/savory/cheesy bread or muffins or to cornbread, where it helps to make the bread moist and light. By the by, if the family turns green around the subject of zucchini late in August, try growing some of the yellow kind next year. The flavor is superb, and grated into cornbread, it really does disappear—providing that you don't get carried away quantity-wise. Start with a cup per recipe, and see how it goes; we like the Basic Cornbread (two eggs) when squashing (page 328).

TOPPINGS   Before you pop your quick bread in the oven, there are various things you can sprinkle on the top for added glamour. Oat flakes, wheat germ, almond meal, sesame or poppy seeds, finely chopped nuts, date sugar—all work well, either alone or in combination.

WHAT IS QUICK?   One last word. The variety possible in quick breads is really limited only by your own imagination and the time you have to spend chopping and measuring. The recipes here are some we enjoy, but you will not limit yourself to these few. Mostly we have tried to include breads that were not only good but also really *quick*—if half an hour goes by while you measure and chop and fuss, and another hour baking, and then the bread has to wait overnight to be ready to slice, from our point of view, it would hardly qualify as a Quick.

Mixing

Ingredients should be at room temperature or a little warmer, even the eggs. This is true for muffins, but it is particularly helpful when making loaves, because cold batter heats unevenly: the crust gets too dark before the loaf cooks in the center.

The traditional method for mixing quick breads is to stir the dry ingredients together, and, in a separate bowl, the wet ingredients. The two are combined with a minimum of mixing, then put in the baking pan and into the hot oven quickly. The speed is intended to insure that the bread loses as little gas as possible before the oven heat can set the dough. Even if you are using double-acting baking powder (which gives you more leeway because part of its reaction begins only in the heat of the oven), this is still a very good method, albeit a little tense if anyone gets in your way, or the phone rings at the crucial moment.

An aside to mothers, fathers, aunts and uncles: Mixing quick breads is not so difficult that you can't involve children in the process. From our experience, making raisin-nut bread or blueberry muffins is quite as much fun as mixing cake or cookies, and more healthful to the family as well. Something that can surprise us "olders" is that oftentimes children are even prouder to contribute an integral part to the family meal than to supply just the dessert.

Baking & Serving

A moderate oven temperature, about 350°F, is good for most loaves, with a slightly higher heat, 375–425°F, for muffins and unsweet cornbreads. The oven should be preheated thoroughly before the bread goes in.

Our recipes call for whole grain flours and a minimum of chemical leavenings and eggs, so they rise less puffily than do standard types. In order to produce nicely shaped muffins and loaves, fill the pans about three-fourths full, sometimes even fuller. For loaves, we have sized our recipes to fill a medium 8″ × 4″ pan. Our muffin recipes make 12 ordinary small muffins, each dip in the tin holding a little over ¼ cup. For the larger size muffin tins—they hold nearly ½ cup each—double the recipe to make a full dozen.

Baking times are given with each recipe, but they will vary with the temperature of the ingredients and the peculiarities of your own oven. In general, allow about an hour for loaves and about 18 minutes for muffins.

If your loaves burn on the crust before they are done in the center, try using shiny metal loaf pans and/or place one pan inside the other as a practical remedy. If you are short on loaf pans, putting your loaf in its pan on a cookie sheet can help, too.

When done, a quick bread will have an inviting aroma and will shrink away from the edge of the pan a little bit. To check, insert a toothpick or clean sharp knife in the middle of the bread; if it's done, the blade will come out clean.

Let muffins cool briefly in their tins; remove them either one by one with a fork, or simply turn the tin upside down over a towel, giving it a firm but gentle tap if the muffins don't all tumble out. (If you ran out of batter before all the cups were full and put water in the empty cup to keep the grease from burning, don't forget to sponge out the remaining water before you turn the tin upside down.)

Recipes for Loaves

Poppy Loaf

Oats and poppy seeds give this loaf a delicacy that harmonizes well with many dishes, from asparagus soup to zucchini Provençale. Makes super muffins.

If you don't have oat flour on hand you can make it in your electric blender or food processor from rolled oats: blend ½ to ¾ cups at a time to make the 2 cups; it will take a little less than 3 cups of old-fashioned rolled oats.

❧

Either soak raisins 5 minutes in ¼ cup boiling water and whirl briefly in blender, or chop them coarsely by hand and then soak them.

Preheat oven to 350°F. Grease an 8″ × 4″ loaf pan.

Put oat flour in bowl and sift in the other dry ingredients. Beat together eggs, oil, and honey or date sugar. Stir milk, raisins and water, poppy seeds, and lemon peel, and add the egg mixture.

Add dry to liquid ingredients, stirring just enough to mix well. Turn into pan, and sprinkle with more poppy seeds. Bake for about an hour.

½ cup raisins
2 cups coarse oat flour
½ cup whole wheat
    bread flour
2½ teaspoons baking powder
½ teaspoon salt
¼ teaspoon mace or nutmeg

2 eggs
2 tablespoons oil (or butter)
2 to 4 tablespoons honey
    OR
¼ cup date sugar

1 cup milk
2 tablespoons poppy seeds
2 teaspoons lemon peel

Wheat Germ Loaf

¼ cup light molasses
OR
2 tablespoons honey
and 2 tablespoons
blackstrap molasses
¼ cup oil
1 egg
1½ cups buttermilk
or yogurt

1 cup whole wheat
pastry flour
¾ cup whole wheat
bread flour
½ teaspoon salt
2½ teaspoons baking
powder
½ teaspoon baking soda
¾ cup wheat germ

1 tablespoon wheat germ

This bread is not sweet but has a pronounced wheat germ flavor, so it plays a good supporting role with soup or salad.

ஐ

Preheat oven to 375°F.

Beat sweetener and oil together with a fork. Beat in the egg and buttermilk. Sift flours, salt, baking powder, and soda together; stir in the wheat germ. Mix the dry ingredients into the wet ingredients, avoiding both lumps and overbeating.

Fill a greased 8" × 4" loaf pan and sprinkle top with wheat germ. Bake for about an hour, but check after 40 minutes to see how it is doing.

FRESH APPLE OR PEAR BREAD

Use butter for the oil measure. Use all honey for sweetener; if fruit is tart, adjust the honey measure. Cream honey and butter together, and add 1 teaspoon grated lemon peel. Follow the recipe as written, and when the batter is ready, fold in 1 cup grated fresh apple plus 1 teaspoon cinnamon; or add 1 cup grated fresh pear plus ¼ teaspoon ginger; and ½ cup toasted chopped nuts, if you like. Either of these breads is good baked as a loaf, but maybe even nicer baked in an 8" × 11" pan, and cut into squares.

The loaf version takes about an hour and a quarter to bake, the cake version, about 30 to 45 minutes.

Zucchini-Rice Bread

If you wish, you may substitute whole wheat pastry flour for the rice flour in this bread: the result will be a little more familiar-tasting, a little less interesting.

ça.

Preheat the oven to 375°F. Grease an 8″ × 4″ loaf pan. Soak the raisins in the hot water. Sift the dry ingredients together, adding the bran after the sifting.

Cream the honey and butter, or stir the honey and oil together; add the egg and lemon peel.

Strain the raisins and measure the soaking water. Add or discard water as needed to make ¾ cup. Mix with the grated zucchini and raisins.

Stir the flour and the zucchini mixture alternately into the egg mixture. Spoon into the greased loaf pan and bake about an hour and ten minutes. This is a moist bread, and when it is done, the testing knife or fork will look a little wet, but it should not be gooey.

½ cup raisins, chopped
1 cup hot water

1¼ cup fresh
    brown rice flour
1 cup whole wheat
    bread flour
2 tablespoons powdered milk
1 tablespoon baking
    powder
¾ teaspoon salt
½ teaspoon powdered ginger
½ cup wheat bran

3 tablespoons honey
3 tablespoons oil or butter
1 egg, lightly beaten
1 teaspoon lemon peel

1½ cups grated zucchini
¾ cup of the raisin water

Kasha-Raisin Bread

This sweet, moist, and hefty loaf is terrific with cabbage or winter squash soup. Toast and cook the buckwheat groats before you begin so they'll have cooled somewhat before you use them.

ça.

Preheat oven to 350°F. Grease an 8″ × 4″ loaf pan. Sift dry ingredients together. Beat oil, honey, and egg yolk; add water, peel, raisins, and buckwheat groats.

Beat egg white stiff.

Stir dry into liquid ingredients, then fold in the egg white.

Turn into the pan and bake about 45 minutes.

2 cups whole wheat flour
¼ cup milk powder
2 teaspoons baking powder
1 teaspoon salt

2 tablespoons oil
3 tablespoons honey
1 egg, separated
1⅓ cups warm water
1 teaspoon grated undyed
    orange or lemon peel
½ cup chopped raisins
1 cup toasted and cooked
    buckwheat groats

This One's for Adele

1½ cups whole wheat
    pastry flour
¾ cup whole wheat
    bread flour
½ teaspoon salt
2 tablespoons powdered milk
1 tablespoon baking powder

½ cup wheat germ
    OR
2 tablespoons wheat germ,
2 tablespoons soy flour, and
⅓ cup wheat bran

¼ cup butter or oil
¼ cup honey
    or light molasses
1 egg, lightly beaten
1½ cups water

Only slightly sweet—suitable for serving for lunch alongside tomato soup, with slices of cheese, or with fruit and yogurt, or anywhere a light/hearty bread is welcome. The recipe is dependable and tolerates a lot of variations, some of which follow.

🍃

Preheat oven to 375°F. Grease an 8″ × 4″ loaf pan.

Sift the dry ingredients together, except the wheat germ (and bran, if used) and stir them into the mixture.

If you are using butter, cream it with the honey; when they are light and fluffy, beat in the egg, and then add the dry ingredients alternately with the water, stirring just enough to mix. If you are using oil, stir it into the honey and then add the egg and water; add dry ingredients and mix.

Bake for 45 minutes to an hour, or until a clean knife or toothpick inserted near the center comes out clean.

DATE-NUT TEA LOAF

Delicate in flavor, this recipe falls halfway between bread and the usual sort of desserty-rich date loaf. It is good just with Better-Butter (page 212) or with ricotta cheese, or beside a fruit salad. Next day it makes fine toast.

Add one tablespoon grated orange peel to the creamed butter and honey. When the batter is mixed, stir in ⅔ cup chopped dates and ½ cup chopped, toasted nuts.

CINNAMON-CURRANT BREAD

Simple and sweet, nice enough for dessert; splendid sandwiching with nut butter or creamy mild cheese.

When you sift the flours, add 1 teaspoon cinnamon. Fold into the finished batter ½ cup currants or chopped raisins. Depending on how you plan to use this bread, you may want to add more honey.

Dark and moist, sweet and plenty festive for holiday fare—but not too heavy for other days. One of our best quick breads.

Follow This One's for Adele but use molasses for sweetener and butter for fat. When sifting the flours, add 1 teaspoon cinnamon, ¼ teaspoon allspice, and pinches of nutmeg and clove. For the water, substitute 1 cup apple juice plus ¼ cup orange juice, and add 1 teaspoon rum or brandy flavoring, or 2 teaspoons booze. When the batter is mixed, fold in ½ cup raisins and 1 cup grated fresh apple. This one may take an extra 15 minutes in the oven.

Persimmon-Nut Bread

Rich in flavor as well as festive in spirit, this bread makes an occasion of dessert, with or without homemade vanilla ice cream.

&

Preheat oven to 350°F. Grease an 8″ × 4″ loaf pan or an equivalent-sized pan (6 cups) of a more festive shape so long as it is not too narrow or deep to bake well.

Cream the butter and honey. Beat in the egg and then mix in the persimmon pulp.

Sift the dry ingredients together. Stir in the nuts. Add them all at once to the liquid ingredients, stirring lightly just until well-mixed. Turn the batter into the pan, place it inside another similar pan or on a cookie sheet, and bake 45 to 50 minutes, until done.

3 tablespoons butter,
    at room temperature
¼ cup honey
1 egg
1 cup persimmon pulp

1½ cups whole wheat
    pastry flour
½ cup whole wheat
    bread flour
2 teaspoons baking powder
½ teaspoon baking soda
½ teaspoon ginger
½ teaspoon salt
pinch cloves

½ cup chopped walnuts
    or pecans

Carrot-Prune Bread

¼ cup honey
3 tablespoons oil
½ teaspoon cinnamon

1 cup water
2 tablespoons lemon juice

1½ cups whole wheat
  pastry flour
¾ cup whole wheat
  bread flour
2½ teaspoons baking
  powder
½ teaspoon salt
½ teaspoon baking soda
½ cup wheat germ

1 cup grated carrots
¾ cup chopped pitted
  prunes
½ cup chopped
  toasted nuts

This sweet and flavorful bread makes good muffins, too.

₰

Preheat oven to 350°F. Grease either an 8″ × 4″ loaf pan or a 12-cup muffin tin.

Beat honey, oil and cinnamon with a fork. Stir in the water and lemon juice. Sift the dry ingredients together, adding the wheat germ at the end. Add dry to liquid ingredients, mixing just enough to combine them thoroughly, but no more. Fold in the carrots, prunes, and nuts.

Spoon the batter into loaf pan or muffin tin. Bake 45 to 55 minutes for the loaf, about 20 for the muffins.

APRICOT-PRUNE BREAD

Soften ¾ cup dried apricots in 2 cups very hot water. Drain, saving 1¼ cup of the liquid to use for the water measure in the bread. Chop the apricots and use them instead of the carrots. Omit the cinnamon and the lemon juice.

APRICOT-NUT BREAD

Make Apricot-Prune Bread but leave out the prunes.

Banana Bread

This sweet bread is at once moister and more flavorful than what we modestly think is an already excellent recipe in *Laurel's Kitchen*. Use ripe bananas, but not squishy half-fermented ones—the bread will be as good as the fruit.

The recipe is designed to use up a lot of bananas—about six—twice as many as most banana-bread recipes we know of. If you haven't got a surfeit of ripe bananas, you can substitute an egg or two for part of the banana measure. The bread will be a little lighter, a little subtler in flavor.

❧

Preheat oven to 350°F. Grease an 8″ × 4″ loaf pan.

Use a fork to beat the sweetener and fat, vanilla and salt. Add the banana and lemon juice. Sift the flours and leavenings and mix the wet and dry ingredients. Fold in the dates and nuts, reserving about 3 tablespoons of the nuts to sprinkle on top of the loaf before baking.

Spoon into the loaf pan and bake as long as an hour and a half, until done. Depending on the bananas, this bread can be very sweet—sweet enough to stand in danger of burning on the outside before it is done; if possible, place the filled loaf pan inside a second pan to protect your crust.

If you want a pretty topping for this bread, brush it with oil or melted butter when done, and sprinkle with date sugar, then return to the oven for a couple of minutes.

APPLESAUCE BREAD

Substitute untart applesauce for the bananas, and add 1½ teaspoons cinnamon (and ½ teaspoon cloves plus ⅛ teaspoon nutmeg, if you like them). Use raisins instead of dates.

½ cup date sugar
  or ⅓ cup honey
3 tablespoons oil or butter
1 teaspoon vanilla (optional)
½ teaspoon salt
2 cups mashed ripe bananas
2 tablespoons lemon juice

1½ cups whole wheat
  pastry flour
½ cup whole wheat
  bread flour
2 teaspoons baking powder
½ teaspoon baking soda
  ½ cup chopped dates
  or dried apricots
½ cup chopped, toasted
  walnuts, pecans, or
  filberts

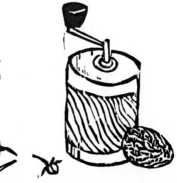

Orange-Cranberry Bread

¾ cup cranberries,
  coarsely chopped
½ cup raisins, chopped
1 tablespoon grated undyed
  orange peel
1¼ cups orange juice
¼ cup honey
¼ cup butter or oil

1½ cups whole wheat
  pastry flour
½ cup whole wheat
  bread flour
2½ teaspoons baking powder
½ teaspoon baking soda
½ teaspoon salt
½ cup wheat germ
½ cup lightly toasted
  chopped walnuts

Seasonal, of course, and all the more special because of it, this tangy-sweet bread is unique, pretty, and delicious.

❧

Preheat oven to 375°F. Grease an 8″ × 4″ loaf pan. Combine in a saucepan cranberries, raisins, orange peel, juice, and honey. Bring to a boil, stir in the butter or oil, and remove from heat. Allow to cool while measuring and combining the other ingredients.

Sift the flours, leavenings, and salt, and stir in the wheat germ. When the liquid mixture has cooled to lukewarm, stir in the dry ingredients and fold in the nuts, reserving 3 tablespoons for the topping.

Spread the batter in a loaf pan. Sprinkle the nuts on top and press them down lightly with your hand or the back of a spoon.

Bake for 50 to 60 minutes, or until done. Test with a clean knife or toothpick, but if you should pierce a cranberry, the testing device will come out wet, so try in more than one spot to be sure.

Let the loaf rest in its pan on a wire rack for ten minutes, and then turn it out on the rack to set for at least half an hour more before cutting. If you can wait longer—it really is worth it—the slices will be less likely to crumble.

Old-Fashioned Scones

These really are good. Since they take only about two minutes to mix up, be sure to start preheating the oven before you begin mixing. The oven should be up to temperature when the scones go in.

ੳ

Preheat oven to 375°F. Dust a cookie sheet with flour.

Sift flour, soda, cream of tartar, salt, and sugar (if you use honey instead, stir it thoroughly into the buttermilk). Grate the cold butter into the mixture and blend with a pastry cutter or with your fingertips until the mixture is like oatmeal flakes. Stir in the buttermilk and currants, and mix gently and quickly, until barely blended together. Immediately turn out onto the floured cookie sheet and pat into a circle about ¾ inch thick, 8 or 9 inches across. Cut the circle into wedges, 4 or 6 as you see fit, and place immediately in the hot oven

Bake about 20 minutes. Serve at once.

PLAIN SCONES

Increase the butter to 3 tablespoons and omit the sweetener and currants.

*2 cups whole wheat
  pastry flour*
1 teaspoon baking soda*
1 teaspoon cream of tartar*
½ teaspoon salt
*1 or 2 tablespoons
  brown sugar or honey*

2 tablespoons cold butter

*1 cup plus 2 tablespoons
  buttermilk at room
  temperature*
½ cup currants

**If you don't have cream of
tartar, use ½ teaspoon baking
soda and 1½ teaspoons baking powder.*

GRIDDLE SCONES

If you prefer, you can bake either kind on a medium hot, un-greased griddle. Flour both sides of the scones, and turn when they are brown on the bottom. Adjust the heat so that the scone cooks through before it burns—that will take a little ex-perimentation and the flour on the griddle will burn for sure. Just dust it off.

Quick Rye Breads

These breads are as remarkable and as distinctive as corn-breads, though in a very different mode. They are not just poor relations of the yeasted ryes, either, but have a delicacy and warm flavor all their own.

Honey-Spiced Rye

⅓ cup honey
1⅓ cups water
3 tablespoons oil
2 teaspoons grated
    orange rind
¾ teaspoon salt
1 teaspoon cinnamon
pinch each
    cloves and anise seed
⅛ teaspoon each
    ginger and allspice
2 tablespoons lemon juice

1 cup whole wheat flour
1½ cups whole rye flour
2½ teaspoons baking powder
½ teaspoon baking soda

½ cup chopped
    toasted almonds

Festive of flavor, with a spicy perfume, this bread is quite nice enough for giving (and eating) on any occasion, holiday or not.

For a longer-keeping, slightly heavier loaf, use all rye flour. Decrease the water to 1 cup and bake about 1 hour and 10 minutes.

⊰⊱

Preheat oven to 350°F. Grease an 8″ × 4″ loaf pan. Combine the wet ingredients and the spices, beating them smooth with a fork.

Sift the flours, baking powder, and soda together. Add them gradually to the liquids to make a mixture that is slightly wetter than other quick bread batters. Stir in the almonds, reserving 2 tablespoons to sprinkle on the top.

Bake about 45 minutes to an hour. Cool before slicing.

Orange-Rye

Reminiscent of Swedish rye bread, but cakier, and wonderfully perfumey.

ᘒ

Preheat oven to 350°F. Grease an 8″ × 4″ loaf pan.

Sift the flours, salt and baking powder together, then add the wheat germ.

Beat the egg yolk into the oil and honey. Add the milk, seeds, and orange rind.

Beat the egg white until stiff.

Stir the dry ingredients into the liquids just enough to mix. Fold in the egg white. Spread mixture in the loaf pan and bake about 45 minutes.

1½ cups whole wheat flour
1 cup rye flour
1 teaspoon salt
1 tablespoon baking powder
½ cup wheat germ

1 egg, separated
3 tablespoons oil
3 tablespoons honey

1¼ cups milk
1 teaspoon anise seeds
1 tablespoon grated undyed
    orange rind

Corn Rye

Dark and moist and flavorful, this bread is not at all sweet.

ᘒ

Preheat oven to 350°F. Grease an 8″ × 4″ loaf pan. Sift the dry ingredients together, adding the caraway seed to the rest after sifting. Beat the oil, molasses, and egg together, and stir in the buttermilk. Add the dry ingredients to the wet, stirring just enough to mix. Put in the loaf pan and bake about an hour.

1½ cups rye flour
1 cup cornmeal
2½ teaspoons baking powder
½ teaspoon baking soda
¾ teaspoon salt
2 teaspoons caraway seed

3 tablespoons oil
3 tablespoons molasses
1 egg
1¼ cups buttermilk

Cornbreads

We'd been told that true Southerners won't touch cornbread made with yellow corn, but at least one authentic Virginian to whom we have an inside line says the crucial factors are *fresh* cornmeal, *coarse* grind, and *no* sweetener, please. We never made perfect cornbread for her until we ground the corn ourselves, and *voilà*—North and South united in applauding! If the cornmeal is not absolutely fresh, the cornbread will have a slight bitterness from rancidity, which some folks prize and others cover up by adding sweeteners.

"Southern" Cornbread in our kitchen turns out to be our Basic Cornbread, with freshly ground cornmeal and no honey.

Without a doubt, cornbread is the quick bread we make most frequently—most often the Basic recipe, which seems to us the very best of all. It also makes 12 fine muffins, when you want muffins.

Basic Cornbread

1 teaspoon salt
1 teaspoon baking powder
½ teaspoon baking soda
2½ cups cornmeal

1 to 2 tablespoons honey
1 to 2 large eggs, beaten
1 to 2 tablespoons oil
2 cups buttermilk*

Preheat oven to 425°F. Grease an 8″ × 8″ pan or muffin tin.

Sift the salt, baking powder, and soda together and combine with the cornmeal. Mix the wet ingredients together, and then add the dry, stirring just until smooth. Turn into the greased pan and bake about 20 or 25 minutes; a little longer if you added vegetables—or only about 15 minutes for muffins.

Add 1 or even 1½ cups grated raw yellow or green zucchini, for a very moist cornbread—the yellow squash is pretty nearly undetectable, the green very pretty. Or add 1 cup grated carrots, also very pretty. It is not a bad idea to include two eggs (reduce the buttermilk to 1½ cups) when adding the vegetables to help the bread cook well.

This recipe makes a rather coarse, grainy-textured bread, particularly when the cornmeal is medium-coarse grind. To maximize the graininess, use a very coarse cornmeal; let the corn soak in the wet ingredients for an hour or so before you sift the leavenings and stir them in. If you prefer a closer crumb texture, use finely ground cornmeal, or substitute 1 cup or so of whole wheat pastry flour for an equivalent amount of cornmeal, sifting it with the leavenings. With the whole wheat pastry flour, the texture will be lighter and the flavor less corny, as it is in the next recipe.

If you haven't got any buttermilk, use regular milk soured with white or cider vinegar (1 tablespoon vinegar plus milk to make 1 cup). Yogurt, beaten smooth, can substitute for buttermilk, but depending on how tart it is, increase the honey to compensate: our yogurt is medium-sour and even with 2 tablespoons of honey in Basic Cornbread the bread is downright tangy.

Yankee Cornbread

Very sweet and moist, this bread browns beautifully. Let it cool for 15 minutes before cutting.

&

Preheat the oven to 350°F. Grease an 8″ × 8″ pan.

Melt the butter and stir in the honey. Combine with the buttermilk and beaten eggs.

Place cornmeal in bowl and sift flour, salt, and leavenings into it; stir to mix. Add the buttermilk mixture and combine. Turn into the greased pan and bake 40 to 45 minutes.

3 tablespoons butter
3 tablespoons honey
2 cups buttermilk
 (at room temperature)
2 large eggs, beaten

1¾ cups yellow cornmeal
1 cup whole wheat flour
¾ teaspoon salt
1 teaspoon baking powder
½ teaspoon soda

Corn Crackers

1 cup cornmeal
*½ cup whole wheat
    pastry flour*
1 teaspoon salt
¼ teaspoon baking soda
¼ teaspoon chili powder
*2 tablespoons grated
    cheddar cheese*

2 tablespoons oil
½ cup buttermilk

It's hard not to use too many superlatives about these crackers. They are super.

Preheat the oven to 350°F.

Measure the cornmeal into a bowl and sift in the flour, salt, baking soda, and chili powder. Stir in the cheese along with any bran that might have been left behind in the sifter from the flour.

Mix the oil and buttermilk, and add to the dry ingredients, forming a soft, moist dough. Form into two balls.

Use two well-greased large (12" × 18") baking sheets without sides. Flatten the balls one at a time, and roll them out to cover the baking sheets—if you have the persistence, they will. Use a piece of waxed paper on top to keep the dough from sticking to the rolling pin. With a pizza cutter, a spatula, or any other method you want, score the rolled-out dough into cracker-sized pieces.

Bake for 5 to 10 minutes, *being very careful not to let them get more than delicately brown.* The recipe makes about eighty 2-inch crackers, depending on how thin you were able to roll them. Please don't let them burn.

A small aside: Should you be tempted cleverly to invert a baking sheet that does have sides, using the back, be warned that unless you support the pan completely under its middle, you will end up after much effort with crackers very thick in the middle of the pan and very thin at the edges, and you with a high level of frustration. (Ask me how I know.)

Muffin Recipes

Nearly everyone enjoys muffins. They are a friendly and comfortable sort of bread, quicker than loaves both in the baking and in the serving: no slicing required, eat them hot from the oven.

For complementing a menu of soup and salad, consider savory muffins instead of sweet ones. We include a couple of good recipes in the pages that follow, and you can easily take off from there. (Most quick loaves, for example, make fine muffins.) If you use our loaf recipes for making muffins, you may end up with some extra batter: either make a few more muffins, or bake the remaining batter in greased custard cups. If you find yourself with unoccupied space in your muffin tin, the old trick of pouring ¼ cup warm water in the unused cups is a good one. It protects the pan and may actually help the muffins cook better.

Our recipes fill a normal muffin tin with small cups that hold just over ¼ cup by measure. For the larger size muffin tins — they hold nearly ½ cup in each dip — double the recipe to make 12.

Basic Muffins

1½ cups whole wheat
    pastry flour
1½ teaspoons baking powder
½ teaspoon salt
½ teaspoon cinnamon
    (optional)
2 tablespoons powdered milk

3 tablespoons butter,
    room temperature, or oil
3 tablespoons honey
    or light molasses
1 egg
½ cup raisins, chopped
¾ cup water

½ cup chopped nuts
    (optional)

Tasty and quick; serve these piping hot for a light but satisfying complement to a simple meal.

℀

Preheat oven to 375°F. Grease a 12-cup muffin tin.

Sift the dry ingredients together. Cream the butter and honey, or stir the honey into the oil. Beat in the egg and add the raisins and water. Stir the dry ingredients into the liquid, mixing enough to moisten. Fold in the nuts, if you want to use them. Spoon into the muffin tin.

Bake 10 to 14 minutes, or until the center springs back when pressed. If you use honey rather than molasses, and pastry flour ground from white wheat, the muffins will be quite pale.

ORANGE-APRICOT MUFFINS

Omit the cinnamon and substitute orange juice for the water. Use ½ cup chopped dried apricots instead of raisins—if they are hard, steam or soak them in hot water before chopping them. These muffins are very good without eggs and butter: use oil, and increase the orange juice by ¼ cup.

FRUIT JUICE MUFFINS

Omit milk powder and substitute any fairly sweet fruit juice for the water.

FRESH FRUIT MUFFINS

Fold ½ cup chopped fresh fruit into the basic batter. Vary the spices: with apples, use cinnamon; with peaches, nutmeg is just right; ginger complements pears very nicely. If the fruit is not very sweet, increase the honey by a tablespoon or so.

Best Bran Muffins

This is a mighty fine recipe. We think it supplies everything you could want from a bran muffin. Make 12 of them, or try 6 muffins and a 3″ × 7″ loaf. Or bake a few muffins and store the batter in the refrigerator for as long as ten days, using it as you need it. The tiny loaf makes a nice tea bread with a creamy tofu or cheese-and-fruit spread, or with nut butter.

ॐ

Preheat oven to 375°F. Grease pan or pans.

Sift flour, soda, and salt together, and stir in the bran. Beat butter or oil and sugar and molasses together, and add egg and buttermilk. Mix dry ingredients into liquids. Place in the pan or pans you have prepared, filling muffin tins about three-quarters full. Bake muffins 15 to 20 minutes; the loaf about half an hour.

VARIATION If you like raisins or currants in your bran muffins, don't be shy about stirring ½ cup of either into the batter.

1 cup whole wheat flour
1 teaspoon baking soda
½ teaspoon salt
1½ cups bran

3 tablespoons butter or oil
2 tablespoons brown sugar*
2 tablespoons molasses
1 egg
1½ cups buttermilk

*Again, brown sugar really does work better in this recipe, but honey or all light molasses can be used instead.

Peanutty Corn Muffins

¾ cup whole wheat flour
1 teaspoon baking powder
¾ teaspoon baking soda
½ teaspoon salt
¾ cup cornmeal
¼ cup roasted peanuts,
    finely chopped

1 tablespoon oil
¼ cup unsalted peanut
    butter (crunchy is best)
2 tablespoons honey

1½ cups buttermilk
1 egg, slightly beaten

Tried and true, and a sure hit with the younger set.

❧

Preheat oven to 375°F. Grease a 12-cup muffin tin.

Sift flour, baking powder, soda, and salt, and stir in the cornmeal and peanuts. (You can skip the peanuts if you don't have any handy, but they do add charm.)

Beat together oil, peanut butter, and honey. Add buttermilk and egg. Stir dry ingredients into wet, mixing until barely smooth. Spoon into muffin cups and, if you like, sprinkle more chopped peanuts on top. Bake in hot oven 12 to 15 minutes.

Cheese Muffins

Use a good robust cheese in these or the flavor won't come through. These are great favorites.

ર

Preheat oven to 375°F. Grease a 12-cup muffin tin.

If you use chives, they need not be cooked, but the onions are best when sautéed until soft in the butter or oil. Let the sautéed onion cool before adding to the batter.

Beat the egg, butter or oil, and onion or chives together. Stir in the buttermilk and seasoned cheese.

Blend the oats in blender to make about 1½ cups of floury meal — or use 1 cup oat flour and ½ cup rolled oat flakes. Sift the other dry ingredients together and then stir in the flakes. Add the dry ingredients to the cheese mixture, stirring just enough to mix.

Spoon into the muffin tin and bake about 15 minutes. These muffins are a pale, creamy color on top, and golden brown on the bottom and sides when done.

2 tablespoons minced
    chives or onions
2 tablespoons butter or oil

1 egg
1¼ cups buttermilk
½ cup grated Swiss
    cheese and
    ¾ teaspoon dill weed
    or parsley
OR
½ cup grated cheddar
    cheese and
    ½ teaspoon mustard

2 cups rolled oats
½ cup whole wheat flour
½ teaspoon salt
½ teaspoon baking soda
2 teaspoons baking powder

Zucchini Cheese Muffins

Like the previous recipe, but a good vehicle for the Green Sorcerer's Apprentice.

ર

Preheat oven to 375°F. Grease a 12-cup muffin tin. Sauté the onions in butter or oil.

Mix the egg, butter or oil and onion, and oats together. Stir in cheese, zucchini, and water. Sift together flour, salt, and baking powder. Add the dry ingredients to the zucchini mixture, stirring just enough to mix.

Spoon into the muffin tin and bake 20 minutes.

2 tablespoons minced onions
2 tablespoons butter or oil

1 egg, slightly beaten

½ cup oat flakes
½ cup grated Swiss cheese
1½ cups grated zucchini
⅔ cup water

1⅓ cups whole wheat flour
½ teaspoon salt
2½ teaspoons baking powder

Blueberry Muffins

1 cup blueberries
¼ cup whole wheat
    pastry flour

1 cup whole wheat
    pastry flour
1¾ teaspoons baking powder
½ teaspoon salt
½ teaspoon cinnamon
½ cup wheat germ

3 tablespoons butter or oil
¼ cup brown sugar*

1 egg, lightly beaten
¾ cup milk

*Honey is good too, but in
this recipe, brown sugar is
better.

These are not your ordinary pale, puffy, supersweet blueberry
muffins; they are brown, spicy, and wonderful. Steam-softened
currants can sub for the blueberries when they are out of season, but we confess that we have made these muffins successfully with frozen and canned berries, as well as fresh. As usual,
pastry flour is best for muffins, but in these, regular flour
works too.

ᕗ

Preheat oven to 375°F. Grease a 12-cup muffin tin.

Wash and drain the berries. Sprinkle with the ¼ cup flour
and let them sit while you prepare the batter.

Sift together the remaining flour, baking powder, salt, and
cinnamon. Add the wheat germ.

Cream the butter and sugar (or honey), and beat in the
egg. (If oil is used, just beat them all together.) Add the milk
and dry ingredients, stirring just enough to mix somewhat,
and then fold in the berries. Spoon into muffin cups—fill them
nearly full—and bake for 15 to 20 minutes or until a toothpick
inserted in the center of one muffin comes out clean.

Date-Nut Muffins

Preheat oven to 375°F. Grease a 12-cup muffin tin.

Sift the flour, salt, baking powder, and soda. Stir in the dates, nuts, and wheat germ. Beat the remaining ingredients together until smooth, then combine all, stirring just enough to mix. Spoon into muffin cups and bake about 15 to 20 minutes.

VARIATION Instead of apple juice, use buttermilk and add an egg. Reduce the salt to ¼ teaspoon. For a Date-Nut Loaf, bake this version in an 8″ × 4″ loaf. Bake at 350°F for about 55 minutes.

1 ¼ cups whole wheat
    pastry flour
½ teaspoon salt
2 teaspoons baking powder
½ teaspoon baking soda

½ cup chopped dates
½ cup chopped nuts
½ cup wheat germ, or bran

3 tablespoons light molasses
2 tablespoons oil
1 cup apple juice
1 teaspoon grated lemon rind
¼ teaspoon allspice

Maple Pecan Muffins

These are subtle and slightly chewy, much lighter than the usual praline-like maple confections.

❧

Preheat oven to 375°F. Grease a 12-cup muffin tin.

Sift flour, baking powder, and salt together. Stir in nuts. Beat syrup and butter or oil, and add the egg. Add water, vanilla, and the dry ingredients, stirring just enough to mix. Spoon into muffin tin, and bake 12 to 15 minutes.

1 ½ cups whole wheat flour
1 ½ teaspoons baking powder
½ teaspoon salt

½ cup chopped pecans

¼–⅓ cup maple syrup
2 tablespoons soft butter
    or oil
1 egg
⅔ cup water
1 teaspoon vanilla

How to Slice a Brick

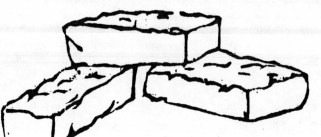

Dear Laurel,

I've been trying for months now to learn how to bake whole-grain bread. When my loaves don't make it I just throw them into the freezer and keep going. I have a freezer full of bricks now, but I'm determined not to give up. Any advice would be welcome—on baking bread, or using up bricks.

K.C.

How many doorstops can you use, really? Sooner or later, some of that good food gone awry must be used constructively (and not for construction either). Until the fine points of breadmaking are perfected, here are a few ploys that can help.

First of all, the point must be made: bread does not have to be light to be good. There are a lot of people who prefer it hefty; maybe you are one of them—though probably you wouldn't be reading this if you were. People who like heavy bread don't use the word bricks. They take the gourmet stance, waft their French vegetable knives, and demand of their guests, have you ever tasted such flavorful bread? Usually it *is* delicious. If anyone asks, you can say it is Eastphalian Pumpernickel.

But maybe the whole thing has gone beyond humor; maybe, say, there is someone in your family who has to face the critical eyes of fellow sixth-graders and so must have sandwiches as much like store-bought as possible... or someone else may just want sandwiches that don't look like they were made on theater tickets. Try this: the technique is as effective as it is screwy—remember, we've had plenty of bricks to practice on in the last decade or so!

Cut your brick in half, making two squarish pieces. Now stand one of the squares on its cut side, and starting parallel to the (former) bottom of the loaf, slice downwards, cutting about four 4-inch square slices, quite thin. Repeat with the other half. *Voilà!* Respectable slices, elegant sandwiches. The crust pieces will be formidable, I admit. Our dogs consider this sort of thing to be the last word in treats—cut them into milk-bone sized bars. By this technique you can usually count on getting eight acceptable slices and a lot of doggie treats from one dud of a loaf. Not bad and better luck next time!

A word of encouragement: we were just working on the Loaf for Learning section when the letter from K.C. arrived. We sent a few suggestions from Loaf and very soon another letter arrived, enclosing a picture of a beautiful, beaming K.C., holding in one hand a brick—and in the other, a high, perfectly baked loaf. Before and after! It was grand.

Refreshing Leftover Loaves

Heavy or light, when a loaf has lost its just-baked appeal, it may not be stale, actually, it may be asking only for a little refreshing to bring it back to goodness. A trick that works amazingly well is to wrap the loaf in a towel dampened with hot water and wrung out. Put it in a covered casserole or wrap it in foil or put it in a clean brown bag, and warm it in the oven at medium heat for 15 or 20 minutes.

The steaming can be done on top of the stove, too, and even faster. Put the wrapped bread in a perforated pan or steamer basket over boiling water. Adjust the towels, water level, and the heat so that you end up with hot, soft, unsoggy bread, and no burned towels: it may take a little fussing, but the results are very dependable once you work out your system. This procedure is useful not only for refreshing tired loaves, sliced or unsliced, but also for warming rolls or heating up muffins and cornbread.

Days-old bread is useful in many ways, even if you wouldn't want to make sandwiches out of it. If the bread is light, it can become bread pudding—savory and cheesy or sweet and custardy—or croutons, to add crunch to soup or salad. Dense, heavy bread can disappoint in bread pudding or as croutons, but works fine made into crumbs. Once they are dried thoroughly, crumbs and croutons will keep a long time stored airtight in the refrigerator.

Bread Pudding

Probably the most popular way to use up stale bread, at least with the younger set, is in bread pudding. In general, it is most delectable when made with light and airy breads, but if you give the heavy ones time to soak up the goodies—at least an hour, better two—they can work too, especially in the savory versions. Keep in mind that there is a lot more bread in a cup of heavy bread cubes than in a cup of light ones; sometimes, twice as much. The light bread will soak up a lot more of the custard. With a heavy bread, check the pudding about halfway through the bake, and if the bread is floating on the top of partially set custard, take a big spoon and give it a righteous stir.

After a light meal, a sweet bread pudding makes a substantial and nourishing dessert, and no apologies. Savory puddings can be just as delicious; taking the place of a grain casserole, for example, they make a hearty foil for green vegetables, soup and salad.

Sweet Bread Pudding

The recipe in *Laurel's Kitchen* is still the best we have come across, but here is a much simpler one that you can vary endlessly with raisins, cinnamon, fruit, nuts; top with toasted coconut, cinnamon, date sugar, or what have you! Use plain or somewhat sweet bread.

4 slices of light bread,
    buttered and cubed
2 cups of warm milk
2 eggs, slightly beaten
¼ to ½ cup honey
    or other sweetener

🖙

Put the bread in a baking dish. Mix the milk, eggs, and sweetener and pour over the bread. Bake at about 325°F an hour, or until brown.

Simple Cheesy Bread Pudding

1 tablespoon butter
4 cups of cubed light
    bread (about 4 slices,
    ½ to ¾ inch thick)
2 cups warm milk
1 egg, slightly beaten
⅓ to ½ cup grated
    sharp cheese

This is a standby for us. Vary it as you like to suit the rest of the menu, and the mood of the bread that wants using. (Sweet or fruity breads aren't well suited to this recipe.) Bear in mind that the bread "slices" we use are good hefty ones. If you've got really thin slices left over, you'll need more.

❧

Use part of the butter to grease an 8″ × 8″ inch pan and put the bread cubes into it. Mix the milk, egg and cheese and pour them over the bread. Dot with the remaining butter. Bake in a moderate oven, about 350°F, until the custard is set and the top nicely brown.

    Let it cool before you eat because it is incredibly hot when it comes out of the oven.

FANCIES

Sesame bread is wonderful in this dish, using cheddar cheese — top it with a tablespoon of toasted seeds.

Rye bread, especially sourdough, is particularly good with an aged Swiss cheese. Add a sautéed onion and a half cup of chopped celery for a delicious casserole.

Croutons

The best croutons come from bread that is airy and not too sweet—light sourdoughs are superb.

For croutons in a hurry, toast bread slices in a toaster, butter them, and cut into cubes. Croutons made in this way will be soft in the middle and are not meant for storing but for eating up right away.

To make plain croutons that will keep a long time, cut bread into ½- to 1-inch cubes, trimming off the crust if you think it is necessary. Spread the cubes on a shallow pan and keep an eye on them while they bake very slowly until they become 100 percent crunchy. (Chomp on one: no other way to be sure that I know of.) If the bread contains milk or much sweetener, take care when toasting it to prevent its getting too brown. Cool thoroughly and store airtight.

Just plain, good crunchy croutons add extra interest to soups or salads. Or you can flavor them either before or after the toasting, to complement whatever you will serve them with. The traditional method uses considerable fat: either spread slices of bread with herbed butter, cube, and toast in oven or skillet; or toast already cubed bread in a skillet with herbs and olive oil or garlic and butter or whatever suits. Usually a little extra salt is welcome, but keep a light hand.

Whether the bread is already cut and toasted or not, you can flavor it using a whole lot less fat, sometimes none at all. Select savory flavorings: sautéed onion, garlic; herbs like celery leaves, parsley, thyme, or dill weed; salt, soy sauce, lemon juice or peel—to mention just a few possibilities. Blend the seasonings with a compatible liquid—water, broth, milk, tomato juice, whatever, allowing about half a cup of the flavoring brew per quart of croutons (four slices of a normal-sized loaf). Toss the cubed bread with the liquid and put into the oven until crisp.

Stuffing

1 medium onion, chopped
⅓ cup oil
2 stalks celery,
    chopped (about 1 cup)
1 teaspoon basil
½ teaspoon salt
    (reduce or omit if
    salted stock is used)
½ teaspoon oregano
¼ teaspoon thyme
⅛ teaspoon sage
shake of pepper
⅔ cup water or
    vegetable stock

4 cups whole-grain
    bread cubes
½ cup pecans, optional

What does a vegetarian stuff? Why, tomatoes, green peppers, oversized zucchinis, winter squash—or, with this delicious dish, simply oneself and one's friends.

≈

Sauté the onion in the oil and add the celery and herbs, cooking until the celery is crispy-tender. Add the water or stock, then the bread, stirring to be sure it is evenly moistened. When hot through, add the pecans if desired.

Serve at once, or bake to make a crispy top. Serves about four people as a hearty grain dish at lunch or dinner.

Crumbs

Truly heavy bricks don't make the best bread pudding or croutons, but grated into crumbs, then tossed in a skillet with olive
oil, garlic, and herbs, and toasted crisp, they find honorable
service atop casseroles or stirred into steamed sliced carrots or
broccoli chunks. Toasted buttery rather than garlicky, crumbs
function nicely in fruit betty, too; or use them plain or flavored
to coat patties, to top stuffed tomatoes or peppers, or to make a
crumb crust. More good ideas follow, and there is no need to
limit your crumbing to heavy breads. The lightest ones are delectable, needless to say.

There may be as many ways to make bread into crumbs as
there are cooks to make them. If the bread is not sliced and is
dry or firm, it is easy to grate it on a normal food/vegetable
grater, using whatever size grate works best. Keep your touch
light, especially if the bread is a little moist. When you are doing a whole loaf's worth, it is a big help to have a bowl that fits
comfortably under the grater; otherwise, use a sheet of waxed
paper or a chopping board, and turn the crumbs into a bowl as
you work.

Maybe the easiest way, and surely the noisiest, is to make
the crumbs in the blender or food processor. Follow the manufacturer's directions. Usually, cut the bread into chunks about
1½-inch maximum; put in just enough to cover the blades,
plus a little. Turn the machine on for a few seconds, then
check. Repeat as needed. *Between blendings,* stir the crumbs
with the handle of a wooden spoon to keep them from packing
under the blades. This method works even if the bread is quite
fresh.

Herbed Crumb Muffins

1½ cups whole wheat flour
¾ teaspoon salt
2 teaspoons baking powder
1 cup whole-grain bread
    crumbs
2 tablespoons grated
    Parmesan cheese

3 tablespoons oil
1 tablespoon honey
1 egg
2 tablespoons chopped
    chives
    OR
minced raw or
    sautéed onions
3 tablespoons finely
    chopped parsley
1 cup milk

Hearty but not heavy, these make a satisfying accompaniment
to soup and salad.

                              ❧

Preheat the oven to 375°F.

Sift flour, salt, and baking powder. Stir in the bread
crumbs and cheese.

Combine oil, honey, egg, onion, parsley, and milk, stirring to dissolve the honey.

Add the dry ingredients to the liquids, mixing just enough
to moisten them. Spoon into greased muffin tins and bake in
preheated oven for 15 to 20 minutes.

Makes 12.

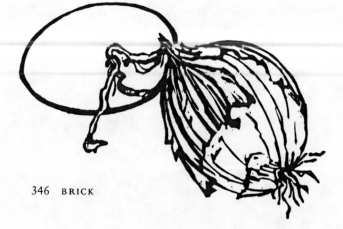

Crumby Greens

A delicious way to use garden greens, whether you serve as is, stuff into tomatoes or steamed ripe bell peppers, or bake in patties.

ᒿ

Sauté the leek or onion in the oil until soft. Remove from heat, and stir in the remaining ingredients. If you're baking these, form 6 small patties, roll in more crumbs, and bake in a greased pan at 350°F until the crumbs on top are nicely browned.

This recipe is a happening: add whatever sweet vegetables are in season. These are good: fresh corn off the cob, diced red bell pepper, chopped coriander leaves.

1 leek or a medium onion, chopped
¼ cup oil
½-inch slice of fresh ginger, minced fine
1½ cups fresh greens, cooked and very well drained
1 cup lightly toasted crumbs
salt and pepper to taste

Crumb Pancakes

These are very flavorful, and if the crumbs are made from light bread, the pancakes are at least as light as normal ones. If you have rye bread crumbs, serve the pancakes with yogurt and applesauce: wow!

The taste, the texture, and especially the sweetness of the bread you use will make them different every time, so vary the amount of the added sweetener as seems appropriate to you.

ᒿ

Soak the crumbs and flavoring in the milk for several hours. Sift together the flour and soda. Add these and the eggs to the bread crumb mixture and drop like pancakes on a hot, seasoned griddle. Makes 6 to 8.

1 cup bread crumbs (not dried)
1 tablespoon sweetener,
  OR
whatever flavoring seems right
1 cup buttermilk

½ cup whole wheat flour, scant
½ teaspoon soda
1 large or 2 small eggs, slightly beaten

Tykmaelk

This simple and satisfying dish could be breakfast or lunch or a midnight snack. It is presented as fondly remembered from a year in Copenhagen, where it is a specialty at the famous Strawberry Cellar restaurant.

ELEGANT VERSION, QUITE AUTHENTIC

Choose large shallow soup bowls that hold about 1½ cups. Heat enough rich, unhomogenized milk to fill them, warming it slowly so that it is gradually reduced in volume by one-fourth. Cool to 120°F. Stir in fresh yogurt, about a teaspoonful per bowl, and pour the inoculated milk into the bowls. Keep them at about 90° to 100°F for 3 to 4 hours, or until set. The result should be softer than regular yogurt, and less sour. There will be a delicate creamy-yellow skin on the top. Chill.

Over each bowl of cultured milk, sprinkle about ½ inch of crunchy-chewy sourdough rye bread crumbs.

Serve with a small bowl of coarse brown sugar, which is to be sprinkled on top to taste.

QUICKER VERSION & NO EXCUSES

Use mild yogurt, kefir, or even good buttermilk. Put it in a cereal bowl. Over the top, sprinkle crumbs; if you don't have sourdough rye, any innovation is fair. The sugar is optional if you aren't being authentic.

Using (Accidentally) Saltless Loaves

A word here on the sad subject of (accidentally) saltless bread. Many people simply can't abide the taste of toast or sandwiches made on such bread, and if you or yours fall into this group, use the loaves to make bread pudding, flavored crumbs, or any of the other recipes in this section that seem appropriate, depending on how heavy the bread is. Add 1¼ teaspoon of salt for each *loaf's* worth of bread, mixing it into the recipe wherever it will be best absorbed by the bread. Note that if the bread did not rise well, you will not get 1 cup of cubes per slice: gauge the salt by the portion of the loaf that *is* included, whatever it is.

Dissolve the salt in the liquid, and give the pudding a little time to sit before you bake it, especially if the bread was heavy. Note that for most people, even sweet bread pudding needs *some* salt if the bread doesn't have any.

BREAD PUDDING

Dissolve the desired salt in the flavoring mixture or in plain water or broth if you don't want to add fat. Shake the mixture into the cubed bread or crumbs, making every effort to mix them evenly. Bake until crisp.

CRUMBS & CROUTONS

A Breadmaking Handbook

A Breadmaking Handbook

There are some wonderful gadgets that can make baking easier and even better, and in this section we talk about a few of them and give a lot of tips and information that can be helpful, too. But all this aside, the most important thing is that you get in there and *start baking,* however timid you're feeling, whatever equipment you have at hand.

Whenever I begin to be dazzled by shiny pans, hand-turned bowls and fancy equipment, the figure of Walter Reynolds comes vividly to mind. I met him in the late sixties in Berkeley, a towering, white-bearded Dutchman, broad of chest, big of heart. Just then he was teaching a Free University course, Baking and Giving Away Bread. Even in those days, it was whole wheat all the way for him — but then he was ahead of his time in a lot of ways.

Walter's class met in the Reynolds' kitchen on Wednesday evenings. He would prepare for it by stirring up a vast batch of dough as soon as he got home from work. When his students arrived a couple of hours later, the dough would be rising in a big plastic garbage can. As soon as people walked in they would roll up their sleeves and start to knead up a loaf's worth of Walter's dough. Those first loaves would come out of the oven about the time the students' own dough was ready to rise. Everyone went home with a hot loaf of bread and a very good idea of what breadmaking was all about.

Walter originated a no-equipment method of baking: measure with a coffee can, mix, then turn the dough out on floury newspaper. Knead it well, let the dough rise in any convenient container, grease the coffee can, put in the dough, and let it rise again. Bake, of course, in the can.

Coffee-can bread had become famous two summers before, when Walter and others turned out hundreds of loaves a week from the basement of a church in the Haight-Ashbury district of San Francisco, using donated flour to provide what was sometimes the only sustenance for many of the 'flower children' that received it. A few years later, during the Poor People's March on Washington, the coffee cans reappeared in Resurrection City, where the bread came off the back of Walter's pickup truck, hot from a gas oven converted to propane. The country was just catching on to the idea that whiteness and goodness are not necessarily the same, and Walter and Ruth Reynolds believed good brown bread had a part to play in the drama.

We don't bake in cans anymore, but we still carry with us what Walter taught: a lesson deeper than words about recognizing hunger and doing something pretty daring and friendly to address it. To make nourishing bread, and to reach out with it, continues that loving gesture in some small way.

Sometimes *partway along in a baking* you find that something is wrong. Possible setbacks are listed here, along with suggestions for snatching victory from the jaws of disaster.

The yeast does not bubble up

See page 61.

You forgot to take the flour out of the refrigerator

Flour cold from the refrigerator will make cold, slow-rising dough unless you compensate by using warmer water. To calculate precisely how warm the water needs to be, plug into the formula on page 398 — or, roughly:

> for a 7 hour dough:
> 100°F water
> for a 4 hour dough:
> 120°F water
> for a fast dough:
> 140°F water

Mix the really warm water with the cold flour before you add the yeast, of course. If the yeast comes in contact with 140°F water, it won't survive.

This method should really be considered an emergency measure, not standard procedure. The flour will perform better for you when it has a chance to warm slowly to room temperature overnight.

The dough won't knead up

See page 65.

If you have to give up on it, here are some possibilities: roll the dough thin and make flat bread or crackers instead (millions of them). You can make Chapathis — Indian flat breads, see page 262; they'll be good (if unauthentic) so long as the dough doesn't have too much sweetener in it. Or, make piroshki. (The *Laurel's Kitchen* kind, for example.)

As for the flour, if you bought it with the understanding that it was bread flour, return the rest to the store; they may not know that they are selling low-gluten flour as bread flour. Otherwise, keep it to use for muffins and quick breads, and as dusting flour.

You overkneaded the dough:

Make English Muffins, page 259.

First Aid

The kneaded dough does not rise in the bowl

Somehow, the yeast is not on the job. Dissolve another measure of yeast in ½ cup of properly warm water, with ¼ teaspoon of sweetener stirred in. If the new yeast bubbles to the top in a few minutes looking vigorous and enthusiastic, take your dough and press it out on the kneading board. Drizzle the newly activated yeast and water on the dough, and work them together well.

When the now very wet dough has incorporated the yeast and is smooth, knead in a mixture of about a cup of flour and a ½ teaspoon salt to regain the proper consistency. Let it rise as if you had just mixed the dough.

If there is no good yeast in the house, wrap the dough in plastic or put it in a covered bowl, and refrigerate it. Sometime in the next week, you can get fresh new yeast, bring the lump of dough to room temperature, and proceed as suggested above.

If you want to use the unyeasted dough right away, you can make Chapathis (see previous problem) or even a naturally leavened bread. For the latter, keep the dough at room temperature or cooler until it ripens, about 18 hours. (If there is any life at all in your yeast, it will take less time than that, and may rise, too.) Form the loaves and bake as suggested in the recipe for Manuel's Seed Bread (page 238); it may not be light, but it can be very tasty sliced thin.

You are unexpectedly called away

If you have to leave the rising dough and won't be back for hours, deflate it and put it in the refrigerator (see page 399). Since it will continue to rise until it cools (and even afterward, slowly), allow room in the container, but cover it to keep stray refrigerator flavors out. The dough will be good for a couple of days; after that, since the yeast is still at work, it begins to get old and may make grayish bread. (There is less leeway with fruited dough, by the way, because the fruit gets winey.)

You think you may have forgotten the salt

Whatever stage the dough is, you can taste a pinch of it. You really can trust your guess about whether it has salt or not. If you have to add salt, unless the dough was over-kneaded in the first place, it is worth rolling it out on the kneading board, sprinkling the salt measure evenly over the dough, rolling it up, and kneading until you think the salt is distributed evenly. One way to be sure is to mix the salt into a tablespoon of molasses or poppy seeds so that you can see when it is all mixed.

The dough rips when you shape the loaves

The most usual and least serious cause of tearing is not letting the deflated and rounded dough rest long enough before you shape the loaves. Give it more time. If for whatever reason the gluten is fragile, handle the dough gently to prevent further tearing. Use plenty of dusting flour on the board, or water if you prefer, to minimize friction.

With weak dough, extra handling will just make matters worse, so press the tear with your wetted fingers, repairing it as best you can. You may have to turn the loaf in the pan to find a smooth top surface. The final rise should be not too warm and not too humid — and, for sure, not too long.

The shaped loaves collapse in the pan

Although it may mean a yeasty-flavored loaf, turn the dough out, shape it again, and let it rise once more. If you suspect that the dough has gotten old, adding ½ cup of chopped toasted walnuts will mask the beery taste.

The bread is underbaked

If the loaf has cooled, it is too late to put it in the oven for more cooking. Pull the wad of raw dough out of the center of the loaf and throw it away. Make the rest into crumbs or croutons, toasting them well.

The bread is overbaked

Dry and hard, it will make good crumbs, croutons, or French toast.

Troubleshooting

Sooner or later—mostly sooner—every baker produces a real bomb. The bread didn't rise, or it rose and fell, or the inside is gray and it tastes like old beer. It's embarrassing, to say the least, but you can use the disaster to learn something about breadmaking. This section has been designed to help you figure out what went awry and, we hope, to prevent a recurrence. By the time you finish these pages, you'll be congratulating yourself for all the things that *didn't* go wrong!

If you are a beginner, a few basic things cause the most trouble:

Adding too much flour when kneading.

Not kneading the dough well enough. (Or, in a food processor, maybe too well!)

Keeping the dough too warm, or not warm enough, while it rose. Not giving the loaves long enough—or giving them too long—to rise in the pan.

It is really worth reading through A Loaf for Learning again, and baking bread from it more than once.

If you are not so sure that it was one of the above, here are more specifics that may help.

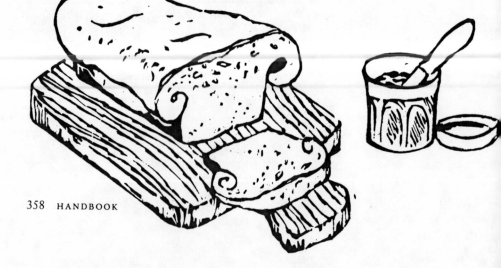

The Bread Didn't Rise Well

Yeast

Was the yeast fresh? Did you dissolve it according to the manufacturer's instructions? Was it exposed to water that was too hot, too cold? That had salt, or too much sweetener?

Rising

Is the bread grayish and strong-tasting? Is the crust thick and the inside crumbly? These are signs that the dough rose too long or too warm. Perhaps you used too much yeast.

Does the bread have a somewhat flat taste? The dough may not have had enough time to ripen. (If that's it, the bread will stale quickly too.) This can happen if the temperature is too low or the time given is too little; or possibly the yeast was old or its measure short.

Proofing

Is the bread coarse and holey near the top? Maybe it rose too long in the pan. Did it (yoik!) collapse? Maybe you jarred it as you put it into the oven, over-proofed or not.

Is the loaf undersized and dense? Here's a tricky one: are the bottom edges of the loaf rounded rather than square like the pan? Did the crust lift away from the loaf and/or seem darker than you expected? If it's a hearth-style loaf, is the bottom rounded and the loaf cracked around the side? Very likely the solution to all these problems is to let the shaped loaf rise warmer or longer.

Flour

Only hard wheat bread flour has the gluten content to make bread rise. All-purpose and pastry flours do not, nor do flours made from anything other than wheat (see page 78). Is the slice dense and hard? Perhaps you simply used too much flour. Next time measure very carefully, and when kneading, try not to add any flour at all on the board, even if the dough seems really sticky at first.

Other ingredients

Adding wheat germ, milk powder, or raw honey can reduce your loaves' size, especially if the bread rises longer than 4 hours total.

Kneading

Did you knead long enough, keeping the dough in a ball and pushing into the center? Did you keep at it for the full count or time? Did you overknead? Not impossible, but unlikely by hand—and easy with a food processor. Look at the slice: is the texture coarse and holey? Next time work it less.

Pan size

Is the loaf squat, but inside, the slice is plenty airy? It sounds like the pan was too big.

Crust Problems

Is the crust pale, thick, and tough?

Probably the oven temperature was too low.

Did you use the sweetener and/or milk the recipe called for? Breads without sweetener or milk are best when baked with steam at a higher temperature (see page 106). If you did include sweetener, but you can't taste it in the bread, the dough may have risen too long or got too warm, or both.

Is the crust terribly dark?

Is it dry inside? It just baked too long. If there are dark areas, or if the top or bottom are particularly affected, your oven has a hot spot. Rotate the bread partway through the baking or move it down or up in the oven to compensate.

If the bread has a lot of milk or milk products or sweetener, the crust will brown deeply perforce. Bake at a lower heat, usually 325°F.

Are there dark spots?

Condensing steam dropping on the loaves causes these.

Did the top crust lift off?

If the bottom edges are rounded, as well, probably the bread was underproofed.

The dough may have been too stiff because of too much flour.

The dough may have dried out and crusted over during the final rising period.

Slightly overproofed bread made from rather slack dough will often collect a pocket of air just under the crust. Slashing helps, but best of all is not to overproof.

Does the crust have blisters?

These can be caused by not deflating the dough completely when you round and shape the loaf; by overproofing a dough that was underfermented; by letting condensed steam drip down on the loaf while it proofs.

Crumb Problems (All that is not crust is crumb)

Is the crumb coarse and holey?

Big holes in an otherwise even crumb come from careless shaping of the loaf.

Did you grease or oil the bowl in which the dough rose? Some of this fat may not get absorbed; the dough separates at these points and gas accumulates. Using too much dusting flour can cause the same problem and so can letting the dough dry out during the second rise, or while it is resting.

If the holes are only at the top of the slice, while the bottom is pretty dense, and maybe the loaf even collapsed a little, it was overproofed. Did you forget the salt? It is easy to overproof saltless bread. If your oven was not hot enough at the beginning of the bake, the bread will continue to rise when it should be baking.

If all the crumb is open and also moist, the dough was too wet.

Is the crumb crumbly?

Usually, the crumb is crumbly if there was too much flour and too little kneading, but it can also be caused by "overing": overkneading, overfermenting, overproofing. Too much wheat germ, bran, oat flakes, and such will do it, too.

Is the crumb uneven?

Cold dough proofed warm may have an open texture on the outside and be dense in the center. Warm dough that is cooler in the final rise may be holey in the center and dense near the crust.

Are there streaks or hard spots in the crumb?

You get hard spots when you pick up bits of hard or gummy scrap from the kneading table; the best place for the stuff that rolls off your hands after kneading is the compost bin. Avoid using too much dusting flour.

You also get streaks when the dough is chilled or dries out during the risings. If fermenting dough gets really crusty there will be gummy places in the bread where it couldn't bake properly.

Flavor & Staling

Is the flavor poor?

If the bread tastes bland and flat, you probably forgot the salt. Bread that is underfermented will also be a little bland and will stale quickly.

If the bread tastes yeasty and looks gray, its rising was too long or too warm or both. Or did you use too much yeast?

Is the flour old or the oil rancid? Did the butter spend the night alongside a half onion in the refrigerator? Fats, flour, milk, eggs—all of them can absorb off-flavors in storage.

Were you experimenting? A new combination of good ingredients doesn't automatically work well.

Does the bread get stale too quickly?

Most of the factors that make poor flavor also make for poor keeping quality. Since no one wants to eat the stuff, it can be around a long time, which doesn't help either.

Overbaked bread is dry and hard, and seems stale from day one.

Bread made in a short time can never keep as well as leisurely loaves do, even when it is made properly.

Some ingredients help bread stay moist and fresh-tasting longer: cooked cereal, stewed or steamed fruit, fat, honey, milk (particularly cultured milk).

Check your storage conditions (see page 426).

About the Ingredients:

Flour

COMMERCIAL MILLS & THEIR PRODUCTS

In the old days most towns had a small grain mill where everyone went to buy flour. We still have a mill in our town, and from across the river it probably looks like it did a hundred years ago. But today inside the Great Petaluma Mill are thirty-three Unique Shoppes, including two restaurants and a candy store.

It was after the invention of the roller mill that small local mills gave way to huge, centralized factories. Freshly ground brown flour from home couldn't compete with the manufactured white flour the new machines produced. With its nearly eternal shelf life and ability to tolerate travel, white flour was not only more glamorous but cheaper and less variable, too.

The modern commercial roller mill is a gigantic affair many stories high. The grain enters on the top and passes through the first, shearing rollers. These break the grains and produce the first powdery-fine flour, which is sieved out through fine cloth. Strong air currents lift off the lightweight bran. What is left is "middlings." These are again milled and separated several times into many distinct flour "streams." The first fine powdery flour from the center of the kernel is *patent flour*. What is taken out of the middlings is *clear flour*. When they are combined, the result is *100 percent straight flour*. It may be 100 percent flour, but it is only 72 percent of the wheat — *72 percent extraction*. All these are kinds of *white* flour. The white flour in the supermarket will be a blend of them, and very likely a blend of different kinds of wheat too, tested and standardized for gluten content and other characteristics.

The other 28 percent of the wheat—the nutritious bran, germ, and "shorts"—is not considered flour and usually becomes animal feed. *Shorts* is whatever won't separate into any of the mill streams, a mixture of everything, about half of the 28 percent. Another milling product, red dog, is taken from the last reduction or tail of the mill, somewhere between low-grade flour and feed. To get whole wheat flour from a big commercial mill of this sort, all these different products are mixed together again in their original proportions.

Big mills have laboratories for analyzing their products. In addition to blending different varieties of wheat to standardize flour quality, various enzymes and chemicals may be added, some of which must be listed on the label. For example, diastatic enzymes may be added in the form of malted barley flour or malted wheat flour. Chemicals used to "bleach" or "improve" the flour include oxides of nitrogen, chlorine, acetone peroxide, ascorbic acid, and potassium bromate. These chemicals are used more often with white flour than whole wheat.

FLOUR FOR
BREADMAKING

If you mean to use the flour for making yeasted bread, don't buy all-purpose or pastry flours: they have too low a gluten content to make light bread. Flours high in gluten are often labeled bread flour, or if the flour comes from a small mill or is stoneground, it may tell on the package the kind of wheat it comes from. You should be able to count on *hard red spring wheat, hard red winter wheat,* and *hard white wheat* to have enough gluten for breadmaking. These are bread flour: the hardness of the kernel is an indication of high protein content. Soft wheats, red or white, have less gluten, and are used either for pastry flour (including whole wheat pastry flour) or as animal feed.

Much of the best wheat in the country comes from Montana, with its long summer days and good soil, but other wheat-growing areas may offer good wheat too: look for a protein content of at least 14 percent for making yeasted whole wheat bread. (Most all-purpose whole wheat flour is around 12 percent, and pastry flour about 6 to 8 percent.) White flour for breadmaking is about 12 percent protein—anything higher would make rubbery bread. Not so with whole wheat, though, because as much as one third of its protein content comes from the brown parts of the grain. Their portion of the protein, since it is not gluten protein, doesn't help make the bread lighter.

Once you have made sure that the flour you buy is high in gluten, the second requirement, no less important, is freshness. Whole wheat flour, unlike white flour, is perishable. Stored at room temperature, it will keep a month; refrigerated, two. After that, unless there are preservatives in the flour or in the packaging, the natural oils in the flour will be getting rancid, and the quality of the bread cannot help but be affected.

If you buy in bulk at a natural food store, find out how often they get flour, from how far away, and how they store it. Taste a pinch of it; it should have a bright flavor, be a little sweet, with no bitterness. If they know you will be wanting fresh flour regularly, they may be glad to get it for you.

If you're buying packaged flour off the shelf, watch out for the date it expires. The trouble is, sometimes these dates are given in a code the consumer isn't privy to. Ask your store-keeper to tell you how to read it, or at least find out how long the flour has been on his shelf. He may not know that whole wheat flour should be stored cool, or that it doesn't keep a long time. Once you get the flour home, store it airtight in the refrigerator.

There are subtler differences in baking quality that come from the wheat, and some from the milling. The most obvious difference in flours is how finely they have been ground. Hammermilled or rollermilled flour, even when it comes from a small mill that grinds in only one step, will be extremely fine, making light bread of a fine, resilient texture. Stone-ground flour can also be finely ground, but our own favorite among commercial stone-ground flours is quite rough. It makes wonderfully nubbly loaves of excellent flavor that are very tender. The large bran particles, softened in fermentation, make excellent dietary fiber. Properly stone-ground flour should feel smooth except for the bran particles — the white part shouldn't be grainy feeling.

Stone grinding is as controversial as it is full of mystique, but it *is* true that the flour is different; whether it is better is perhaps debatable, but we very much prefer it for our daily bread. It is true that commercial stone-ground flour from a reputable mill is usually more expensive, because these mills can never match the volume of the faster hammermills or rollermills.

Advocates of stonemilling — ourselves included — have felt that the flour might well taste better and keep fresher because the slower speed of stone mills protects the flour from heating up as it is ground. This may still be true as a general rule, but now we know at least one conscientious commercial miller of whole grains who has air-coolers for *both* his stone mill and his hammermills to make sure neither heats up as it grinds. The only way to be sure about flour is to see how it works.

GAUGING FLOUR QUALITY If you shop around and try all the flours you can find in your area, you will hit on some you like much better than others, and probably settle on two or three that you like for particular strengths they have: a super high-gluten, finely ground flour for making fruited and mixed-grain breads, for example; a coarse, slightly lower-gluten flour with outstanding flavor for French and other plainer loaves.

One thing to keep in mind is that whole wheat flour will also vary noticeably from year to year. Spring wheat is harvested in the fall; winter wheat, in early summer. Millers let newly harvested wheat cure for 90 days before they grind it, so some time in November, the first of the new spring wheat flour makes its debut. You will notice the difference in your bread.

Baking Test for Flour Quality

If you want to make a choice about what flour to get regularly, or, even more, if you want to choose a wheat to buy in bulk for grinding in your own mill, you may find it useful to take a more careful look at the baking qualities of the flour or wheat you are considering. This baking test is modeled on one professionals use for this purpose, and it can be very helpful in evaluating the strengths and weaknesses of any flour. Use these ingredients to make bread according to the basic Whole Wheat Bread recipe (page 80).

2 teaspoons active dry yeast (¼ oz or 7 g)
1 cup warm water (235 ml)
6 cups whole wheat flour (900 g)
2½ teaspoons salt (14 g)
1½ cups water, approximately (355 ml)
2 tablespoons honey (30ml)
2 tablespoons bland oil (30 ml)

Date: Type of wheat: Type of grind:

1. CHARACTER OF FLOUR: coarse/granular/fine/powdery/rough/soft
   Bran flecks: large/medium/small   Taste: fresh/stale/musty/sour/rancid/mild

2. AMOUNT OF WATER ABSORBED: cups

3. KNEADING TIME: minutes by hand/by dough hook/in food processor

4. DOUGH ELASTICITY: elastic/not very elastic/not at all elastic

5. GASSING POWER AT 80°F:
   First rise: less than double/double/triple.   Time:
   Second rise: less than double/double/triple.   Time:

6. ROUND & REST   Spring of tense dough to finger poke: strong/slow
   Time required to relax: minutes.   Dough stability: stable/runny

7. GASSING POWER AT 90°F PROOF: sluggish/vigorous
   Time required to proof: Rise: inches above/below pan rim

8. OVEN SPRING Baked height above pan rim   inches.   Spring: inches.

9. CRUST COLOR: pale/medium/dark   10. BAKED   minutes at   °F

ll. BREAD CRUMB Color: pale and bright/gray/dark/streaked
   Grain: even, uniform, thin, elongated cell walls/uneven, dense, coarse, thick cell walls
   Texture: velvety/silky/soft/elastic/rough/furry/crumbly/harsh/brittle
   Moisture: moist/dry/gummy

12. TASTE: wheaty/gluteny/nutty/pleasant/sweet/flat/sour/acid/rancid

COMMENTS:

Separated Wheat Products

As we've seen, wheat germ and bran are separated out by commercial mills when they manufacture white flour. Both bran and germ have received a lot of attention lately from nutritionists and the medical profession because of the impressive contribution they can make to health — and it's about time, too. But to us, wheat germ alone or bran alone just can't compare to what they have to offer when used as part of the whole grain. And so we do not often use them individually, but celebrate their virtues within the perfect balance of the whole.

WHEAT GERM Wheat germ is the seed's embryo, 2 to 3 percent of its weight, or a full two tablespoons in the three-cup pound. It is packed with nutrients — good-quality protein, unsaturated fats, vitamins, and minerals. Because the fats are unsaturated, they are quite unstable, and once milled, wheat germ gets rancid after several days at room temperature. Since heat treatment, either wet or dry, helps to inactivate the lipase enzymes that cause rancidity, we suggest if you buy wheat germ, unless you can get it within a few days of milling, buy the kind that is toasted at the mill. Buy small rather than large quantities at a time and store airtight in the refrigerator.

Cereal scientists who have studied wheat germ because they wanted to use it to fortify white bread have decided that 2 to 3 percent raw germ is all that the dough will tolerate, because wheat germ contains a reducing substance called glutathione that breaks down gluten. Fascinatingly, this is almost exactly the amount that occurs naturally in whole wheat flour. (As the saying goes, What do you know? God got it right.)

BRAN Bran is the protective, fibrous covering around the wheat kernel, comprising 13 to 17 percent of its weight. That is a little less than two ounces of bran in a pound (3 cups) of flour — one loaf's worth — but if you could sift all of it out, it would fill a whole cup. Whole wheat bread, then, already has a generous amount of bran in it, but there may be circumstances where you would want to add more, either for the culinary effect or for its roughage. Yeast fermentation softens the bran, making it gentler on the digestive tract (though still effective). It also helps to make some of the plentiful minerals the bran contains easier to assimilate.

From the baker's point of view, added bran cuts into the gluten, reducing its rising strength. Soaking the bran in hot water or overnight to soften it seems to help somewhat: for example, see the recipe for Spicy Currant Bread on page 234.

It is true that we included gluten flour in some of the bread recipes in *Laurel's Kitchen*, but we've learned a lot about breadmaking since then! We hope that once you've mastered the skills described in A Loaf for Learning, you will agree that gluten flour is not only unnecessary but downright unwelcome. We have parted ways with gluten flour for several reasons: with good flour you don't need it to make bread light, for one thing; it is a superrefined product, for another (even more so than white flour); and it makes cardboardy bread, for a third. Besides, the amino acids in its protein are far out of balance.

GLUTEN FLOUR

Well, so what is the stuff, anyway?

When the bran and germ are removed from wheat, what is left is white flour: mostly starch and gluten. The starch can be washed out, leaving the tough gluten. This is dried, broken up, ground again and combined with patent (fine white) flour. Fifty percent protein gluten flour is the result. Some bakers add gluten flour to their dough: if there is more gluten, you expect a higher loaf. But if there is more gluten, much more kneading is required to develop it, and more time to ferment it adequately, too. Gluten-enhanced breads have a characteristic taste and texture reminiscent of corrugated paper, and they tend to stale quickly.

If you have bought some flour that time after time refuses to make bread light enough to suit you, we would like to suggest that you use it along with some other, better bread flour in a recipe like the Scottish Sponge Bread. "Weak" flour often has outstanding flavor and can make splendid bread when used in such a recipe. However, it *is* possible to strengthen a flour's rising power by adding gluten flour. One teaspoonful per cup of whole wheat flour will increase the protein content by about 1 percent; a tablespoonful per cup would, for example, make a strong composite bread flour of approximately 15 percent protein out of an all-purpose whole wheat flour of 12 percent protein. *Be sure to allow extra kneading and extra fermentation time.* This is definitely cheating (but it does work).

Incidentally, another gluten product, vital wheat gluten, is also available in some places. It has a higher protein content and is specially processed to prevent the denaturation of the protein by heat.

Because of its high protein content, some people add gluten to foods as a supplement, but it is severely deficient in the essential amino acid lysine (which is supplied in the bran and germ), so in the rare case where a protein supplement is needed, gluten would be a particularly poor choice.

Milling Your Own

If you have a convenient and dependable source of good-quality whole grain flours, you probably don't need to invest in a home mill. But if your local sources disappoint you, there are several advantages to preparing your own flours and cracked cereals at home.

For one thing, whole, unbroken grain keeps very well for a long time, even for several years, without exotic storage requirements. It is only after the grain is ground that the oils begin to oxidize and the flavor and nutritional quality deteriorate. When you grind your own flour you can use it at its freshest, getting the best for both taste and health. Wheat is quite a bit less expensive than flour, and often, especially if you buy in reasonable quantities, you can choose what varieties you want.

Wheat flour keeps most of its goodness for a month at cool room temperature, but it is best stored airtight in the refrigerator, especially if you don't know how old it was when you bought it, or if you don't bake daily. Whole-grain rye flour is even more perishable, which is why it is so hard to find on the shelf: dark rye flour is fractioned, with some of the more spoilable (and healthful) parts removed.

Home-ground rye flour is really special, flavorful and sweet, but the biggest flavor difference in the home-grinding department is corn. Before we got our mill, we were puzzled by what should have been so obvious: why is cornbread bitter sometimes? We investigated leavening combinations and varieties of corn, called experts, and wrote letters to the big natural foods companies. No one could tell us, though a few actually suggested that people like the bitter taste! When we first ground our own corn and made cornbread, no one could believe the difference in flavor: it was amazingly sweet and delicious, without a trace of bitterness.

Later a nutritionist said, oh yes, corn oil goes rancid very quickly. And shortly thereafter we came across the information that years of breeding corn for high yields have created a grain with elevated levels of polyunsaturated oils—so that all corn products, even commercial products like corn flakes, become rancid quickly. While the food scientists address the problem, if you are a cornbread fan, do contrive to mill your own, and enjoy the incomparable sweetness of it. Keep fresh cornmeal in the refrigerator, for a week or so at most.

Incidentally, brown rice flour also spoils in a short time, and home-ground is vastly superior to store-bought.

With any grain you take the trouble to grind yourself, be sure to check it over and make sure it is clean and free from mold. If you grind fairly small quantities, it is worth the trouble to pick out discolored or moldy grains, rocks, sticks, etc. But to make life easier, buy good quality grain.

A few enthusiastic people have suggested to us that the cheapest place to buy grains is at the feed store. No one is denying it is cheaper! But animal feed may have quite a few things you wouldn't want in your bread: rocks, sticks, mouse droppings, dust, weed seeds. Even when the flour ground from such grain is not actually harmful to eat, the bread may taste dirty and gray; professionals refer to it, in fact, as a "feedy" taste. One prominent brand of whole wheat flour that we tried has this flavor—it is unmistakable. In addition, feed wheat is likely to be so low in gluten that bread made from it won't rise.

We do not have the expertise to discuss the merits of all the home mills on the market. A book on the subject or even a thoroughgoing study in the *Consumer Reports* style is much needed. Meantime, in their book *Home Food Systems,* the Rodale people have provided a helpful comparative guide.* Our own experience with a few representative mills we gladly share here.

The first and perhaps least obvious thing to take into account when you consider buying a mill is your own comfort. If the mill is electric, is it going to be so outrageously noisy that no one can stand to be in the same room? If it is a hand mill, are you really strong enough to run it regularly, or will it end up gathering dust in the attic? The best hand mills have a flywheel built in to make turning them easier; these are exquisite tools, versatile and well-made, but they are expensive, too. A lot of our friends have been enthusiastic about converting their hand mills to pedal power, (bicycle pedals, right?) but so far not one of them has been efficient to run. Be practical.

Home grinders, hand or electric, vary in size and shape from the smallest, about like a milk carton, on up. They generally sit on or clamp to the top of a table, and grind by rotating two grooved plates — usually steel — against each other.

*Corliss A. Bachman, *Home Food Systems* (Emmaus, Pennsylvania: Rodale Press, 1981)

CLEANING   As far as the grain is concerned, the most important factors are cleanliness and temperature. The mill has got to be cleanable, and this becomes most critical when it is the convertible kind that can grind seeds and nuts and beans as well as grains. These oily foods especially, if not cleaned out of the mill immediately after grinding, can turn rancid and even mold in the nooks and crannies, contaminating everything that comes after. The Corona-type mills, for example, are fabulous for the price, but they simply must be taken apart *completely* after use for cleaning. Until you see it you'll never believe what can grow on a little crushed sunflower seed.

TEMPERATURE   Unless you have the strength of ten, (or your mill is dull) it is not too likely that you can overheat the flour, grinding by hand. The electric mills, particularly the high-speed ones, are much more likely to raise the temperature of the flour higher than you would like. Temperatures above 115°F will destroy vitamins; above 140°F, even the best wheat will suffer a loss of baking quality. Any such heat gives the flour's oil a push toward rancidity; it is possible to grind flour and not have it even warm to the touch. Your small chef's thermometer measures the flour's temperature easily, by the way.

VERSATILITY   Last, consider what you want to be able to do: most mills have their limits. Stone-mills grind *only* grain—you'll ruin them with beans or nuts or anything oily. But they will adjust to make fine or coarse flour or cornmeal, or will crack grain for breakfast cereal. Some of the high-powered electric mills will grind any dry grain or bean, even soybeans, into dust in just seconds, but they can't make anything coarser than fine flour. Cornmeal is out for them, and so is breakfast cereal. Very few mills will grind sprouts or nuts, though hand mills with interchangeable plates can grind whatever you are strong enough to put through. Usually that excludes beans, especially soy. The only mill we know that accommodates every challenge is the Dimant, that expensive hand mill we mentioned that has a flywheel. It converts to motor power readily, by the way, is easy to clean, and pretty. (See its portrait on pages 194 and 195.)

The best millstones are at once hard and porous, so that they wear slowly and do not become smooth even with long use. The last known quarry that produced such stones was in France, and it has been exhausted; the best natural stones now are cut from hard pink granite, and these are the only natural stones available today, that we know of. Many of the big natural foods firms that sell stone-ground flour use mills with such stones, 30 inches across. Our own 8-inch version—scarcely home-size—is the smallest the Meadows Mill company sells: with it we grind wheat, corn, rice and rye for a dozen families.

Like the larger stones, ours has to be sharpened after about 100 hours of milling. It definitely requires the kind of

care that you expect to give a fine tool: we have learned how to face (sharpen) the stones, adjust them, and grease the running parts. When the stone is sharp and properly adjusted it grinds very cool and as fine as needed for our purposes. The mill is not terrifically easy to clean or pretty to look at, unless you really appreciate the no-frills approach—but after more than three years of regular use, we like it very much indeed.

We do not know of any small home-sized stone mill that has nautral stones. Most have composite stones made of hard bits of abrasive, bonded together, and we feel there is some question about whether this is safe. No matter what the mill is that grinds your grain, you can count on traces of the grinding surface finding their way into the flour.

One home mill, the Samap, uses hard natural Greek Naxos stones instead of Carborundum. These mills are not inexpensive, but they do adjust to grind flour very fine and will grind coarsely enough for cereal grain, too, though like other stone mills, they can't handle seeds or wet grains (sprouts), beans or such.

About the Ingredients:
Yeast

There are millions of species of yeast, but our familiar baking yeasts (and brewer's yeasts too) are all from the species *Saccharomyces cerevisiae,* a highly refined sort. Before the turn of the century and the advent of dependable commercial baking yeast, breadmaking was an art surrounded by many mysteries. Getting bread to rise wasn't easy, and getting it to rise and taste good was even more challenging. Brewer's yeast, barms, home-made "potato yeast"—there were many methods, and some of them involved days or weeks of fussing. A good starter was a great treasure, and secrets were not easily shared. Our friend Sultana, who grew up in a tiny village in northern Greece, recently asked her mother where you would get a starter like the one they used to make the family's bread. Her mother was incredulous: Why, you would get it from your mother, of course. What if you didn't have a mother? Well, maybe your aunt would give it to you. What if you had no family? Then you wouldn't make bread!

The yeast we take so much for granted is produced commercially by a rather simple but highly controlled process. Different yeast strains are used for active dry yeast and compressed yeast, each one developed to withstand the storage conditions it will have to face while still maintaining its leavening power and other baking characteristics. Huge vats of a diluted solution of molasses, mineral salts, and ammonia are seeded with carefully selected strains of yeast. Sterile air bubbles through and the seed yeast grows until literally tons of it are ready for harvest. The yeast is separated from the solution, washed, then mixed with water and emulsifiers for compressed yeast or dried over a period of hours for active dry yeast. Sometimes preservatives are mixed in; if so, they have to be listed on the ingredient label.

Yeast is a simple one-celled plant, and like all living things it grows best in a certain climate, with adequate food and water. Dough meets all its requirements: calories, minerals, vitamins, and simple nitrogen for making protein. Yeast likes a neutral to slightly acid pH, and some oxygen too, though it can get on without it for a while.

When plenty of oxygen is available, yeast metabolizes its food completely, multiplying energetically and giving off carbon dioxide and water as waste products. This efficient metabolic process is called respiration, and its discovery by Louis Pasteur was what made the commercial manufacture of yeast possible: bubbling air through the nutrient solution keeps the yeast metabolism efficient and its waste products harmless. When there is not much oxygen — as in bread dough, where the oxygen is rather quickly used up — yeast adapts by changing its metabolism from aerobic respiration to anaerobic fermentation.

Fermentation burns the available carbohydrate food less efficiently, producing carbon dioxide and alcohol as by-products. Beermaking capitalizes on this process, but with bread dough that is left too long, the accumulated alcohol will eventually kill the yeast. Deflating the dough, kneading, shaping, and so on, all remove alcohol through evaporation. They also move the yeast to new pastures, aerate the dough somewhat, and break up the accumulated carbon dioxide bubbles into smaller air sacs, making a finer-textured dough that can hold the gas better and produce a lighter bread.

Releasing carbon dioxide to leaven the dough is the flashiest thing yeast does, but it is not the only one. Many minute chemical by-products of fermentation give the bread flavor; and in some mysterious ways the action of the yeast both develops and mellows the gluten so that it can do its gas-retaining work better. During the fermentation period, other changes take place: the starch and proteins of the dough continue to absorb water into themselves (one reason that longer-fermented bread keeps better), and there is a lot of enzyme activity.

One enzyme that does important work during the whole fermentation time is amylase, which we have discussed elsewhere. Another, probably even more important to us who eat the bread, is phytase. Like amylase, phytase is an enzyme that the new plant would use when it needed to gain access to nutrients stored in the seed. These essential nutrients are locked up by a substance called phytic acid, which safeguards them until they are needed by the growing sprout. With amylase the nutrients in question are sugars, which the enzyme releases from its storage form, starch. With phytase, the nutrients are minerals: phosphorus, zinc, calcium and others. As bread ferments, stored minerals are released, and this is one reason that leavened bread has nutritional advantages over unfermented wheat products, and one reason for choosing the longer fermentation times when that option is open to you.

Baking yeast comes to us either in dried granules or moist pressed cakes, and technologists have put a good deal of energy into seeing that they are both exceedingly good at their job of raising bread.

The commonest kind of yeast for home baking is *active dry yeast,* the granular kind found in tiny flat foil packets at the grocer's, or in bulk at natural food stores. This is the kind we call for in our recipes: it is available everywhere, convenient to keep, and very dependable. A typical recipe in this book calls for 2 teaspoons (1 packet) of active dry yeast (¼ ounce or 7 grams). When we wrote *Laurel's Kitchen,* one packet measured a tablespoon, and when we started this book, it measured 2½ teaspoons; now it is 2—but it still weighs the same, and still raises two loaves. The yeast companies are always trying to improve their products, and maybe from their point of view, less bulk means less storage and shipping space.

For moist (or "cake," or "compressed") yeast, the equivalent amount is one square (⅗ ounce or 17 grams). When you buy either of them in bulk, or want to substitute one for the other, think of moist yeast as composed of about half water by weight, so that active dry yeast weighs 45 percent as much as cake yeast of the same leavening power.

The most important thing to keep in mind when you buy yeast is to be sure it is fresh. If active dry yeast is kept airtight and cool, it maintains its potency for several months. Try to encourage your storekeeper to keep his supply refrigerated, and even so, don't buy yeast whose pull date has gone by. Sometimes active dry yeast is sold in open bins, and you are encouraged to scoop out what you want, put it in a paper bag, and take it home. Because exposure to warmth and air damages yeast over a period of time, bulk yeast of this type has been responsible for some densely disappointing loaves.

Whatever kind you buy, be sure to read the manufacturer's directions for that particular yeast. (Ask to see the label if you buy in bulk.) Until recently there were just two kinds of yeast, cake and active dry, and the directions for using them appeared in every cookbook. Lately, however, several new kinds of active dry yeast have appeared on the scene, and each one of them has its own particular requirements: if you use one of them, you'll get the best results from it if you follow the manufacturer's suggestions exactly. Some of these yeasts are designed to work very fast, and do. They make bread that is exceedingly light, with the other characteristics of quickly raised bread, too: uninteresting flavor and poor keeping quality.

Professional bakers have long preferred moist, or compressed, yeast for its greater dependability and gassing power. It can be activated at a wider range of temperatures, making it a little easier to use. It keeps for only a week or two in the refrigerator, but since bakers buy so much of it, it is convenient for them to keep a fresh supply on hand. Sometimes they do not object to selling a pound of it, or even half a pound—so if you like to use moist yeast and have been having a hard time finding it in the stores, try your nearby bakery. Fresh moist or compressed yeast is creamy-smooth looking, beige in color, *not crumbly or grayish*. A pound is enough to raise 64 normal loaves of bread—a serious consideration.

You can store compressed yeast wrapped airtight in the refrigerator for about two weeks; frozen (at 30–32°F) for as long as two months. If you purchase a large quantity, we suggest cutting it into one-baking-sized chunks, and wrapping them airtight in foil before freezing them. To prepare refrigerated compressed yeast for baking, dissolve the yeast in water that is no warmer than 85°F. Soften frozen yeast in water that is even cooler.

NUTRITIONAL YEAST

Before leaving the subject of yeast, it is perhaps worth mentioning that nutritional yeasts—torula, brewer's, etc.—are quite dead and will never raise bread. Even if you are using them for the sake of their nutritional wallop, in addition to regular yeast, their overpowering flavor does not add much to the appeal of the loaf, and one protein (glutathione) present in the pulverized yeast cells can actually keep your dough from rising well.

About the Ingredients:
Water . . .

As a general rule, water that is good to drink is good for bread-making. Some minerals in the water strengthen the gluten and act as food for the yeast, but exceptionally hard or alkaline water can retard the yeast's action. If your water is very hard, you may find that you get a better rise if you add a tablespoon of cider vinegar or lemon juice to the water measure (not the yeast-dissolving water, please!). Very soft water will make a soft, sticky dough that does not rise well. For this reason, distilled water (the softest of all) works poorly in baking.

The amount of chlorine normally used to treat drinking water is in low enough concentration that it does not disturb baker's yeast, but where a less vigorous leaven is working—for example, in Flemish Desem Bread—don't use chlorinated water.

Many liquids can be used in bread—water, milk, fruit juice, soymilk, potato water, applesauce, egg, cooked cereals, and others. Water, though, is the most universal and one of the very best: it lets the full vital flavor of the wheat shine out strong and clear. Please note that whatever liquid you use, the yeast should be dissolved in water only, and at the proper temperature.

. . . & Salt

Salt's most obvious contribution is flavor: if ever you find you have made an unexpectedly strange-tasting bread, there's a fair chance you forgot the salt. If you left it out, the bread will probably have other problems, too: saltless loaves are usually crumbly, have a characteristically porous top crust, and they often collapse. Salt strengthens the gluten and regulates the growth of the yeast.

It is possible to make good bread without salt, as we describe in the section on Saltless Bread, and many people, for reasons of health and/or taste, prefer it that way. In the recipes in this book we have used what most people who are accustomed to lightly salted food find acceptable, but you will easily adjust our quantities to suit your own taste and needs.

Most salt available in retail stores contains anticaking agents, and often "free-flowing" agents as well. These additives do not affect breadbaking in any noticeable way, but if you prefer to avoid them, check to see if your natural food store sells additive-free salt. If it lumps up a little, you can usually crumble it easily, but do protect it from moisture so it won't turn into a hard rock. When you make bread, if your salt is not finely ground, dissolve it in part of the water measure rather than stir it into the flour so that you will be sure it gets mixed evenly into the dough.

Much has been made lately of the superiority of sea salt, and you can pay an outrageous amount for it if you are willing. There are bakers who swear by the beautiful lilac-colored salt from a particular bay in South France, and others who pine for the petal-pink sea salt of Hawaii. It is true that bread dough is conditioned by many minerals, and perhaps these exotic salts contain some of them. However, even if the water you use in your bread is so soft that it is practically distilled, we question whether any minerals that might be present in these salts could be worth their exotic price.

As for normal sea salt, whether you find it on the supermarket shelf or in a specialty store, most likely it originated in the vast red salt-drying ponds that stretch along the southern part of the San Francisco Bay: it is there that the Leslie Salt Company manufactures virtually all the sea salt sold in this country. Ocean water is dried, scraped up, washed, redried, redissolved and precipitated, so that what is left is very nearly pure sodium chloride. If it were not purified in this way, there would be a substantial amount of ocean pollution along with the salt—not only bits of seaweed and fish but some toxic minerals like lead and cadmium, and residues of pesticides, as well. Leslie's sea salt is 99.95 percent sodium chloride. To be "food grade," salt must be very pure indeed; and this is true whether the salt was mined from the earth or evaporated from seawater, and no matter how much you pay for it.

About the Ingredients:
Sweeteners

There is a persistent myth that added sugar or honey is necessary to provide food for the yeast. Yeast does prefer added sugars and will choose them first over those from the dough itself, but truth to tell, the yeast can convert dough starches into sugars perfectly well, and these are adequate for it in all but the very longest-rising doughs. The classic daily breads of Europe contain no added sugar or fat, but Americans seem to prefer their breads a little on the sweet side, and most of our recipes do call for some sweetener.

Sugar in any form—honey, fruit, molasses, or granulated cane—not only affects the bread's flavor but also makes the crumb tenderer; and when you slice the finished loaf and put it into the toaster, the toast browns faster. In small quantities—about 1 tablespoon per loaf or so—the type of sweetener you use will not make too much difference in taste, but when there is more, the sweetener should be considered a flavoring agent as well.

We use honey because the flavor harmonizes well with whole wheat, and for ecological and other reasons we prefer it to refined sugar. For many of us, besides, there are real advantages to keeping granulated sugar completely out of the kitchen but if you want to substitute brown sugar in any recipe that calls for honey, you should have good results. In breadmaking quantities, the nutritional differences between sweeteners are insignificant.

Honey is fascinating stuff. Books have been written about it, and songs and poems as well. One tiny bee works her whole lifetime to produce one teaspoonful, so we use it with a certain appreciative awe. Honey gives a bright sweetness to bread, and because it holds moisture, bread made with honey keeps well.

Since its character reflects the flowers it comes from, there is considerable variation from one jar of honey to another. This is of much practical interest in breadmaking. We have had

HONEY

honey as black as molasses that was so acid or so full of enzymes (or *something* mysterious!) that the bread made with it simply would not rise. Commercial bakers, when they use honey at all, generally pick the pasteurized kind because even the lightest honey is a biologically active entity, with properties that can interfere with the dough's development. The home baker can deal with these vagaries better than the professional, whose livelihood depends on being able to produce identical loaves day after day; but even at home if you are making a long dough, one that will take more than four or five hours to rise, we suggest scalding raw honey before adding it to the dough. For the least damage to its flavor, heat it in a double boiler, and don't let it get over 180°F. Or if you prefer, heat it in part of the liquid from the recipe, then cool to the proper temperature. Some honeys are acid enough to curdle milk if the two are heated together, but that won't hurt the bread.

MOLASSES

Molasses is one of our favorite sweeteners, especially for the heartier breads, which its dark flavor complements boldly. There are many varieties of molasses, most by-products of sugar refining. Sugarcane is pounded, the juice extracted, and from the juice comes sugar. What remains behind is first extraction molasses, the lightest. Second extraction is darker because more sugar has been removed. Finally, third extraction molasses, or blackstrap, is left. It still contains some sugar, but so little that it is not commercially practical to take any more out. Blackstrap is well known as a rich source of iron and other minerals, partly because sugar extracting used to be carried on in iron vessels. Nowadays this is not necessarily so, and the iron content varies a lot from brand to brand (and so does the flavor).

Because sulfur is used in the refining of sugar, there is residual sulfur in the molasses — highly objectionable to people who are sensitive to it. *Unsulfured* molasses is available most places; it is this that we have used in testing our recipes. Which kind you prefer is very much a matter of your own taste. As a rule of thumb, the darker the molasses is, the more sugar has been removed, and the stronger the flavor. Blackstrap, by far the darkest of the lot, is more a flavoring agent than a sweetener, and it should be used with caution by those who haven't become addicted to its tangy bite. *The Joy of Cooking* (at least our vintage edition) pronounces thus on its pungency: "Blackstrap molasses is a waste product . . . and is unpalatable." To its fans, blackstrap is marvelous. *De gustibus.* Whatever kind of molasses you use, of course, it will make your bread darker in color than if you had used another sweetener.

Malt is extracted from sprouted barley, usually, and sometimes MALT from other grains. It has a rich taste and so enhances the flavor of grain that manufacturers of white-flour products often use it to help approximate the satisfyingly warm flavor of whole wheat.

The form of malt that is most concentrated and most easily available is barley malt syrup, a thick, viscous semi-liquid: this is the kind that we have used in recipes in this book. When you buy it be careful to get the plain-flavored kind—hop-flavored malt syrup, sold for brewing, is quite bitter. Look for a brand that has not been diluted with corn syrup, certainly.

This malt syrup is *non-diastatic:* it has been heated in its manufacture, and contains no active enzymes that would affect your bread. *Diastatic* malt, or dimalt, does contain active enzymes. Dimalt is most often sold in natural food stores in the form of flour. The flour is much less concentrated than syrup in sweetness and malty flavor, but because its enzymes convert dough starches into sugars, a small amount sweetens a whole loaf, making dimalt a good choice for people who want to make bread without added sweeteners. The dimalts that are available to the home baker vary in potency, but as a rule, a quarter-teaspoon per loaf is just about the maximum you can use without having the bread become a gooey mess that can't bake properly.

For more about malt, including instructions for making your own, see pages 273 to 275.

Pure maple syrup is one of the most delicious sweeteners, whether you pour it on pancakes or use it to sweeten bread dough. Be alert to its freshness, though. It does not keep well, even in the refrigerator. If mold forms on the top, skim it off. The molds can't survive in the syrup itself, but other micro-organisms can, and they can alter the flavor drastically. If there is any question in your mind, bring the syrup to a boil—often that revives its usefulness. But even then always taste it before you cook with it, because when its flavor is off it can ruin a whole baking. The crystallized version keeps longer.

Sorghum syrup, from a grain that grows well in most places in the United States, is rather sour, and we did not like its flavor in bread. There may be many good ways to use it, but we are not familiar with them.

Crystallized fruit sugars (date, banana, and the like)—and for that matter turbinado, demerara, and the whole health-food-store panoply—may have some subtle advantages over supermarket varieties, but they are expensive for what you are getting, which is—sugar. Some are far less sweet than their more plebeian counterparts, so you may find it necessary to add much more to get the same sweetening effect.

Finally, a word here about fructose, which not long ago received a whole lot of attention as a sinless "natural" sweetener. It does occur naturally in honey and fruits and vegetables, but commercial fructose is a highly processed sugar, usually manufactured from corn syrup, which is itself a highly refined sugar. We can't recommend it at all.

About the Ingredients:
Fat

Most of our recipes call for a tablespoon or so of oil or butter per loaf because even this small amount helps the bread keep longer, enhances its flavor, and makes it tenderer. A tablespoon of cool butter or two to three tablespoons of oil per loaf make what bread scientists call a "conditioning amount": it actually helps the loaf to rise higher in the oven. More oil is required because liquid oils have less of the fatty acids that are solid at fermentation temperatures, and these fatty acids are the conditioning element. Different kinds of oil have slight differences in composition; as a general rule, the higher the melting point, the more conditioning effect you can expect.

Be sure it's fresh: rancid fat can spoil a loaf completely. Refined oils don't contribute flavor of their own to the bread, but unrefined oils do. The ones we have found successful are sesame oil, which has an emphatic taste (best when there are also seeds on the crust), and olive oil, good especially in sandwich bread and rolls where you don't want sweetness. Olive oil has a high melting point and therefore some conditioning properties; bread made with it usually rises beautifully.

From the nutritional standpoint, it is best to minimize the use of any fat or oil, and for this reason we have tried to use as little as possible while still providing a wide variety of flavor and texture to the breads. You can, however, follow the recipes in this book, or any other bread recipe, for that matter, with no oil or butter at all; the slice will be chewier, the crumb more open; in most cases the bread won't keep as well — though there are other ways to help bread keep well.

If you are looking at your bread with an eye to lowering fat content, we suggest you take a canny look at just how much you spread on the slice. It is very easy to put a full tablespoon of butter on a piece of toast, and building the habit of using less takes a continuing, conscious effort. If you are reducing the fat in your diet even more drastically and have given up fatty spreads on your bread altogether, why not try the European custom of breaking fresh bread rather than slicing it? The exposed crumb is then much softer and more appetizing. On this score, too, hearth breads and sourdoughs, rolls, and breadsticks, are good eating without the butter.

Grease

Nearly everything you bake on or bake in has to be greased to prevent sticking. In our experience, vegetable oil does not work reliably for this job unless it is hydrogenated — the solid white stuff sold as vegetable shortening. We kept a can of this around with a small cloth napkin inside — using it *only* for greasing — until our friend and baking wizard Manuel Freedman suggested this alternative, which works beautifully.

Buy some lecithin, either the granule or liquid form, at the supermarket or any natural food store. Mix ½ cup lecithin and 1 cup liquid vegetable oil, blending smooth in the blender. Keep it in the refrigerator. Use this for greasing anything — it works like magic. For best results, apply a *very* thin coat only, being careful to cover the entire surface. "It's the best release product in the business," says Manuel, and he knows whereof he speaks.

Timing

If you're a canny baker, you can manipulate the quantity of yeast and the temperature of the dough so that its rising times suit your convenience, and so that you produce the bread you like.

As you've seen, most of the recipes in this book make yeasted dough that is ready for the oven in three or four hours, but if you want to let the dough rise longer nearly any recipe can be adapted to accomplish this. Similarly, you can reduce the preparation time so that your fast dough is in the oven in 2½ hours.

There are other reasons to vary the timing of your bread. More yeast and warmer dough make a higher loaf. Cool dough and a longer rising time produce a slightly smaller bread, but one that is flavorful, keeps well, and is very nutritious.

There are some tricks to making good bread on your own schedule. Some of them are obvious, others are not. In this section we try to explain the possibilities, but if you are a beginner, we would urge you most earnestly to set aside time to make A Loaf for Learning at a leisurely pace once or twice before you try changing timings. When you get fancy it helps to know what you're about.

When you vary timings, it's particularly important to keep alert to what is happening to the dough; that is your tipoff to how well you are adjusting the amount of yeast and the temperature of the dough. After each rise, look really carefully at your half-inch finger-poke (page 48). Does the dough come back a little, shrinking the hole? For the next rising, you will want to give the dough a bit more warmth so it can ferment

Bakers call doughs that rise slowly "long" and those that rise quickly "fast." It isn't strictly grammatical, but it is a convention, and we've followed it in this book.

adequately in the amount of time you have allotted. If the dough not only doesn't fill in the hole but sighs profoundly with alcohol on its breath, next time keep it cooler, for you are courting a gray, yeasty-tasting loaf. The final rise, or proof, is the most important to time closely. Especially if you're new at this, try to arrange to work nearby so that you can keep an eye on the loaf.

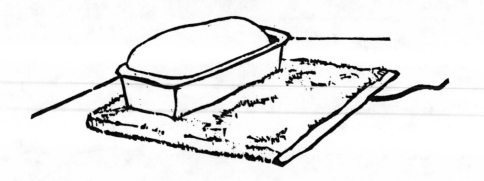

Timings for Straight Doughs

A *straight dough* is one that has been mixed using all its ingredients from the beginning. Most of our recipes follow this model. In the next pages we present the four basic straight dough timing patterns. Most of the breads in this book can be made following any one of these timings, if you make the suggested adjustments.

A *sponge dough* is mixed in stages and offers further possibilities for timing variations. See pages 401 to 405.

Bread in a Tearing Hurry

"FAST" DOUGHS: about 2½ hours plus baking time				YEAST: 4 teaspoons per 6 cups flour
Mixing & Kneading	*First Rise*	*Second Rise*	*Shaping & Proofing*	DOUGH CONSISTENCY: quite soft
½ hour	1 hour or less	about ½ hour, or less	about ½ hour	
about 85°			95°F	

Very high, with mild bakery-made flavor, loaves or rolls produced by this timing come in handy when you want bread fast. We have seen recipes that purport to produce yeasted bread even faster, but we have not liked their raw-gluten taste: you would do better to make a quick bread leavened with baking powder! (See pages 309 to 337.) We believe that the timing presented here is the fastest way to have *real bread* from dough that has actually developed and ripened properly.

This pattern will work for any recipe that doesn't call for unusual timing. Basically, you double the yeast and keep the dough very warm; if you manage it just right, the dough moves so quickly that you really have to stay on your toes to avoid letting it get away from you. For light buttery dinner rolls, this timing is a natural; if you are making loaves, it isn't a bad idea to choose a recipe that has interesting ingredients to add taste and texture, since the bread will not in itself have rich flavor. Including dried fruit, potato, or cooked cereal, for example, would enrich the flavor, and also offer the advantage of increasing the bread's keeping quality, which otherwise is quite limited.

Good Morning (or Good Afternoon) Bread

SHORT-NORMAL DOUGH: about 4 hours plus baking time				YEAST: 2 teaspoons per 6 cups flour
Mixing & Kneading	*First Rise*	*Second Rise*	*Shaping & Proofing*	DOUGH CONSISTENCY: soft
½ hour	1½–2 hours	about 1 hour	1 hour or a little less	
about 80°			slightly warmer	

In general, the recipes in this book follow this pattern because it is the one most of our friends find convenient. It fits comfortably into a day at home, with plenty of time on either side: if you start at ten, the bread will be out of the oven by midafternoon; or, begin about lunchtime if you want fresh rolls for dinner without any rushing.

The dough is really a fairly fast-rising one, and will produce very light bread. Still, the timing is not so fast that the bread does not have good flavor and keeping quality, and the nutritional value is respectable, too. For best flavor, don't let the dough get warmer than 80°F during its first two rising times. If the dough is kept cooler, it will rise a little more slowly, but the bread will be very good: see next page.

Early Riser's (or Night Owl's) Delight

LONG-NORMAL DOUGH:	about 7 hours plus baking time			YEAST: 2 teaspoons per 6 cups flour
Mixing & Kneading	First Rise	Second Rise	Shaping & Proofing	DOUGH CONSISTENCY: soft, but not too soft
½ hour	3–4 hours	1½–2 hours	about 1 hour	
about 70°			slightly warmer	

With the same measurements of the previous choice, this timing is more leisurely both for you and for the dough. We usually start the bread about 5:00 A.M. and take it out of the oven at lunchtime. Another household we know begins in the afternoon and finishes just at bedtime. (They have some truly enthusiastic midnight snackers in that house.)

With the longer rise, the bread has rich flavor and very good keeping quality, plus some nutritional advantages from the extra fermentation. Since it rises at room temperature, no special arrangement is necessary for warming the dough, so long as it is protected from drafts. Doughs like this do not demand such precise timing as those with a faster pace, but they still have plenty of energy to rise high.

Simple breads are at their best made in this way because the flavor of the wheat really has a chance to bloom. Flemish Desem and French Breads definitely require the longer rise, but any recipe in this book that does not specify an unusual timing will work beautifully on this schedule.

Night & Day Doughs

TWENTY-FOUR HOUR DOUGH, plus baking time

Mixing & Kneading	First Rise	Second Rise	Shaping & Proofing
½ hour	about 20 to 24 hours deflating about every 8 hours		about 2 hours
about 55–60°	warm the dough a little toward the end of the rising period		warm

YEAST: (active dry only) ¼ tsp per 6 cups flour
SWEETENER: increase by 2 teaspoons per 6 cups flour; do not use raw honey
DOUGH CONSISTENCY: stiff
BAKING TIME: increase by 15 to 30 minutes

TWELVE-HOUR DOUGH, plus baking time

Mixing & Kneading	First Rise	Second Rise	Shaping & Proofing
½ hour	about 8 hours	about 2 hours	1½–2 hours
65–70°		warmer	quite warm

YEAST: (active dry only) ¼ tsp per 6 cups flour
SWEETENER: increase by approx. 1 tsp per 6 cups flour; do not use raw honey
DOUGH CONSISTENCY: moderately stiff

Our friends Delores and Gregg are enthusiastic about 24-hour bread because it fits effortlessly into their work schedule: they just mix it up one day after work, punch it down before bedtime and again in the morning, then shape, proof and bake after work the next day. The twelve-hour version can follow the same pattern, except it has to be mixed in the morning before work, not always such a leisurely affair. Both versions benefit from longer baking time, about 15 minutes extra — more if the loaf is heavy.

These breads have exceptional flavor, nutrition and keeping quality providing that they are kept cool enough to ferment properly in the time allotted. The loaves will not rise so high as they would with more yeast on a more accelerated schedule, so if making a large loaf is important to you, adjust the recipe you choose so that you can increase the amount of dough in the pan slightly — or else consider following a long-rising sponge pattern for your bread instead of this one. (See page 401.)

Lengthening the Rising Period

For longer-fermented breads in particular, we like to use a rough stone-ground flour. It is not just that the larger bran particles, softened in the fermenting dough, make ideal dietary fiber that is especially beneficial (which they do), but the coarser flour makes a particularly delectable texture, too, and the full wheatey flavor seems to sing out most appealingly. If the dough is made into freestanding hearth loaves, coarse flour seems to hold up better than finer flours do.

FLOUR

The recipes in this book and the suggestions in this section are based on the high-gluten whole wheat bread flour that is standard in the United States. In most of Europe and Australia, and other parts of the world, too, flour is often lower in gluten. Doughs made from these lower-gluten flours can make delicious bread—classic French Bread is an outstanding example—but they do not tolerate either very fast or very long fermentation periods as well as doughs made with high-gluten flour.

In a long dough, the yeast may consume a considerable amount of the available dough sugars. To compensate, add a small amount of extra sweetener. Don't use diastatic malt in longer fermentations; some of its enzymes weaken the gluten and soften the dough, making these breads dense and wet. (Also, see next paragraph.)

SWEETENER

Any ingredient that would normally reduce the size of the loaf will have an exaggerated effect as the fermentation time increases. (Raw honey, for example, which ordinarily reduces the rise of bread very slightly may do so considerably if the dough is a slow-rising one.) When the culprit is an active enzyme or a competing organism, as it may be with honey or cultured milk products, or with fruits, you can minimize the effect by steaming or scalding the ingredient beforehand. Be sure to cool it before adding to the dough—you don't want to warm the dough if it is going to rise a long time.

OTHER INGREDIENTS

The most critical variable of all is temperature. If you can keep your dough within five degrees of what you intend, you can time it very closely to be ready when you want. Suggestions for making these calculations are given here, but you will quickly learn to make the adjustments necessary for your own flour and room temperatures, even without the mathematics. In this respect, cooler doughs are more tolerant, fast ones very demanding.

SOME CALCULATIONS
FOR CLOSE TIMINGS

Breadmaking need not be a matter of guesswork. You can control the timing of your dough's risings very accurately by controlling its temperature. Of course, even if it starts out warmer or cooler, dough will eventually come to the temperature of its surroundings, but in the meantime it will be rising too quickly or too slowly for the best fermentation at your selected timing. With one or two loaves, following normal timings, this is not crucial because the dough changes temperature in a relatively short time; but when you have a large dough (many loaves) or are planning on a very fast rise, the mixing temperature makes a bigger difference.

DOUGH KNEADED BY MACHINE

Here's a way to figure how to get the right dough temperature:

*multiply the
dough temperature
you want by 2
subtract the temperature
of your flour
result: the temperature
your liquids need to be*

For example,
80°F×2=160
160−65=95°F

Using an electric dough hook or a food processor to do the kneading will raise the temperature of the dough. For this reason, you will have to use cooler liquids in the recipe itself (but of course *not* to dissolve the yeast). In fact, though this is important, you have to be finicky only with recipes like French Bread where the dough must be really cool.

Calculations have been devised to compensate for the warming effect of the machines, but they are exceedingly cumbersome. Just measure the temperature of the dough when it's mixed, and then again after you finish kneading to find out how much your machine warms the dough. The next time you can compensate by using cooler water. Except for the ½ cup or so for dissolving the yeast, lower the temperature of the liquids by almost twice as much as your machine warmed the dough. For example, if your machine heats the dough by 10°F, you'll want to use water that is 20°F cooler than you would otherwise.

Refrigerating Dough

Beyond all this, you can also retard your dough by putting it in the refrigerator during one of its rises. We have never had very good luck with bread when it has spent more than one rise in the cold but there are several possibilities that do work nicely for us.

In general, whenever you keep dough in the refrigerator, seal its container to prevent it from absorbing stray flavors. Since the dough needs to cool evenly, and later will have to come to room temperature before you use it, help keep the yeast action as even as possible by forming the dough into a flat disc rather than a ball before you put it in the refrigerator. Raisins and such have a tendency to become winey, by the way, and their limit in the refrigerator is about one day.

Knead up a normal recipe, using cold liquid (except for dissolving the yeast). Refrigerate for a day or two or three, deflating the dough from time to time if it rises. When you want to make a loaf or rolls, take out what you need and let the dough warm through. If it has risen once or more in the cold, and you have punched it down, the dough may be ripe by now, and ready to shape; or, it may require another rising period: gauge that by the feel of the dough. Shape, proof, and bake as usual.

A dough that has risen in the normal way one time can go into the refrigerator afterward, to have its second rise there. Deflate the dough, divide it in two for loaves, or into smaller parts if you will be making rolls. Press into discs not more than an inch thick. Place in a flat baking dish or some such container, and cover securely. When you are ready to resume, put the dough in a warm place, covered, until it has softened, warmed through, and fully risen. Round the dough, let it rest, and shape as usual. For the final proof, keep the loaf only just a little warmer than the dough. If the dough is still cool, and is proofed in a very warm place, there will be a dense core in the loaf when it is baked.

A normal warm dough can have its final rise in the refrigerator, surprisingly: it will take about three hours, depending on how warm the dough is, and how quickly your refrigerator can chill it. This is tricky, but the bread can be baked after about three hours, when it is fully risen, or as late as the next day *if* your refrigerator is cold enough to prevent the loaf from overproofing. The cold loaf, fully risen, can go directly into a hot oven. It will probably need a little more baking. Watch carefully and test for doneness. (See page 57.)

These are mostly daredevil schemes, but you can make them work with a little experimentation. An even more radical suggestion we've heard is freezing dough, but after some research and experimentation, we don't really recommend that for home bakers.

Sponge Doughs

Sponge doughs were probably invented by old-time professional bakers who were tired of never getting home from work, and wanted to have a chance at a night's sleep before they had to get up to start the bread for the breakfast customers. Before leaving in the evening, the baker would mix up a portion of the dough for the first of the next morning's bakings. It would ferment overnight, giving him a head start on the day. Such a prefermented portion of a larger dough is called a sponge.

The need to make bread quickly without sacrificing the good nutrition, flavor, and keeping quality of longer-rising dough is no doubt even nowadays the most frequent impetus to follow the sponge pattern. But there are other good reasons for making sponges, too.

A *sponge* is part of the dough that is mixed up and allowed to ferment ahead of time.

A *sponge dough* is bread dough that is made from a sponge.

A *straight dough* is one that has been mixed using all the ingredients from the start.

Sponges offer a lot of flexibility. When your schedule is unpredictable, a sponge will be hurried up or will wait awhile, without so much damage to the bread as if it were a straight dough. Besides, sponges can be made to move faster or slower as you like: suggestions follow.

FLEXIBLE TIMINGS

It is pleasant and even fairly easy to prepare dough for two loaves of bread by hand. When you are faced with kneading twice that, though, some serious muscle and endurance are required. By kneading in stages and letting the yeast do some of the work, the process can become a lot more manageable. For example, you can make five loaves of Scottish Sponge Bread (page 90) if you're in fairly good shape. The sponge also gives you the option of making different kinds of bread — say, wheat, rye, and raisin-buckwheat at the same time.

BIG BATCHES

Low-gluten wheat flour and flours from other grains as well as beans have a lot to offer nutritionally, and they may have outstanding flavor, too; but in some cases adding them at the beginning of the fermentation period can make poor bread. However, you can make a sponge with the high-gluten wheat flour, let it ferment, and then add the weaker flours with the other dough ingredients, and get the best use of each. Both Scottish Sponge Bread (page 90), which is designed to include some pastry flour (or other low-gluten whole wheat flour), and Busy People's Bread (page 163), which uses bean flour, are examples of ways to do this.

A sponge dough ordinarily requires four risings: one for the sponge, and two plus the final proof for the full dough. When you use a weaker flour in the dough, only one rising between sponge and shaping may be required. Be alert to the state of the dough, and evaluate it cannily before you decide to let it rise again prior to shaping. If it seems nearly ripe, round it and let it have a little longer rest than usual, then go ahead and shape without further ado. Consult A Loaf for Learning if you need to review these techniques.

Most recipes can be adapted to the sponge method. For best results we suggest you choose the sponge pattern that is closest to the timing you want to follow, and divide your own recipe's ingredients similarly. The amount of flour and water, the temperatures of the sponge and dough, any other ingredients that may be included— all these affect the fermentation of the sponge and the success of the bread. Still, with a sponge, there is always leeway. Ideally you use it to make your dough when the sponge has risen as much as it can and started to recede or fall back. But if you need to, you can take it up much sooner or let it go much longer and still have good bread. Longer-fermenting sponges, like longer-fermenting doughs, give you more flavor, nutrition, and keeping quality.

A professional baker's sponge usually contains half to three-quarters of the flour, the yeast, part of the sweetener, and enough water to make a *stiff* dough. That is what we recommend. A variation that is popular with home bakers is the so-called wet sponge, made from part of the flour and all of the liquid, but we find it ineffective, messy, and unpleasant to work with — not worth the trouble.

The chart on the next page is intended to give a quick overview of the basic possibilities for making sponges of various timings. What it comes down to is mixing up about half the flour and water with enough yeast to let the mixture ferment in the time you have for it. To lengthen the time, use less yeast, mix a stiffer sponge, include the salt, and keep it cooler. To hasten its work, include more yeast, make it softer, hold the salt until you make the dough, and keep it warmer. Though sponges are accommodating and flexible, it isn't a case of anything goes. If you are just trying the method out, we suggest following one of the recipes with the sponge procedure fully explained so that you can get a feel for the process before you do your own adaptations.

Scottish Sponge Bread, page 90
Busy People's Bread, page 163
Yogurt Bread, page 176
Overnight Started Bread, page 180

Making Sponge Doughs Suit Your Timing

SPONGE	INGREDIENTS					STIFFNESS
Time & Temperature	Yeast	Flour	Salt	Water Temperature	Sweetener	
24 hours in refrigerator	⅛ teaspoon	half or less	all	cold	some or all	stiff
18 hours at about 55–65°F	⅛ teaspoon	half or less	all	icy	some or all	very stiff
12 hours at about 65–70°F	⅛ to ¼ teaspoon	half or less	all	cold	some or all	stiff
8 hours at room temperature	1 teaspoon	half or less	all or part	cold	some or all	stiff
5 hours at room temperature	2 teaspoons	half or more	all or part	cool	all, part, or none	stiff
3 hours at room temperature	2 teaspoons	half or more	none	cool	all, part, or none	medium
1½ hours at 80°F	2 teaspoons	half or more	none	lukewarm	all, part, or none	soft

FLOUR: *Don't use low-gluten flour in a sponge.*

YEAST: *Use active dry yeast only in long sponges (8 hours or longer). Dissolve in ¼ cup warm water in the usual way.*

SWEETENER: *Do not use raw honey or raw fruit in long sponges (8 hours or longer).*

Dissolve the yeast as you would for a normal dough, using whatever amount is called for to make the sponge. It is necessary to dissolve the yeast according to the manufacturer's directions in warm water, but if your sponge is to stand for more than a couple of hours, you will want to use as little warm water as possible so that the sponge will not be too warm and ferment too fast.

Stir the yeast mixture and the other liquid into the flour, mixing thoroughly to the desired consistency, and then knead only briefly, about five minutes: enough that the dough can hold the gas generated by the yeast, but not completely, since there will be more kneading later when the dough is made.

Put the sponge in a container that will let it rise quite a lot before it falls back—more than double, at least. Cover the container with a plate or a thick damp towel so that the contents don't dry out and crust over; keep where it will be the right temperature, and protected from drafts.

Soften the sponge in the liquid called for in the recipe that has not already been used in the sponge and then add the rest of the ingredients according to the instructions in the recipe. If you want the dough to rise quickly, use warm liquid; if you want a more leisurely rise, cooler; but expect the dough to be livelier than it would be without the sponge, and if you use warm liquid, the dough will probably rise and be ready to deflate in about an hour. For a *very* fast dough, add an extra teaspoon of yeast; the first rise may take nearly an hour, but the second rise and the proof will be exceptionally fast. Keep this version very warm for rising and proofing.

TO MAKE THE DOUGH

If the sponge did not include the salt, don't forget it now!

The Rising Place

Everybody's home is different, and so each baker has to play sleuth to find the warm place or the cool one where the dough can rise best. Drafty log cabins with wood heat present the greatest of challenges because the heat is dry and prone to extreme ups and downs, but apartments boasting air conditioning and forced-air heating have their problems, too.

Some entrepreneur will someday invent and market a compact little warming box, good for breadmaking and also for incubating yogurt and tempeh. It will be well-insulated, use little power, be adjustable from 70° to 110°F or so, keep steady heat (oh, especially, let it keep *steady* heat!) and offer a method of humidifying the atmosphere inside in a controlled way. In our dream, this wonderful box is easy to clean and not too expensive, a home version of the commercial bakery's proof box. Until the happy day this comes along, here is a very funky, very simple version you can construct.

Place a heating pad under a towel; put a cake rack on top and then the dough in a big covered bowl. On top of this struc-

ture set an inverted corrugated box or styrofoam ice chest. Stick the thermometer inside the dough's snug house to keep tabs on the temperature. Adjust the temperature by changing the setting on the heating pad or by lifting the box a little to let in air. For the final rise you can get a humid atmosphere by putting the shaped loaves in covered casserole dishes, or in loaf pans in sealed plastic bags that have a little water inside.

Of course you don't have to go through all this if you're working with a dough that rises more slowly at normal room temperature, or if your house has a place like a sunny porch that is already just warm enough for your rising dough. Whatever the temperature, be sure to protect the dough from drying out by covering it with an effective lid, and from exposure to drafts with a layer or two of toweling or newspaper, a box, or some such.

If your oven has a pilot light or an incandescent bulb, the easiest thing is to set the dough in its bowl or pan in the oven to rise. But watch out! Most ovens are warmer than you might think—we have mentioned this before—so experiment by keeping the door ajar (say, with a rolled-up towel) until you get it just right. The heat in the oven will be steady but dry, so be sure to protect the dough from crusting over.

OVEN RISING

The usual method for keeping the dough from drying out on the top is to cover the bowl with a damp towel. Usually we have a lot of respect for such conventions, but this one is a mystery. What happens every time is that either the towel dries out and doesn't do the job, or the dough rises into it, and becomes one with the towel forever. A platter, a lid, a matching bowl inverted on top—any of these is much better.

When you are covering the shaped loaf, *if the dough is ripe* so that there is no trace of stickiness to it, a damp towel will not adhere to the loaf—but it can still dry out. Keeping the loaf in a closed plastic bag or in some other closed space like a big covered pan or canning kettle will protect the shaped dough during its final rise. Provide extra humidity if it is needed by putting a little hot water in the bag or kettle.

Halfway through the final rise, the time comes when you have to preheat the oven. The bread's inside: what to do? Here are some ideas:

ها Set the nearly risen loaves in a draft-free place, turn on the oven, and don't worry about it.

ها Float the loaves in their loaf pans in a dishpan of warm water, covered over with another dishpan. This astonishing idea is super-effective because of the humidity; the water will stay warm for as long as half an hour if there is enough of it. Add some boiling water should the bread need more time after that.

ها When the bread is about three-quarters risen, simply turn the oven on with the proofing loaves inside. They will continue to rise while the oven preheats. Start a little sooner if your oven takes a long time to get up to temperature, a little later if it preheats very quickly. This is definitely a daredevil technique, but it can work well if your timing is just right. Note that for breads that require high initial heat, especially heat plus steam, this method won't do; save it for recipes that include milk or plenty of sweetener. (Please remember to remove the plastic bag or whatever you have used to keep the bread from crusting over while it was rising. Thermometers, too. You'd be amazed at how hard it is to get melted plastic off the oven rack.)

ها You can set the loaves on a heating pad for the last part of the rise. A hot-water bottle will work too; it is good for about half an hour. Since it will be *very* hot at the beginning, cover it with towels to even out the heat and protect the bread.

So far all this has had to do with finding or devising a Warm Place, but if you are making Desem or French Bread or want to have a long cool fermentation for an eight- or ten-hour dough or a long-rising sponge, what you want is a Cool Place. This can be much harder to find, unless your climate is temperate and there is a porch, cellar, or garage that stays cool without being drafty. Sometimes a low cupboard on the shady side of the house is just right.

French bread requires dry proofing, which makes it a poor choice for any humid day even on a cool porch. For other doughs, here is an option that sounds fantastic but works: make a secure bundle of the dough tied up in a muslin or linen cloth and *float* it in a tub of cool water. When you return to it the bundle will have become a soccer ball, bouncy and nicely fermented. The timing has to be careful, because there is no finger-poke testing! Less spectacular, also effective: just leave the dough in its bowl and place it in in an ice chest, keeping its temperature steady and proper with cool water around the bowl. *Again, a thermometer is most helpful in adjusting all these.*

Paraphernalia
Kneading Machines

FOOD PROCESSORS

There is nothing like the satisfaction of making bread by hand, feeling the dough develop its own life and supple strength as you knead it in a rhythm as old as mankind, etc.—but. If you make a *lot* of bread or have a time schedule that is snugger than tight, or if you have a physical problem that makes kneading difficult, it is a whole lot better to use a dough hook or food processor than to give up the idea of making your own bread.

Most readily available, and admirably efficient, is the now ubiquitous food processor, fitted with a special dough blade. Some brands (Cuisinart for one) even have a special *whole wheat* dough blade! Whole wheat dough is substantially different from white flour dough, and the method we present takes these differences into account, but please compare them with those of your own machine's manufacturer before you begin.

Most processors can handle only one loaf at a time, and sometimes only part of one, but they are so fast that if you have nerves of steel, you could do several loaves in sequence in less time than it would take you to knead two loaves by hand. (Better yet, since it is so quick and easy, do one loaf at a time, and bake often.) When you want to prepare a standard two-loaf recipe, measure out the ingredients for each loaf separately, with the exception of the yeast. Prepare the yeast according to the directions in the recipe, and then when it is time to add it to the bowl, stir it thoroughly and pour in just half.

Keep in mind that the pitfall of using this wonder device is that it works so fast and so efficiently that it is very easy to overknead the dough. Stop the machine often and feel the dough to see whether it is ready, using the criteria described in A Loaf for Learning.

Mixing & kneading whole wheat bread with a food processor

Dissolve the yeast in the warm water required in your recipe. Assemble all the other ingredients. Use *cool* liquids for the rest of the recipe. The processor will heat the dough by as much as 25°F because it kneads so vigorously. If you take the temperature of your mixed ingredients before and after processing the first few times you make bread, you can learn to gauge the actual amount your own machine heats the dough, and use this information to plan how warm the water should be in future bakings.

Put the dry ingredients in the work bowl and process until mixed—about 15 seconds. Add the yeast mixture, then add the rest of the liquids in a steady stream while the processor is running. Add them as fast as you can and still give them a chance to mix well. If you work too slowly here, the dough will become stiff. Add liquid until the flour comes together as a dough ball, then stop the machine to feel the dough.

It may take a little practice to learn how much liquid to add how fast. If the liquid measure is too much for the amount of flour, the dough will be mushy and sticky. This will probably cause it to stick underneath the blade and strain the motor —the machine may even stop. If it does, scrape the sides and bottom of the bowl with a rubber spatula and bring the dough up over the blade and center post. Sprinkle a tablespoon or two of flour over the dough and process, repeating until the dough is not so soft.

If you're not adding enough water the dough will be dry and hard—so much so that the blade may turn without moving the dough. If this happens, cut the dough up, put it into the bowl, and sprinkle it with a tablespoon of water. Turn on the processor and, with the machine running, gradually add more water until the dough softens.

If the water has not blended evenly into the dough, the underside where the blade is turning will become very soft, even sticky, while a hard ball forms on top. If this happens, remove the dough and cut up the hard part. Replace it in the work bowl with the softer part on top. Then process the dough again, adding more water, a tablespoon at a time, if necessary to soften it.

Once the dough feels reasonably soft, process it very briefly; then feel again carefully to evaluate its water content. Moisten your fingers with water and squeeze the dough. It should be soft enough that you don't feel any strain on the muscles in your fingers when you squeeze it, yet not so soft that it loses all feeling of substance and feels almost runny. (Ignore the fact that the dough is sticky.) Process for another very short time, adding water or flour a tablespoon at a time as needed to make a soft dough.

When you mix up a recipe that calls for adding cold butter to a partly kneaded dough, add it about halfway through the processing.

The machine will complete the kneading of one loaf's worth of dough made from high-gluten flour after about 125 revolutions once the dough ball forms, but a lower-gluten dough may take only half that many. If the dough ball suddenly falls apart and spreads against the sides of the bowl, stop the machine. The processing has been a little too long; check the time or count, and with the next loaf, allow a little less. Meantime, the dough is probably fine. Remove it from the bowl, shape it into a smooth ball, and set it aside. Process the next part of the dough if you are doing two loaves, and then go back to your recipe to let the dough have its first rise.

Many home mixing machines have a dough hook attachment.
We've seen only one or two widely available machines that are
powerful enough to handle whole wheat dough. If you have a
mixer with a dough hook, try using it to knead one loaf at a
time. You'll know very quickly whether your machine can handle the job. There are relatively inexpensive hand and electric
kneaders, but we don't know of any that are good for whole
wheat dough. We'd like to.

Of course, you can get wonderful, expensive machines
specifically made for kneading dough. Our own is a 30-quart
Hobart mixer, and it kneads bread for a dozen families. All our
recipes have been tested both in single batches by hand, and in
big batches in this machine: they all do beautifully both ways.
If you have a mixer with a dough hook, compare the instructions from its manufacturer with the following, the method we
use to knead whole wheat dough. (The rye instructions are
different and follow.)

Mixing & kneading whole wheat bread with a dough hook

Dissolve the yeast in warm water. Measure the flour and salt
into the bowl. Turn the machine on slow speed to mix them.

Using unbreakable cups, pour the liquid ingredients and
the yeast mixture in a steady stream into the bowl while the
hook runs on slow speed. Add the liquids without haste, but
without dallying, either. The flour will look like it is getting
evenly moistened; then when most of the liquid is in, it will
begin to look like mud.

Stop the machine and feel the consistency of the dough.
Moisten your hand with water and squeeze the dough. Is it soft
or is it stiff? Ignore the fact that the dough is wet and sticky.
Does the dough resist your touch? Does it strain the muscles in
your fingers when you squeeze it? Then it is too stiff. On the
other hand, the dough must have enough flour to hold its
shape. Does the dough feel waterlogged, as if the flour is not
contributing much substance to it? Does it have a runny, liquid
quality to it? Then it has too much water. Feel deep into the
dough, not just the surface.

If the dough is not right, thoroughly mix in more water or

flour, a little at a time, and reevaluate until it is right. If you are using a coarse, stone-ground flour, it will take up the water more slowly, so it is best to let it rest for 5 minutes before making the final adjustment in water content, at least until you are familiar with the whole process and feel comfortable about making adjustments while the dough is being kneaded.

The first few times you mix the dough in your machine, you may want to do the mixing all on slow speed, so that you can observe the changes in the dough more carefully. Normally, though, this would be the time to turn the machine to medium speed. As you continue to beat it the mudlike mixture will suddenly come together into a soft claylike dough. The gluten begins to form, but the dough's surface continues to look rough and bumpy, and if you feel the dough—stop the machine first!—it feels quite sticky. The next big change comes when the dough reaches cleanup—all the dough comes off the sides of the bowl to form a ball. The dough feels a little drier. Soon after this the dough becomes fully developed, so watch it closely: the dull, rough surface develops a smooth, satiny sheen, and it stretches rather than tears over the hook. The dough feels drier, and if you stretch it gently, it will form a thin uniform translucent membrane without thick strands or lumps in it. If you hold it up to the light, it is faintly webbed inside. Look for brown flecks of bran against the bright white gluten sheet.

If the kneading is continued on too far, the dough loses its elasticity, softens, and pulls into long rubbery strands. Finally the dough gets wet, runny, and quite sticky again. Loaves made from such dough will tear in the shaping or proofing, and they will not rise high.

The amount of time it takes a dough to develop fully depends most of all on the amount of gluten in the flour and the speed of the mixer. With a good strong flour the dough may be mixed and developed in a little less than ten minutes at medium speed, somewhat longer at slow speed. This will vary with the quality of the flour, so watch the changes in the dough and don't depend on just how much time the machine has been running.

Using your dough hook to knead rye bread

Collect all the recipe ingredients so that they are measured and handy. Dissolve the yeast in the warm water. Mix the flours and salt in the bowl. Add the liquids slowly but steadily, using the flavored liquids first, plain water last. When you have added the first two-thirds of the wet ingredients and a stiff dough forms, drizzle the last third or so of the liquids down the side of the bowl in small increments over about 10 minutes, keeping the machine on slow speed. Each time you add water the dough will fall apart against the sides; wait until it comes back together, and then once again add a little water.

Keep checking as you near the end of your allotment of water and stop adding it when the dough reaches proper consistency. *The larger proportion of rye flour there is in the dough, the less kneading it will tolerate;* ten minutes is about right for a normal recipe with four cups wheat and three cups rye flour, but there is no set rule. Ideally it will take the same amount of time to add the liquid as it takes to knead up the dough, but if you think that the dough can take more kneading — if it is more than half wheat flour, it might — keep the machine going a little longer. Always be alert to the condition of the dough so that you can stop as soon as it begins to get sticky.

Dough Cutter/Scraper

This tool is truly indispensable for dividing dough for loaves or rolls, and also for scraping the kneading surface clean afterward. Ours came from a bakery supply store more than a decade ago; now they are available everywhere in kitchen shops and hardware stores. The edge is square and not sharp, protecting the tabletop, but it goes through dough without fuss.

There is also a flexible plastic version of this which works beautifully for scraping dough out of the bowl, but not quite so well for the other uses.

Dough Knob

I can't imagine getting along without the dough cutter, but *this* bit of practical woodcraft is definitely just for pleasure. For mixing up the dough, no spoon can match its efficiency. We have never seen one in a store or catalog, but anyone who knows how to use a wood lathe could make one in a jiffy. The dough knob is turned from a 1½-inch dowel about 11 inches long. The handle is about ¾ inch in diameter. This is the shape:

Pans & Other Miscellany

Bread may not be better-tasting when it is baked in a standard size pan, but it does make predictable slices for sandwiches and for putting in the toaster—not unimportant considerations for most of us. However, you can bake in almost any heatproof utensil that gives room for rising and that will let you remove the loaf after it is baked. (We know someone who thought it would be groovy to use a rustic clay bean pot. The bread *did* bake well, and he eventually managed to get it all out by various methods.)

We have sized our recipes carefully so that they will fit into two medium loaf pans: 8″ × 4″ (or, if you measure the top, 8½″ × 4½″)—21 × 11 cm. We greatly prefer this size of pan for whole-grain breads. The larger (5″ × 9″) standard pans were designed for cardboardy white bread, and unless an extremely high-gluten flour is used by a really terrific kneader, slices of whole-grain breads made in these pans tend to fall apart when they are spread with anything stiffer than pea soup. Besides, it is not so easy to cook the bread thoroughly in the large pans without drying out the crust. The smallest standard pans, usually called fruitcake pans, are about 3″ × 6½″. The slice is too small for a reasonable sandwich, though the bread bakes well enough, and in less time. You would have three or four loaves from one recipe using these.

It would be impossible to discuss the merits of all the pans and crocks and stones and whatnot that are available to the enthusiastic and well-financed baker; but sometimes normal kitchen equipment does just as well as some of the expensive stuff. For example, stainless steel bowls: grease them well and dust them with cornmeal or sprinkle with seeds to be sure the dough doesn't stick. The 1½-quart size is just right for one loaf's worth of dough. If the bowl is fairly shallow or squarish, the loaf will be shallow or squarish too, and look as if it were baked free-form. If the bowl is deep and round, the bread will come out looking like a soccer ball with a slightly flattened top. These loaves can be very pretty, but note that whenever the loaf becomes rounder and deeper, is more spherical, or is larger because there is more dough in it, it will take extra baking time. When it is flatter (but well-risen) or longer and narrower than the norm, it will take less time to cook through. *Bread that has not risen well takes the longest time to bake.*

The recipes in this book work beautifully baked in two eight- or nine-inch pie tins; or free-standing on a cookie sheet if the dough is not too soft. (If it is too soft, it will sag and make a large, flattish, crusty, airy—but delicious—loaf.) Two normal loaves can also bake side by side in an 8 inch square baking dish. To be sure that they don't cling to each other after they're baked, a little fat between them does the trick. They will require extra baking time: to check, turn them out and let them fall apart. Touch one loaf where it was next to the other, as if you were testing a cake for doneness with light finger pressure. It will spring back if it is done. If it doesn't and your finger-mark stays wetly there, put the loaves back for another 10 minutes of baking, more or less.

Try to bake your breads or rolls as close to the center of the oven as possible, or a little above center. If you have to use the bottom rack, it is helpful to use two baking sheets or two loaf pans one inside the other to deflect some of the heat from the bottom of the bread. Check halfway through to see whether you should reverse the pans for an evener bake. Be sure there is at least a couple of inches of air space all around the edges of the baking sheet.

If your baking pan or dish is pottery or glass, take time to warm it up a little before you put in the dough. Very cold pans can chill the dough on the crust, making the bread dense there. The result may just be a tough crust, or the crust may actually separate from the loaf where it was chilled.

Readers of *Laurel's Kitchen* will be surprised to see that we have not recommended baking in the 46-ounce juice cans. Our enthusiasm for cans has been dampened by recent findings that the lead solder in their seams does find its way into the food stored—and perhaps baked—in them. We are really sorry about this: cans do have many advantages for breadbaking. More loaves fit into the oven, for example, with better distribution of heat. Enclosed in its can, the dough rises nicely and doesn't dry out in proofing or in baking. Also, before we did the research for this book and learned how to make splendid bread every time (ahem!), we loved the cans because they hid our mistakes: if the bread didn't rise, the slices were still the same chic round shape, and sandwiches were still possible and not embarrassing.

Now we use ordinary pans or bake on the hearth for our daily loaves, saving the cans for steamed bread on rare occasions. Until the industry manages to get the lead out, we can't recommend cans for regular bakings.

Ovens

Every oven has its own peculiarities, and bakers learn, usually by error and trial, how to work with the challenges presented by the ovens that bake their bread.

Typically, the hottest place in the oven is the bottom, with the heat rising up the sides, across the top (next hottest), and down into the middle. The evenest heat is in the middle. Modern gas and electric stoves have thermostatic controls but most thermostats have a wide range between their on and off temperatures. When you preheat to 400°F, the burner goes on high and heats the oven to 500°F. Then the thermostat registers, and the big burner goes off, leaving a tiny "holding flame." Gradually the temperature goes down to 400°F. You put the bread in with efficient speed because you know that leaving the door open causes loss of heat. Even so, the inside temperature descends to 350°F. The relatively cold loaves further cool it to 300°F, and the thermostat registers. The burner blasts on again, raising the inside temperature to 450°F.

Because of its very uneven heat, a "flashy" oven like this bakes poorly. If your oven performs this way (one of ours does), try to preheat well, and be sure to put the bread in when the temperature is *up*. This is one place where an oven thermometer is useful: let it help you chart the pattern of your thermostat's ons and offs.

One way to even out oven heat is by putting quarry tile on the bottom rack. These are clay tiles about 6 inches square and ⅜ inch thick, which you can get cheaply at any building supply store. Nine of them would do the trick for most small household ovens. Be sure to allow at least 2 inches between the sides of the oven and the tiles so that the rising heat can circulate. Preheat for *at least* half an hour to get the tiles hot. Since they hold the heat, if your oven is insulated well, it will use less fuel to maintain the temperature, so the extra preheating shouldn't mean much extra fuel.

Given that no oven is perfect, do what you can to use the one you have to best advantage. For example, the thermostat on the top of the oven should be allowed to do its job: let the heat reach it. Don't use an 18-inch cookie sheet in an 18-inch oven: the heat will be trapped below, the bottom will burn, and the top will never get hot. Allow at least 2 inches around the edges, and 1 inch between whatever loaves you have inside. Since a lot of heat is lost when the door opens, arrange the racks *before* you turn on the oven—and allow an extra five minutes of baking time for each opening of the door. Never open the door during the first 15 minutes of baking. Another tip: black pans or cookie sheets concentrate heat, making things brown fast where they touch, so never use them on the bottom rack.

For breadmaking, the convection oven has the advantage of recovering very quickly the heat lost when the door is opened; for this reason, loaves should have a fuller proof than those baked in a normal oven. The heat is very dry, though, and if the dough is soft and even slightly *over*proofed, a characteristic long tubelike hole may form just under the crust. Slashing the loaf before you put it in the oven will help, but being careful not to overproof is the best protection.

CONVECTION OVENS

Small, relatively inexpensive convection ovens for home use are available everywhere. Our experience with them is limited to one breadmaking demonstration we gave at a local community college. Two loaves were rising in their pans on top of the oven while the demonstration progressed: it seemed like a nice warm place, but the bread rose with agonizing slowness. Later we figured out that the oven was vibrating the bejabbers out of those poor loaves! It did bake them beautifully, however.

After years of rubbing sticks together for fire and eating in a place that allowed about half an inch per person, we finally were able to build ourselves a kitchen and dining place. We decided to include a brick oven for reasons of economy and ecology—and because we had become addicted to Flemish Desem Bread, which is traditionally baked on the hearth.

A brick oven bakes well because it provides steady, steamy, intense, radiating heat at the beginning and steady, gradually descending dry heat for the rest of the bake. This gives old-fashioned, so-called lean breads (no added fat or sugar or milk) crispy-tender, shiny, ruddy crusts and full, sweet flavor.

We've been using our brick oven for three years now, and we love it—not only for the bread it bakes but also for the continuing adventure of firing it, for the marvelous smells, and even for the small measure of independence it gives us from our utility company. Wood-fired bake ovens are still used wherever

people make bread, their many styles adapted to the climate of the place they're built. To give you an idea, here are a few examples.

The oldest and most straightforward kind is one that is also a firebox: a fire is built inside the oven itself, and then when it is hot enough, the coals are raked out and the ashes mopped. The oven is closed down for a while to let the temperatures even out; then the bread is put in and the opening sealed with one or another sort of door. The simplest of these, the beehive oven, is used all over the world in hot climates. Made of adobe or brick, it usually stands outdoors to keep its heat isolated from the living quarters. Our friend Alan Scott, who loves his desem as much as we do, has built a number of four-loaf-sized beehive ovens in his backyard, using heat-resistant concrete. They work wonderfully well.

The most sophisticated and complex design we found came from Finland and is perfect for very cold climates. The oven is part of a mass of brickwork intended to keep the house well-heated. The fire from the fireplace or stove chamber enters a chimney that winds around the oven on at least three sides, heating the brick from the outside. By the time the draft from the fire leaves the building, it has relinquished all its heat into the brick mass and passes from the building cold.

Our costal Northern California climate is cool but not so

cold that we need to use the fireplace all year. We made our hearth oven part of the fireplace, but separate from it so that they can be used independently. They share a common chimney, which also vents the kitchen stoves.

To tell the whole story would take another book, but if you are thinking of going this route, here are some things to consider.

WOOD   Well-seasoned hardwood burns hotter and requires less fussing. Sometimes hardwood mills will give mill ends free for the hauling. Once cut, the wood must cure for at least six months to a year so it will burn hot and clean.

STEAM   We finally settled on a system that pipes (stainless steel pipes! Copper pipe threw blue flakes onto the bread) tap water along the sides of the oven so that it drips down the masonry, turning into steam. A simpler method that also worked was to fill a punctured loaf pan with boiling water, letting it drip onto the hearth. We abandoned that because it was hazardous to the bakers and wasted space.

HEAT   It takes a little while to learn how to get the heat just right at the moment the bread is ready to load. We fire the oven slowly for a couple of hours, then keep the temperature at 1000°F for another hour. After that, shut down the oven for half an hour to even out the heat before the bread is loaded. By then the heat is about 550°F, which is just right. After loading and steaming, the temperature is about 400°F, or a little higher. A thermometer (pyrometer) in the ceiling of the oven makes gauging this easier.

EQUIPMENT   Once the oven has been fired, it is brilliantly self-cleaned except for a few ashes that can easily be mopped out using a long-handled mop and clear water—and care to prevent burning arms!

Essential for loading the bread into the oven is a baker's peel, a sort of paddle about an arm's length longer than your oven is deep. Load and unload the loaves with a deft push-pull that comes quite naturally.

Knives

Every home baker needs a good knife. This is especially true if (like some authors) you can't wait to slice the bread until it is completely cool: a bad knife can *really* wreck a fresh, soft loaf. Fortunately, although you can spend upwards of twenty dollars for an elegant knife, a truly splendid bread cutter lurks on the supermarket rack for about two dollars. (They call it a ham slicer, but don't let them fool you.) These knives have a *long, thin* blade with the wavy kind of serrated edge—not the sawtooth sort, which is inferior. They keep their sharpness for a year or two of daily slicing—not forever, granted, but in the meantime they are great. They're very hard to sharpen at home. Electric knives, if you have one, work very nicely.

A short-bladed knife is for the birds, by the way. One of our favorite catalogs advertises a "bread" knife that has a 7-inch blade—ridiculous!

On the other hand, for loaves of the dense, firm sort, that want to be sliced thin, a long, razor-sharp French vegetable knife serves better than the one described above. If you like *really* thin slices, favor the firm breads, and have a rich uncle, there is a hand-turned Dutch all-purpose slicer that is truly remarkable. The brand name is *eva,* and it effortlessly cuts slices of any thinness out of the densest bread. There are probably other such gizmos, too, that we haven't seen.

To slice a loaf, cut with a smooth, gentle, sawing motion —*lots of sawing and not much downward pressure.* If you can, grasp the loaf on both sides with your noncutting hand. The secret of perfect, even slices is fierce concentration, even more than manual dexterity.

The Bread Box

You've just put a lot of work and a lot of good stuff into making this great bread. How to store it so it keeps its splendor to the last slice?

First, *always* let the bread cool completely (protected from flies, when they are around) before you wrap it up. It will get soggy otherwise, and be more likely to get moldy.

If the bread will be eaten in a day or two—or, if it is a good keeper, three or four—it is best stored at cool room temperature, loosely wrapped in clean cloth or a clean paper bag or kept in an old-fashioned breadbox. Bread kept at room temperature in an air-tight container or wrapped tightly in plastic is likely to mold quickly, so if you use a breadbox of any kind, be sure it has some ventilation. Between loaves, clean the box out to prevent any mold spores from passing from one batch to the other. We like to use our "granite-ware" canning pots as breadboxes. Their loosely fitting lids suit them well for storing bread a day or two or three; and they're mouseproof and easy to clean.

To store bread for longer than a few days, wrap the cool loaves in plastic bags, seal them, and keep them in the refrigerator. For even longer periods of time, freeze them. (Friends who freeze bread suggest that it is helpful to slice the loaf first, so you can remove just what you need. It is pretty hard to saw through a frozen loaf.)

Sources of Wheat & Flour

Look for a natural foods store near where you live. If they don't already sell good, *fresh* flour, they may be glad to order it for you. If you can gather a group of people of like mind, you'll be able to order in bulk at considerable savings.

If you find no satisfactory source of flour near at hand, consider investing in a home-size mill; then you can buy top- quality wheat in bulk and mill it fresh whenever you need it. Wheat, unlike flour, travels well and keeps indefinitely.

The following companies sell excellent products by mail. There are certainly others, but these we can recommend from personal experience. See *Home Food Systems* (Rodale, 1981), pages 81 to 83, for a more extensive list.

Giusto's Specialty Foods
241 East Harris Avenue
South San Francisco, CA 94080

Al Giusto has supplied quality organic grains to Northern California for more than thirty years; we have used his wheat flour and cereals for a decade. For breadmaking he sells a superb high-protein Montana spring wheat flour, very finely ground, and also a flavorful stone-ground winter wheat flour —coarse, medium, or fine. The winter flour is lower in protein and so best used in breads; beginners may want to stick to the higher-gluten spring flour, or use the two in combination.

Either wheat is available unground, as are other grains and flours of all kinds.

Walnut Acres
Penn's Creek, PA 17862

Organically grown wheat and flour, and all manner of other good things besides: the beautiful Walnut Acres catalog is a tribute to forty years of hard work and loving dedication to high ideals of care for man and earth.

Little Bear Trading Company
Rt. 1, Box 266A
Cochrane, Wisconsin 54622

A small, dedicated group of people with a strong commitment to organic agriculture and natural foods. They sell freshly ground flours as well as seeds, beans, and grains.

BARLEY

Valley Seed Company
P.O. Box 1110
Phoenix, Arizona 85001

If your nautral food store doesn't sell whole-grain hull-less barley, you can order it from Rob Huntington at the Valley Seed Company. Specify that you want it for eating.

BRICK OVENS

Alan Scott
P.O. Box 838
Point Reyes Station, California 94956

Are you thinking of building a wood-fired backyard oven for baking your hearth bread? Alan Scott has built many and would be glad to share his working plans and advice with you.

Suggested Reading

We haven't tried to list here the many recipe books you can find in any bookstore. We *have* listed several books which have nothing directly to do with baking bread, but which helped convince us of the wider significance of this "homeliest" act.

For a historical account of what bread has meant, in the European tradition anyway, we strongly recommend a passionately written and engagingly idiosyncratic book written toward the end of World War II, *Six Thousand Years of Bread*. *The Breads of France* is here primarily for the bakers' own stories, which give a glimpse of the rich tradition of French breadmaking.

The books by Alexander and Barnet might seem farthest removed from our subject, but they're very helpful in focusing on larger economic realities, making it abundantly clear to what extent corporate greed has eroded the quality of our lives — and providing strong motivation to Do Something about it.

Anyone seriously interested in a cereal-based diet will have questions about where supper is coming from. *Merchants of Grain,* by Dan Morgan, a veteran reporter for the *Washington Post,* gives a most revealing look at the international grain market.

The 10th Anniversary Edition of *Diet for a Small Planet* sketches a picture of food resources that is in some ways even grimmer than that of the original edition. But one is left feeling oddly buoyant and hopeful, perhaps because ten years in the hunger movement have renewed the author's faith in that most underestimated resource, the human spirit.

Finally, for the most resonant, far-reaching exploration of the agricultural crisis, do read poet-farmer Wendell Berry.

C. F.

SELECTED READING LIST

Alexander, Josephine. *America through the Eye of My Needle: Common Sense for the Eighties.* New York: Dial Press, 1981.

Barnet, Richard J. *The Lean Years: Politics in the Age of Scarcity.* New York: Simon & Schuster, 1978.

Berry, Wendell. *The Unsettling of America: Culture and Agriculture.* New York: Avon, 1979.

Clayton, Bernard, Jr. *The Breads of France: And How to Bake Them in Your Own Kitchen.* New York: Bobbs-Merrill, 1978.

The Cornucopia Project [Rodale Press]. *Empty Breadbasket? The Coming Challenge to America's Food Supply and What We Can Do About It.* Emmaus, Pa.: Rodale Press, 1981.

David, Elizabeth. *English Bread and Yeast Cookery.* Viking Press, New York. 1977.

Food Monitor. Published bimonthly by World Hunger Year, Inc., 350 Broadway, Suite 209, New York, N.Y. 10013.

Jacobs, H. E. *Six Thousand Years of Bread.* New York: Doubleday, 1944.

Kramer, Mark. *Three Farms: Making Milk, Meat and Money from the American Soil.* Boston: Little, Brown and Co., 1980.

Lappé, Frances Moore. *Diet for a Small Planet.* Tenth Anniversary Edition. New York: Ballentine Books, 1982.

Lappé, Frances Moore, and Joseph Collins. *Food First: Beyond the Myth of Scarcity.* 2d revised ed. New York: Ballentine Books, 1978.

Morgan, Dan. *Merchants of Grain.* New York: Viking Press, 1979.

Perelman, Michael. *Farming for Profit in a Hungry World: Capital and the Crisis in Agriculture.* Montclair, New Jersey: Allanheld, Osmun & Co.; New York: Universe Books, 1977.

Pyler, E. J. *Baking Science and Technology.* 2 volumes. Chicago: Siebel Publishing Co., 1973.

Sultan, William J. *Practical Baking.* Westport, Conn.: AVI Publishing Co., 1965.

Index

[432]

THE LAUREL'S KITCHEN BREAD BOOK
*was prepared for Random House entirely by Laurel and
her friends. The full-page woodcut illustrations and the
endpapers were designed by Ed, the Loaf for Learning
by Victor, and the others by Laurel; all three worked at
cutting the blocks, with Victor doing the lion's share.
Terry designed the book on Nick's model and mothered
it (and Laurel) through production with loving care.
The text type is Sabon, set by Hassan; the titles are
Monotype Centaur and Arrighi. For all those who donated time to it, this book is a labor of love, offered in
the hope that it will open the way not only
to better breadmaking but to a fuller,
more intentional way of life.*

ABOUT THE AUTHORS

The authors' first book, Laurel's Kitchen: A Handbook
for Vegetarian Cookery and Nutrition *came from the
daily experience and meticulous research of a group of
people with a shared commitment to spiritual values. To
hundreds of thousands, Laurel has become a guiding
spirit whose kitchen symbolizes whole-food cookery at
its best. Carol, who voices the authors' larger concerns
about food and economics, writes the syndicated col-
umn "Notes from Laurel's Kitchen," and is working on a
book on Christian mystics. Bron is a nurse with a deep
interest in nutrition, whose desire to make whole-grain
breadmaking available to everyone prompted much of
the research and testing that went into this book.
Behind these three authors stand the many unnamed
cooks and bakers of "Laurel's kitchen" whose work has
given these books the authority of so
much personal experience.*